Relativity, Philosophy, and Mind

THE NOTEBOOKS OF PAUL BRUNTON

(VOLUME 13)

RELATIVITY, PHILOSOPHY, AND MIND

PAUL BRUNTON

(1898–1981)

An in-depth study of
categories nineteen, twenty, and twenty-one
from the notebooks

Published for the
PAUL BRUNTON PHILOSOPHIC FOUNDATION
by Larson Publications

International Standard Book Number (cloth) 0-943914-38-8
International Standard Book Number (paper) 0-943914-39-6
International Standard Book Number (series, cloth) 0-943914-17-5
International Standard Book Number (series, paper) 0-943914-23-X
Library of Congress Catalog Card Number: 88-80798

Manufactured in the United States of America

Published for the
Paul Brunton Philosophic Foundation
by
Larson Publications
4936 Route 414
Burdett, New York 14818

Distributed to the trade by
Kampmann and Company
9 East 40 Street
New York, New York 10016

88 91 92 90 89
2 4 6 8 10 9 7 5 3 1

The works of Dr. Brunton

A Search in Secret India
The Secret Path
A Search in Secret Egypt
A Message from Arunachala
A Hermit in the Himalayas
The Quest of the Overself
The Inner Reality
(*also titled* Discover Yourself)
Indian Philosophy and Modern Culture
The Hidden Teaching Beyond Yoga
The Wisdom of the Overself
The Spiritual Crisis of Man

Published posthumously

Essays on the Quest

The Notebooks of Paul Brunton

volume 1: Perspectives
volume 2: The Quest
volume 3: Practices for the Quest
Relax and Retreat
volume 4: Meditation
The Body
volume 5: Emotions and Ethics
The Intellect
volume 6: The Ego
From Birth to Rebirth
volume 7: Healing of the Self
The Negatives
volume 8: Reflections on My
Life and Writings
volume 9: Human Experience
The Arts in Culture
volume 10: The Orient
volume 11: The Sensitives
volume 12: The Religious Urge
The Reverential Life
volume 13: The Reign of Relativity
What Is Philosophy?
Mentalism
(*titled* Relativity, Philosophy,
and Mind)

CONTENTS

PART 3: MENTALISM

EDITORS' INTRODUCTION

The three topics in this volume together constitute a critical turning point, a stage of profound deepening, in our understanding of self and world: properly understood, they provide a fresh basis for conduct, tap a deeper inspiration for living, and catalyze daily spiritual practices.

Relativity, Philosophy, and Mind is our own composite title for categories nineteen, twenty, and twenty-one (*The Reign of Relativity, What Is Philosophy?,* and *Mentalism,* respectively) in the personal notebooks Dr. Paul Brunton (1898–1981) reserved for posthumous publication. Because of a unique light these three sections lend to one another, we have chosen to publish them together as one book, the thirteenth volume in *The Notebooks of Paul Brunton*. The *Notebooks* format should be very helpful to readers who need clarification and development of similar, but not entirely identical, ideas presented earlier in *The Hidden Teaching Beyond Yoga* and *The Wisdom of the Overself.* It should also be inspiring to new P.B. readers, giving them important keys to getting more from those two earlier books than was possible for many of us in previous years.

Many of us who read those earlier books, for example, were able to follow P.B.'s ideas on relativity without much difficulty. Intellectually, we could acknowledge the relativity of observer and observed; we could assent to the *epistemological* notion that all we experience, all we *know* is a product of our own minds. But we were considerably less amenable to the *metaphysical* premise that the natural universe itself is mentally constructed, that Mind is the essential substance of all that is. In the way that it addresses this particular problem, the *Notebooks* structure is a significant improvement on the earlier books.

P.B. here distinguishes much more carefully the ideas on relativity from those on mentalism. He also gives much more detail about what the essential intermediate step that bridges them involves—the step of achieving a balanced individual wholeness and assuming a philosophical perspective. The present structure of first, the ideas on relativity, second, the components essential to a philosophical perspective, and third, the ideas on mentalism makes this final section much easier to appreciate. His elaboration of the important distinctions between these three sets of ideas makes the transformative power of mentalism considerably more obvious. In the process, however, the reader will still have to do some real thinking: the *Notebooks* format does not provide a continuous sequence of reasoning intended to transform outlook from materialism to mentalism; the "missing" key is the reader's own mind, which must discover, develop, and apply this sequence for itself. P.B. has simply provided here the ideas needed to accomplish that discovery under one's own power.

The Reign of Relativity, Part 1 of this volume, encompasses the current scientific development of Einstein's widely acclaimed Theory as well as the ancient observations of Shankaracharya. P.B.'s interest here is not so much to reiterate that Theory in layman's terms as to show the extent of relativity's domain and to explore the implications of its principles for spiritual development. His approach combines intellectual analysis and the cultivation of intuition through straightforward mystical exercises. His intention is to take us deeper than the superficial familiarity with the *concepts* of relativity and on to a full awareness of the substantial questions to which it gives rise.

Insight into the nature of relativity brings an understanding that what we see and know is directly related to our organs of perception and knowledge. Through exploring both the subjective and the objective elements of relativity within becoming, as well as the relativity between being and becoming, we learn that what we perceive has neither more nor less reality than our own perception. The world of our everyday experience is consequently understood to possess, at the very least, a different reality than we had unconsciously assigned to it. It is clearly *not* what it appears to be—that is, among other things, it is not a field of fixed material objects that necessarily exist in their own right with the same forms that our perception gives them. Our physical senses, our awareness (or unawareness) of motion and location, our states of consciousness—in short, all the various elements of our mind-body complex—are at the very least contributing factors to the world of our experience. We say *at the very least* because even at this level of the teaching the question arises as to whether or not the so-called objects possess any self-identical extension *at all* independently of the relational factors in perception.

Recognition, *real* recognition, of the inexorable relativity both of 'objective' phenomena and 'subjective' faculties is a major, and usually unsettling, event. The unsettling feeling that accompanies it has a genuine basis: deep inside ourselves, we *know* that the faculties we are currently using are unreliable vehicles for ultimate truth, and we feel the urgency of discovering a more reliable means to knowledge.

Reactions to this situation have been dramatic, with implications reaching into a variety of fields. For some, the sense of the world's reality is undermined; for others, the sense of reason's reliability is threatened; for almost all, the possibility of authentically objective knowledge, non-psychological knowledge, is seriously challenged. If everything is relative, the cry goes out, is there then no Truth but only truths—tentative truths totally dependent on the standpoint taken? For some, the only ultimate Truth is that everything is relative; for others, Truth remains as that which is beyond the relative, revealing the relative as totally illusory. Each of these extreme viewpoints lends itself to a variety of interpretations, and there exists a spectrum of viewpoints between them. The range extends from the nihilistic "nothing is sacred" to the Buddhistic "sacred No-thing," and from Pantheism to Theophany. Each interpretation serves as a basis for action and has tangible repercussions in daily living. Each is eminently challengeable. Each is an idea in our minds. How do we test the reality of these ideas we have about Reality? This is where philosophy meets us: now we need it, and now its disciplines become genuinely meaningful.

Part 2, *What Is Philosophy?*, meets us at the core of this so called Kantian dilemma and points beyond psychology to reliable knowledge and durable selfhood. Everything now points to the need for a more reliable faculty of knowledge, and philosophy sets out to develop one. It brings in the dimension of "the moral law within" and outlines a complete system of self-development oriented toward the awakening of an entirely new and non-psychological faculty: insight. *Relativity* having turned our minds to the apparent dichotomy of being and becoming, *What Is Philosophy?* turns them toward a deeper level of our own being in which they can be realized as twin poles of a single reality that is our own truest self.

The philosophic training addresses the need for individual wholeness, and for the ability to distinguish between the reliably real and the merely apparent. Each faculty of the human psyche is fulfilled: neither feeling nor intellect nor will nor sensation is allowed to dominate all the others or to improperly subsume the role appropriately filled by one of the others. Then these faculties are all integrated under the guidance of the developing intuitive faculty and brought to a balance appropriate for that particular psyche. When this balance is achieved, insight arises: a faculty latent in all of us but active only in the few who have achieved sagehood.

Once the philosophical viewpoint and experience is made more clear, the ideas on mentalism become more transparent. These ideas are not intended to produce a devaluation of the natural universe and practical experience; neither are they intended to evoke despair with respect to the possibility of ontological knowledge. They are intended to awaken us to what mind really is.

Part 3, *Mentalism*, addresses the fact that most of us, without really investigating the knowledge-situation, assume that we know what we mean when we say "my mind." We find out that we don't. And as we awaken to what mind in its deeper layers is, mentalism becomes a celebration—not only of the mind's deeper reality but also of the intelligent universe.

The *presentation* of mentalism involves two levels. On one level, we are simply requested to try a different approach to reasoning about the knowledge-situation. Showing how unsatisfactory the materialist presupposition proves to be, P.B. asks us to try a different premise. Let's see what happens if we work with the presupposition that mind is first, rather than last, in the perceptual series. Does this presupposition prove more satisfactory? For many of us, nothing more than honest, scrupulous thinking is required to evoke a resounding Yes! On a deeper level, P.B. tells us that this premise, experimental to reasoning, is in fact a firsthand experience in advanced stages of meditation. Its verification is available to anyone who will intelligently pursue the enterprise.

At this deeper level, we see mentalism not as reality *reduced* but as reality *revealed*. Rather than to reduce the world to *mere* ideation, it shows the *importance* of ideation. It reveals the presence and accessibility of fathomless untapped power within us to improve—through improved ideation—our immediate selves and consequent circumstances. But most importantly, P.B. takes great care to assert that he is not here presenting just another form of philosophic idealism, and certainly not a solipsism. He does not challenge the superpersonal reality of the natural universe—only our materialistic conception of that universe. Implicit in his position is that the materialistic conception that has such power over our thought-processes is itself an idea, and a thoroughly unsatisfactory one. His final stance is that "science, which began by repudiating mind and exalting matter, is being forced by facts to end by repudiating matter and exalting mind." More detail on the relationship between the individual mind and a deeper, universal mind appears in volume 16, *Enlightened Mind, Divine Mind*.

Editorial conventions with regard to quantity and structuring of material, spelling, capitalization, and other copy-editing practices for this volume are the same as have been outlined in earlier introductions. As in earlier volumes, (P) at the end of a para indicates that the para also appears in *Perspectives*, volume one of *The Notebooks* series. Once again we have many friends at Wisdom's Goldenrod and the Paul Brunton Philosophic Foundation to thank for this volume's being ready for press. We would also like to thank, on behalf of the foundation, the still growing number of readers throughout the world whose additional financial support is helping to make it possible for these books to be published at their current rate.

With this volume, we have for the first time reached a stage in the editorial process from which we can foresee the completion of the "Ideas" series. Three more volumes will take us to that goal. For further information about publication schedules and related projects, please write to the

Paul Brunton Philosophic Foundation
P.O. Box 89
Hector, NY 14841

Part 1: THE REIGN OF RELATIVITY

There are three stages on the path of world enquiry. The first yields as its fruit that the world is but an idea, and this stage has been reached from the metaphysical end by thinkers such as Bishop Berkeley, and nearly reached from the scientific end by such a man as Eddington. The second stage involves the study of the three states, waking, dreaming, and deep sleep, and yields as its fruit the truth that ideas are transitory emanations out of their permanent cause, consciousness. The third stage is the most difficult, for it requires analysis of the nature of time, space, and causation, plus successful practice of yoga. It yields as its fruit the sense of Reality as something eternally abiding with one.

The ordinary mentalness of the world and the superior reality of Mind illustrate the reign of relativity. This does not mean that the world is so utterly illusory that it is non-existent. It has a relative existence for everyone. But the enlightened ones are aware of the truth that Mind-in-Itself is there. They know it also by the wonderful experience of cosmic consciousness when everything falls away—including their own personal ego—and only THAT remains. This is not merely their point of view but something far and away beyond it that can only happen in the state of contemplation; hence it is a temporary one but—as Plotinus mentioned—a recurrent or accessible one.

1

THE COSMOS OF CHANGE

The universe comes, exists, goes, comes again, and repeats this cycle. Man does the same until he breaks the illusion of common experience and penetrates into the reality behind it all *and behind himself.*

2

The discovery of relativity leads to the conclusion that we know only the appearances—and partial ones at that—of an incomprehensible creative Mystery.

3

All existence is stamped with these two characteristics—a coming-to-be and a passing-away. Where is the reality in, or behind, them?

4

Once we understand the true nature of Mind, and the universal law of Karma under which it operates, we can understand why the cosmos, as a series of dependent evolving mental images, has no end and no beginning and must be as eternal as Mind itself.

5

We live in a cosmos wherein infinite being is forever expressing its own inexpressible self. But as the limitations of it are done in time space motion and form, we are in a never-ending never-successful process.

6

Maya is inexplicable: Reality is ineffable.

7

Because the world-thought issues ultimately from the World-Mind, it cannot be wholly excluded from Reality. It may even be called Reality because it is the ground of everything else, yet is itself derived from Nothing.

8

Nothing that is to be found in space and that exists in time can continue in perpetuity. It will, it must, disintegrate and disappear.

9

All things are either changing or will be affected by change: physical things like peas and mountains, mental things like impressions and imaginations. Is there no unchanging element at all in this ever-changing world?

10

The region of real power, real knowledge, is not in duality, not in the contrast of good and evil, light and dark, but in THAT which transcends them. Can we gain access to it?

11

We live in the Real—all of us—but only few know it.

12

This is a paradox of existence: that the Real is beyond the illusory and yet the illusory is derived from the Real.

13

Only when one stands upon this mystical mountaintop does one begin to see how, in a made universe, there cannot be the pleasurable, the joyful, and the sweet alone. Wherever there is birth there must be death; wherever there is a possible pleasure there must be a possible pain. The recognition of the unpleasant things may sound quite inhuman, and in a certain sense it is; but then, it was not a human being who fashioned the universe.

14

The notion that the world is not what it seems to be, that it is an appearance quite other than the reality behind it, is a true one. But it ought not to be misused to support escapism, apathy, the sense of futility and of the uselessness of life. Fit it to the other half of truth, that the Reality from which the world (which includes oneself) is derived, is divine, with all the wonderful meanings of the word. The correct consequence should follow—inspiration and invigoration.

15

The upward spiral course of the line of Eternal recurrence reveals the relativity of this phenomenal world, not only in time but also in space, and in a kind of substance—from which it is formed.

16

If there is one thing that is forever what it is, itself unchanging and unaffected, it cannot be found in this world of time and space.

17

The world is seen and man must live in it. But he can do so deceived by the feeling of its reality, or awake to the reality itself, which hides behind the appearance.

18

The unseen energy from which atomic physics derives the universe is beyond investigation by scientific apparatus. But the first effect is not so exempt. The split atom reveals itself in the cyclotron as nuclear particles which have definite form. From them the universe is built and thus matter appears. Energy form—matter—this is the sequence but where is mind in all this? Consciousness and intelligence exist in man. He is only a part of the universe. The whole is greater than the part (that is, mind). Therefore mind exists in the universe (that is, Nature). Careful analysis combined with its opposite, profound meditation, shows using the knowledge derived from atomic physics, this universal mind to be none other than the unseen power—God.

19

If the world is unreal, as Advaita asserts, it nevertheless *does appear*. As Brahman it does not appear; this is the function of *Maya*. Brahman, however, is the reality underlying the unreal appearance of *Maya*.

The world appearance

20

The world is not illusion: it is relative, or an appearance, a changing phase of reality. Nor is it purposeless. It exists to evolve the individual entities to their goals.

21

There is a view that human existence is a kind of sleep-walking, that it is God imagining himself to be man but that one day he wakes up and discovers his real nature: this is a view which needs deep careful consideration before summary rejection.

22

Both philosophy and metaphysics and even some religions agree in calling the universe an illusion. But they do not all agree in their attitude towards it. Only philosophy draws attention to the fact that even if its existence is an illusory one, it is still there, for we are aware of it. Mental denial does not lead to physical non-reporting of it by the five senses. It is better to admit this existence and to put it in its proper place rather than to say it is nothing, that it is not there.

23

We are trapped in the world of time, embedded in our earthly selves, limited by this five-sensed body, and entirely deceived by the seeming reality of things into believing it to be the final reality.

24

There is no thing, be it as vast as a sun or as small as a cell, which is not subject to the law of opposite polarities and which therefore does not manifest itself in two entirely contrary ways. Yet man, because his senses are so limited, sees it in only a single way. It is this incompleteness which creates his illusion that the thing really exists in time, is measured in space, and is shaped in form.

25

Not only is this world not the real world, it is not even its shadow, but only the shadow of its shadow.

26

The world does exist, we are surrounded by it, and usually we apply the term to something that does not exist. It will be more correct to translate the term *Maya* not by "unreal" but by "not what we think it to be." We must not deny the existence of the world—that would be lunacy—but we must try to get a correct understanding of its hidden nature.

27

It is a mistake to translate the Sanskrit term *lila* as play in the sense of sporting idly. The correct meaning is play in the sense of a theatrical show.

28

"All the world is but a dream," sang the Mahratta mystic, Tulsidas, thus echoing the misunderstanding which has stamped mystical thought throughout India.

29

A "delusion" is wholly false and untrue, whereas an "illusion" has some kind of basis beneath it.

30

There is no need to insult intelligence by denying existence—whether the world's or the body's—but we can try to understand that there are different forms of existence and only one formless essence of it.

31

The world-illusion: it projects the unreal but hides the real.

32

Here is the essence of both the Theory of Relativity and philosophy's development of it. Two men standing on two different planets moving at different speeds and at disproportionately different distances from the same object at the same instant of time, will differently perceive this object and differently estimate both its character and the measure of the forces working upon it. How can it be said that one of these results is wrong and the other right? Both are correct, for both must be what they are from their respective standpoints. But the same object and the same forces cannot at one and the same time possess contradictory measurements and properties. Therefore these men are not really dealing with *it* but with *their own* observations of it. On the other hand, two entirely different objects may produce two entirely similar sets of sense-impressions, as in the case of the meteor called shooting-star and a genuine star. Hence the things and forces in the world are not really the world-in-itself but what we individually see and experience as the world. All that we really know of them in the end is the picture which forms itself out of our sense-impressions, and this picture alone has genuine existence. Anything beyond it has only a supposed existence. But these impressions when thoroughly analysed are found to be only forms which the mind has unconsciously made for itself, just as a dreamer unconsciously makes his dream world for himself. The world of man's experience is always entirely relative to the individual man himself. All that he sees and smells lies wholly within his consciousness and not outside it.(P)

33

It is, of course, almost impossible for a non-mathematical brain to be able to comprehend processes which are essentially mathematical. However, I cannot agree with the criticisms that the ancient philosophical form of this doctrine was no more than a guess. Certain mental powers of insight into the nature of things were developed by a few ancient philosophers through concentration and reflection. By the exercise of these powers they arrived at a result which is different only in form, but not in essence, from the modern theory of Relativity.

34

Whatever the universe be in human experience, it is, in important ways, like a dream. That is, we must grant existence to a dream world as an indubitable fact because it is a perceived and experienced world; but at the same time we must refuse its form ultimate existence, and hence enduring reality, because it is neither perceived nor experienced after we awake from sleep. This twofold character of the dream world also belongs to the familiar and so-called real universe. It is plain, yet paradoxical at the same time. For this reason, ancient Tibetan philosophers declared the world to be both existent and non-existent. To the unenquiring mind it vividly is what it seems to be, but to the awakened insight of the sage its form presents itself like a more enduring version of the transient form of a dream world. Both forms are thought-constructions. Both have Mind as their underlying "substance." Therefore Mind is their reality. Apart from Mind the world could not even exist, just as apart from the dreamer his dream could not exist.(P)

35

When the analysis of his life is made he sees that it sums up as (1) a series of changing experiences through which he passes physically and (2) another series through which he passes mentally. Impermanence is stamped upon them. However welcome at first, they are disenchanting in the end.

36

In this matter of the real and the illusory, it is not enough to hear or to read about what is real; it must also be *known* by experience following intuition, which itself offers glimpses.

37

The world is not as real as we ordinarily see it: but neither is it as illusory as some metaphysicians see it. For insofar as it is an illusion there must be something behind it to create the illusion.

38

The world-illusion not only obscures the Reality behind it but deceives us into thinking of the Many as being Real, instead of being One.

39

When the old worn-out phrases about Brahman and *maya* are parroted from Shankara it is better to answer simply, "So what!" For still things remain the same as before, all the denunciation of the world has been merely *maya* and does not change its very real presence and actuality to us. The same applies to the other persons and individuals. Is it not better to say that the ego, with its body, emotion, and intellect, is part of the person's experience than to deny it altogether?

40

In itself the universe is not eternal, but its intermittent appearances are. If it were eternal, there would then be a pair of supreme realities—the Divine and the Material, God and Matter—each separately existing.

41

When they come out of their dreams and studies, these pedantic dismissers of the universe of their own selves still find the world and the body waiting for them and still confronting them with problems and cares.

42

To say that the world is *maya* is to say that it is changing, dependent, relative, mysterious, and illusory.

43

A thing becomes an illusion only when its reality becomes inferior to a higher reality that has already been found. Until then, it is still a reality. Only the sage has the strict right to call this world an illusion. If anyone else does so, such talk is mere babble.

44

Are the lake waters and massive Alps which present themselves to my gaze nothing but an illusion? Do those terrible wars and tragic events through which the human race has lately passed deceive us about their reality?

45

We think we are experiencing a real world, but that is because we know so little and are deceived so easily. For we know only the appearances of things, see only the illusions of the senses.

46

Without an immeasurably swift vibratory movement of the flashes of energy which constitute it, our illusion of a world around us could not exist.

47

The actions and movements of figures on the cinema screen are optical illusions. The screen really registers thousands of individual *still* photos. The illusion of motion is created because the eyes cannot register each picture separately, the speed of release per second being too high for its own power to do so. Thus the sense organ deceives us into thinking that the actors are moving, when really each and every photo shows them still. If the reels of film were turned just slowly enough to depict each photo separately, the illusion of living movement would disappear altogether.

48

The senses tell us that a star is only a speck. Reason corrects their judgement and tells us that it is an object of immense size.

49

The world's reality is only apparent, its eternality is only relative. Its true nature eludes the senses, its timeless essence eludes the mind.

50

What the Hindus call *maya* is what the Westerners often call "illusion"; it is also what Gandhi called "appearance," Fichte called "idea," and Schopenhauer "representation."

51

The world as it appears to our eyes is not the same as the world as it would appear to the eyes of a two-dimensional being.

52

We live in different worlds which interpenetrate each other, for there are simply different levels of consciousness. This is as true of the so-called dead as it is of us and it explains the coexistence of heaven and hell.

53

It is more careful to admit that our experience of the world is *both* real and illusory than to dogmatize that it is *only* illusory.

54

All things are relative to other things and are subject to change. Every object which seems completely real is only so for a limited time and in a certain form.

55

It is truer to say that the world is an appearance than that it is an illusion, an experience rather than an unreality.

56

Philosophy does not advocate belief in the orthodox Christian theory that the universe was created from nothing, nor its related notion of a sudden first creation, which is an equally untenable assumption. There is no moment when the universe has not existed, either latently or actively, and consequently there will be no moment when it will not continue to exist, either latently or actively. This is so because the world does not arise by a sudden act of creation but by a gradual process of manifestation. Since there is no particular moment in the universe's long history when it could be said to have been first created, it has never had a beginning and consequently will never have an end. It has never been started so it can never be finished. It is eternal and self-sustaining because it is the body of God, who is eternal and self-sustaining. Creation begins and ends nowhere and nowhen. The conception of the universe which presumes to assign a date to creation is a nebulous one and will vary with the mere caprice of the "dater." He will hatch out a creation theory to suit himself, depending therefore on human temperament and taste. Philosophy repudiates the mentalistic theory as generally interpreted, for external Nature is not regarded as unreal. It is a fact that our experience of the world's appearance is ephemeral but our experience of the world's existence is essentially real. It follows therefore that those who would turn the world into an illusion to which no value should be attached are compelled to recognize its presence and evolve their theory to account for it. The truth is that the cosmos is truly a self-revelation of the World-Mind. It is spun out of God's very self. Thus instead of an absentee God, we have an everywhere-present one who is the very essence of the world.

57

He must not let the *Ashtavakra Samhita* be misunderstood. It does *not* preach mystic idleness and indifference. The world is there for both sage and student, and both must work and serve—the difference being mental only. Illusionism is not the doctrine except as an intermediate stage towards truth, which is higher. One must participate in God's work by assisting evolution and redeeming the world, not squat idly in peace alone.

58

Although we live in a world that is basically unreal—if we define reality as that which never changes, which ever was, is, and will be—we have to live in this world as if it were real, substantially real. We are compelled to do so, because we find ourselves here and we have to be active here. What it amounts to is that the *maya* of the Indians has to be treated as if it were Brahman, but we can only do so safely if we know the Truth.

59

The Hindu metaphysicians write off the Universe as our own fault, because we are deceived by the power of illusion, while our personal ego receives the same labelling: it is a fiction. At the same time they propound the teaching of a constant series of reincarnations in other forms which we have to undergo. Thus, their idea of immortality takes a different shape from the Christian one. We forget what we suffered and enjoyed, only to fall into new memories and new resurrections. Thus they deny we have any personal ego at all, yet go on behaving as if it is really there. The serious man may be forgiven his bewilderment. He is promised liberation (from the existence which at the same time is denied) if he rises to a height not only of incredible moral virtue but also of incredible psychological subtlety and semantic penetration, while we too have to go on attending to the earthly matters which are quite illusory.

60

There is a wide assortment of smiles. They can be prompted by traits as far from each other as hypocrisy is from sincerity, as selfishness is from compassion, as the falseness of treachery is from the realization of truth. They may look alike; this is an indirect, remote, but not unconnected illustration of the teaching that the universe is in reality not what it appears to be.

61

Of what use or help is it to tell the enquiring Westerner, "The Hindu sage does not see the world; he sees only Brahman"? If he does not see the world, then he does not see food in front of him, nor even his own body—both being parts of the physical world. Such statements merely create confusion for others. The Greek philosopher saw the world but understood it for what it really was. He did not need to deny its existence.

62

The status of the world is contradictory. It is a thing because it exists but a no-thing because it is only an appearance. It is like the hazy twilight, which is neither day nor night, yet in one sense day but in another night. It is like a dream, which is real enough while we are within it but unreal when we are not.

63

Alice in Wonderland: "You're only one of the things in his dream. You know very well you're not real," said Tweedledum. "If I wasn't real," Alice said, "I shouldn't be able to cry." Interrupted Tweedledum: "I hope you don't suppose those are real tears?"

64

The Hindu doctrine of world illusion is itself an illusion because it denies its own experience instead of admitting but reinterpreting (that is, understanding) it.

65

The first momentous discovery with metaphysical implications of the first order towards which science arduously laboured its way was that matter is in the end only an illusory appearance. The next great discovery of a similar character has already begun and it will finish with the corollary that time and space are also in the end illusory appearances. But as the world in which we live and the only one which we ordinarily know is a material, temporal, and spatial one, it follows that mankind is beset by the profoundest illusions. Thoroughly to understand the significance of illusions, however, is to understand that in the end it is the working of the Mind alone that plays these tricks on man and clothes the world for him in matter, time, and space. If therefore he wishes to free himself from these three universal illusions he must achieve conscious control of the mind's activity. This he can succeed in doing through Yoga; concentration on a single thought theme or object, when persisted in to the bitter end, stops such mental activity and thus the illusions which accompany it also stop.

66

The relativity of things, ideas, and experiences should not be used to assert that one thing is as good as another, one truth as valid as another. That would be idiotic. All is illusion but all is not equally illusive.

67

When the meaning of relativity is only half-understood, and its place in the scheme of things wholly misunderstood, then all statements are equally true, or equally untrue.

68

The doctrine of relativity has a grave danger of its own. When we see that numerous standpoints may rightly exist, we may claim despairingly, "Beauty, truth, and righteousness have no real existence but only an imagined one."

69

The sceptics who deem this world-appearance impenetrable, who would say that the only truth is that there is no truth, only opinion, are honest but not fully informed.

70

All knowledge presupposes both a subject and an object, the two thoughts "I" and "another."

71

From one standpoint Relativism reveals all knowledge to be but a bundle of illusions.

72

Such is this relativity of all things to their knower that because the world we experience is *our* mental world, we never see the world as it really is in itself or as a being who was observing it from outside would observe it. The consequence is that we never see the world without unconsciously seeing the world mixed up with the self. The "I" plus something other than the "I" constitute our field of consciousness. We never know the world-in-itself but only the world-in-a-state-of-interaction-with-the-self. We never know the self-in-itself but only the self-in-a-condition-of-interaction-with-the-world. Such are the actual and compulsory conditions of the so-called experience of the world and our so-called experience of the self.(P)

73

What does experience mean in the light of this analysis? It means not only that the world in itself is never known in isolation but also that the "I" is likewise never isolated.

74

Can the observer who sees, the knower who knows be himself made an object to be perceived? No! says the intellectual; Yes! says the mystic philosopher.(P)

75

In the awareness of a thing, a scene, or an event there is awareness inside time and space, and hence inside their limitations. The subject is present, tied as ever to an object; the observer is involved as always with the observed.

76

Whoever claims to possess an absolute knowledge of Truth is suspect. Without going to the opposite extreme and agreeing with French novelist Anatole France that "all is opinion," and without proceeding to his dry conclusion, "My opinion is to have no opinion!" we may grant that the personal status of a man and his particular standpoint lead to the kind of "truth" he attains.

77

The spectacle of this world is subject to change, but the spectator himself never changes. These constant transformations are plainly to be seen but he who sees them is deeply concealed.

78

If the relativity of human knowledge is so striking a fact, how then, it will be asked, can philosophy be of any service to the quest of truth? It can only destroy the intellectual positions of others but cannot establish an absolute final position of its own.

79

To take the world as it really is demands a profound insight which arises as all the old dualisms dissolve.

80

If anyone proclaims it to be Truth, then it must be portrayed as living truth, something with a living God behind it.

81

As a man grows more aware of philosophy's truth, he grows more aware of the ephemeral nature of things.

82

Both the subject and object of consciousness are only one.

83

Man sees the world all right, but seldom sees himself in the act of seeing the world.

84

Which, amongst so many conflicting teachings, is the true one? Their effect upon the thoughtful seeker is to produce bewilderment. But he who understands the relativity of ideas may move through them all with unruffled detachment.

85

Man himself is an evolving and therefore a changing entity. His perceptions and his understanding are growing in range. How then dare he claim that any of his knowledge is final, any of his truths absolute?

2

THE DOUBLE STANDPOINT

All experience may be regarded from either the practical or the philosophical standpoint, but best of all from the double standpoint.

2

We use a twofold standpoint in this quest. This is because it is the minimum possible. Yet even this would seem to contradict and negate itself. But each serves a purpose of its own. It is possible, because of the reign of relativity in the universe, even to trace a sevenfold standpoint, all the levels coexisting.

3

Mentalism says we can make sense of our experiences only if we apply to them, and to our understanding of them, the double standpoint: Immediate and Ultimate, or Appearance and Reality, or Relative and Absolute. The ordinary, normal point of view takes the world as the five senses find it—that is, as it appears to be. This is easy for everyone to understand and accept. But the deepest possible examination and analysis by philosophic intelligence, as well as the highest possible insight of mystic experience, presents a totally different result: The One, That which IS, has undergone no change at all.

4

Can we ever escape from the relativity which affects everything from an ant to an aeon? In a universe where everything is in process of continuous change and is ever becoming something else, where nothing has a self-existence that is really enduring, where every ephemeral change seems the only reality at the moment, can we hope to find something that exists by its own right and forever exists unchanged in itself? Reality that IS? The answer is provided by philosophy. Our intellects and senses may misapprehend it and perceive form without perceiving its essence. Nevertheless, reality interpenetrates everything and goes out into all things. There is nothing here in this space-time without its share in reality. Hence philosophy bids us see *through* the multitudinous forms of the world into the unity upon which they are grounded, without, however, letting our consciousness lose, as the mystic loses, the forms themselves. And this unitary substance is none other than Mind-essence itself.

5

If we think, "I strive to become one with God," or, "I am one with God," we have unconsciously denied the statement itself because we have unconsciously set up and retained two things, the "I" and "God." If these two ultimately exist as separate things they will always exist as such. If, however, they really enter into union, then they must always have been in union and never apart. In that case, the quest of the underself for the Overself is unnecessary. How can these two opposed situations be resolved? The answer is that relativity has taught us the need of a double standpoint, the one relative and practical and constantly shifting, the other absolute and philosophical and forever unchanged. From the first standpoint we see the necessity and must obey the urge of undertaking this quest in all its practical details and successive stages. From the second one, however, we see that all existence, inclusive of our own and whether we are aware of it or not, dwells in a timeless, motionless Now, a changeless, actionless Here, a thingless, egoless Void. The first bids us work and work hard at self-development in meditation, metaphysics, and altruistic activity, but the second informs us that nothing we do or abstain from doing can raise us to a region where we already are and forever shall be in any case. And because we are what we are, because we are Sphinxes with angelic heads and animal bodies, we are forced to hold *both* these standpoints side by side. If we wish to think truthfully and not merely half-truthfully, we must make both these extremes meet one another. That is, neither may be asserted alone and neither may be denied alone. It is easier to experience this quality than to understand it.

This is puzzling indeed and can never be easy, but then, were life less simple and less paradoxical than it is, all its major problems would not have worried the wisest men from the remotest antiquity until today. Such is the paradox of life and we had better accept it. That is, we must not hold one standpoint to the detriment of the other. These two views need not oppose themselves against each other but can exist in a state of reconciliation and harmony when their mutual necessity is understood. We have to remember both that which is ever-becoming and that which is ever in being. We are already as eternal, as immortal, as divine as we ever shall be. But if we want to become aware of it, why then we must climb down to the lower standpoint and pursue the quest in travail and limitation.

6

It would be an error to believe that the two standpoints are in conflict with each other; they are not because they cannot be. They can never produce a logical antimony; they are different readings of the same thing, a difference rendered inevitable because referring to different levels of knowledge, experience, and position.

7

One of the helpful notions which philosophy contributes to those who not only seek Truth through the intellect alone, but also seek to know how they are to live with that Truth in the active world itself, is the idea of the twofold view. There is the immediate view and there is the ultimate viewpoint. The first offers us a convenient way of looking at our activities in the world and of dealing with them whilst yet holding firmly to the Truth. The first tells us to act as if the world is real in the absolute sense. The second viewpoint, the ultimate, tells us that there can be only one true way of looking at everything, because there is only one Reality. Since it deals with the Absolute, where time and space disappear and there is no subject to view, no object to be viewed, there is no thought or complex of thoughts which can hold it; it transcends intellect. Therefore it could be said that philosophy uses duality for its practical viewpoint, but it stays in nonduality for its basic one, thus reconciling both.(P)

8

What is the practical value of the teaching about time? The full answer to this question would embrace many fields, but here is one of the most important. Philosophy teaches its student to apply the double point of view to the outward happenings of his life as it does to the inward contents of his sense-experience. From the ordinary point of view, the nature of an event determines whether it is a good or an evil one; from the philosophic point of view, the way he thinks about the event will determine whether it is good or evil for him. He should always put the two points of view together and never separate them, always balance the short-range one by the long-range one.

The higher point of view enables him to escape some of the suffering which the lower one would impose upon him. An event which to the worldly man seems staggeringly important and evil from the point of view of the moment, becomes smaller and smaller as the years recede and, consequently, less and less hurtful. Twenty years later it will have lost some of its power to shake him; fifty years later it will have lost still more—indeed, it may have lost so much as to cause him no further pain; one incarnation later it will not trouble him at all. When the student adopts the long-range point of view he achieves the same result in advance and by anticipation of time. It is said that time heals all sorrows; if we seek the reason why, we shall find it is because it insensibly gives a more philosophic point of view to the sorrowful. The taste of water in a jar will be strongly sweetened by a cupful of sugar; the taste of water in a bucket will be moderately sweetened by it; the taste of water in a bathtub will be only slightly sweetened by it; and water in a lake will be apparently quite unmodified by it at all. In exactly the same way, the stream of happenings which makes up time for human consciousness gradually dilutes the suffering which each individual event may bring us.

The student is not content, however, to wait for such a slow process in order to reduce his suffering. By bringing the philosophic attitude to bear upon each event, as and when it occurs, he immediately reduces his suffering and fortifies his peace. Every calamity which is seen from this standpoint becomes a means whereby he may ascend, if he will, to a higher level of understanding, a purer form of being. What he thinks about it and what he learns from it will be its real legacy to him. In his first fresh anguish the unawakened man may deny this; in the mental captivity which gives reality to the Present and drops it from the Past, he may see no meaning and no use in the calamity; but either by time or by philosophy he will one day be placed at the point of view where the significance of suffering will be revealed to him and where the necessity of suffering will be understood by him. This, indeed, is one of the great paradoxes of the human development: that suffering leads him step by step from the false self to the acceptance of the true self, and that the true self leads him step by step back to the acceptance of suffering.

If the worldly man agitatedly sees the event against the background of a moment, if the philosophic student calmly sees it against the background of an entire lifetime, the sage, while fully aware of both these points of view, offsets them altogether by adding a third one which does not depend on any dimension of time at all. From this third point of view, he sees both the event itself and the ego to whom it happens as illusory. He feels the sense of time and the sense of personality as unreal. Deep within his mind he holds unshakeably to the timeless character of true being, to the eternal life of the kingdom of heaven. In this mysterious state time cannot heal, for there are no wounds present whereof to be healed. So soon as we can take the reality out of time, so soon can we take the sting out of suffering. For the false self lives like a slave, bound to every passing sensation, whereas the true self lives in the timeless peace of the kingdom of heaven. As soon as we put ourselves into harmony with the true self, we put ourselves into harmony with the whole universe; we put ourselves beyond the reach of calamity. It may still happen, but it does not happen to nor is it felt by our real self. There is a sense of absolute security, a feeling that no harm can come to us. The philosophic student discovers the mission of time; it heals sorrows and, under karma or through evolution, cures evils. The sage solves the mystery of timelessness, which redeems man.(P)

9

Philosophy would not be worthwhile if it did not take the view that for the practical purposes of life, it must turn around and adopt a non-metaphysical approach. Thus a twofold attitude is the only complete and therefore correct one which it may approve. We have the right and bear the duty to ask ourselves in what way is a teaching related to everyday living; in what way is it connected with the world we know? If both relation and connection are absent, it is fair to say that the teaching is inadequate and lacks the necessary balance of interests.(P)

10

Metaphysically, every thing and every thought contains in itself the form of its opposite. We must try not to be attached to one opposite and not to be repelled by the other in a *personal* way. This does not mean that we may ignore them—indeed we cannot do so, for practical life requires that we attempt at least to negotiate them—but that we deal with them in an equable and impersonal way. Thus we keep free of the bonds of possessiveness. If we try to cling to one of the opposites alone whilst rejecting the other, we are doomed to frustration. To accept what is inherent in the nature of things is therefore a wise act. If, through being personally hurt by it, we are unwilling to do so, if we rebel against it, then we shall succeed only in hurting ourselves all the more. To run away from one of the opposites and to run after the other is an unwise act. We must find a balance between them; we must walk between the two extremes; we must ascend the terrace above the standpoint which affirms and above that which negates: for the entire truth is never caught by either and is often missed by both. For the way in which our consciousness works shuts us up, as it were, in a prison house of relativistic experiences which are the seeming real but never the actually real. To accept both and yet to transcend both, is to become a philosopher. To transcend the opposites we have to cease thinking about what effect they will have upon us personally. We have to drop the endless "I" reference which blinds us to the truth about them. We must refuse to set up our personal preferences as absolute standards, our relative standpoints as eternal ones. To do this is to cease worrying over events on the one hand, to cease grabbing at things on the other. It is indeed to rise to an impersonal point of view and enter into harmony with what Nature is seeking to do in us and in our environment. We have to find a new and higher set of values. For so long as we cling to a personal standpoint we are enslaved by time and emotion, whereas as soon as we drop it for the philosophic one, we are liberated into a serene timeless life.(P)

11

All concepts are dualistic; each implies its contrary concept. We cannot think them without silently posing their counterparts: the Void and the All, the "I" and the not-Self. This is why we have to abandon dualism in the end for nondualism if we want truth. We cannot have one foot in each camp.

12

Once the double viewpoint is understood and set up as the necessary starting point, the timed measure and the timeless order fall into his scheme of things. Practical experience carries him through the ordinary existence, and divine experience—the eternal Now—is not displaced by it. Success in living the philosophic life and maturing the mentality it requires makes this possible.(P)

13

Only by accepting the double standpoint concurrently, rejecting neither the Real nor the Illusory, can we achieve Truth's wholeness.

14

Unless one looks at life from this double point of view, one can get only an inadequate unbalanced and incomplete perspective. It is needful for the everyday practical routine of living to regard it only at the point of personal contact. Here one sees its momentary, transitory, and finite form. But it is also needful for the satisfaction of the higher interests of mind and heart to regard the living universe as a whole. Here one sees an eternal and infinite movement, cored and surrounded by mystery.

15

That which IS is not moved, affected, or changed by events or things, by cosmic calamities or human thoughts. For these are all in time, THAT is out of it, has always been out of it and must therefore always be out of it. To us, all is happening in successive moments, but that is the timed view.

16

Hegel in Germany and the Jains in India taught the relativity of truth. They showed that by taking up different positions different aspects of truth would be revealed. But where the Jains put forward seven positions as covering the range, Hegel put forward three. Any relative truth is limited, one-sided, incomplete, and may even contradict the others. While philosophy endorses the truth of relativity present in both positions, it cannot endorse their exclusive character. It paradoxically adopts a positionless position free from their rigidity and limitations. It comes into no conflict with any sect, system, or religion, with any fixed dogmatism or freethinking scepticism. It is a rival to none, competes with none. It reconciles the varied expressions of human thought and belief, accommodates them all by refusing their one-sidedness, bias, prejudice, but avoids their errors and incompleteness. It *knows* what it teaches, the final incontrovertible truth that there is nothing beyond Mind. It experiences the final uncontradictable reality where no distorting ego is present.

17

Science has pushed forward its exploration and operation into the immense distances of the cosmos without being able to conceive an end to them, as it has penetrated the unbelievably tiny world of the atom with a similar result. This is the mathematical infinite. But there is another. No instruments and no apparatus can be applied to objects of thought which imply its existence, for measurement and quantity are not concerned. That is the *metaphysical* infinite.

18

(a) "The one without a second" reappears in the universe as "no two things alike." (b) Nonduality, not two, means mentalism; the world is my idea, in my consciousness, hence not separate from me. There are not two—me plus world.

19

The World-Mind itself dwells in the Timeless Present, the Eternal Now. But for human beings all things happen, are experienced and observed, in succession.

20

Why did Emerson remark when he had to examine a quantity of wood he had ordered: "We must see to these things, you know, as if they were real"?

21

Unless these two standpoints are recognized as necessary, only bewildered minds, confused thinking, and false conclusions will follow. The immediate must be distinguished from the ultimate, the obvious from the profound.

22

Just as *The Hidden Teaching Beyond Yoga* defines Reality as that which is always real and never changing, so Truth is that which is always and everywhere true and not necessarily under certain conditions.

23

Consciousness can assume different forms, can operate on different space and time levels, so that it is relative. But it can also remain itself and assume no form; it is then what has been called absolute, not relative. But to reject the possible existence of all these other forms, however temporary they may be, as do those Indians who limit themselves solely to the doctrine of nonduality—fascinated as they are by the reality of the Real and the illusoriness of the unreal, so that they forget whether they are real or unreal—is to forget that he who holds the doctrine is himself a human being. He who comes back from the mystic experience of universality comes back to a human form, is himself a human being, however divine in his inmost essence. The Absolute is not a human being and can have no possible point of view, but the human being must have a humanized philosophy and can have a point of view. What is he to do after recognizing the opposition between the absolute and the relative consciousnesses, between the real and the unreal? The answer is and must be the double point of view. Not, mind you, the double nature of Truth, but the double point of view for us, humans: the one being empirical, practical, earthly and rational, the other being ultimate, divine, intuitive.

24

The enigma of existence cannot be solved on the single basis of the Void alone, nor on the basis of manifestation alone. Both must be taken into account together and at the same time in order to constitute existence for human entities as incarnate individuals.

25

This recognition of the dual principle governing all manifested existence does not cancel recognition of the Unmanifest as being the Final, the Unique, the Real. For the two are derived from it; into it their appearance and working vanish at last, but they themselves, as part of the World-Idea, never. Each universe follows the Divine Order of Yin-Yang.

26

The attempt to reduce truth to a single focal point fixed at the highest possible level suffices for the meditator and the dreamer. But it is too limited to suffice for life itself: thought and action, insight and practice, require two distinct points of view—the immediate and the ultimate.

27

The way out of the to-and-fro wanderings of his moods, to spirit and then away from it, is to accept the double nature of his being and the double polarity of Nature, the double viewpoint of truth and the double aspects of God. Then struggles cease and harmony prevails. There is then no warlike confrontation within himself, but peaceful reconciliation.

28

We have learned that time is but the succession of our thoughts. We have learned also that in all our experience of time and irrespective of the particular series to which it belongs, whether it run with the rapidity peculiar to dream or with the slowness peculiar to wakefulness, there must exist in us a background of rest, of stillness, against which we unconsciously measure our time-sense. The problem is how to bring this background into the field of consciousness. The answer is partly provided for us by this brief analysis. If the thought-succession were stopped—if awareness were determinedly pinned down to a single immobile point—then we would become enfranchised in the kingdom of Infinite Duration. This, however wonderful it be, could nevertheless only be a temporary process because life itself demands that we return to world-consciousness, to the knowledge of experience in space-time. It is indeed the condition which the successful mystic evidently arrives at, the condition of sublime trance which is regarded by him as the perfection of his quest.

29

The ultimate truth refers to the essence of a thing, its real nature. The immediate truth refers to its shifting conditions or passing states, the thing as it appears at the moment of perception.

30

Paradox is the only way to view both the immediate and the ultimate at the same time.

31

Philosophy says that its highest teaching is necessarily paradoxical because the one is in the many and the many, too, are one, because nonduality is allied to duality, because the worldly and limited points to the Absolute and Unbounded: hence the doctrine of two Truths.

32

Paradox is the only proper way to look at things and situations, at life and the cosmos, at man and God. This must be so if as full and complete a truth as mind can reach is desired. To express that truth there are two ways because of its own double nature: there is what the thing seems to be and what it really is. The difference is often as great as that yielded by an electronic microscope with five thousand-fold magnification when it is focused on an ant, compared to the view yielded by the naked eye.

33

If we question time and matter—those foundations of all our worldly experience—for their real nature, we come up against paradox and contradiction, against irrationality and logical absurdity. The only proposition which can properly be affirmed about them is that they exist and do not exist at the same time.

34

You cannot put It into any symbol without falsifying what It really is. Yet you cannot even mention It in any way whatsoever without putting It into a symbol. What then are you to do? If mystics declare, as they so often do, that you should keep silent, ask them why so many of them have failed to obey this rule themselves? In their answer you will find its own insufficiency and incompleteness. For although, like everyone else, they too have to function on two separate and distinct levels, yet the truths pertaining to one level must in the end be coupled with those pertaining to the other.

35

Paradox is the bringing together of two elements which are antagonistic yet complementary.

36

The worship of God in the ordinary and personal sense is quite valid for those who wish to practise it, and for the masses who cannot rise to the highest nondual conception of God. If it involves this phenomenal world, and keeps the worshipper in duality and relativity, he is not wasting his time. As soon as the human mind insists on indulging its imagination or its thinking capacity and tries to understand where it ought to stop and let go of its egoistic effort, it must accept such a paradoxical situation as the double standpoint. The sixth-century Chinese philosopher Chi Tsang, in his "Essay on the Double Truth," which accepted both the immediate or relative and the ultimate or absolute standpoints, felt the difficulty but could do no other than accept it.

Its cultivation and application

37

The necessity of employing the double viewpoint leads to the acceptance of paradox as being the nature of truth. The practising philosopher finds that he must live in time as well as simultaneity, extension as well as infinity, mind as well as MIND. Were he to be simplistic he would create confusion.

38

He has to practise living on two different planes of being at once, the immediate and ultimate, the short-range and long-range, the relative and the Absolute, not as if they were in eternal contradiction but as if they were one and indivisible.

39

We *have* to cope with the world and the problems it brings us with the body and its needs. There is no evading them. Yet on the other hand, we *have* to recognize that in Absolute Truth there is no world, no body, no problems—only the one infinite timeless Being. How can we meet this enigmatic dilemma? Christian Science denies the dilemma in theory, but is untrue to its denial in practice. This is why so many have passed into its portals only to emerge again in later years. Philosophy counsels us to admit the plain fact, *to cultivate a bifocal vision*, and to see the relative truth where and when we want it but always fitted into the larger absolute truth.

40

There are two viewpoints: a qualified truth for the lower stage of aspirants which admits duality, and the complete viewpoint of nonduality for the highest student. Thus for practical life, when dealing with other people or when engaged in some activity, those in the first stage must accept the notion of the world being real, because of expediency; yet even so, when they are alone or when keeping quiet, inactive, they ought to revert back to regarding the world, which includes one's own body as a part of it, as idea. Only for the sage is the truth always present, no matter whether he is with others, whether he is working, or whether he is in trance, and this truth is continuous awareness of one Reality alone and one Self alone.

41

Two simultaneous states of awareness are present in him.

42

We must perceive unity in diversity, and diversity in unity.

43

There is no loftier metaphysical standpoint than that of nonduality, but man cannot live by metaphysics alone. He is in the body, which in its turn is in the world. He needs a second standpoint to deal with both body and world. He needs the relative, the finite, the immediate one of personal experience. Metaphysics may tell him that the world, when examined and analysed, is but an appearance, and not even that when it is taken into the deepest meditation; but the five senses tell him that he must come to terms with it.

44

The world exists in precisely the same way for both the simpleton and the sage, but whereas it exists only as it appears in the first case it exists *both* as it appears and as it really is in the other.

45

In order to remember that we are godlike in essence we do not need to forget that we are human in existence.

46

We exist as beings in time and space, but as Being in the Timeless and Spaceless. For an Advaitin to deny the first statement is as futile as for a materialist to deny the second one.

47

Does this double standpoint mean that there is a constant oscillation between the two aspects, a mind which flutters from one to the other over and over again? Of course not! Just as the small circle can be contained within a larger circle, so the mind can be at once in the practical and the metaphysical yet able to concentrate on the one needed at any moment.

48

He has a double existence, with the frontal part of his consciousness in time and the real part out of it. All the miseries and misfortunes which may enter into the one part will make no difference to the blessed tranquillity which permanently reigns in the other.

49

He is to be not only an actor in the world's drama taking part in the events, but also a member of the audience watching them, not only in the very midst of the happenings but also their detached observer. This sounds too contradictory: are the two roles irreconcilable?

50

His awareness of the relativity of things relieves the philosopher of any compulsion to identify himself with any particular viewpoint. His liberation from dogma enables him to take the viewpoint which best suits the circumstances. This does not at all mean that chaos will enter into his affairs, insincerity into his attitudes, and anarchy into his morals. He is safeguarded from such perils by the link he has established with the Overself's infinite wisdom and immeasurable goodness.

51

The knowledge of its essence thrusts itself up between him and the world so that the physical sensed-envelope is seen for what it is.

52

Only by having a philosophic perspective on whatever happens to him, by balancing the day's events against the timelessness of Reality, can he find and keep peace of mind.

53

He lives in this fixity of consciousness deep within his heart, a fixity which makes the passage of time seem illusory and which makes the happenings of time seem appearances.

54

Live among men as if the world-appearance is what they feel it to be—the reality—but know for yourself the inner truth about it and about yourself.

55

Coming down here into the body of flesh and blood is *our* confusion. Experiencing the sufferings and distresses which we do is our fate. The satisfactions are there also, yes, and induce us to cling to life and return anew after each reincarnation. We need always remember that all this experience which a human undergoes is relative to time and place and must pass on and away. To what? To that higher order of the universe where we are with God as higher creatures.

56

With this larger outlook comes a larger acceptance of the past, of bygone deeds and thoughts, however one may regret actions or feel guilty or embarrassed about emotions. For if there is to be a forgiveness of others, there must also be forgiveness of one's self. And if one has outgrown one's past self, it should be as if one were looking upon another being, a stranger being.

57

This duality of his life will go on until he is ready for the Great Truth which displaces all the lesser ones but which he cannot grasp while clinging to them. If he persists in doing so, he will never be able to make the transition to understanding that there is only the One Infinite Life-Power, the One Ever-Existent Mind, and that all else is mere illusion, idea, or dream.

58

We hear from the East that the world is unreal and that the ego is unreal, or that the world does not exist and that the ego does not exist. It is here that semantics as developed by Western minds may perhaps be of some service in clarifying confused thinking leading to confused statements. The body is a part of the world. Do we or do we not dwell in a body? If we do not then we should stop feeding it and stop taking it to the physician when it gets sick. Yet even those people who make such extraordinary statements do continue to eat, to fall sick, and to visit a doctor. Surely that disposes immediately of the question whether or not the body exists. In the same way and by the same pattern of reasoning we can discover that the world also exists. What then has led these Indian teachers to proclaim otherwise? Here we begin to intrude upon the field of mentalism and as a necessary part of the key to mentalism we must turn to the dream state. If we dream of a world around us and of a body in which we live in this dream world and of other bodies of other persons moving in it, the Indians say that these dream persons and this dream world are seen to be non-existent when we wake up and hence they deny its reality. But the experience did happen, so let us scrutinize it. There was no such thing as this world, true, but something was there; what was there? Thoughts. All this world and all these persons about whom we dream pass through consciousness as thoughts, so the thoughts were there. Whether we consider dream or hallucination, the pictures are there in the person's mind; they exist there, but they exist there only as mental creations. But when we say they are merely mental creations, we are bringing in an attempt to judge them, to judge their nature, what they really are. The statement that they are unreal is therefore a judgement and is acceptable only on the basis of a particular standpoint, the standpoint of the observer who is outside the dream, outside the hallucination. It is not acceptable on the basis of the person who is having the experience at that moment. Thus we see that the existence of the ego, the body, and the world need not be denied; it is there, it is part of our experience, but what we have to do is to examine it more closely and attempt a judgement of its nature. And this judgement does not alter the fact that they are being experienced. This is a fact of our own, of everyone's experience, including the highest sage, only the sage and the common man each has his own judgement from his point of view, from his knowledge. In all these topics we can see how much easier it is to pick our way if we adopt the attitude which was proclaimed in *The Hidden Teaching Beyond Yoga* that there is a double viewpoint and a double standard in this teaching in order that we may be clear about our experiences and about our ideas and not get them mixed up. These two standpoints, the immediate and the ultimate, the common and the philosophic, are absolutely necessary in all talk and study about such metaphysical topics. Otherwise we get lost in mere verbiage, words, words, words.

59

The illumined person must conform to the double action of nature in him, that is, to the outgoing and incoming breaths. So his illumination must be there in the mind, and here in the body. It is the two together which form the equilibrium of the double life we are called upon to live—being in the world and yet not of it. In the prolongation of the expiring breath, we not only get rid of negative thought, but also of the worldliness, the materialism of keeping to the physical alone. With the incoming breath we draw positive inspiring remembrance of the divine hidden in the void. Hence we are *there* in the mind and *here* in the body. We recognize the truth of eternity yet act in time. We see the reality of the Void, yet know that the entire universe comes forth from it.

60

The exterior reality being *Maya*, our universe becomes both an enigma and a paradox until nonduality is accepted as the final and only solution.

61

The difficulty in accommodating the practical and philosophical views of existence is understandable. However, these dual views should not be mistaken for contrasting and opposing ones. The ultimate insight synthesizes them although it cannot prevent the continuance of their seeming variations. It is as though the foreground of the mind must hold the practical view while the background simultaneously holds a philosophical view. This is true for the developed aspirant, but in the adept there arrives, after long practice and profound experience, a condition of illumination which treats all experience for the idea that it is and at the same time keeps bright the light of the ever-burning lamp of reality—Pure Mind.

62

The idea of illusion is a necessary discovery for the beginner, but with deeper knowledge he discovers that the illusion is also the real because it is not apart from reality. The truth is that reality is attainable.

63

The philosophic view does not depose the empiric everyday view of the world. For practical purposes, the rules of the latter will always remain dominant.

64

To live in the ego is to live in time, to live in the Overself is to live in timelessness. But because man must live in both to live on earth at all, let him learn the art of resting in the eternal Now, the continuing moment which opens on to eternity.

65

The double viewpoint doctrine is as useful as it is convenient, for it enables the philosopher to live among the ignorant who believe they inhabit a totally real world as if he shared their belief. Otherwise they might segregate him from his fellows on a charge of insanity and put him in the special institutions built for such cases.

66

We live in the limitations of relativity but pursue the freedoms of divinity. Only later do we discover both are counterpart ideas—to be transcended.

67

The statement "to be" is to be "in time" or "in timelessness." Most limit its meaning to the first phrase only. But the more enlightened know that the higher possibility has been realized by some.

68

Where time is dismissed as unreal, attention to historic change must necessarily wane, and where form is regarded as illusory, the need of a cosmogony will not be felt. The correctness of this position cannot be argued away but its one-sidedness can. For we still have to live in time and form, with our bodies at least.

69

So long as you think there is variety, as in dream you feel the differences are real, you are in the illusory plane. In the unenquired stage, when you don't enquire into the reality of your experience (as in dream) you hold the illusive view.

70

The practical standpoint cannot be dispensed with because it is not humanly possible to find time to gather all the facts and so we have to take many matters on trust or on authority. We use it with confidence because it is based on a fairly uniform experience. The fact remains, however, that the knowledge it affords is not true but only probable knowledge.

71

World-Mind has truly made an image of itself in man who has his pure Mind state in sleep and his active state in waking. Hence space-time relations are introduced only with manifestation and not in Mind. The eternal stillness of Mind is broken by the birth of a cosmos, but it is broken only from the low standpoint of human ignorance.

3

THE STATES OF CONSCIOUSNESS

Consciousness is a property of Mind operating at various levels—sub, super, and ordinary. It is not nullified when it passes out of the ordinary level.

2

There are different levels of consciousness through which a man may progress but only one level of the Real Consciousness.

3

When the Bible says, "No man hath seen God at any time," it means that the sense and thought perceptions of man, being finite and limited in range, cannot comprehend what is infinite and unlimited. That Jesus knew of a Real beyond intellection may be gleaned from his saying, "Which of you by taking thought can add one cubit unto his stature?" which is curiously reminiscent of an Indian saying by Ashtavakra: "A million thoughts will only yield another thought." Simply because it eludes conscious grasp, we can form no conception of Mind as reality. For consciousness of anything particular is a signal that the thing is intellectually graspable—that is, finite and limited. But that whose holy presence itself makes thought possible, cannot be expected to step down to the level of denying its own grandly immeasurable and timeless infinitude. The moment particularized consciousness appears, that moment there will also be relativity, and the moment relativity appears, that moment duality with all its transience and destructibility must be there too. Consequently, we cannot have our Overself with all its nonduality and non-limitation and have this kind of consciousness too.

4

Consciousness is the parent of consciousness, as the greater circle includes the smaller.

5

Consciousness ordinarily implies some object which confronts it, or some idea which occupies it, or some image which appears in it. Hence there is some duality, some relativity, present.

6

The boundaries of his present consciousness have been set up by physical sensation and logical thinking.

7

The consciousness which inheres in the personal self is the palest possible reflection of the intensely real consciousness which inheres in the Overself.

8

Consciousness is the first kind of existence, however limited it may be. But at its best it is divine.

9

The mistake too commonly made is to believe that the ordinary level of consciousness is the only possible one. Successful meditation is one way of getting free from it.

10

If we carefully study Descartes' use of terms, it becomes clear that "I think, therefore I am" refers not to the capacity of being self-aware, but of being somehow conscious.

11

The principle of consciousness in every human being is indeed the same thing as his spiritual consciousness and not a second thing, but he interposes so many clouds of thoughts, sensations, emotions, and passions into it that he seldom comes to this knowledge. He seldom isolates this consciousness principle.

12

There are different modes of being among living creatures, and different modes of consciousness sometimes appear among human creatures.

13

Consciousness is a continuum but, at deeper levels, changes its form until its projection, the little ego, is shut out as in deep sleep.

14

The doctrine of opposites and complementaries, of Yin and Yang, applies not only to the relativity of the universe itself, but also to the human being, to his physical body and mental states.

15

When the mind unites itself with the world outside, we call it waking; when it withdraws attention from the world and unites with its own thoughts or fancies, we call it dreaming; and when it lies settled in itself, uninterested in anything, we call it deep sleep.

16

If anyone could fully perceive the astounding implications of the dream and sleep states, he could not become or remain a materialist. For he would perceive that there is something within him which is able to announce a fact of his experience but which is nevertheless outside his conscious experience. That fact is deep sleep; that "something" is the witnessing element, the soul.

17

Mind is the most mysterious of all things pertaining to human life, yet it is also the most significant. Take its three states of waking, dreaming, and deep sleep and you will find they not only contain wonders for ordinary observers but also great instruction for thoughtful inquirers, for Mind has cast so deep a spell upon us, its projections, that we have forgotten what we were and why we are here.

18

In unwittingly setting up waking consciousness as the sole arbiter of all his knowledge, Western man limits that knowledge unnecessarily. And in regarding other forms of consciousness as mere copies or aberrations of waking consciousness, or else denying their existence altogether, he bars himself from the supreme insight and the highest felicity open to him. Unless he brings the dream and the deep sleep states also into his reckoning, he will continue to be deceived by the Unreal and to mistake the shadow for the substance.(P)

19

Unreflective life is often impatient with such enquiries into the relative value of the waking state, for to them its superior reality in contrast with dream is completely beyond all question. They denounce the sleep enquiry as being altogether too flimsy a premise on which to build great conclusions. Yet when we remember that all living creatures from ant to man are plunged into intermittent sleep for substantial portions of their whole lives, how can we hope to grasp the meaning of their existence and the meaning of the universe of which they are parts, without examining the full meaning and proper value of sleep-states? Whatever we learn from a single state alone may always be liable to contradiction by the facts of another state. Therefore unless we coordinate and evaluate the truth of the waking state with the truth of the sleep state we cannot hope to arrive at ultimate truth in its fullness. But when we venture to make such a coordination we shall discover that in sleep there lies the master-key of life and death!(P)

20

This comparison of the three states offers a clue to the real nature of first, the self; second, the world; third, consciousness; and lastly, Mind—the deepest mystery of all.

21

It would not be hard for a man who has thought much about this situation to ask: Am I only dreaming that I am awake? If I attain the transcendental consciousness will both states vanish, and I with them?—an empty-handed triumph!

22

The forms taken by consciousness when it appears within time can be quite variable. Each variation seems a real experience while the others seem dreamlike or even illusory.

23

Waking is but a unit in a triad of facts about the world's existence. All waking investigations into the universe do not exhaust its meaning; they will always leave a residue too important to be ignored. The world as known to the dreamer is not the whole world. But it is equally true that the world as known to the waking man is just as limited. The facts offered by the dream state differ from those offered by the sleep state while both differ from those of the waking state. Each standpoint will necessarily arrive at a different conception of the world from others.

24

Now it would be too much to expect that any human being could collect all the facts about human experience. But it is possible to collect the principal facts about the three different categories of human experience—wakefulness, dream, and deep sleep—and this is precisely what metaphysics does.

25

It is an ironical fact that even the most ardent subscribers to the doctrine of materialism cannot for long endure material existence but must repeatedly escape from it in sleep or dream. Unfortunately they fail to see the metaphysical significance of this necessity.

26

Even animals have to pass through the experience of three states.

27

The mysterious significance of sleep has yet to be realized by the Western thinkers as it has been by those of the East. It is an independent and distinctive aspect of life with special characteristics too important to be undervalued and too decisive to be ignored. Our great error has been to neglect its investigation, to relegate it among the curiosities of nature when we should have vigorously pursued its ultimate meaning. The secret of life cannot be got from the study of one side of it only—the waking. Man's research must embrace its obverse side too—the sleeping.

28

That mental images and mental facts, emotional trends and intellectual tendencies still exist in a deeper level of mind when they are absent from our consciousness; that the very ego itself still exists therein even when our conscious existence has become utterly blank in deep sleep—these facts indicate how wonderful a thing the mind is.

29

Here, in this wakeful state, on this physical plane, we may move towards the fulfilment of life's higher purpose. But in ever-changing dream or ever-still sleep there is no such opportunity. Hence the New Testament suggests that we work "whilst it is day, for the night cometh when no man can work."—John 9:4

30

Waking world is the crux. Realization must be won here and now.

31

The term "waking state" suggests the actual moments of passing from one state to the other, the transition itself, and is therefore inaccurate to describe as a static condition. Hence I try to use the term "wakefulness" or the "wakeful" state instead.

32

The first question is also the final one; it is quite short, quite simple, and yet it is also the most important question which anyone could ever ask, whether of himself or of others. This question is: "What is consciousness?" Whoever traces the answer through all its levels will find himself in the end in the very presence of the universal consciousness otherwise called God.

33

An evolutionary process in Nature has given a higher quality of consciousness to the waking state over the dream state precisely because of the greater usefulness of the waking state in carrying out the essential, as well as ultimate, purpose of Life Itself.

34

The dream state is the key to the mystery of *who* he is, while the more advanced deep sleep state indicates *what* he is; but it only indicates, points, and does not reveal. However, the problem of sleep is humanity's great study because it solves many others.

35

Sleep is such a disparate fragment of man's life that the dismissal of its silent offering of fact as unimportant is an act of emotional prejudice and one harmful to intellectual honesty. This partial view of life is not enough. The man who confines his views of existence only within the limits of its waking field is really a narrow specialist whose conclusions cannot be trusted beyond their empirical boundaries. Nay, his conclusions are positively dangerous because within such boundaries they may be indubitably *correct*. He has separated a fragment of universal existence—most important, doubtless, but nevertheless a fragment—yet expects to discover the whole truth of that existence from such incomplete data. He has come to believe that his knowledge of the waking world suffices to cover the other two worlds. The instant this belief arises he falls into the trap of imagining that he understands the others when in fact he does not understand them. This delusion is dangerous also because it prevents further enquiry, hinders his advancement, and ultimately renders his mind incapable of apprehending truth.

36

It must not be thought that either the mind of dream or the unconsciousness of profound sleep is ultimate reality. They are not. They are only illustrations drawn upon to help our limited finite minds to form a truer conception of that reality.

The mysterious significance of dreams

37

Is there nothing real during the experience of dreams? Is it completely illusion? The sharpest analysis enables us to detect a residue of reality. The consciousness itself, carried over from waking, was real.

38

Usually each dream is not a complete cycle but a jumble of separate dreaming moments. The fact of this discontinuity of the dream state cannot be used as proof of its unreality. There is an evolutionary process in Nature which gives a different quality to the working of consciousness in the waking state from that of the dream state, precisely because of the greater utility of the waking state to the outworking of its purposes.

39

Nobody dares deny that dream ideas act in so powerful a manner upon the dreamer's mind as to give him the feeling of all that intensity and reality of experience which he possesses during the waking state. People are plainly seen; objects are solidly felt—as much in one case as in the other. The powerful effects of a very vivid dream will sometimes be remembered for days afterwards. And who that has experienced that awful form of dream called the nightmare can find any waking experience which can surpass it in intensity, in immediacy, and in actuality? Yet the same experiences which are accepted as being so real during dream are repudiated as being so unreal after waking! When we consider that this same paradox holds good of all the millions of dreamers throughout the world, we must indeed admit there is something wholly mysterious and momentous in it.

40

A comparison of the waking with the dream state yields two striking similarities. Firstly, neither in one state nor the other do we make our planetary environment, or the other persons who figure in it, or cause all its happenings. We are born into our waking world—it is there ready-made. We find ourselves abruptly in our dream world. The other persons just happen to be in both worlds with us. We do not deliberately prefabricate most of the everyday happenings in the waking world and we do not do this with the dream happenings either. Secondly, in neither world can we predict exactly how we shall behave, react, or feel in all their situations. This is all intended to say that our waking life is really a kind of sleep, from which we need to wake up; that just as the dreamer only awakens when his fatigue exhausts itself or when someone else arouses him, so we, too, only awaken from life's illusions when we are exhausted with all the many different kinds of experience we get from many different incarnations or when a teacher appears to reveal the truth to us. Further, what we have done or desired in former incarnations predetermines a large part of the picture of our present one. Yet, the connection between this cause and this effect is unseen by us until someone else, a master of insight, shows it to us. Until then we are like sleeping dreamers.(P)

41

While he is inside the dream he is outside its real nature, unable to measure its true dimension.

42

There is an intermediate mental state which lies between the unconsciousness of pure mind and the wakefulness of full consciousness. It corresponds to dream, to reverie, and to trance. It is the subconscious.

43

The adept not only knows when asleep that his dream-world is only mental, but he also knows when awake that his wakeful-world is also mental.

44

It is only *after* you awake that you consider your dream to be only a spurious imitation of real life and to possess a pseudo-existence. This difference of view, as against your view during the actual dream itself, must be carefully borne in mind. However trivial you think it now, when you were experiencing the dream it seemed as important as your present waking phase.

45

The contents of dream experience are as external in space as the contents of wakeful experience. But their mutual relations are not governed by the same intrinsic conditions.

46

We know that the dreamer's mind produces a world which not only proceeds wholly from and is substantially dependent upon itself, but is also wholly confined within itself at the time of dreaming. But the world which is experienced during waking is, on the contrary, common to all men. This, it would seem, is an important difference.

47

A dreaming body which believes itself to be running away from a tiger is really lying flat and motionless in bed. Behind the dream figure of a tortured man projected by the dream mind stands the dreamer himself. He is actually undergoing no torture at all. Similarly, if a waking-world tortured man could penetrate deeply enough into his own mental being, he would find the deeper portion of his mind which has projected his own waking self and which is likewise undergoing no torture at all. To achieve this, however, he would have to be as able to stand aside from the waking standpoint as he already is able, after awaking, to stand aside from the dream standpoint. But it must never be forgotten that the waking, dream, and deeper selves are three standpoints of one and the same mind, are all parts of the complex character of ourself. The mind wears three faces, as it were, two of which are visible and the other invisible.

48

A nightmare is the strongest example of what reality dream life can apparently attain. Suppose for a minute that one's own body has become the imagined body belonging to one in a vivid dream. During the period of dream, men may gash it with knives and stab it with daggers. The skin will be cut, the flesh penetrated, the nerves severed; pain will be felt, and blood will pour out of this body. All may happen during such a horrible nightmare precisely as it may happen during the waking state and with the same dramatic vividness. Yet during the whole ghastly experience the skin, nerves, flesh, and blood were merely imagined, were only ideas! The whole apparatus of sense, whether it be eye or ear or skin, and the whole mechanism of nerves, are themselves mental experiences no less than those dream ideas and those dream perceptions which we unhesitatingly accept as such.

49

The truth is that the so-called unconscious has an immensely wider and more wonderful range of activity than the conscious mind. It can accomplish much more in less time, too.

50

The unconscious is very conscious.

51

Stimuli involved in the dream state are not identical with those of the waking state. In the dream state they are entirely self-suggested, whereas in the waking state the results of World-Mind's activities take precedence over self-suggestion.

52

Every experience possible to the physical body—even that of awakening from a dream!—can find its perfect parallel in an experience possible to the dream body. It is utterly impossible to mark out any difference between the two bodies in this respect.

53

Descartes: When I considered that the very same thoughts which we experience when awake may also be experienced when we are asleep, while there is at that time not one of them true, I supposed that all the objects that had ever entered into my mind when awake had in them no more truth than the illusions of my dreams.

54

The intelligence which sometimes solves our problems for us during dreams is of a higher quality than that which ordinarily solves them during wakeful hours. It is indeed of the same order as that which we call intuition.

55

The space-time sense is so modified in dream that you may be here at one moment and across the world at the next.

56

The state of dream is purely an intermediate one between the seeming life of wakefulness and the seeming death of sleep.

57

The sense-experiences of the dream world occur without the use of any of the body's sense organs at all. They give us the experience of colour, without the eyes and without light; of form, without the touching hand and without an external object. Do they not point to the independence of the mind, to its reality in its own right, to the separateness of its sensations from physical causes?

58

It is true that the mind imposes its own ideas in dreams but this is only one of several factors to be considered. It is necessary to distinguish between the different classes of dreams. Some are dramatizations of physical disturbances but others are symbolic messages from the higher self. Thus most of our dreams are unimportant, but some are significant.

59

A dream may be trivial or important, inspired or commonplace, prophetic or symbolic, irrational or significant, an imagination or a revelation, terrifying or satisfying, uplifting or degrading, an echo of the day or an invention of the night, other-worldly or this-worldly, quickly forgotten or long remembered—it can be any of these because the mind's possible workings are widely varied.

60

Dreams occur for several different reasons. And two parts of one and the same dream occur for two different reasons. It is unscientific to say—as the materialistic medicos, many psychoanalysts, and the fortune-tellers stubbornly say—that dreams are determined by a single particular cause. And it is just as unscientific to say that dreams have only one function to perform. Therefore the student must move warily when trying to understand dream processes or to interpret individual dream happenings. It is quite true to assert, for example, that some dreams or some parts of a dream represent unconscious desires or repressed emotions, but it is equally true to assert that most dreams don't represent them at all. It is fallacious to make the dream a metaphor pointing to future events. More often, it is a stew cooked up out of past ones. For most dreams merely reveal what happens when the image-making faculty breaks loose from the general mental equipment and works out a series of self-deceptive illusions based on real material picked up during the previous day's experiences.(P)

61

Just as the spiritual ignorance of man reveals itself during his slumbers by his total lack of knowledge that the dream-experience is only a series of ideas, so the evil character of man reveals itself during his slumbers by the rule it imposes—unrepressed by legal sanctions or social codes—upon his dreams. This is one of the elements of truth in Freud's otherwise grossly materialistic teaching. The dream is partially a self-revelation. Hence it is the teaching of the mystical order of Turkish Sufis that the progress of a disciple is partially to be measured by his teacher by the progressive purification attained in the character of his dream life.(P)

62

The meaning of an event which eludes him on the ordinary world level may reveal itself on the dream, meditational, or psychic levels.

63

You may have a dream which puts itself in a purely symbolic form. This taken literally may seem ridiculous but interpreted becomes meaningful.

64

Sleep is a strange affair; dreams are even stranger. Few know that they can be converted into coherent rational experiences, that they can be consciously shaped.

65

If waking life events contribute to dream life, so do dreams themselves contribute to waking life.

66

In that mysterious moment when blankness falls upon the mind and sleep supervenes, the cross-over into conscious sleep is possible.

67

The fact that most dreams are merely mechanically formed and do not signify anything important should warn us not to fall into superstition about them or to be guided unduly by them.

68

Dreams are often mixed because the mind is more negative to other minds and thus a telepathic receptivity is set up, which works so loosely, however, that a kaleidoscopic presentation results.

69

The same sleeping man plays several roles in a single dream. And he plays them all at once. More, he even creates the varied environments in which these characters perform.

70

Our dream-self passes through five-sensed experiences and space-timed events which would entirely justify its assertion that the dream world is a material one. Yet the enlightenment gained on awaking entirely proves that the dream world is only a mental one.

71

Such is the extraordinary working of the dream-mind that a single remembered person, idea, incident, or emotion is quite enough to arouse instantly a whole string of associations, near or remote, rational or fantastic, whose images it forms effortlessly and projects into its own external world.

72

The belief of psychoanalysts (of the older schools) that all man's dreams are either a projection of his repressed sex wishes or an atavistic reversion to his primitive past, may sometimes be correct but is more often incorrect.

73

Both dream and delusion prove the creative power of mind.

74

He detaches, albeit without loss, a fragment of himself and gives it a new shape and a new life. Yet all this is an unconscious process.

75

Dreams give us the forms of reality, but do they give us the content of reality? If we take the general experience of nearly all dreams, the answer must be that they do not. If, however, we take the special experience of a few dreams which synchronize perfectly with the wakeful state in their memories, figures, or predictions, the answer is that they do.

76

It is rare that in a dream anyone *knows* that he is dreaming.

77

A dream can condense the events of a whole day into a few minutes. Where has the change taken place? The mind that experiences both wakeful and dream events has changed its condition, and with that its sense of time.

78

A single idea will henceforth dominate all his dreams—the idea that he *is* dreaming.

79

In dream we find a key to comprehending some occult phenomena that would otherwise be quite incomprehensible. Take, for instance, the appearance of an adept to his disciple hundreds of miles distant from his physical body.

80

As he lifts himself out of the dreaming state, the focus of his awareness becomes sharper and the field of his activity becomes a shared one.

81

That physical conditions produce many dreams is indisputable. *But not all dreams.* That many dreams are merely echoes of happenings during the past day or two is also indisputable. But they have passed into the sphere of memories—that is, mental events, ideas which are non-physical things. Mind can affect brain, brain can affect mind: they are separate things.

82

Most dreams are produced by imagination, but most dreams are not guided from unusual sources.

83

It is quite possible to visit in dream a place where the individual has not been during his present and waking life. This is not a trick of the mind; rather it is one of the powers of the mind to be able to see or be at a distance from the body.

84

Usually each dream is not a complete cycle, but a jumble of separate dreaming moments; hence most dreams are worthless and prove nothing.

85

In the very midst of his dream he knows what in it is true and what is only imaginary.

86

While yet sleeping on his bed, his conscious mind unites with his dreaming mind to wake into a new world.

87

Too many dreams are broken fragments or random mixed-up pieces or chaotic unhelpful stories.

88

Most dreams are too hazy and incoherent to be worth special study, but some dreams are so vivid and so reasonable that they might be taken from waking life.

89

Millions of dreamers enter their private dream worlds every night. It is then that the image-making power of the mind becomes quite extraordinary. It creates seemingly independent beings and living personalities during its dream state.

90

Ordinarily dreams lack a constant rational quality. The controlling hand of reason and coherence seems curiously but fitfully absent, while materials drawn from waking life seem curiously and irrationally mixed together.

91

The bedside notebook and pencil will be better used for the intuitions with which we may awake from deep sleep than for the pictures which may survive from dream.

92

The mistake in J.W. Dunne's theory of dreams is the belief that what was quite true of his own personal dreams was equally true of all other persons' dreams.

93

It is a startling moment when he wakes up to the fact that he is dreaming without waking up to the physical world at all. For then he is able to *know* as a scientific observable fact that the measurable space around him, the sensations of resistance and solidity in his feet and the hardness or smoothness of objects in his hands, are nothing else than mental creations.

The deep stillness of sleep

94

There is a strange happening which comes often to every man: first he is embraced by sleep, then during sleep he is embraced by imagination in the form of dream. All this is happening outside his ordinary awareness and independently of his personal control. What happens when he is embraced by deep dreamless sleep? The answer is that he has been *taken* to the source of his being for renewal of his forces physical, emotional, mental, and spiritual. That which took him there is Grace.

95

When we step into the deep pool of the sleep state, mysterious yet momentous things happen. The worst pains of a disease-tortured body vanish as though they never were, as the worst anxieties of a troubled mind are cast aside completely. We find healing peace and strength. We rotate in a cycle of waking dream and slumber. It is therefore not enough and cannot be enough to examine our waking state alone.

96

In sleep, which supervenes when the intellect becomes fatigued, the latter retires to rest in the higher mind, when no thoughts arise.

97

The presence of the personal ego in the dream state accounts for the presence of joys and sorrows in that state too. Its absence from deep sleep accounts for the latter's satisfying tranquillity.

98

Deep dreamless sleep removes anxieties from the mind because it removes the ego which suffers them. It removes exhaustion from the physical body because the complete relaxation of tension consequent upon the ego's absence allows the universal life-force to permeate every cell.

99

If the sleeping state is completely deep, this return to the source leaves an afterglow. The newly awakened man is loath to get up, not only for obvious physiological reasons, but also because of this one. It vanishes quickly, this delightful feeling, because the ego takes over with its tendencies and memories and, above all, its outward-turned world-seeking nature. The informed person will not miss the chance to surrender to that glow and bask in its serenity, letting the ego wait. "I dozed, and my book fell from my weary hand. When I woke up, I was full of joy and smiled silently," wrote Ts'ai Ch'o, a Chinese poet of Ts'ai, the Taoist mystical-philosophic school.

100

If advantage is to be taken of the solar currents of magnetism, the main axis of a bed should lie north-south.

101

Sleep provides a highly valuable counterweight to the ego's activity, a denial of its real existence, and a lesson in the true meaning of mind.

102

Those who think that sleep is all we need to remove the body's fatigue after activity and work may be surprised to learn that this is only true of deep dreamless slumber. In the case of dream-filled sleep, it is not more than partially true.

103

There is a kind of sleep which has a special quality about it—intensely deep and refreshingly blissful. Those who are physically ill awake from it feeling much better, sometimes quite healed. Those who are practising meditation just before passing into it get as much spiritual benefit as if they had continued to practise in a state of wakeful alertness. The ancient priest-physicians called it "temple-sleep" and the modern Oriental mystics (Indian and Muhammedan, *not* Japanese) call it "yoga-sleep."

104

He may be dead or he may be living but the sleeping man does not know what his condition is.

105

If the finite human mind cannot form any correct idea of the Unknown Infinite and Eternal Mind, it can make something of the fact that it itself exists, apparently unknown and unexperienced, in deep sleep.

106

What I saw in this jungle hermitage of The Andavar reminded me of an ancient attempt to banish sleep by Syrian holy men who seated themselves at the top of a 300-foot obelisk which was planted in front of the celebrated temple of Emesa. There, on this lofty perch, the *fakir* rang a handbell so frequently through twenty-one days and nights that he hoped to evade sleep. It reminded me, too, of what Ramana Maharshi once told me about yogis who, with the same object in view, had themselves tied to a ladder planted upright so that they could not fall into a sleep-inducing recumbent position. In the Maharishee's opinion, these forms of asceticism were extreme and violent attempts to force a premature evolution.

107

When the ego suspends its action and falls—without an object for its consciousness or a body for its working—into profound slumber, it has returned to its source. The real "I" then rules.

108

The belief that the two hours before midnight are most valuable for recuperative purposes is an old one. It was propagated by Manu the lawgiver, as well as by the rishees of ancient India, in whose ashrams and schools all retired to sleep at ten, to rise again at four or five.

109

If there are no pains in deep slumber there are no pleasures either. The ego is then not annihilated, but only withdrawn.

110

During those serene moments which follow immediately after an awakening from dreamless and undisturbed slumber, the erstwhile sleeper *feels* inexpressibly rested, divinely at ease. Those moments do not and cannot last, however, and with his speedy absorption into the affairs and cares of the new day, the man soon loses their delightful and unusual quality.

111

The necessity of sleep humbled even Alexander the Great, for it reminded him that he was mortal.

112

"In Cuba, as a young subaltern, Churchill learned the habit of afternoon siesta. Later, as the First Lord of the Admiralty, he found he could add two hours to a long working day by taking an hour's sleep after lunch. His gift for hard work is incredible."—from a London newspaper

113

"Sleep is the idea based upon the conception of absence."—Patanjali, *Yoga Sutras* I:10

114

The need of an unconscious is demonstrated by the need of deep sleep and represents the need of biological self-preservation. For an excess of memory would paralyse all possibilities of active life. We would be unable to give to the immediate everyday duties that definite attention which they require. The great number of such memories would utterly destroy all possibility of concentrating on the practical needs. And similarly, an inability to bring the thought-mechanism to rest regularly would end by overwhelming the individual with a myriad of unwanted thoughts and again render the simplest concentration difficult or impossible. The senses do not provide merely the conditions under which we become aware of the external world but also the inhibitory mechanism which prevents us from becoming aware of too much. The range of visual vibrations, for instance, is but a fraction of those which are actually present. Similarly, Nature has ordained that the individual mind should shut out of consciousness more than it is able to attend to, should be a representative mechanism which permits us to concentrate on what is relevant in our personal life without distractions that would render life intolerable.

115

In the state of deep sleep the things of the world are put far from us and we emerge refreshed, calm, and happy. Let dreams, with their confused memories of the world which has been left behind, enter into this sleep and at once it loses some of its peace. Does anyone ever trouble to put the two together in connection, the absence of the worldly life and the presence of a happy mind?

116

The definition from Blavatsky of dreamless sleep is correct insofar as no impression upon the physical brain is left. Her statement that the higher self then reverts to the original state is, however, very loosely expressed. It is the lower ego that thus reverts.

117

Saint Francis Xavier's achievements were impressive, even amazing, yet he slept only three hours at night.

118

With the onset of deep sleep we retreat into a timeless world, which swallows up and holds in suspension all our past and present existence.

119

Animals which hibernate in winter are the bear, whose sleep is light; the bat, whose sleep is heavy; the woodchuck, whose eyes are tightly closed; and the raccoon, which rolls itself into a ball. What is to be noted is that during this period, lasting many weeks or even several months, the rate of breathing is gradually reduced to a mere fraction of what it is during the period of ordinary activity. The Columbian ground squirrel almost stops its pulse-beat during its half-year-long hibernation.

120

Why do so few know the exact moment when they enter into the sleeping condition? What happens to their consciousness then?

121

During deep sleep we experience the sublation of the whole pluralistic world. What has become of it then? Has it lost its reality? This we may not say. Has it kept its reality? This too we dare not assert. Thus the nature of the universe is seen to be indeterminate.

122

Once he has attained the philosophic realization of the Overself, he goes nightly to sleep *in it*, if the sleep is dreamless and deep, or inserts it into his dreams if it is not. Either way he does not withdraw from it.(P)

123

What is known during deep sleep is the veil of ignorance which covers the Real. That is, the knowing faculty, the awareness, is still present, but caught in the ignorance, the veiling, and knowing nothing else. The sage, however, carries into sleep the awareness he had in wakefulness. He may let it dim down to a glimmer, but it is always there.

124

It is hard for Western-educated minds to accept this Vedantic view that in deep sleep consciousness goes on. Sir William Hamilton, one of the best of British metaphysicians of the early part of last century, in a lecture asked, "Can I know without knowing that I know? This is impossible."

125

If the nightly return of the man to his Overself were really full and complete, he would not awake the day after into spiritual ignorance. Instead, he would consciously enjoy the peace and presence of the Overself.

126

That which is present during the interval between two thoughts is also present during deep sleep.

127

Is it not strange to observe that the same men who are so attached to their personality when active in the waking state, become indifferent to it when inert in the sleeping state! Can it be that there is something which transcends it and which ordinarily is hidden, covered up by the thoughts of the waking state? That in the stillness which dissolves such thoughts, the Overself can reveal itself? That deep sleep stops short of the revelation because, although it dissolves thoughts, it annuls consciousness?

128

Chandogya Upanishad VIII.3.2,3: "Just as people, who do not know where wealth lies buried, walk over the ground without securing the wealth, even so owing to their covering of ignorance people do not attain divinity within their hearts, though they come in contact with It during deep sleep. . . . The true Self lies within the heart. That is why the heart is called [*hridayam*] (He is within the heart). He who knows that self is within the heart realizes divinity during the state of deep sleep."

129

Although the sage withdraws with the onset of sleep from wakeful awareness, he does not withdraw from all awareness. A pleasurable and peaceful sense of impersonal being is left over. In this he rests throughout the night.

130

Muhammed: "I am not as one of you. Verily, I pass the night with my Lord, and he gives me food and drink."

131

Ernest Wood, *Practical Yoga*: "In this philosophy sleep is not regarded as a total cessation of the mind's activity. There is still an idea there. The mind dwells upon the idea of the absence of everything; so this idea needs a class to itself. It is not considered to be an unconscious state. That is why, it is argued, when we wake in the morning we may say: 'I slept well,' meaning not that we now feel refreshed and we therefrom infer that we slept well, but that we remember that we slept well, that we enjoyed the pleasurable idea of absence of anything. We may note here that the mere suppression of ideas—not the system of control propounded in the aphorisms—would be only the concentration of the mind on absence, which would not lead to yoga."

132

Koran: "And one of His signs is your sleeping."

133

If the sage's sleep is wholly without those varied mental experiences of persons and places which manifest as dreams, then it will pass so swiftly that an entire night's sleep will take no longer than a few seconds of wakeful time.

134

In slumber the *activity* of consciousness disappears but the *possibility* of consciousness remains.

135

What happens to the feeling of one's physical body, to all the thoughts in awareness of one's personal self, to the perceptions of all the things outside, when one falls into a sleep without dreams? Everything vanishes and yet the next morning everything reappears. Therefore not one thing was lost. Where were they all? The sleep itself provides an answer. Its own deeper level receives and holds the self and its objects of attention and then projects them forth again. That level is the Mind, the Real, Consciousness-in-Itself.

136

No one gets out of deep slumber with the feeling that he did not exist during that period, nor even out of dream-filled sleep when he may have assumed a different identity. Both states are looked on as different but not as annihilatory: so deep sleep shows that consciousness can exist despite the person's ignorance that it is an entity by itself apart from him and his body, thoughts or emotions.

137

No ordinary man thinks of himself when he is sleeping but not dreaming. Why is it that the idea of "I" is then lost? Obviously the mind itself is not lost, only its products are. But is not consciousness associated with mind? It too could not have been lost. Then why does it seem to be absent? No answer to this last question can possibly be found. The reason is that it is *not* absent at all. This is why consciousness goes on during deep absorption, in listening to music, *even though I have forgotten myself*. The more complete the absorption, the more complete is the forgetfulness.

138

Behind the dreams or the unconsciousness of ordinary sleep there is, also, for some seekers upon this Quest, another form of life where contact is made with, and instruction obtained from, sources which are remote from the physical environment. Ultimately, the results filter through the subconscious mind, expressing themselves in a general way through mental direction and emotional ideals.

139

Sleep is a condition which nature imposes on man. No one, not even the sage, can alter its general course and therefore even the sage has to accept this condition as an inevitable part of his own human lot. But if he is to attain full self-realization, this must eventually pertain to his sleeping state as much as to his waking state, else it will not be what its name suggests.

140

When we assert that there is emptiness in deep sleep we overlook the fact that some mind must have been present to note the emptiness and thus enable us to make the assertion afterwards.

141

The objection that self-consciousness disappears in deep sleep and hence is not real and lasting is incorrect, for we know afterwards that it existed and disappeared. When we awake we *know* it and *are conscious* that we experienced deep sleep although we do not know it at the time of the sleep. So it is known *after* sleep that consciousness persisted in it.

142

This state of conscious transcendental sleep is symbolized in some mystical figures of antiquity by forming or painting them without eyelids.

143

Sleep comes when attention goes down to the throat centre.

144

When a man falls totally asleep, when no thoughts and no dreams are active, he has withdrawn (or more accurately been withdrawn) into the centre of his being. He can go no farther inwards. He is really alone with the Overself but, being unable to harmonize with it, the principle of consciousness is not active.

145

Bhagavad Gita, Chap. II, sloka 69: "That which is night to all beings, in that the self-controlled man wakes. That in which all beings wake, is night to the Self-seeing Muni."

146

Sleep, by shutting off conscious thought and conferring oblivion of the ego, relaxes tense nerves and pacifies agitated hearts. During its reign, the mind merges back into its source. With the difference that he seeks full awareness and permanent continuance, the mystic seeks this same result.

147

In sleep the non-existence of things is *not* known to you; therefore sleep is a state of ignorance, not of Gnanam, for the Gnani knows everything to be Brahman. The nonduality of sleep is not the nonduality of Gnanam. Brahman is not known in deep sleep but is known in Gnanam.(P)

148

In the ordinary waking state, men are well aware that they are not sleeping; but in the dreaming state they mistakenly believe that they are in the other one. A few, however, have come to a degree of development where they know that they are dreaming, and fewer still know that they are in deep thought-free sleep. They are the sages.

149

The moments between sleep and waking or between waking and sleep are very sensitive and very important. They should be used to switch thought to the highest ideal one knows.

150

As taught in *The Wisdom of the Overself*, use the last few minutes in the twilight state of consciousness before falling asleep at night for constructive self-improvement. The best form this can take during your present phase of development is to relax in bed, empty the mind of the day's cares, and make definite, concrete suggestions about the good qualities desired and imaginatively visualize yourself demonstrating these desired qualities. Furthermore, you should go even farther and visualize yourself in possession of the Higher Consciousness, attuned to the Higher Will and expressing the Higher Poise. All this will be like seeds planted in the inner being and growing during sleep.

151

Character can be bettered and weaknesses can be overcome through the regular use of constructive exercises in meditation, either at any time during the day or just before falling asleep. Whatever the fault, weakness, or vice may be, it should be firmly coupled in meditation with pictures of its dangerous consequences, and then with a mental attitude of its dangers and their horror. Such an association of ideas will tend to produce itself automatically whenever the fault manifests itself.

152

Pre-sleep exercise: If he is trying to cure himself of a bad habit, for example, let him think of a situation which gives rise to it and then of the physical and mental miseries which result from it. Then he must picture to himself the development of such a situation and of his reaction to it in a positive reformed way. If this exercise is repeated night after night, he will one day find that when the situation occurs in real life, he will react rightly to it, resolutely turning his back on the bad habit. No special effort of will need be made; the change will be natural easy smooth and without strain. It will be as though some external force had intervened and resisted the bad habit on his behalf, achieving instantaneous triumph.

153

This pre-sleep exercise of recalling the day's events would be worth doing for the sake of its value to anybody in developing memory and fostering observation. But to the disciple it has very much more to give. This will be given, however, only if his self-examination is rigorously impersonal; if he does not let the personal self or animal nature interfere with it.

154

The late President Kennedy was another man who drew many of his best ideas intuitively from the waking-up period each morning. He was also one of those, like Napoleon and Churchill, who fall asleep immediately the eyes are shut.

155

In those delicious moments where sleep trembles into waking, there is some sort of a beginning Glimpse but alas, it vanishes without fulfilling its promise as soon as the world of objects comes more fully into the circle of attention. And this is precisely where the value of such a state lies, both for the ordinary man and for the would-be yogi. *It has no objects.* It is "I" without a world. It is awareness-in-itself. True, it is fleeting and does not last, but a man can learn to practise holding himself to it.

156

Two of the mysterious psychological moments when a good thought can be thrown into fertile soil are on the verge of falling asleep and on the verge of awakening from sleep.

157

The returning consciousness waking from sleep or withdrawing from reverie is in a better position to sense intuitive truths than when actively and entirely wakeful.

158

Ask yourself before sleeping the questions that puzzle you and the answers may be there, waiting for you, on waking.

159

In those first moments when awakening from the nightly sleep, we may enter a heavenly thought-free state. Or, if we cannot reach so high, we may receive thoughts which give guidance, tell us what to do, warn us against wrong decisions, or foretell the future.

160

The moment he awakens in the morning he should turn his attention for a few minutes to the thought of the Quest. If this is done faithfully every day, it becomes a useful exercise with excellent results in the subsequent hours.

161

On awakening from the night's sleep, take the inspired book, which you are to keep on a bedside table for the purposes of this exercise, and open it at random. The higher self may lead you to open it at a certain page. Read the paragraph or page on which your glance first rests and then put the book aside. Meditate intently on the words, taking them as a special message to you for that particular day. In the course of your activities you may later find this to be so, and the message itself a helpfully connected one.

162

If, in the act of falling asleep, he invites the higher self through aspiration, he may one day find that in the act of waking up an inner voice begins to speak to him of high and holy things. And with the voice comes the inspiration, the strength, and the desire to live up to them.

163

Plato's precepts to Aristotle: "Do not sleep until you have put three questions to yourself: (a) Have I committed any sin? (b) Have I omitted any duty by accident? (c) Have I left anything undone intentionally?"

164

The point where one can pass from wakefulness to pure consciousness is naturally most difficult to find. Everyone misses it because habit-patterns compel him to do so. Much patience is needed for these exercises. This is indeed a task for one's whole lifetime. But there are easier objectives and more accessible goals which are quite excellent for most people of the present day.

165

Pre-sleep fourth state exercise: The secret of a successful passage into the transcendental state consists in insisting on retaining consciousness but not on retaining self-consciousness. For if, at the moment when you are about to slip into the fourth state, you suddenly become aware that you are doing so, then you will at once be hurled back into the ordinary condition. The ego-sense has therefore to subside completely before the pass-over can be effected. So long as the ego knows what is happening to it, so long does the cross-over remain impossible. It must not be allowed to intrude itself at the fateful moment yet neither must consciousness itself be allowed to lapse.

166

What is this magic that hides in sleep? The founder of Alcoholics Anonymous, an organization of redeemed inebriates for helping men master the liquor habit, felt he had reached the end of his tether through drink. The habit was beyond his power to overcome, its results proving too dangerous and disgusting even for him to tolerate any more. Suicide seemed the only way out. He uttered a last prayer to God to help him and fell into a long deep sleep. He awoke cured!

167

Method of falling asleep by Su Tung-po, poet and mystic: "I lie perfectly still. I listen to my respiration and make sure it is slow and even. After a short while, I feel relaxed and comfortable. A state of drowsiness sets in and I fall into sound sleep."

168

The ruling ideas with which he falls asleep will form a connection with the wakeful life and profoundly influence it.

169

This exercise need not necessarily be practised just before or after sleep. These periods are most effective for novices. But for those who have made progress with meditation, it may be done at any time of the day during a meditation period.

170

The famous "Battle Hymn of the Republic," to which great armies of soldiers marched during the American Civil War, was the fruit of this mysterious sleep composition. Julia Ward Howe had often tried to think out the words for a new marching song but without success. But one morning she awoke in the grey dawn with the verses of the new hymn forming themselves spontaneously in her mind. She rushed to write them down before dressing and before they fled away.

171

Some who have attained sufficient proficiency in meditation have cured themselves of insomnia by affirming the divine Presence when they close their eyes in bed at night, and holding on to this affirmation.

172

There are certain intervals of consciousness between two thoughts—such as those between waking and sleep and those between sleep and waking—which normally pass unobserved because of the rapidity and brevity associated with them. Between one moment and another there is the timeless consciousness; between one thought and another there is a thought-free consciousness. It is upon this fact that a certain exercise was included in *The Wisdom of the Overself* which had not previously been published in any Western book. But it is not a modern discovery. It was known to the ancient Egyptians, it was known to the Tibetan occultists, and in modern times it was probably known to Krishnamurti. The Egyptians, preoccupied as they were with the subject of death and the next world, based their celebrated *Book of the Dead* upon it. The *Tibetan Book of the Dead* contained the same theme. Between the passing out of the invisible vital-forces-body at the end of each incarnation and its entry into that state of consciousness which is death, the same interval reappears. If the dying man can lift himself up to it, seize upon it, and not let it escape him, he will then enter into heaven—the true heaven. And it was to remind him of this fact and to help him achieve this feat that the ancient priests attended his last moments and chanted the pertinent passages from these books. This mysterious interval makes its appearance throughout life and even at death, and yet men notice it not and miss an opportunity. It happens not only at the entry into death but also in between two breaths. It is possible to go even further and say that the interval reappears for a longer period between two incarnations, for there is then the blocking out of all impressions of the past prior to taking on a new body. Plato must have known it.

Trance and the 4th state of consciousness

173

There is a deep, very deep, level of meditation where we have the same experience as dreamless sleep but keep our awareness. Because the ego with its thoughts and emotions, its motives, desires, and calculations is no longer present, it must be described as a condition of generalized being. (The oft-used term "universal" is not quite accurate.)

174

If by yogic concentration and withdrawal the body-thought is expunged from consciousness, it vanishes together with the world it sensed. This is no longer there. But this does not entitle the yogi to assert after his trance has ended that the world is still not there.

175

Professor Sen Gupta, on the "Four Buddhist Jnanas": "It is again stated that the process of contemplation of 'emptiness' and of the negation of self-hood leads to a sense of joy. Both of these concepts, 'emptiness' (*Sunyata*) and the negation of self-hood (*nairatmya*), however, seem to signify the same type of transformation of consciousness, the growth of a plane of non-relational experience of the *nirvikalpa* stage. The stage of 'emptiness' as defined above is said to develop through the practice of *Pratyahara*, with withdrawal of the senses from the objects. Man's mind loses in this way its contact with things outside: desires no longer fixate upon things that fulfil them; mind, so far as its operations can be observed from outside, is asleep. In earlier Buddhism, in which the discipline of the Yoga was generally followed, we find mention of *pleasant emotions*: 'When, aloof from sensuous ideas, aloof from evil ideas, he enters into and abides in "First Jnana," wherein attention is applied and sustained, which is born of solitude and filled with zest and pleasant emotion.' In the 'Second Jnana,' again, there is an 'inward tranquillizing of the mind self-contained and uplifted from the working of attention' and there arises 'zest and pleasurable emotion.' In the

'Third Jnana' likewise the individual is said to 'experience' in the body that pleasure of which the Aryans speak. 'It is only in the last stage that man goes beyond joy and sorrow.'"

176

The awareness of this higher self need not annul the awareness of the ordinary self, although in the deepest mystical trance it will certainly do so. But man does not live by trance alone.

177

In this strange condition he is neither asleep nor awake. He is free of the flesh. It is a dream-like state without the irrationality, the pictures, or the happenings of most dreams.

178

It is a condition of the wakeful and dream phases of human existence that thoughts should flow through the human consciousness. For they are the active phases of the divine entity wherein it is incessantly creative. Only in the negative phase of deep sleep can thoughts be absent. This is the normal truth. For in a fourth phase, attainable through intense self-absorbed meditation and for a brief interval only, the thought-free state can be induced without any loss of awareness.

179

Consider the fact that our individual lives are totally suspended during sleep, that the waves of personal consciousness then merge utterly in the ocean. How clearly this shows the Divine to be also the Infinite and Universal, our lack of true spirituality, and our possession at best of its pale reflection! For where else could we go to sleep except in this Infinite and Universal Mind? Yet we know it not! To get rid of such ignorance, to attain transcendental insight into the fourth state of being, is the most wonderful of all the tasks which this philosophy sets before us.(P)

180

It is the presence of the physical ego in the wakeful state that paralyses all spiritual awareness therein. It is the absence of the personal and physical ego in the deep sleep state that paralyses all material awareness therein, too. By keeping it out and yet keeping in wakefulness, the transcendental consciousness is able to provide the requisite condition for an unbroken spiritual awareness that is not only superior to the three states but continues its own existence behind theirs.

181

Ordinarily we simply cannot grasp this amazing concept of "pure consciousness." All the consciousnesses of ordinary human experience imply a consciousness of some object and an entity to whom this happens.

182

There are two kinds of consciousness, one is in ever-passing moments, the other ever-present. The one is in time, the other out of it. The ordinary person knows only the one; the enlightened sage knows both.

183

A man never leaves Consciousness. The world comes into it as perception, that is, as idea. Whether anything, object or state, comes into it or not, Consciousness remains as his unchanging home. Whether asleep or awake, wrapped in himself or out in the world, his essential being remains what it is. His thoughts and sense-impressions, feelings and passions are produced by it or projected from it: they exist in dependence on it and die in it.

184

In our view, even deep sleep unconsciousness is a form of this "consciousness" which transcends all the states we ordinarily know—waking, dream, and deep sleep—yet includes them when they merge back into it. Such a "consciousness" is unthinkable, unimaginable, but it is the true objective awareness. It is also the *I* you are seeking so much. But to reach it, then you have to let go of the I which you know so well. (P)

185

The transcendental being is not an unconscious one. The absolute consciousness could not be other than self-conscious in its own impersonal way. Hence the fourth state is not the same as deep sleep. (P)

186

Is it not a strange thing that after a night's dreaming sleep when we may become some other person, some other character during our dreams, we yet wake up with the old identity that we had before the dream? And is it not equally strange that after a night's sweet, deep, dreamless slumber when we actually forget utterly that same previous identity, we are able to pick it up once more on awakening? What is the explanation of these strange facts? It is that we have never left our true selfhood, whether in dreams or deep slumber, never been other than we really were in essence, and that the only change that has taken place has been a change of the *state* of our consciousness, not of the consciousness itself. (P)

187

We must see it as ordinary experience transcended into a consciousness which defies comprehension.

188

We exist for a fragment of time only and therefore relatively. But is there something behind time itself which is absolute, a principle of Foreverness? The Buddhists firmly deny it; the Advaitins just as firmly proclaim it, while philosophy accepts and reconciles both schools.

189

Every man is conscious being, even in deep sleep. This then is his real being: this consciousness as it is in itself, not in the limited form it takes in his ego.

190

The deep sleep of night, when nothing is known or remembered, followed by the wakeful activity of day, when the world is perceived and self-identity recollected, must have some principle common to them on which they depend and in which they are linked. Otherwise we could not have understood that we slept or picked up again the continuity of consciousness from the previous day.

191

"I would that thou hadst passed right through thyself as one who dreams in sleep yet sleepless."—"The Secret Sermon on the Mountain," Chapter 14 of Volume 2, *Thrice Greatest Hermes* by G.R.S. Mead

192

In his inmost being every man is rooted in the World-Mind. The three states pass away—sleep, dream, and waking go—but the fourth still remains: it is this root—being.

193

In the waking state we experience the physical world, in the dream state our experience corresponds to the etheric astral world, in the deep sleep state we enter a still higher level of experience which is that of the God whose will is expressed in the other and lower two worlds. This God the Hindus call Ishvara; I have called it World-Mind. Now underlying these three states and therefore the Reality, the consciousness, the real consciousness underneath them, man experiences as enlightenment. The other three are states whereas this is the Reality supporting those three states—waking, dream, and deep sleep. In deep sleep man reaches God, it might be said, but owing to his ignorance he is unaware so he does not benefit by it.

194

Psychological states are quite distinct from pure consciousness: they are thrown up from it and have, relatively, only a transient existence.

195

One of the first things a student of philosophical psychology must learn to understand is that the different states of consciousness are not the same as pure basic essential consciousness-in-itself. The states are like little circles within larger ones. They possess various limits and limitations, belong to lower levels, and are subject to alteration. Basic consciousness transcends all these things, all these conditions, and may therefore be called transcendental consciousness.

196

What is called *Turiya* or the "fourth state" in Sanskrit, although it is neither waking, dreaming, nor sleeping, is related however to all three as their background. Therefore, before one falls asleep it comes into play. Before one wakes up in the morning it also comes into play. Or before a dream comes to an end and deep sleep supervenes, it comes into play. This is why either the practice of meditation or the brief practice of spiritual remembrance at any of these three natural pause periods takes the fullest advantage of them. This is also why during the interval between two separate thoughts, it comes into play. Thus, throughout a man's life, he's comfortably being brought back into touch with his divine Self. But because his face is turned the other way and he's looking in the wrong direction, he never takes advantage and becomes aware of that Self.

197

The fourth condition is attained when the true nature of the other three is fully comprehended, so fully that all the thoughts, feelings, and acts of the man are henceforth based upon the unshakeable conviction that the three are only appearances within the Real.

198

Intellectual standpoints and emotional moods may change, and do, but this heavenly consciousness stops all that, for it belongs to a timeless world. There, no arguments can begin, whether with others or oneself: no feelings can toss the man about with each new event or circumstance. There, a superior wisdom reigns, so lucid, so penetrating, that it certifies its own worth, debate being quite unnecessary. And there, finally, the self is at last purified and stabilized in its higher identity and is therefore at peace.

199

The most extraordinary thing about it is that this Supreme Principle, which is the fundament of all things, runs like an underground stream through all the three states of man yet he knows it not. His ignorance is due to heedlessness, his refusal to turn inwards and pay attention to what is going on inside.

200

How paradoxical: that the fourth state should be the First Principle of Being!

4

TIME, SPACE, CAUSALITY

The three thought-forms of space, time, and cause necessarily dominate the universal experience of mankind. They are the relations wherein we experience that aggregate of objects which makes the world of Nature. They are not open to choice or rejection by anyone but are forced on all alike and felt by fool and philosopher.

2

The time-space-causality reference is an essential part of human nature, a governing law of human thinking. These three hold good solely within such thinking and can have no possible or proper application outside it. Man does not consciously or arbitrarily impose them upon his thought; it is beyond his individual power to reject them.(P)

3

Living in time and space as we do, we perforce live always in the fragmentary and imperfect, never in the whole, the perfect. Only if, at rare moments, we are granted a mystical experience and transcend the time-space world, do we know the beauty and sublimity of being liberated from a mere segment of experience into the wholeness of Life itself.(P)

4

We are forced by our mental and physical constitution to submit to time with its succession of moments and to space with its extension of points. But mystics *know* that both can be transcended in certain experiences, and a freedom attained which is ordinarily never felt even to be possible.

5

We know that each object in the universe, as certainly each living creature, and the entire universe itself, must have had a commencement in time as well as a source in space.

6

Through the limitations set up by time, space, and sensation, the perceptions of forms and the experience of events by the personal ego become possible. That is, its own existence becomes possible. Therefore any change in these limitations would bring about a change in its existence. The world which it knows here would vanish and another would take its place.

7

Our thinking process is bound by time and space relations, but there is something in us which is not. Ordinarily, we have no awareness of it, although it never leaves us.

8

Knowledge of the world is only possible because the world is cut up into spaced and timed fragments, which are simultaneously thrown into the relation of cause and effect.

9

When the personal ego is withdrawn from consciousness, its time-and-space perceptions are withdrawn alongside of it.

10

Space and time constitute the world-cross on which we are crucified until a Deliverer comes to show us how to rescue ourselves.

11

The mind must locate its objects in space and time or it could not have any objects at all.

12

Everything that is manifested must be manifested in some space-time world—that is, it must have a shape and it must be subject to "Before" and "After."

13

We are given forms embodied in space and minds working in time whereby we may come to decipher meanings in life and the world, develop awareness of the Infinite Being that is behind both, and know our true self.

14

So long as man's awareness is trapped in space and time, so long will he be unable to know the reality that transcends them.

Their relative and mental nature

15

Just as there are different heard sounds, seen objects, and felt things, so there are different kinds of experience and different levels of space and time.

16

There is, however, no single frame of time in which thoughts can be molded. For time, as we have seen, is a variable because it is an idea; it offers an unlimited variety of ways in which events might arrange themselves. There are a number of different frames and one of them is used for waking sensations while another is for dream perceptions. For the experience of a clock hour spent suffering the pangs of acute toothache will be much longer than the hour spent with a sweetheart. Time is ultimately mental.

17

Materialism is compelled to hold that there is only one uniform time. Mentalism holds that there are different kinds of time, not only for different kinds of beings but even for one and the same being.(P)

18

The most valuable metaphysical fruit of the quantum theory is its finding that the processes of the universe which occur in space and time, emanate from what is fundamentally not in space and time.(P)

19

Nothing in the universe is permanent: all things are time-bound. No form is continuous: all forms are broken down in the end.

20

Time is an efficient undertaker and puts all things, neatly coffined, well away in their appropriate cemeteries in the end.

21

Time, first ignored, then a friend, is lastly an enemy.

22

Who is to say how many events can happen within one second? Even waking experience offers conflicting testimony on this point, as the drowning man who sees his life pass in backward review well knows. And dream experience, too, often crowds a whole drama into a few minutes.

23

Sometimes under abnormal conditions a man's sense of time may travel backwards and relive events in reverse (as when drowning) or travel forwards and live in events which come to pass later (as when dreaming).

24

Daily we return to activity and nightly to repose, while time is measured by a metal pointer circling around a graduated dial.

25

Who does not know the healing powers of time, which ends the memory of sorrow and the feeling of pain?

26

We humans find it normal to experience in the way we do astronomical time and geometrical space, but it would be foolish to expect that other inhabitants of other worlds could do the same.

27

Einstein proved by purely scientific and mathematical methods the relativity of time and space, but the Jain masters of India knew it without such helps—and this teaching was imparted three thousand years ago.

28

The mathematical frontier of the present moment has only an illusory and not a real existence.

29

We shall understand the movements of time better if we understand that it is neither a straight line nor a round circle. It is a beginningless endless spiral.

30

The theoretical significance of time is unaltered, although invention has altered its practical significance for human life through the departments of travel and communication.

31

Einstein has taken two fundamental human experiences—time and space—and proved them to be relative variables dependent on man himself, while he has dispossessed them of any other than a mathematical reality.

32

It is only custom and familiarity that make a particular kind of time seem real to us and all other kinds seem fantastic. But to creatures with different sets of perceptions from ours, our human-experienced time would seem quite fantastic and theirs quite normal.

33

The alternation of day and night—that is, *time*—depends on the daily turning of our earth; but to a man standing on another planet and observing ours, the same suggestion of a particular time-order would arise.

34

Time is a form (one of many) taken by consciousness. All measurements of it, whether taken on precise instruments in the laboratory or felt by the nerves of the physical body, are relative, because they are dependent on bases which are themselves forms of the mind.

35

Whether we gain it from the mystic experience or from the deepest reflection, we shall come to see that time is the great deluder of men. The past which has gone, the future which has yet to be, and the present which is in flux are not what they seem.

36

Just as there is no particular point in a circle which is the true beginning or true end of it, so there is in reality no point in time which is the true past or true future.

37

Time obliterates memories, cancels hates, annuls loves, diminishes or destroys both passions and illusions. Yet the most singular change is what it does to the sense of reality. More and more, material life seems like the stuff of dreams.

38

In some dreams time shrinks a whole day into a mere half hour or, in others, it expands a single minute into several hours. This is what happens to the mind under the influence of certain drugs: nay, even still more fantastic disproportions between waking time and sleeping time have been brought about.

39

Our attitude towards time, our sense of its quick or slow, short or long passage, depends on the feelings with which it is filled.

40

Time is purely relative to the standpoint, to the position taken up. But this is the superficial view. When we enquire deeper, we find that our notion of time varies also according to the mental (and not merely physical) position which we adopt. Thus a lover will find one hour passing like a few minutes when in the presence of his beloved, whereas his impatient, waiting rival will feel that every minute is counting its full weight! This reveals that time is ultimately mental, an idea in the mind. It comes and goes; it is illusory.

41

If, in the dimension of space, only a single page parts this chapter from the previous one, in the dimension of time several months lie between them.

42

Let us reflect upon this mystery of space. It is the one element which has no opposite. Even shape and form of every kind are included within space and do not constitute its antithesis.

43

What does the word "space" stand for? Does it represent the image of something actually known? Does it represent the imagined concept of something not actually known?

44

To say that the World-Mind is diffused throughout all space would be true but would also be untrue if the statement were left there. For all space is itself a state in the World-Mind.

45

The point will be clearer to non-metaphysical readers if you always couple *Time* with *Place* rather than with Space.

46

Height, length, and breadth equals space. This continues into the fourth dimension, Time; hence the space-time continuum.

47

This would necessarily make space prior in existence to all things, that is, the world itself. But if space really has such an absolute existence, it would itself need a location wherein it must be put.

48

We are geared by nature to a particular set of space-perceptions. We are not free to measure experience just as we please.

49

Ultimately the spatial outlook is a part of the dream just as the time-sense is. When you awake from the dream, even space—the sense of here and there—is divorced from reality. However, it is our best symbol of the Mind.

50

We hardly realize the immense emptiness of universal space. The suns and planets and stars are mere tiny points of light and heat and matter surrounded by so many million miles of the great void that, relatively speaking, they are of ludicrous unimportance.

51

Space is as illusory as Time. Both are mental creations.

52

The student has moved in thought from the circumference to the centre, from all things in the universe to their source in the self. The universe is something which, spiritually, exists within himself. He and the world are verily inseparable. Space is only an idea.

53

If the investigation of time made in depth by intelligence shows the real essence of it to be an eternal Now, so a similar investigation of space shows its real essence to be an eternal Here. Both these results are also to be reached in actual experience sharply and clearly in meditation in depth. But where are they? The answer is given briefly and precisely by mentalism: they are in consciousness.

54

Time is not quite what it appears to be if carefully analysed. It will be found on the one hand to be a mental experience and on the other to exist only in the present.

55

As we try to think away all the objects which space contains, we must not forget to think away the *light* with which we unconsciously fill all space. We shall find if we succeed in this admittedly difficult exercise, that space itself will then disappear. Thus the common belief in space as a kind of vast vessel containing everything, as depending on and being determined by the distances between two or more objects and the relative positions occupied by these objects, is hardly a correct one. Both "inside" and "outside" are merely relative terms. All this again is because, as mentalism declares, space is really the idea which we subconsciously impose on. Hence, when for a few brief moments the mind transcends its creations and returns to itself in mystical abstraction, we lose the feeling of the "outsideness" of things and the world fades into being our own unreal dream. This happens because, as mentalism has already taught us, space is needed by the mind to contain its images, to measure its forms, and therefore mind accordingly makes it. Now the same considerations apply to time, for if we think away all the objects which have their life in the past present or future, there will be no time left to flow onwards. There will be no independent thing called time. Nevertheless, the mind is not left in a wholly negative state after this is done. Whatever we may possibly experience or know in the external world must necessarily be experienced or known under the forms of space and time; to be at all, they have to be as they are. But these forms are variable and changeable, relative and dependent. Therefore these events or things are not themselves eternal and enduring realities. Space and time are ways in which we experience existence; they are not things in themselves.(P)

56

The relativity theory brings space and time together as having no existence independent of each other. Mentalism explains why this is so. They are both inherent in one and the same thing—imagination; they are two ways in which the creative aspect of mind functions simultaneously.(P)

57

Just as there is really no such thing as "matter," so there are no such things as substance and time. These are abstract concepts, useful for certain purposes, but imaginary, just mental constructs.

58

Time slips away all the time! Amid its inexorable movement one thing remains unmoving—the sense of "I."

59

It is not a human feat to put a beginning to the cosmos, or to time which is connected with it, for then the human entity would need to be existing individually and consciously before both.

60

Although you will probably feel, like nearly everyone else, *outside* the experience of time and apart from it, you will in reality be *inside* it. For it will be deep in your consciousness and involved in the making of its shape.

61

We get all our experience in the form of space relations, time relations, and cause relations. It has already been shown that all this experience is, however, the fruit of mind's working. The mind makes its own times and its own spaces as the forms furnished to thought.

62

The mind makes a space relation with its objects and a time relation with its events. These relations may alter to every imaginable extent; hence they are only relative ones.

63

We have now to ask, "How do we come to look upon the snake as real? What persuades us to take such illusions on their face value?" When we examine the position of perception—upon which they are based and within whose sphere they appear objectively—we find that we always see the world in clothes of four dimensions, three of space and one of time. Kant has laboriously demonstrated how the mind superimposes these two characteristics on its vision of the world; that is to say, they lie *within* the mind and not outside it. It is therefore perfectly possible for mental constructions to be extended in space and occur in time, thus assuming all the characteristics of conventional reality, and still remain nothing more than mental workings after all. Buddha's ultra-keen insight noted this illusoriness of the spatial relation and so he likened the world to a bubble.

64

Planets may revolve and clocks may tick but in the end our experience of time depends upon our consciousness of it.

65

We have never experienced a time which is independent of space. The two are interdependent.

66

If for the human mind there can be no visible beginning in time of the universal order and, equally, no ending of it, if this is the meaning of eternity, then we must remember that for the most brilliant intelligences of our race and the deepest mystical seers, time itself is in the mind.

67

Where is the present when you try to catch hold of it? What indeed is time itself? All three tenses, all time, are mental states.

68

Do we move along in time or does time move in us?

69

Time cannot be separated from the experience of it.

70

Although there are nostalgic interludes when those unexpected memories become utterly vivid, the truth that "time is in the mind," once quoted to me by Wei Wu Wei as we parted, also returns often enough.

71

Ljudevit Vulicevic, Yugoslavian nineteenth-century writer: "We divide time into epochs, centuries, years, and give names to these fanciful divisions, regarding them as something real in themselves and outside our consciousness. Time is nothing in itself. It is not a reality but a thought, an idea in man."

72

The world seems hung in space and strung through time. What is the responsible factor in this illusion? It is mind.

73

Now if it is impossible to get at all the causes it is equally impossible to get at all the effects. We shall never comprehend in its fullness any structure in the universe, any event in history, any purpose in human consciousness or consequence of human action.

74

From "Greek Doctrine of Non-Causality," by Mary M. Patrick in *Aryan Path*: "There was a man in Alexandria named Aenesidemus, in the first century B.C., who formed a bridge between the old and the new Pyrrhonism. He was originally an academic sceptic. But when the Academy renounced its sceptical standpoint he turned to Pyrrhonism, then becoming very strong, especially in Alexandria. He may be called the prophet of later scepticism, and we find the sources of his authority in the teachings of the Academy, in early Pyrrhonism, and in the Empiric School of Medicine which had its seat in Alexandria. It is to Aenesidemus that we owe much of our knowledge of scepticism for he was a voluminous writer. He formulated the 'Ten Tropes of (Epliche)' or 'suspension of judgement' some of which date back to Pyrrho himself. His greatest work however was 'The Eight Arguments Against Causality' which have quite a modern ring. He taught that while there is a logical connection between cause and effect in nature as we know it, the idea of causality is after all only a physical conception, for science reveals no final truth and no cause in itself."

75

Notes on Causality/Non-causality:

All our thinking is shaped into the mold of causality and this not by our own choice but by Nature's.

Nothing can enter experience which is not thrown by the mind into a causal form. The mind being capable only of experiencing in this way is incapable of grasping the essentially real in experience.

All that we know of Nature is our own mental experience of it; and all that we know of causality in Nature is likewise only the way in which that mental experience arranges itself.

The causal habit, like that of time and space, is one of the cardinal habits of thinking and one of the fixed forms of awareness. It is our lack of comprehension of the way in which the mind works, the relation between consciousness, ego, and mind, which makes it inevitable for us to fall victim to these three great illusions of the race.

The bias towards belief in causality is so universally ingrained in mankind that religious teachers had to explain the world in causal terms first. But the Vedantists used such causal explanations as steps to mount up towards non-causality. They taught that the world is a creation and its creator the pure spirit Brahman, and then led the pupil to enquire into the nature of Brahman, gradually showing him that Brahman is one, indivisible and partless. Such a partless being cannot change or produce change, therefore there can be no creation, that is, the truth of non-causality. In this way the pupil was led from religion to philosophy.

Creation as an act is different from creation as a fact. Advaita challenges the reality of the first but admits the second in the sense that it does not deny the existence of the world. But the question "How did God create the world?" does not admit of a simple accurate answer. In the first place it is oversimple and therefore inadequate; secondly it is mis-stated and omits at least two other questions the answers to which are prerequisite to an answer to the question in its present form. The infinite principle of Mind does not will or create the Universe, but within its seeming darkness there arises a point of light which becomes the centre of a potential universe. A first beginning of the Universe has never happened, because the Universe is a manifestation of Mind, the reality which, existing in timeless duration as it does, has never had a beginning itself.

Causality functions in the ordinary world. To doubt that would be to doubt all human experience. But when we enquire into its ultimate abstraction we find causality contradicts itself, it is relative and an appearance. At the same time we see that the causal thought-form must be added to the percepts of space and time to bring experience into ordered relationship during the manifestation of the universe, and lapse when the mind sinks again into consciousness.

Even so supreme a teacher as the Buddha had to confess, "Unknowable is the beginning of beings."

What it is in Mind that impels it to make these myriad appearances as ideas we do not and cannot know. The question itself is based on belief in causation, which is another idea, and is therefore invalid because it is without meaning to Mind.

One valid application of the tenet of non-causality is this—when water is converted into steam we cannot say steam is a new creation, for it is still nothing but water albeit its expression has changed.

The world being but an expression of the Overself is not a new creation, for fundamentally no new thing has come into being. The world is but a changed expression of Overself, and as cause implies effect, that is, duality, and as there is no duality, so there is no causal relation behind the universe. From the empiric standpoint—that is, disregarding fundamentals and looking at secondary elements only—within the universe causality clearly reigns. V.S.L.'s application of non-causality to the interrelations within the world is illegitimate.

If causality were not a practical working truth we should plant grass seed in the hope of getting grapefruit.

We must get our minds quite clear about this position. It is all a matter of standpoint. From a practical standpoint the world is composed of many entities affecting and inter-reacting with each other in a causal manner. From the ultimate standpoint the world is Mind-essence, and this being the only existence cannot change its nature and come into a second birth; it cannot fall into the duality of cause and effect. But the Mind's finite productions, ideas, can do so.

Therefore it is admitted that causality fully reigns in the realm of ordinary experience. But when we seek to understand Mind in itself we seek to transcend ordinary experience. Mind in itself is not subject to causality.

The question of causality depends, like the question of the universe, on the particular point of view which we take up. It is real when considered as pertaining to two things, just as a dream table and chairs are real when considered by the dreamer himself. It is fictitious when we look not at the multiplicity of things but at the essence wherefrom they are derived, just as the dream table and chairs are fictitious when looked at from the broader point of view of the man who has awakened with the dawn.

Whereas experience presupposes the relation of causality, reality itself stands out of all relations. Causality is a condition of knowing and thus confines us to the familiar world. The category of causality is inapplicable to Brahman.

If there is one rigid law in nature it would seem to be none other than the law of causality, for how can the chain of causation ever be broken?

The reticence of the Buddha in discussing problems concerning the First Cause is made explicable by his knowledge of non-causality.

Sub-atomic science—indeterminacy, Heisenberg's Quantum Theory; Super-atomic science—Einstein's relativity; milliards of galaxies which made the universe.

Sub-atomic physics reveals that the ultramicroscopic electrons and protons are disobedient to the law which science took as the best established of all laws—that of cause and effect. This revealment may even bring the theoretical search for reality into a cul-de-sac. What was once a philosophical tenet may become a scientific one too. What was once the consequence of man's keenest reflection may become the consequence of his ascertainment of facts.

Scholars often use the words cause and effect with less warrant than truth demands. The phrase is profusely sprinkled over lecture and book until we accept their statement as unquestioningly as we accept today's sunrise. But it behooves the few who would root up the reason for all things to look a little closer into this usage. When we do this, those smooth and finished doctrines which have held us captive so long may be compelled to open their doors and set us free. We may discover, as did David Hume, that whether in the behaviour of matter or of mind, much that we accept as causal is nothing of the kind, it is merely consecutive.

Hume said that a thing or self was only a bundle of relations, being nothing in itself.

It is very easy to fall into what may be called the fallacy of the single cause, as when Hitler—conveniently overlooking himself and those like him—asserted that the Jews were the cause of Germany's worst troubles. The truth is that most problems are many sided, and behind the simplest effects there lie usually a combination of causes.

Causality is a misapprehension from the philosophical standpoint, but quite correct from the physical and practical.

In the last reckoning life is really a process whereby the individual becomes conscious of his own true identity. The spiritual nature of man does not exist potentially, but actually. The discovery of his own identity is simply man's destruction of the hypnotic illusions of Ego, Time, Space, Matter, and Cause—his moment of release from untruth.

The Overself is not subject to causality, but the ideas which appear to arise in it are. This is where students become confused.

We must not ascribe activity to the Overself. This does not mean that it is wrapped in everlasting slumber. The possibility of all activity is derived from it. It is the life behind the Cosmic Mind's own life.(P)

76

The very idea of a First Cause of the universe is a false one. For a "first" involves the denial of any historic past, a "cause" involves the existence of a "before" and an "after"—that is, of time. But time is infinite and "first" denies it. So a "First Cause" is a contradictory idea.

77

If there were no infinite power there would be no finite things.

78

To say that one event "causes" another is really and only to say that, under certain conditions, the second event always follows the first one.

79

Wherever there is change there must be cause also. When, however, we discover on deeper enquiry that the change is illusory, the cause also becomes illusory. Thus the philosophic work reveals itself as a work of disillusionment.

80

The consequence of disbelief in causality inevitably must be disbelief in the theological assertion that God is the creator of the universe.

81

And what is here true of a part is likewise true of the whole, for the principle of unconscious mind gives birth not only to the aggregate of ideas which constitute a human personality but also to the aggregate of ideas which constitute an entire universe. The unconscious is therefore the region of all causes, of all possibilities.

82

The concept of evolutionary progress is entirely based on the notion that one thing can produce another—that is, of cause and effect. Such a concept is essential to practical life and to the *practice* of science; it must be closely enquired into, however, when we wish to know the final truth of things and not merely their appearance. When such enquiry is made, it will be found that the notion of causality is an *a priori* one, that it inheres in the framework of human thinking and thus prejudices the issue. The study of Kant, Max Planck, and others will show that this idea may be approached from another angle. Evolution as a theory rises and falls with causality; the destruction of the latter destroys the former. Consequently, from the viewpoint of *ultimate* truth, which is our concern, we may say that evolution is unproved and we must disregard it. The seeker after truth cannot concern himself with theories and fancies. He must deal in proved facts.

Perpetuity, eternity, and now

83

Do not confuse infinite time, which is duration, with timelessness, which is eternity. The first is just the lengthening of the ego's past, present, and future; the second is their dissolution in ecstatic smiling ego-free being. (P)

84

When in deep sleep we have absolutely no sense of Time's existence at all. We are then in eternity! When we become thoroughly convinced of the illusoriness of time, and make this conviction a settled attitude, eternity reveals itself even during the waking state. This is life in the Overself. This is not the same as totalizing the past present and future; all those belong to illusion. This realization gives perfect peace.

85

The concept of time's eternity and space's infinity is not intelligible to a finite intellect.

86

The idea of Eternity, which is a prolongation of time, is not the same as the idea of the Eternal Now, which is a cancellation of time.

87

So long as we think of eternity as being a long-drawn waiting period stretching through millions of years, so long will we fail to understand the true meaning of Spirit, and hence the true meaning of spirituality.

88

There is a difference between eternity and timelessness. It is one of kind, not merely of extent. Too many people fail to perceive this and so slur the one into the other.

89

Neither intellect nor common sense can understand the mystic's experience of timelessness, although both can hold some sort of vague concept of eternity, which is not the same.

90

The Eternal is that which is changelessly the same, but the Perpetual is that which is ever-changing.

91

Memories of past events added to anticipations of future ones stretch out our notion of time like a piece of elastic. But that does not give us infinite eternal being; it merely gives added burdens which the mind must carry.

92

In Arabic the syllable "La" is negative. Hence Allah = the no-beginning.

93

A vague, dreamlike, shapeless, shadowy, and selfless future seems unappetizing. But the Real is not of this kind at all, not a part of past or future. It is not in time; it is in the Mind.

94

The totalization of past, present, and future does not constitute eternity; accumulated experience does not confer eternal consciousness, but merely prepares the requisite condition for its reception.

95

Duration, which is the passage of time without end, is not the same as Timelessness. Yet this is the kind of survival which those who ordinarily talk of belief in immortality usually mean. They want the ego to go on endlessly, to endure forever, even if they want only the better side of the ego to continue. They want this spurious self to be perpetuated and ignore the real being whose shadow it is.

96

The English novelist Graham Greene says that he several times had dreams of happenings which later were realized. What does this mean? Its simplest meaning must obviously be that the present and the future are already joined together. The second meaning must be that since the present quickly becomes the past, the past and the future are also joined together. The total meaning must be that time is a single unbroken line. In metaphysics this can be called eternal duration, and in metempsychosis this explains how actions done now are echoed back in a later birth. For us humans, mentalism puts past, present, and future within the mind and their separateness from each other within illusion. From this illusion we can be set free only by experiencing and knowing the timeless, which must not be confused with eternal duration. The timeless transcends the past, present, and future. What we experience now in the present is abstracted from the whole of experience, the totality, but the abstraction is illusory. The reality which we give to the present and deny to past and future is again within us, within the mind, but it is within the deepest layer of the mind and that deepest layer is connected with timelessness, for that is the reality in us.

97

Thoughts and time come up together and thus humans are kept captive by the sequence Past, Present, and Future. They believe from this experience that this is the only form taken by consciousness. But another kind of experience is possible. Whether by yoga or by philosophical thinking, stillness supervenes and time rests.

98

No other moments are so worth living for as when one experiences the meaning of timelessness.

99

In timelessness there is no past to remember, no future to foresee, no sense of one moment succeeding another which is the present. In timelessness we experience only being, whereas in time we experience what the metaphysicians and the Buddhists call becoming. Whereas our experience is in fragments, whether it be now or later or in the past, in being experience attains wholeness, totality.

100

Eternity contains, undivided, the past present and future. How it can do so is a mystery which human perception and human understanding may not ordinarily grasp. The unaided intellect is powerless to solve it. But there is, potentially, a fourth-dimensional intuitive faculty which can succeed where the others fail.(P)

101

The feeling until now was one of living *in* time. Imperceptibly or suddenly this goes and he finds himself in a timeless condition, with the tick-tock of thoughts following one another absolutely stilled. It is temporary but it is also glorious.(P)

102

The mystery of the atom has resolved itself into the mystery of light, which is now the greatest mystery of physics. Einstein demonstrated the dependence of time upon the position and speed of motion of an observer. He showed, too, the amazing consequence of placing the latter in a stream of light wherein if he moved with the same velocity as light, the observer would then possess no sense of the passage of time. If this happened, what sort of a sense would he possess? Einstein could not tell us, but the mystic who has conquered mind can. He will possess the sense of eternity. He will live in the eternal, in the Kingdom of Heaven.(P)

103

When time is abolished, history is annulled. The man who emerges into this kind of consciousness finds the peace of eventless existence.

104

So long as the mental faculty operates in time, so long must it fail to cross the limits into timelessness.

105

When one experience is different from another, when consciousness flows through a series of changing episodes, successive thoughts, and varying pictures, our life is then within time. But when experience is continuously one and the same, when consciousness knows no past behind it and no future ahead of it, our life is then set free in eternity, the feeling of movement vanishes.

106

All that had happened in time and everyone that he had met in place, all events and persons that were external to him, ceased gently to exist. He found himself stranded on the shore of eternity—a happy and exalting experience.

107

Some find themselves fascinated by the prospect of infinitude in space providing the contrast to our narrowly limited condition, and by the thought of infinity beyond time, that is, timelessness liberating us from the momentary and transitory existence that is our human lot.

108

The emotions of the ego bind us to experiences in time. The stillness of the Overself is the truth that sets us free in timelessness.

109

The Overself is not in time and consequently has no history. It *is*, with no beginning and with no end. The intellect which flits from past to future, from one chronological event to another, finds such ideas strange, hard to comprehend, and puzzling.

110

Acts which are done in time cannot of themselves disclose the Timeless which transcends them, which ever was and ever shall be.

111

The events of time are continuous but the experience of timelessness is not. It simply *is*.

112

The sun and the clock make time move for us, but the mind can beat it into utter stillness.

113

Buddha: "He who conquers time is the greatest victor."

114

If in meditation he feels as if he had always been sitting there, it means he touched eternity, timelessness.

115

Caught inexorably in timeless being but knowing of the capture only after returning and lost to the world—what is this mystery of time?

116

When time stops, he feels that he has found his higher Self, that the ordinary everyday self is a shallow one. The other never changes, whereas the lower one changes during the years and with moods during the day.

117

We should look neither in the past nor in the present for what is to be found only in the Timeless.

118

The meaning of eternity reveals itself when the stillness suspends time.

119

We are always in the Timeless but the individuality may pass in and out of time.

120

The eternal Now is not to be confused with the temporal Present. In the latter, "I " am the chief actor. In the former, "I" am acted upon. In the latter, the "I" stands in its own light and complains of the darkness. In the former, the "I" gets out of the way and that which *is*, is revealed.

121

The "now" of what has become the past, the "now" of what is to be the future, and the "now" of what is the present are all contained within time. The "now" of the World-Mind holds all these three together, simultaneously. But the "now" of divine Mind is not in time at all, but rather transcends it.

122

That there is an insight where all times lie side by side—the past, the present, the future—the twentieth century B.C. and the twentieth century A.D., may seem impossible to the ordinary mind.(P)

123

The fourth dimension is in everything existing in the three-dimensional space and at the same time exists in its own dimension. *Now* in the fourth is the same as *here* in the third dimensional world.(P)

124

If reason, properly and metaphysically applied, tells us that time is not really real, experience tells us that the present moment holds the reality.

125

The Now which is existence in time is not the same as the NOW which is essence in timelessness.

126

The "now" of the ego and the "Now" of the enlightened man are two different things. For the latter's is the Eternal Now whereas the former's is fugitive and passing.

127

There is no moment in time which may not be opened out into the eternal Now.

128

Eternity is hidden in every moment; that which historically was and shall be is screened by the Now, which is infinitely timeless and timelessly infinite.

129

To live in the eternal NOW is to escape the traps of time, whether time past or time to come. It is the open door to Reality.

130

Whether in imaginative recollection of the past or in creative anticipation of the future, that which can transcend both—the Ever-peaceful Now—is grandly superior.

131

There is no feeling of succession of one instant by another—that is, of time—in this awareness of what IS.

132

To have mastered this knowledge, to have grasped the secret behind time, is to lift him out of the past, the future, and the fleeting present. With him is a benign companion, the ever-tranquil eternal Now.

133

Why does the actual present seem so much more real than the shadowy past or the distant future, although the first was not less real *then*, nor will the second be less when it is fulfilled? It is because consciousness, by means of which we know the present, in its final nature exists in a timeless NOW.

134

Time can be measured on a clock but the Infinite is measureless and unapproachable. Thought can push out to greater and greater magnitudes but still remain time-bound. The Eternal Now if it exists belongs to metaphysical and mystical worlds.

135

All time is in the Now. It is the circle of eternity which closes on itself.

136

"Moment to moment" simply means the eternal now.

137

The present, despite its constant changes of form, is always with us. Why? Because our innermost real being, without those changes, is always with us.

138

According to the *ultimate* standpoint of the relativity doctrine of the hidden teaching, past present and future are simultaneous and not continuous as is popularly believed. Consequently there is no *fixed* time between two events in a man's life or between epochs in a planet's life.

139

The concept of simultaneity defies our comprehension when applied to the World-Mind's holding of the World-Idea. How could our extremely limited finite intelligence do any justice to it? How could it take in all aspects of all things and of all happenings at once? It might be expanded beyond its present limits under special conditions but still come nowhere near such superhuman feats.

140

If our own consciousness seems bound by time to this brief life in the body, the glorious experience of the Eternal Now is the best witness to the existence of timelessness.

141

We live inside time; yet real life is outside time.

142

There is the real present but there is also the illusory present. To live in the past is to die, to live in the future is to dream, but to live in the real present is to be awake, enlightened.

143

Eternity is in this imperturbable Now, the All is in this Here.

144

There is really no progress from materiality to spirituality. There can be no shifting of the mind through time in the hope of finding eternity en route. The present moment is also the eternal *now* and, when properly understood, never changes.

145

An alert comprehension of the true meaning and precise inward significance of the present moment is the same as a comprehension of eternity, for the present slips and merges into eternity as the raindrop slips and merges into the ocean. Thus the transient is not only an inlet to the everlasting, but *is* in reality. Nothing begins, nothing ends.

146

This is the Timeless Now: the contemporary of all possible moments in past present and future. It is pure spirit. It is the true self behind and beyond man.

147

Time concepts, be they of the past or of the future, seem vague and hazy as they recoil into this Eternal Now. Is there then no sense of time left at all? In the practical mood, there is.

148

This basic Consciousness was never really in "before" or in "after." It was even then where it is now.

149

The present moment holds all past, all future within itself. The immediate experience contains the ultimate one, too.

150

The past can be known in the individual finite consciousness only as a present idea, but it is otherwise with the infinite mind. Yet when you say that all time is present time, that past present and future are coexistent, you can say this only at the price of eliminating all the sense-experience content of time. But as soon as you can do this, then the whole meaning of temporal existence changes completely and neither past nor future events can come into visibility of any kind. For everything that is individual and finite dies and disappears in the new temporal form.

Living with time

151

You can begin the quest by trying to get rid of your idea of time. This will be your honourable diploma, this will be your certified matriculation, when you succeed in turning time's illusion into the reality hidden behind it, into the Ever-Presence.

152

Time is woven inextricably into all our thinking and the only way to escape its domination is to escape the bondage of thought.

153

Metaphysics tells him that he has all the time there is. Misery prods him into doing something to get relief, and doing it quickly. This is a paradox.

154

We may live in the mere succession of events and so remain victims of time, or we may, while still noting them, raise our consciousness out of such involvement to a level so high as to become a mere spectator of them.

155

If he could bring himself to extend toward the future that same calmer attitude which he extends toward the past, he would be better able to avoid mistakes.

156

Science has immeasurably extended the time-scale which governs the human outlook on the life of the race and planet. The few thousand years of the biblical view have grown to millions of years, which science assigns to the past and future ages of man and his home. The sense of urgency will gradually be displaced as the implications of this view penetrate educated thinking.

157

Do what we will, we do not seem able to dispute the fact of the irresistible onward movement of time. It is therefore beyond the ordinary capacity of the human mind to accept the concept of a static time, of a dimension of existence wherein there is no passage of hours and years. Such a thing is as inconceivable as it is incomprehensible. Yet such is the surprising elasticity and adaptability of the mind that if only we frequently put the whole problem of time up for consideration and familiarize ourselves with the evidence for this concept, we shall eventually begin to experience strange flashes.

158

What every human being may bring within his own personal experience is the "stuff" out of which both past and future are made, the mind-essence from which their successive thought-structures are born; he may know the One, even if he may not know the many.

159

When we begin to understand the true nature of time we perforce revise our attitude towards it. We learn never to be in a hurry, to work without haste, and to build slowly but surely like corals.

160

His work is to keep still even though time is rushing by; the more it hurries the more firmly he is to remain outside the rushing current, implacably set in timelessness.

161

Time seems to ebb; he rests in the eternal Now, all haste gone, all urgent pressures stilled. He feels there is enough time to do all that has to be done, however slowly he moves to and through it.

162

Our best time occurs when we forget the passing of time. Here, for those who can appreciate it, is a clue to the nature of real happiness.

163

This indifference to the events of time will eat away his passion for activity, as the Ganges waters are eating away the walls of the great houses which rise from the riverside at Benares. The author of *Om*, that novel of Buddhistic mysticism, Talbot Mundy, perceptively wrote, "The consciousness of Wisdom is quiet, and in no haste."

164

A stateliness and stability inheres in the realization that time is illusory. It is as though a myriad worlds pass by, a million years are lived.

165

The man of forty years ago is now a stranger to me. What can I do but disapprove of a number of his bygone actions? Indeed they are unbelievable. Yet he too was myself at that time.

166

Where is the human being who is not really affected by the past, present, and future? It is easy to make the claim in talk or print, but even if this were granted, the effect of mass history (for example, a world war) must shape personal life even for the reputed "spiritually self-realized souls."

167

How infinitesimal is the period of a human lifetime against the background of Time itself!

168

He reacts to reminders of a distant, unpleasant, or pleasant past as if it were emanating from some stranger.

169

If man is inwardly already godlike, pure Spirit, only the development and evolution which are gained from experience—that is, time—can bring him to conscious realization of the fact.

170

Each past experience as it happened did so in the present. It was happening NOW. The same will be exactly true of each future one. This seems simple and true, yet it is really the result of a profounder analysis than people usually make of their human situation. Then if both past and future are not different from the present, we are *always* in the NOW. This is what is meant by timeless existence, by the illusory nature of time.

171

It is our innate inertia which keeps us set in habitual outlooks and thus keeps us victims of our own past experience. We copy again every day what we did before, what we thought and felt before. We live in both the conscious and the subconscious memories, desires, fears which time has accumulated for us, and that the ego has created to bind us to itself. We are ruled by compulsions, fixations, and neuroses—some of them not even known—that freeze us, preventing further real advancement. We rarely enter the day to gain really fresh experience, think really new thoughts, or assume really different attitudes. We are prisoners of time. This is because we are so ego-bound. The compulsion which makes us conform ourselves to dead yesterday's ideas and practices, concepts and habits, is an unreal one, an illusory one. In letting ourselves become victims of the past by letting it swallow up the present, we lose the tremendous meaning and tremendous opportunity which the present contains. Whereas the Overself speaks to us from tomorrow's intuitive understanding, the ego speaks to us through memory. Its past enslaves us, preventing a new and higher way of viewing life from being born.

But it is possible to arouse ourselves and to begin viewing life as it unfolds in the Eternal Present, the Now, with wholly fresh eyes. Every morning is like a new reincarnation into this world. It is a fresh chance to be ourselves, not merely echoes of our own past ideological fixations. Let us take it then for what it is and live each moment anew.

When a master mystic like Jesus tells men to refrain from being anxious about the morrow and to let today's evil be sufficient for today, he speaks out of his own consciousness of living in this Eternal Now. Consequently, he spoke not of periods involving twelve or twenty-four hours, but of pinpoints of a moment. He told them to live timelessly, to let the dead past bury itself. He is indeed a Christian, a Christ-self man, who lives cleanly and completely in the present—free, uncontrolled, and unconditioned by what he was, believed, or desired yesterday.(P)

172

During the night when Gautama entered Buddhahood and the great revelation of the Good Law was made to him, he discovered that existence was from moment to moment, discontinuous. The Hindu sages deny this and assert it is *continuous* in the Self. The pity of it is that both are right. For what happens in every interval between two moments? We then live solely and exclusively in the Self, the Absolute, delivered from Relativity and Finitude.

Many "still" photographs make up a cinema film. The break between every pair of pictures is not reported to the conscious mind because fast movement outruns attention. The symbolism is interesting: see *The Wisdom of the Overself*, Chapter 14, seventh meditation, for a more detailed explanation. Whoever attempts this exercise should practise it with the eyes only slightly open.

Then why did not the Buddha finish his announcement and give the entire truth? For the same reason he carefully kept quiet on several other points which could disturb men dependent on religion—on its representatives and rites, its customs and dogmas, and especially its past—to the point of enslavement. He likened the human predicament to being in a burning house and directed attention to the urgent need, which was to get out *now* and thus get saved. Here is a key word: the Present, manipulated rightly, can open the practitioner's mind. Then the Timeless itself may take him out of time (he, the personal self, cannot do it), out of the now into the Eternal NOW. If it is no easily successful way there is always the long detour of other ways found by men.(P)

173

We are victims of both the concept "time" and the feeling "time." They keep us captive to a limitation which is only one side of existence: there is another side wherein we could claim our freedom. But that would require a power to concentrate which cuts through the mesmeric suggestion holding us down and penetrates into the real Now. This is not a new dimension so much as it is above all dimensions. It is not a leaving-off of time so much as a discovery of the source from which time itself—chopped up and measurable as it is—is projected. That source is infinite being: it is measureless.

174

Not only will all men be saved in the course of time and series of reincarnations, but they are already saved in the timeless Now.

175

The magic word which gives this power is *NOW*. In its realization the eternal triumphs not only over the past and the future, but also over the present with its dismal circumstances. In pronouncing this word, life will no longer be a mere echo of what went on before, with the appalling consequences which lie visibly all around us, but a manifestation of something entirely *new*, something creative, as spirit is creative.

176

By suppressing the time-conscious element of his attention, he may unfold the timeless element of it.

177

Those moments when his mind is at its highest level and his character at its best also withdraw him from being embedded in the limited personal identity and focalized in its narrowness. It is this concentration—necessary though it be to pursue his individual life—which becomes so excessive and so exclusive that it screens off the so-called material world until it seems to be the only and real world. It is this too which keeps him in passing Time, in the fleeting Present, and hides the Eternal Present from him.

178

The Now is forever ours, forever with us, but it must be recognized, understood, accepted for the reality that it is, and not as the present *time* which it is not.

179

How much that seemed, say forty-five years ago, so important or so exciting, now in retrospect seems so trivial and flat and ordinary! It is said that time and circumstance have made this change of attitude, but why and how? The answer must be because we *really* live in the unchanging NOW—whether as worldling in spiritual ignorance, and hence only on the surface of self, things, and events, or as sage in spiritual knowledge in their inmost being.

180

To be free is to live, as far as possible, unconditioned by the past and unburdened by its memories. Equally is it to reject the future, to be without its anticipations, its hopes and its fears. But all this is only possible if one lives in the timeless Present, or what Krishnamurti calls "from moment to moment" and Eckhart "the eternal Now."

181

Living in the present moment means living according to truth and principle (but not according to hard rigid dogma) flexibly applied in the particular way required by the immediate situation in which you are. Such a way of living leaves you free, not ruled tyrannically by imposed regulations which may not at all suit the particular case.

182

The illumined mind must live in the eternal Now, which is not the same as the temporal Present. Because it is beyond the reach of events the Now is saturated with Peace. Because it is forever drifting on the surface of events the Present is agitated with change. Each of us can learn to live in the happy presence of this peace if he will prepare the way by (stoically) disciplining the thoughts he brings into every moment. He alone is responsible for them, he alone must have the hardihood to reject every one that reduces his stature to the little, time-bound, desire-filled ego.

183

The space in which the process of thinking takes place, is time. It could not exist without the dimension of time. If thought is ever transcended, time is transcended along with it. Such an achievement throws the mind into the pure present, the eternal now, "the presence of God" of all mystics.(P)

184

In contemplating deeply Nature's beauty around one, as some of us have done, it is possible to slip into a stillness where we realize that there never was a past but always the *NOW*—the ever-present timeless Consciousness—all peace, all harmony; that there is no past—just the eternal. Where are the shadows of negativity then? They are non-existent! This can happen if we forget the self, with its narrowed viewpoint, and surrender to the impersonal. In that brief experience there is no conflict to trouble the mind.(P)

185

When his consciousness comes to maturity, it comes out of the prison which time is. The past cannot now hold him there. The future can only be this new timelessness, so that he "takes no thought for the morrow."

186

The kind of eternal life which philosophy seeks involves a change of quality rather than of dimension. It seeks a better life rather than a longer one. Incidentally, it gets both.

187

Remembrance of the past, and especially attachment to it, supports the ego, maintains and preserves it. The quester must hold his memories loosely for, after all, this present life is only one of a string which in itself is only a dream.

188

Memories keep a man fastened to the old ways of life, however stupid they have proved themselves to be and however worthless their values have shown themselves. There is no way out of them except to put the destructive ones, the limiting ones, the useless ones, and the obstructive ones to the stake, burn them, and be done with them—and be done with them ash and all.

189

Attitudes and habits formed in earlier years or picked up from one's social heritage belong to the past and often hinder this living in the NOW. To become independent of them at any moment, if needful, without destroying their admitted usefulness at other times, is an art to be achieved.

190

A silly yet serious error made by beginners, intermediates, and proficients alike is to declare that because they live in the eternal "Now" they need not concern themselves with the future. They live, and want to live, only one day at a time. Consequently they throw prudence to the winds and forethought to the dogs. Such a course invites trouble and may even end in disaster, although it is true that both may be mitigated if they have honestly surrendered the ego to some extent. The mitigation will depend on, and be in one way proportionate to, the extent. In that case, what they refuse to do for themselves may be done by the Overself. But where there is only verbal surrender, or imaginary surrender, they will have to take the consequences of their shiftlessness.

191

Recollections of the desired or feared past snare you still further in the ego. Anticipation of a desired or feared future do the same. But by letting both go, living in the eternal Now, you weaken the ego.

192

The ever-moving nature of time is not allowed to oppress him into forgetfulness of the ever-present background of timelessness.

193

It is the way of those who withdraw from time's tyranny to cease looking forward to the future or backward to the past. They live from day to day—nay, from moment to moment. For theirs is a divine care-less-ness.

194

If he will take up, and hold firmly to, this standpoint of the Eternal Now, how many matters that trouble, afflict, and depress his mind would cease to do so! How trivial and transitory they would seem then!

195

To free himself from the bondage of time, he must free himself from the claims, the demands, the relationships, and the grievances of the past. He need do this only inwardly and mentally, of course. He is to come to the beginning of each single day as a new beginning, not letting the familiar, the routine, the habitual, the environmental, impose its old ties upon his thought, his faith, or his imagination.

196

This life, which is for most people an uneasy balance between hopes and fears, can be confronted in a different, more satisfactory way: and that is by a shift to the ever-present Mind behind the present moment.

197

All that memory belongs to time gone: it has served to make the present. *Now* must he travel on, must look for new developments, must liberate mind and heart from ways which no longer help, must create and invent what is *now* needed.

198

He begins to live as if he has enough time to do everything; more particularly he is not too busy to attend to spiritual concerns.

199

What we recollect of the past and what we expect of the future do not exist. But what we experience now does exist. It stands out uniquely from all this series of events in time. We *can* deal with it and in doing so we may affect the future.

200

This feeling of being in a dimension outside time confers a sense of being really alive. The past fades away and no longer hangs heavily over him. To help the birth of this new awareness Jesus advised: "Let the dead bury their dead." [Luke 9:60]

201

There are moments when he pauses during a walk and lets time drift away to the void.

202

We cannot renounce the world, much less the ego, unless we renounce also our own past memories which build it; they must go, the dead outgrown personality left to bury the dead pictures of bygone experiences. So doing we claim freedom, the possibility to lead a new, perhaps better life, even the possibility of being open to the grace of being born again.

203

The idea of the everlasting Now is a fascinating one, but it is something more than an idea alone, it is also a Reality. Whoever keeps on reflecting upon it with intense concentration and wholehearted absorption will discover its Reality, for he will dispel the illusion which time casts upon the mind.

204

A little enquiry shows that we never actually experience a past or a future, because we continually *live* in a now. This is all we experience, whether we are a child in age or an elderly person. This now is really out of time and it is certainly out of the past, because the moment you attempt to grasp the past it is not there, there is only the now. The same applies to the future. In that sense, existence in time is illusory. In the higher mystic experience there is complete stillness and no movements of the mind in thought, and there is also a lapse of the feeling of time and an entry into a purely timeless condition. This condition is a true condition for happiness, for it confers an indescribable peace of mind which is the only kind of happiness we can expect to experience on this earth.

205

Living in the eternal Now does not mean living a whole lifetime all at once; the finite human being could not do it.

206

A man must choose: does he wish to live in the moving instant or in the fixed eternal? Waiting for what the subsequent years will bring him, whether he waits in joy or in anxiety, is to be imprisoned by time. But remaining in the place where time pauses, the mind is to be kept serenely unrippled. He is to apply this attitude of detachment not only to objects but also to thoughts, not only to present possessions but also to past memories.

207

This does not mean that he is impervious to all the correction taught by experience, but that he accepts only those which truth bids him accept.

208

The page is closed; the more you try to return to it, the more you suffer. The old threads cannot be picked up again. Let them go. Accept the responsibility of the present, be willing to look at, and for, the new.

209

Memory of the past warps his attitude, anticipation of the future distorts it. He is unable to bring a genuinely straight mind to his problems.

210

We are so enmeshed in the past, in its obsessive memories, tendencies, and drives, that we tend to repeat and perpetuate its errors and stupidities.

211

Present time never stands still, it is always moving away. That is one reason why we are enjoined to "*Be still*," if we would know we are like God at base. In the mind's deep stillness we live neither in past memories nor future fears and hopes, nor in the moving present, but only in an emptiness which is the everlasting Now. Here alone we can remain in unbroken peace, paid for by being devoid of expectations and free from desires, cut off from attachments and above the day's agitations or oscillations.

212

Must we reject time and history in order to live in the eternal Now? Must we pretend in order to acquire the consciousness of Overself that this human drama is not being acted out by the "I"?

213

It takes no account of the years, rejects all sense of pressure from moving clockhands; time comes to a standstill. This is peace, this is detachment, call it what you like.

214

Every man is a victim of his own past until he awakens to this recognition—that at his best level he is divine in a timeless way, that there he may rise above this past and free himself from it.

215

To let go of his past is to let go of memories, with their various identities he has assumed.

216

We must look for eternity in the present moment now, and not in some far off afterlife. We must seek for infinity here, in this place, and not in a psychic world beyond the physical body.

217

He lives, as I once wrote, on the pinpoint of a moment. He has no clear idea of his next move forward and less of his probable position in the future generally.

218

We must refuse to chain ourselves either to the past or to the future by refusing to chain our thoughts to them. That is to say, we must learn to let them come to rest in the timeless Void.

5

THE VOID AS METAPHYSICAL FACT

Even inside the timed world, what is a thousand years here could be a single year in another area of the universe. Time itself would be a relative changing measure to a traveller through it. It is the same with space. What of this vacuum which is timelessness? It is the Void.

2

Learning detachment from the world comes at the beginning of the path. Learning that the world is not even there comes at the end.

3

What I am trying to say is that this indescribable Void out of which the universes appear, this utter Nothing between and behind them, this unknown Power between and behind the atoms themselves, is God.

4

How hard for the unprepared ordinary man to understand that the world of objects and persons, things and planets, is unreal whereas the world of the Void is real!

5

The fathomless Void seems, as a concept to someone who has never experienced it or, failing that, correctly understood it, like nonbeing. Yet it is the most important concept of all Oriental wisdom, the last possible one of all Occidental theology and metaphysics.

6

Every conceivable kind of form comes out of the seeming Void into time and space.

7

The Void is the state of Mind in repose, and the appearance-world is its (in)activity. At a certain stage of their studies, the seeker and the student have to discriminate between both in order to progress; but further progress will bring them to understand that there is no *essential* difference between the two states and that Mind is the same in both.(P)

8

What we have called "the void" is the same as what medieval German mystics like Tauler and Boehme have called "the abyss." It is the Eternal Silence behind all activities and evolutions, the Mother of all that exists.

9

This is the great miracle of our existence, that out of the Void it comes forth, out of Nothing it receives consciousness, power, and life.

10

All phenomena are ultimately empty and relative. This is a large part of the meaning of the Void.

11

In a precise scientific sense, the Void is beyond explanation since it is not really a Void at all. It is a perpetual paradox.

12

The universal existence is an ever-developing process, an activity and not a thing. There is no cessation of this process anywhere but only the mere show of it. THAT out of which and in which it arises is alone exempt from this vibration, being formless, intangible, inconceivable void.

13

There are no relativities in It, no timed events, no places, no creatures: nothing that can ever be known by finite perceptions.

14

This unthinkable Void is, for those who want one, the First Cause of all existence.

15

Our thoughts pass out and evaporate into a seeming void. Can it be that this void is really a nothingness, really less existent than the thoughts it receives? No, the void is nothing other, can be nothing other than Mind itself. The thoughts merge inward in their secret essence—Thought.

16

On one hand there is the emptiness of the Void, on the other hand there is the fullness of the cosmos which comes into being to occupy it.

17

In the Void the Real is hidden, all time is rolled up there: the entire world and the space holding it dissolves there, everything and everyone emerges and vanishes there. THAT alone is the ever-Real, ever-Being. That is what man must learn to consider as his own hidden being, a task of re-identification.

18

The Void is empty of matter, yes, of all material universes—but it is not lacking in Reality. It is in fact the mysterious support of all material universes.

19

In the Void there is no one particular thing or creature. It is Pure Consciousness with no personality.

20

Atomic physics shows the world as derived from a mysterious No-thing.

21

That which is called the Void, Emptiness, is not the total annihilation of all things but the total lack of that matter of which they were supposed to be composed.

22

The Void is called so only as it is empty of all *forms*, of all things shaped or patterned, of all creatures drawn in any image whatsoever. It is *their* annihilation, but only to be followed at a later period by their self-unfolding again.

23

It is not the annihilation of being but the fullness of being.

24

You may get rid of every object of thought and, seemingly, of every thought itself until there is only a void. But even then you will still be thinking the void and consequently holding a "thought." It will not be the true void. The *thinking* "I" must itself be eliminated. Only when this is done will all activity truly cease and the stillness of the Eternal be truly known. This can be realized by some kind of mystical practice only and not by conceptual effort.

25

The Void is not beyond the reach of human consciousness, not a condition that is unknowable or inexperienceable. This is testified by the Buddhist Sage Nagasena: "O King, Nirvana *exists*. . . . And, it is *perceptible* to the mind. . . . that disciple who has fully attained, can *see* Nirvana."

26

The momentary pause in every heartbeat is a link with the still centre of the Overself. Where the rhythm of activity comes to an end—be it a man's heart or an entire planet—its infinite and eternal cause is there. All this vast universal activity is but a function of the silent, still Void.(P)

27

What Eckhart calls The Nothing is not dissimilar from what Buddha calls The Void. The ordinary human mind recoils from such a conception and human knowledge keeps no place for it. The five senses want a tangible world, even if it be only an illusionary appearance.

28

The Void does not mean that there is ultimately nothing at all but that there is ultimately nothing within finite human intellectual and sense perception. We cannot strictly assert that reality is this or that because the moment we make such an assertion we imply that finite reason knows enough about infinite reality to make it. However, although it is true that we cannot describe this state except in negative terms, that need not deter us from searching for symbols and similes which have an intellectually positive character, so long as we understand that they are only symbols and similes.

29

Even in Pali Buddhism there is the Void, called *sunnatta*, meaning emptiness. *Nibbana* can be realized by the sole path of contemplating all conditioned things as empty, soul-less (*anatta*), devoid of a permanent and personal entity. *Nibbana* is the Unconditioned and hence "It is just because there is no sense experience that in *Nibbana* there is happiness," said Buddha.

30

Men are too deceived by their perceptions of the world around them, too ignorant of the ultimate in scientific atomic research, to believe that its "substance" is totally immaterial, is in short a Void. In this matter, their infatuation with their bodily senses makes the deep subtle thinking required to pierce this ignorance even harder still.

31

Man has no faculty whereby he can perceive the absolute and infinite Power as clearly as he can perceive any material thing.

32

The most meaningful of all figures in the domain of numbers is the nought. Consider! It is there even before you can start with the one. The Void is also the most mysterious of states in which to find one's mind. It holds both the least and the most.

33

The notion of the Void when it is first encountered is somewhat frightening. The reason for this is that it bears no identity, this great emptiness has no self-being. It is like a confrontation with annihilation, this unidentifiable and unique non-thing.

34

The Void is not a mere nothing as ordinarily meant: nor is it something the mind can hold for unlimited periods.

35

Is there any difference between what Christian Saint John of the Cross called "the Nada (Nothing)" and what Buddhist Nagarjuna called "the Void"?

36

Tibetan wisdom-knowledge equates the Void with the Inner Stillness.

37

The Void is not an experience limited to the Buddhists and Hindus. It has also been mentioned in the works of Western mystics such as Saint John of the Cross, in *The Hermit* (unknown author), and in the medieval English work *The Cloud of Unknowing*.

38

The whole of truth cannot be given in a single statement when the whole universe is based on the dualities and opposites. One aspect without the other would be a misleading half-truth. For instance, to speak of the Void as the Source of All, to tell men that the universe is a No-thing, would seem meaningless to common sense, although it is metaphysically correct. "It would not be the Tao unless people of inferior intelligence laughed at it," said the sage Lao Tzu. As Tenshin, a great teacher of art in the last century, explained: "Truth can be reached only through the knowledge of opposites." It was Tenshin, too, who said, "Nothing is real except that which concerns the working of our own minds."

39

If the Void is not taken into account or has not yet been experienced, the individual will still have an inadequate idea of existence.

40

Not all minds are fitted to comprehend the tremendous truth of the Void, which science has discovered and philosophy proclaims. It would be in vain to ask the untutored to accept No-thing as the cause of Things, to believe that there can be effects without causes, and that all is in the mind. They would need education in the most advanced nuclear physics, capacity to cope with the most difficult mathematical formulae. And even more than education, the tutors themselves would need inspiration. For though the facts are there, only a genius like Heisenberg, or a mind like his disciple von Weizsäcker, can quickly see their sublime meaning—*God is*.

41

Thus the Void must become the subject of actual meditation. It must be dwelt on as unbounded and immaterial, formless and relationless, and the effort used in meditation must combine the imaginative with the rational faculties, the intuitive with the aspirational.

42

The One behind the Many is not to be mistaken for the figure one which is followed by two, three, and so on. It is on the contrary the mysterious Nought out of which all the units which make up multiple figures themselves arise. If we do not call it the Nought it is only because this might be mistaken as utter Nihilism. Were this so then existence would be meaningless and metaphysics absurd. The true ineffable Nought, like the superphysical One, is rather the reality of all realities. From it there stream forth all things and all creatures; to it they shall all return eventually. This void is the impenetrable background of all that is, was, or shall be; unique, mysterious, and imperishable. He who can gaze into its mysterious Nothingness and see that the pure Divine Being is forever there, sees indeed.(P)

Part 2:
What Is Philosophy?

It was the custom among Chinese, Indian, and Persian sacred writers to preface their writing by an introductory invocation, so this author does the same. He entrusts this new enterprise to divine guidance, to the loftier inspiration of his Masters during his own apprenticeship to Truth, and pays his due debt of acknowledgment to them. May they deign to guide his pen, and accept these pages as part of his silent recompense for the help and hope he received from them, which he now ventures to pass on in his turn.

We may begin by asking what this philosophy offers us. It offers those who pursue it to the end a deep understanding of the world and a satisfying explanation of the significance of human experience. It offers them the power to penetrate appearances and to discover the genuinely real from the mere appearance of reality; it offers satisfaction of that desire which everyone, everywhere, holds somewhere in his heart—the desire to be free.

1

TOWARD DEFINING PHILOSOPHY

The old Oriental idea is to be *lost* in the Infinite. The new Occidental ideal is to be *in tune* with the Infinite.

2

Neither the psychoanalyst nor even the religionist seeks that full purification and total transformation of the human being which philosophy alone seeks and alone achieves. All other paths—including the mystical ones—seek to effect a particular purpose or a partial one: only this is informed enough and willing enough to fulfil the complete purpose for which man has been put on earth by the World-Mind and surrender absolutely to it. If the philosopher has any desire at all, it is to know, understand, and co-operate with the infinitely intelligent and perfectly efficient World-Idea.

3

It is a transcendental idea that the mind gets hold of and knows. It is a gathering of clear supra-mental perceptions. It is the higher reason, the discriminating understanding. It penetrates the whole being and remains. Thus it becomes naturalized and continues the natural consciousness of the man.

4

It is not only a right intellectual attitude towards life. It is also an exalted emotional experience of life. Nor is it only an occasional attitude and an intermittent experience. It is sustained through the day and throughout the year.

5

Philosophy is an explanation of life and a distillation of its highest knowledge. Consequently it includes metaphysics. But it is not identical with metaphysics, being far greater.

6

The complaint has been made not seldom that the Indian version of this quest is too largely a process of dehumanization. I must leave it to the public propagandists of Indian teachings to give their own defense in this matter. But the philosophic attitude seeks a balanced wisdom, a removal of negative, ignoble, sensualist, narrow-minded, unpractical, and fanatical traits from character and action. Beyond that it welcomes the fine flowering of human culture, the refinement of human living, and the enchantment of human quality.

7

There are two sets of critics who match themselves against philosophy. There are the hard materialists, on the one hand, and the imperfect mystics, on the other. The first are guided by reason but limited to sense-experience; the second are guided by intuition but limited to meditation-experience. Both are incomplete. Both are opposed to each other as well as to philosophy, which understands, appreciates, and accepts both as expressing necessary but partial views which should be included in a fuller and more integral view.

8

Philosophy overcomes the mystic's fear of worldly life and the worldling's fear of mystical life by bringing them together and reconciling their demands under the transforming light of a new synthesis.

9

Ours is a complete synthesis of mysticism, metaphysics, science, religion, ethics, and action. It offers a higher and wider objective than the earlier yogas.

10

Because its concepts are not merely the productions of a mechanical logic but the inspirations of a living soul, they are powerfully creative, dynamically stimulative. In philosophy, art consummates itself.

11

There is nothing spectacular in philosophy. Reasoned thought pitched at the highest level and directed inwards upon itself is one of its chief features.

12

Yoga is primarily the method and result of meditation. Philosophy accepts and uses this method and incorporates its results. But it does not stop there. It adds two further practices, metaphysical reasoning and wise action, and one further effort—the mystical insight into, and distinction of, the ego. Therefore we are justified in saying that the hidden teaching does go beyond yoga.

13

The battle to secure mental stillness must first be fought and won before the battle of the ego can be brought to an end. For it is only in that deep state wherein all other thoughts are put to rest that the single thought of "I" as ego can be isolated, faced, fought until its strength is pitilessly squeezed out and destroyed at last. The attainment of this inner stillness is yoga; this conquest of the ego in it and after it is philosophy.

14

Philosophy is not satisfied with a merely intellectual reflection of the truth, as in a mirror, but seeks direct vision of the truth.

15

Its evaluation of mankind is neither materialistically contemptuous nor mystically rosy. It sees the bright permanent essence along with the dark passing form.

16

Philosophy offers a manner of living which is a natural part of, and outgrowth from, its cosmically derived principles.

17

The practice of philosophy is an essential part of it and consists not only in applying its principles and its wisdom to everyday active living, but also in realizing the divine presence deep, deep within the heart where it abides in tremendous stillness.(P)

18

People sometimes ask me to what religion I belong or to what school of yoga I adhere. If I answer them, which is not often, I tell them: "To none and to all!" If such a paradox annoys them, I try to soften their wrath by adding that I am a student of philosophy. During my journeys to the heavenly realm of infinite eternal and absolute existence, I did not once discover any labels marked Christian, Hindu, Catholic, Protestant, Zen, Shin, Platonist, Hegelian, and so on, any more than I discovered labels marked Englishman, American, or Hottentot. All such ascriptions would contradict the very nature of the ascriptionless existence. All sectarian differences are merely intellectual ones. They have no place in that level which is deeper than intellectual function. They divide men into hostile groups only because they are pseudo-spiritual. He who has tasted of the pure Spirit's own freedom will be unwilling to submit himself to the restrictions of cult and creed. Therefore I could not conscientiously affix a label to my own outlook or to the teaching about this existence which I have embraced. In my secret heart I separate myself from nobody, just as this teaching itself excludes no other in its perfect comprehension. Because I had to call it by some name as soon as I began to write about it, I called it philosophy because this is too wide and too general a name to become the property of any single sect. In doing so I merely returned to its ancient and noble meaning among the Greeks who, in the Eleusinian Mysteries, designated the spiritual truth learned at initiation as "philosophy" and the initiate himself as "philosopher" or lover of wisdom.

Now genuine wisdom, being in its highest phase the fruit of a transcendental insight, is sublimely dateless and unchangeable. Yet its mode of expression is necessarily dated and may therefore change. Perhaps this pioneering attempt to fill the term "philosophy" with a content which combines ancient tradition with modern innovation will help the few who are sick of intellectual intolerances that masquerade as spiritual insight. Perhaps it may free such broader souls from the need of adopting a separative standpoint with all the frictions, prejudices, egotisms, and hatreds which go with it, and afford them an intellectual basis for practising a profound compassion for all alike. It is as natural for those reared on limited conceptions of life to limit their faith and loyalty to a particular group or a particular area of this planet as it is natural for those reared on philosophic truth to widen their vision and service into world-comprehension and world-fellowship. The philosopher's larger and nobler vision refuses to establish a separate group consciousness for himself and for those who think as he does. Hence he refuses to establish a new cult, a new association, or a new label. To him the oneness of mankind is a fact and not a fable. He is always conscious of the fact that he is a citizen of the world-community. While acknowledging the place and need of lesser loyalties for unphilosophical persons, he cannot outrage truth by confining his own self solely to such loyalties.

Why this eagerness to separate ourselves from the rest of mankind and collect into a sect, to wear a new label that proclaims difference and division? The more we believe in the oneness of life, the less we ought to herd ourselves behind barriers. To add a new cult to the existing list is to multiply the causes of human division and thence of human strife. Let those of us who can do so be done with this seeking of ever-new disunity, this fostering of ever-fresh prejudices, and let those who cannot do so keep it at least as an ideal—however remote and however far-off its attainment may seem—for after all it is ultimate direction and not immediate position that matters most. The democratic abolishment of class status and exclusive groups, which will be a distinctive feature of the coming age, should also show itself in the circles of mystical and philosophic students. If they have any superiority over others, let them display it by a superiority of conduct grounded in a diviner consciousness. Nevertheless, with all the best will in the world to refrain from starting a new group, the distinctive character of their conduct and the unique character of their outlook will, of themselves, mark out the followers of such teaching. Therefore whatever metaphysical unity with others may be perceived and whatever inward willingness to identify interests with them may be felt, some kind of practical indication of its goal and outward particularization of its path will necessarily and inescapably arise of their own accord. And I do not know of any better or broader name with which to mark those who pursue this quest than to say that they are students of philosophy.(P)

19

We may generally distinguish three different views of the world. The first is that which comes easily and naturally and it depends on five-sense experience alone. It may be called materialism, and may take various shapes. The second is religious in its elementary state, depending on faith, and mystical in its higher stage, depending on intuition and transcendental experience. The third is scientific in its elementary state, depending on concrete reason, and metaphysical in its higher state, depending on abstract reason. Although these are the views generally held amongst men, they do not exhaust the possibilities of human intelligence. There is a fourth possible view which declares that none of the others can stand alone and that if we cling to any one of them alone to the detriment of the others we merely limit the truth. This view is the philosophic. It declares that truth may be arrived at by combining all the other views which yield only partial truths into the balanced unity of whole truth, and unfolding the faculty of insight which penetrates into hidden reality.(P)

20

The worth of religion's contribution toward human life is admitted. The transcendent character of mysticism's goal is admired. The offering of metaphysics is respected. The necessity of disinterested practical service is accepted. The attitude which is attracted by one and repelled by the other is defective and incomplete. The coming age will require their synthesis. But these things, however good, are not enough. For there is need of adding to them another and still farther milestone on mankind's great march. And this is philosophy—that which harmoniously brings all these together and then transcends them.

21

Science suppresses the subject of experience and studies the object. Mysticism suppresses the object of experience and studies the subject. Philosophy suppresses nothing, studies both subject and object; indeed it embraces the study of all experience.(P)

22

It is perhaps the amplitude and symmetry of the philosophic approach which make it so completely satisfying. For this is the only approach which honours reason and appreciates beauty, cultivates intuition and respects mystical experience, fosters reverence and teaches true prayer, enjoins action and promotes morality. It is the spiritual life fully grown.(P)

23

The esoteric meaning of the star is "Philosophic Man," that is, one who has travelled the complete fivefold path and brought its results into proper balance. This path consists of religious veneration, mystical meditation, rational reflection, moral re-education, and altruistic service. The esoteric meaning of the circle, when situated within the very centre of the star, is the Divine Overself-atom within the human heart.(P)

24

Philosophy refuses to compromise with truth; hence it refuses to place itself at the point of view which attempts to comprehend the Infinite with finite equipment.

25

The basis of philosophic living is simply this: the higher self feels nothing but the good, the true, and the beautiful; we are its projections and are to become its reflections. Why then should we not, here and now, discipline ourselves until we also feel only the same?

26

Philosophy is not a matter of theory alone. It is also a matter of conduct. It imposes responsibilities on the conscience and restraints on the will.

27

It accepts and endorses the modern method, that is, the inductive method as applied to facts which are universally verifiable, the way of cautious approach, the insistence on a habit of calm examination, the passion for clear truth and ascertained fact rather than mere opinion and personal emotionalism: in short, a scrupulously honest rigorous outlook and an impersonal attitude of mind more than anything else.

28

To separate the essential truth from its accidental overlay, the permanent fact from the personal dream, the full insight from its temperamental colouring—this is one task of philosophy.

29

The purpose of philosophy is to expel illusion from the mind and correct error. Truth will then appear of itself.

30

On Spinoza's Doctrine

(a) Spinoza taught that God was the whole of things in the universe. This brought him into the category of Pantheist. Philosophy says this is true, but only part of the truth. For God is not only immanent in the universe but also transcends it. God still would be God even if there were no universe.

(b) He declared that the unknown reality was Substance. Philosophy says this is only an attribute of Reality and as such still not the ultimate itself, no more than the quality of fragrance is the flower itself.

(c) He believed in Causality as science did in the nineteenth century, and as all must do who do not comprehend the final truth that Reality is nondual, and hence leaves no room for the duality of a cause and an effect.

(d) Spinoza's pantheism made him declare that everything is God. This is the theological outlook. The philosophical one declares that everything is a manifestation of One Infinite Reality. For if the ego also is God, then who is God?

(e) Spinoza's teaching that God has two attributes, Mind and Matter, that reality has two aspects, mind and body, made him a dualist. Philosophy knows only one reality—Mind. It admits causality only for the immediate and practical purposes of the illusory world.

(f) His teaching on how to live so as to fulfil the proper purpose of life is identical with philosophy's teaching. He saw that man so far must become wholly free inwardly and as free as possible outwardly. This is to be achieved by self-mastery, by overcoming desires, subjugating passions, and simplifying existence. This brings true happiness.

31

Philosophy is not only a body of doctrines to be believed because they cannot be found except by higher revelation, but also a way of life to be practised and a discipline of thought to be followed.

32

It is a grave error to regard philosophy as being identical with metaphysics. It is quite true that every philosopher is also a metaphysician but he is not a metaphysician only. He is also a mystic, a religionist, an activist.

33

It is the essential office of philosophy to declare the supreme worth of truth.

34

It is a doctrine inspired by divinity, founded on truth, and applied to life.

35

Every man has his own abstract view of his relation to the universe. In most cases it is either an unconscious or half-conscious one. But still it is there. To the extent that he seeks to make it a fully conscious and completely true one, he becomes a philosopher.

36

It is significant that in Sanskrit the term which stands for philosophy is also given the meaning of "insight." Hence an Indian philosopher was someone who not merely *knew* about things, like a metaphysician or scientist, but who had an insight *into* them.

37

It is the method of philosophy to direct each student, to show him the way, but at the same time to warn him that no one can travel the way for him.

38

Here is realism of an uncommon kind, for it mingles the spiritual and material, the ultimate and material realities.

39

The philosophy of truth is universal in outlook, all-comprehensive in scope. Consequently it makes no claim to displace any religion or to supersede any mystical or metaphysical system.

40

Philosophy interprets, after due reflection, the whole of the data supplied by the sciences. It generalizes and synthesizes the results of scientific observation and experiment.

41

It is not only a metaphysical doctrine to satisfy the reason in its acutest questionings; it is also a religious power to sustain the ego in its darkest hours.

42

Philosophy is the higher culture of life. To be philosophic is to live more fully.

43

Philosophy is at one and the same time a doctrine, a practice, and a realization.

44

Philosophy sets out to decipher the meaning of life. But it asks first if there be a meaning. It does not dogmatize, does not start with initial assumptions.

45

Philosophy is not a set of doctrines so much as an attitude of mind.

46

Here is a teaching which the intellect may accept and the conscience may approve. Here are complex ideas which will need time for the modern man to work them out in his own way; here are germinal conceptions whose full significances may at first remain unrecognized, but will disclose themselves as gradually as trees disclose themselves out of seeds.

47

The philosophic conception of spirituality is not of a state to be reached in the world beyond death or in an Oriental ashram or Occidental cloister beyond active life, but of a state to be reached here and now and within.

48

It is the first operation of philosophic training to instill doubt, to free the mind of all those numerous suggestions and distortions imposed on it by others since childhood and maintained by its own slavish acceptance, total unawareness, or natural incapacity.

49

We call ourselves students of philosophy because we cannot take any name derived from a human teacher. We are not followers of this man or that man exclusively, but of the inner light.

50

It is comprehensive enough to suit the modern taste, especially the modern Western taste which, while appreciating the simplicity and purity of a life like the best Indian yogi's—its freedom from desires and its indifference to possessions—nevertheless feels that it cannot and should not deny its own inclinations toward a fuller, more comfortable, and more artistic external life. Such a complete ideal, uniting the seeming opposites of contemplation and activity and combining apparently incongruous items like self-discipline and susceptibility to beauty, is more attractive and better justified to us. Without undue asceticism and without undue abnegation of the world, it yet inculcates the following of virtue and the pursuit of wisdom not less ardently than does the Indian ideal.

51

It is so all-comprehensive that it can be taken as far from the realities of ordinary living as the human mind can soar or brought as close to them as the human heart may desire.

52

Philosophy adjusts its spiritual help to suit the needs of those it seeks to help. It is religious with the religious believers, metaphysical with the metaphysical-minded, mystical with the mystically experienced, practical with the active. But with those who can appreciate its own breadth and integrality, it is all these things and more at one and the same time.

53

It is a life that is moral and rational, contemplative and active, in the truest and consequently the least conventional sense of these terms.

54

It is a knowledge achieved first in the state of contemplation and then confirmed by the process of reasoning, or vice versa. Thus the result is the same.

55

Certain truths are immovably fundamental to all worthy systems of mysticism and tremendously important to all mankind: there exists a supreme reality beyond the awareness of sense or intellect; there exists a soul in man which is rooted in this reality; the higher purpose of human life is to establish full consciousness of and communion with this soul; a good life increases happinesses and attracts rewards, but wrong-doing increases misery and attracts retribution.

56

Philosophy never ceases to affirm that the soul exists and that human consciousness can be raised to embrace it.

57

This—the recognition of the Soul's factuality—is the only doctrine to which every man may commit himself, whatever his other beliefs.

58

Here is no new cult seeking followers, no new church pleading for members. Philosophy is the wisdom of Life itself. Whether people study it now or neglect it will not affect its eventual destiny.

59

Philosophy affirms, not on the basis of theoretical speculation but on that of direct experience, that every human being has a divine soul from which it draws life, consciousness, and intelligence.

60

The teaching is comprised of three parts: (a) the truth-principles, (b) the meditation methods, (c) the mystical experiences.

61

Genuine philosophy is a living force actively at work in molding the character and modifying the destiny of its votaries.

62

Here in philosophy he will find thought become mature, mysticism become lucid and sane, everything in his life put into balance and proportion. Here all that is bizarre and eccentric, unrealistic and exaggerated has no footing.

63

Philosophy is Greek in that it rejects extremes and seeks a balance of all man's parts, but Indian in that it venerates the transcendental.

64

The Greek quest for an ideal which combined balance with serenity is itself combined in philosophy with the quest for truth and reality.

65

The philosophic ideal is not merely an intellectual one, but also a mystical one, not merely practical, but also emotional. It develops harmonies and balances all these different qualities.

66

In affirming the reality and supremacy of Mind, philosophy lays down both its first and its last principle.

67

To observe physical things or events with scientific accuracy yet think about them on a deeper metaphysical level, to feel in a human way yet without falling victim to the obscuration and distortion of human passion and emotion, to benefit by only the best in art and culture, to withdraw from thoughts into the still transcendental intuition of being itself, and finally to put into one's life in the everyday world the calm balanced result.

68

This is philosophy which opens the way to bigger thoughts, wider minds, and finer ideals; which makes the quest for truth an inner adventure and a religious duty; and which finally points to a supernal divine stillness as the place where the revelation must be made.

69

Why is philosophy the love of wisdom? Because as such it leads to a quest for what is Timeless, the Universal, the True, the Real, the Enduring Peace-Bestowing Satisfaction: that is, the Absolute which alone is free from all relativities.

70

The notion that a man requires no special schooling in philosophy is a nonsensical and superficial one. For philosophy tries to do in complete consciousness and in complete thoroughness what the unphilosophical are always doing in an unsystematic casual and unconscious way. It seeks to impart a proper understanding of the meaning of the world so that those who have to live in this world may live aright, successfully, and more happily.

71

The Buddhist looks forward mainly to the cessation of suffering, the Vedantin mainly to the attainment of bliss. The philosopher looks to both.

72

Metaphysical curiosity is not enough for philosophy. It needs to *know*, not merely to speculate. It also needs the holy uplifts of real religion.

73

Philosophy has its discipline as well as its holiness, its metaphysical abstractions as well as its practical sages. By its very definition it cannot be one-sided and lack balance. Its reactions are emotional as well as intellectual but both exist in equilibrium and harmony. It is not only a way of thinking but also of living.

74

Philosophy does not affirm its facts arbitrarily or dogmatically. They are put forward, *as they are found* by the human mind when at last its development is capable of comprehending the subtlest of all truths, in orderly, rigorous, logical form.

75

Our doctrine provides a scientific case for ethics, for compassion, for service.

76

Philosophy is scientific in that it must deal with facts, not with pious hopes or idle theories.

77

Philosophy usually prefers a balanced position between extreme conventional views. But it prefers its own unconventional view to the others most of all.

78

The popular view merely looks *at* life; the philosophic view looks *into* life.

79

The central point of our program rests, however, on the firm foundation of the ultimate wisdom—hitherto kept in a hidden school for the privileged few but now to be made available for all whose ethical outlook and mental capacity can grasp it.

80

Philosophy does not deal in unverified assertions or mere opinions. If it accepts revelations as part of its teaching, it does so only because the revealers have proven themselves to be utterly reliable, only because they have gone through the most strenuous mental emotional and moral discipline. Much of its teaching, however, may be put to the test of evidence and reasoning, and this test is not only welcomed but required.

81

More than a thousand years ago, Theon of Smyrna wrote: "It may be said that philosophy is the initiation into and tradition of real and true Mysteries." And he mentioned that this initiation begins with purification but ends with felicity.

82

Here in philosophy man's noblest aspirations receive their highest fulfilment. Here his searching after truth achieves satisfying finality.

83

Philosophy is at one and the same time a religious cult, a metaphysical system, a mystical technique, a moral discipline, and a practical guide.

84

Philosophy puts in definite form ideas which meet the subconscious need of some and sets down clearly ideals which express the fine but vague aspirations of others.

85

Note the similarity to Jesus' "Seek ye first the kingdom of heaven and all these things shall be added" in The Wisdom of Solomon: "I preferred Wisdom before sceptres and thrones, and esteemed riches nothing in comparison with her . . . All good things together came to me with her, and innumerable riches in her hands. . . . she was the mother of them. If riches be a possession to be desired in this life, what is richer than wisdom that worketh all things?" The quest of philosophic wisdom is also the quest of the kingdom of heaven.

86

Philosophy not only gives its votaries a doctrine to study but also a method of worship, not only a way of life but also a technique of meditation.

87

This is the gospel of inspired action, of dynamic philosophy, of rational religion, of balanced mysticism.

88

The teaching which philosophy offers deals with matters of permanent rather than topical interest. The counsel which philosophy gives deals with the general course of human life rather than with particular personal vicissitudes.

89

Philosophy is both a tradition of knowledge and an achievement in experience.

90

It prefers individual advancement to the illusion of gregarious advancement. It sees the home as not less holy than the ashram.

91

What is the ultimate explanation of this universe wherein we dwell? What are the final concepts of its meaning which transcend all previous concepts and render them imperfect? It is the business of a philosopher to find out these things.

92

Even after a man's religious faith has fallen to pieces and he stands for a while in doubt and confusion, there will inevitably arise within him the need of finding a fresh intelligible picture of the universe, for he cannot rest satisfied with a merely negative attitude toward life. And he will have to construct it out of the findings of scientific materialism, if nothing better comes to his hand. This mind will necessarily try to make sense of the universe and to harmonize its seeming contradictions into a logical unity.

93

It is not quite the same to go in search of a faith to believe in as to go in search of a truth to understand. Philosophy, however, unites the two endeavours.

94

Philosophy rests upon the basis of intuitive perception and mystical insight.

95

The philosophic view is not only attractive to reason and appealing to emotion, it is also fortifying to conscience. It provides indeed the best dynamic for a nobler life.

96

It is to be judged not only as a metaphysical system but also as a moral influence.

97

Just because philosophy's statements are so definite, this should not be misconstrued as being dogmatic.

98

We are not constructing a closed and rigid system of philosophy but rather revealing an attitude of mind which can lead to truth.

99

Contrary to conventional beliefs, philosophy does no harm to whatever is worth retaining. It makes religion truly religious, rationalism more rational, and mysticism soundly mystical. It takes away their follies, true, but it leaves their facts untouched.

100

Dharma = moral living.

101

Galen, the celebrated Greek physician and thinker, saw this point. Although not a Christian himself, he praised the early Christians of his time (second century) because, "Day and night they strive that their deeds may be commendable and that they may contribute to the welfare of humanity; therefore each one of them is virtually a philosopher, for these people have attained unto that which is the essence and purport of philosophy . . . even though they may be illiterate."

102

Because philosophy provides a view of life's landscape from the mountaintop, it provides the truest fullest view.

103

It is not concerned with theories that might be, but with things that incontestably are.

104

Against the barrenness of materialistic denial, it offers the urgently needed values and explains the practices of meditation, intuition, and aspiration.

105

Philosophy is the quest grown up, equipped with maturity and judgement and balance.

106

It cannot be easily classified for it is at once a doctrine requiring some faith, a teaching needing some study, a morality for obedience, and a technique for practice.

107

It is a doctrine which is alive with ethical feeling, rich with metaphysical truth, rare in its freedom from religious and racial prejudice, the solvent of many problems.

108

Calmness and balance are the most admired virtues in the philosophic code. The first is developed to the extent of becoming superb self-composure, the second until it integrates utter opposites.

109

Plato wrote that philosophy is a kind of death. He meant that the desires and interests, the matters and activities of the outer world must be surrendered in a certain way and at certain times. This is to be done invisibly and secretly in the deepest part of the soul. It is there to become an abiding condition, a permanent attitude, a total withdrawal from what a man normally lives for: thus he dies to the world. It is also to be done differently at specially reserved times by the process of extremely deep meditation. Consciousness is reversed from things and thoughts to its own pure Self.

110

Others besides Plato have compared philosophy to the art of dying while yet still living. In Buddha's case it meant dying to all desires which sought satisfaction in the outer world, renouncing that world in order to enter the monastic world of monks and nuns. In the philosopher's case this is not a necessary outcome, although it was a perfectly logical conclusion for the Buddha to make. The philosopher seeks to free himself as much as possible from worldly chains, but the essence of his achievement is more positive than merely leaving the worldly life.

111

Such a teaching has been called pessimistic. We answer: how can it be so when it teaches the way to the ending of all sorrow, the way to the achievement of all serenity? Where is the pessimism in denouncing the baser joys for the sake of receiving the better ones? The teaching would be pessimistic if it saw no hope at all for humanity and if it denied the worth of all satisfaction, but, on the contrary, it offers an immeasurable hope and shows the way to transmute lower into higher satisfactions.

112

It is the philosopher's desire to think authentically, to push aside prejudice and bias in order to get at the solid facts.

113

Will philosophy ever become, like religion, a social force? The answer is that it is already a social force since everybody has some kind of outlook upon life, however primitive it be—it is only that his philosophy is unconscious. We who study it, deliberately, try consciously to become philosophers.

114

Philosophy cannot be limited to being some metaphysical system, or an ethical code, or a kind of logical enquiry, or somebody's opinions about this and that: it must give a whole overview, a fruit of enlightenment.

115

If this teaching is less dramatic than others, it is also safer. If results take longer to appear, they are also certain and lasting.

116

The advantages of pursuing the path of Gnana Yoga, of an enquiry into Self, are manifold. It starts from the standpoint to which we are accustomed, by taking self as we find it. It does *not* start from some divine Brahman whose existence is initially known to but one man in millions (since it is to be apprehended only in *Samadhi*). The enquiry into Self, moreover, accepts this world as real, and does not ask us to go against every attribute of common sense. It permits our minds to work along their natural lines of thinking. It follows the method most suitable to our Western scientific minds—that is, it works from the known to the unknown.

117

It is a study which imparts gratifying significance to the universe and consoling harmony to its phenomena. It is a study which restores religious faith because it demonstrates that the forces behind our human existence are not blind and unconscious but intelligent and benign.

118

Philosophy constitutes the supreme keystone of all man's evolutionary building. The way to it is the predestined path to which he must ultimately come when he has exhausted all other cultural roads, all personal hopes, all worldly guides. It is the acme of his higher culture and the last lap of his ethical ascension. Its statuesque intellectual grandeur is akin to that of Himalaya. And as that mighty range mingles hard brown granite with soft white snow, so does this unique system mingle hard rational thinking with sensitive mystical meditation.

119

These ideas do not stand alone—not that it really matters even if they did, provided they are true ideas. But we can bring to them the support of high-grade minds, perceptive metaphysicians, fine poets, contemplative mystics who lived in the beatitude of divine union, and even a few top-ranking nuclear physicists and Astronomers-Royal.

120

It begins with the statement that the men of today are not completed beings.

121

The world has yet to discover that the teaching of this philosophy is the most brilliant of all intellectual systems, the most religious of all religious paths, the most mystical of all mystical techniques.

122

Philosophy can smilingly await its hour, for all roads lead to it, none away from it. Life is a mystery. Mystery provokes inquiry. Inquiry leads eventually to discovery. Discovery, by stimulating thought upon itself and by evoking intuition about itself, can end only in philosophy.

123

The teaching is thus both an inheritance from the past and a precursor of the future.

On the term 'philosophy'

124

If you ask what is philosophy, the answer must begin with what it is not. It is not about guesses and speculations, not about beliefs produced by human wishes nor superstitions produced by human traditions.

125

Anyone may become a college professor of philosophy without becoming a mystic, but to become a philosopher he must also become a mystic.

126

The academic teaching of philosophy is a necessary part of educational effort but it is mainly metaphysical and logical, an intellectual effort without soul, without intuitive feeling, and a collection of varying human opinions, speculations, and theories. To become fully worthy of its title it must remake men, awaken their higher possibilities, show also the need and practice of non-thought.

127

It may be asked why I insist on using the word "philosophy" as a self-sufficient name without prefixing it by some descriptive term or person's name when it has held different meanings in different centuries, or been associated with different points of view ranging from the most materialistic to the most spiritualist. The question is well asked, although the answer may not be quite satisfactory. I do so because I want to restore this word to its ancient dignity. I want it used for the highest kind of insight into the Truth of things, which means into the Truth of the unique Reality. I want the philosopher to be equated with the sage, the man who not only knows this Truth, has this insight, and experiences this Reality in meditation, but also, although in a modified form, in action amid the world's turmoil.(P)

128

Viewed from the standpoint of the house in which we all have to live—that is, the body—Advaita Vedanta seems to deal only in ultimate abstractions—however admirable and lofty its outlook. The body is there and its actuality and factuality must be noted and, more, accepted. This is why I do not give any other label to the ideas put into my later books than the generic name philosophy. I do not call it Indian philosophy since there are ideas in the books which do not belong to India at all. I do not identify it with any particular land, race, religion, or teacher from the ancient past or the modern present. Philosophy cannot be limited only to abstract ideas. It includes those ideas but it also includes other things. Its original Greek meaning, "love of wisdom," concerns the whole of man, and not only his abstract thoughts, intellect, feelings, body, or relation to the world around him. It concerns his entire life: his contacts with other people, the morality which guides him in dealing with them, and finally his attitude towards himself. Philosophy must be universal in its scope; therefore, it may embrace ideas which originate not only in India or in America or in Europe, but in every other period of civilization. Not all ideas are philosophical, but only those which are true, useful, in harmony with the World-Idea, and able to survive the test of practice and applicability.(P)

129

There is a kind of understanding combined with feeling which is not a common one here in the West, indeed uncommon enough to seem more discoverable and less puzzling in the Asiatic regions. It is puzzling for four reasons. One is that it cannot be attributed to the intellect alone, nor to the emotional nature alone. Another is that it provides an experience so difficult to describe that it is preferable not to discuss it at all. A third is that although the most reverent it is not allied to religion. A fourth point is that it is outside any precise labelling as for instance a metaphysics or cult which could really belong to it. Yet it is neither anything new or old. It is nameless. But because there is only one way to deal with it honestly—the way of utter silence, speechless when in contact with other humans, perfectly still when in the secrecy of a closed room—we may renew the Pythagorean appellation of "philosophy" for it is truly the love of wisdom-knowledge.(P)

130

I regret to state that most academic people mistake the history of philosophy for the study of philosophy.

131

The term *philosophy* we reserve for the *philosophy of truth*, which is the harmonious and balanced union of all these elements in their perfected state. We shall not here use this term for the academic wordplay, the sterile jugglery of technical terms, the toying with unreal and distant issues which so often passes for philosophy. This integrality is more in accord with the ancient and essential meaning of the word, derived as it is from the Greek *sophia* (wisdom or ultimate knowledge) and *philos* (love).

132

I have avoided the risk of starting a new movement or founding a new church only by taking the risk of causing confusion among those belonging to the old movements, the old churches. For by my giving so broad a name as "philosophy" to this teaching, a name to which they are already accustomed and with which they are already familiar, they will take it to be a harmless barren intellectual playing with ideas remote from us in history time relevance and usefulness. They will fear no rivalry from it and will mostly ignore it and thus leave others, who can appreciate its timeliness, to work at it in peace.

133

If the name "Philosophy" has been wrongly attached to the productions of merely intellectual guesswork, we have every right to restore it to its proper use.

134

Do not confuse the quibbling over phrases and the hair-splitting over words with philosophy. It is nothing of the sort. Their concern with non-problems is entirely outside its own province.

135

The simple name "philosophy" is an old one and it is enough for this teaching. Mentalism is its metaphysical branch, mental quiet is its mystical practice, and the Overself is the ultimate Consciousness of man.

136

The appalling modern misuse of this ancient term, calling anybody's whim, opinion, speculation, guess, or fancy his "philosophy," is reprehensible.

137

I insisted on giving the word "philosophy" its original Greek meaning even though it has been manhandled by this time to mean all sorts of different things from science to religion to opinion.

138

There are questions which people often ask: Is philosophy socially desirable? Has it any practical usefulness? How will it help *me*? Where is the time for it, anyway? Such questions would not be asked if the definition of philosophy had been understood, for they betray the questioner's confusion of it with metaphysics.

139

We do not narrow the meaning of this expressive term down to the merely academic and theoretical. We cling to its ancient significance and declare that there is no other study whose rewards are so great as those of philosophy. But it is to be studied not only from ponderous books, but also from pulsating experience.

140

Philosophy cannot be taught by lectures alone: life in the larger sense is also its classroom. Its best teachers come without prepared notes, without programmed courses, but with the catalytic power to inspire ideas and deeds.

141

It was implicit in the word itself, and well understood by the Greeks who used it, that the term "philosophy" referred not to worldly wisdom—in the sense that the Jesuit Baltasar Gracian used it—but to divine wisdom.

142

If some part of what is here comprised under the term "philosophy" is also discussed in the academic institutions, so much the better for them, but it is certainly not the most important part. Nor is the general attitude, the spirit behind it all, the same. Logic and linguistics have their place, but making use of them merely to get lost in words, in empty abstractions and futile hunts for non-existent meanings, is pseudo-serious delusion.

Philosophy's transcendental "position"

143

Philosophy does not set out to please people but to guide them; not to be commercially successful but to be ethically successful; not to dispense with truth for the sake of holding followers but to dispense with followers for the sake of holding truth.

144

Philosophy occupies an unassailable position, which can endure and survive all the intellectual emotional and practical changes likely to happen in a man's life.

145

The philosophy of cosmic existence, of which human existence is merely a part, cannot change with, or depend on, changing human opinions. It is and must be eternal, the same with ancient peoples as with those yet to be born, independent of individuals who come and go. The intellect cannot deliver itself of such a philosophy.

146

There is nothing new here. It is an old truth and teaching. They are unchangeable, immutable. They do not vary with time.

147

It has the oldest tradition behind it which culture can offer yet it is ever fresh and new because it lives in the NOW: timeless.

148

Those who strive hard to penetrate the core of life's mystery will find their fullest result in philosophy.

149

Philosophy is unique. It alone offers a point of view which includes all other points of view, and yet transcends them. It alone is able to say that it both has a position and has no position. It alone is without particular interest in attacking other positions, yet is able, if necessary, sturdily to defend its own!

150

Although philosophy propounds statements of universal laws and eternal truths, nevertheless each man draws from its study highly personal application and gains from its practices markedly individual fulfilment. Although it is the only Idea which can ever bring men together in harmony and unity, nevertheless it becomes unique for every fresh adherent. And although it transcends all limitations imposed by intellect emotion form and egoism, nevertheless it inspires the poet, teaches the thinker, gives vistas to the artist, guides the executive, and solaces the labourer.(P)

151

Most people look for labels, affix them or accept them, and then are forced to stand up for all the ideas bearing the label they identify themselves with. They limit their search for Truth as soon as they join a group. They must then accept untruths along with truths. Philosophy, as we use the term, cannot be limited to any single set teaching, for it is universal. It approaches the truth universally, free from prejudices, exclusions, and labels.

152

Philosophy refuses to regard itself in an exclusive sense. It admits all labelled points of view. But it refuses to limit itself to any of them. For they deal with apparent truth. The point of view which deals with real truth is really no point of view at all.

153

The would-be philosopher should not feel bound by labels, categories, and other fences which people want to put on others simply because they themselves live quite willingly surrounded by such fences and cannot understand someone who refuses to do so. Philosophy is a path which ends in the pathless—a way to the inner freedom which comes with truth.

154

It would be difficult to put philosophy into any category of its own for it has links with everything and with nothing, with particular religions and with no religion at all, with particular metaphysical systems and with none, with the different theologies and creeds, and so on; it has no organization and no one founder or apostle.

155

Philosophy competes with no teaching, religion, system. It stands by itself, unique.

156

Philosophy is not any man's personal possession. It is itself impersonal.

157

Such is the incontrovertible character of the philosophy of truth that it will always survive, however many civilizations rise and vanish, for both prolonged experience and sustained reflection always lead to and confirm it in the end.

158

Such teaching can never be useless and consequently can never disappear.

Its value and benefits

159

It is good and sensible to seek improvement of one's work. It is idealistic and noble to seek improvement of one's self. It is best of all to admire, know, practise, and realize Philosophy.

160

One of the first fruits of philosophy is perhaps the balanced understanding which it yields. In no other way can men arrive at so truthful, so fair, and so just a view of life, or indeed of anything upon which they place their thinking mind. And this splendid result could not come about if the philosophic quest did not bring the whole man of thought and feeling, of intuition and will, into activity in a harmonious and well-integrated way. Thus wholeness is holiness in the truest sense.

161

Why should we trouble our heads with philosophical study? Why is it not enough to practice goodwill towards men? The answer to the second question is that the feeling of goodwill may vanish at the first bitter experience of being injured by other men. It will not suffice to depend on feeling alone; one must also get thoroughly and rationally convinced that goodwill is necessary under all circumstances, and not only for the benefit of others, but even for our own.

162

Whoever understands philosophy truly will find it basically important not only in his thought but also in his career. He will find all crucial decisions will be influenced by what he has learned from philosophy or made by how it has shaped his character.

163

It provides him with a standpoint wherefrom to measure the correctness or error, truth or falsity, breadth or limitation of the views, theories, and statements presented to him by others. Like a keen cold wind it blows away the mists of superstition and foolishness. The ordinary aspirant is not capable of distinguishing between a sound doctrine and a fallacious one, between a competent teacher and an incompetent one or a self-seeking teacher and a selfless one, between the correct course to pursue in meditation and the incorrect one. The discipline will give him the education which will enable him to make such critical distinctions. It summons all these to the bar of severe scrutiny. It puts thought on its farthest stretch because it starts where science leaves off. It shows up the defects of an improper and unbalanced outlook. It stresses the need of making reason a governing wheel to control emotional adventures. It warns the mystic who would rightly extinguish the tyranny of intellect to develop it at some time or other, because he who would become divine must also fulfil himself as a man. It counsels him to balance the mind-stilling methods used in meditation with the mind-sharpening discipline of metaphysics and science.

164

Philosophy tells us how to *live* whereas the ego-mentality only tells us how to appear as if we were really living.

165

To be an intellectually conscious philosopher offers advantages in every way. For our conduct of life flows naturally out of our understanding of life. If the second is faulty, incomplete, or wrong, the first will be so too! For the appraisal of men and the values of things which determine this conduct are themselves determined by our understanding. Sound principles and correct theory afford the best guarantee that when action is taken it will be rightly taken. It is then possible to understand clearly what is being done and why it is being done. Therefore studies in the metaphysics of truth are not wasting time. It is here that the soundness of the philosophic attitude and the quality of its metaphysical knowledge save us on many occasions from falling into grave blunders.

166

Such studies as my books deal with may seem profitless to those unacquainted with their practical value. More than five thousand years ago the most famous of Indian sages pointed out: "Even a little of this yoga practice saves from great dangers." Quite clearly he did not refer to the common yoga but to the philosophic one, for the utter inability of most Indian yogis to save their own country is obvious to every critical observer.

167

The acquirement of spiritual wisdom does not necessarily prevent the disciple from making worldly mistakes; but because it develops the qualities which will prevent them, and because it takes to heart the lessons of experience, humbly and receptively, it does reduce the frequency of those mistakes.

168

The *practice* of philosophy tends to reduce the number of one's perplexities and to quieten the questioning mind itself. It keeps the thoughts well-balanced and the feelings clean.

169

He who will let these ideas take lodgement in his mind will find that as he penetrates farther and farther into the great hinterland of philosophy, getting to know it better and better, his appreciation of it and devotion to it will grow proportionately.

170

Philosophy explains life, guides man, and—by removing his misunderstanding about his own identity—redeems him.

171

The man who becomes thoroughly imbued with philosophical ideas finds his mind liberated and his feelings liberalized.

172

Not only does philosophical study inform the mind, it also elevates the mind.

173

The quest has three aspects: metaphysical, meditational, and morally active. It is the metaphysician's business to think this thing called life through to its farthest end. It is the mystic's business to intuit the peaceful desireless state of thoughtlessness. But this quest cannot be conducted in compartments; rather must it be conducted as we have to live, that is, integrally. Hence it is the philosopher's business to bring the metaphysician's bloodless conclusions and the mystic's serene intuition into intimate relation with practical human obligations and flesh-and-blood activities. Both ancient mystical-metaphysical wisdom and modern scientific practicality form the two halves of a complete and comprehensive human culture. Both are required by a man who wants to be fully educated; one without the help of the other will be lame. This may well be why wise Emerson confessed, "I have not yet seen a man!" Consequently, he who has passed through all the different disciplines will be a valuable member of society. For meditation will have calmed his temperament and disciplined his character; the metaphysics of truth will have sharpened his intelligence, protected him against error, and balanced his outlook; the philosophic ethos will have purified his motives and promoted his altruism, whilst the philosophic insight will have made him forever aware that he is an inhabitant of the country of the Overself. He will have touched life at its principal points yet will have permitted himself to be cramped and confined by none.(P)

174

The sincere, who are honestly desirous of discovering Truth at whatever cost, will be helped within their limitations; the insincere, who seek to support their petty prejudices rather than to follow Truth, will have their hearts read and their hollowness exposed.(P)

175

He who has sufficiently purified his character, controlled his senses, developed his reason, and unfolded his intuition is always ready to meet what comes and to meet it aright. He need not fear the future. Time is on his side. For he has stopped adding bad karma to his account and every fresh year adds good karma instead. And even where he must still bear the workings of the old adverse karma, he will still remain serene because he understands with Epictetus that "There is only one thing for which God has sent me into the world, and that is to perfect my nature in all sorts of virtue or strength; and there is nothing that I cannot use for that purpose." He knows that each experience which comes to him is what he most needs at the time, even though it be what he likes least. He needs it because it is in part nothing else than his own past thinking, feeling, and doing come back to confront him to enable him to see and study their results in a plain, concrete, unmistakable form. He makes use of every situation to help his ultimate aims, even though it may hinder his immediate ones. Such serenity in the face of adversity must not be mistaken for supine fatalism or a lethargic acceptance of every untoward event as God's will. For although he will seek to understand why it has happened to him and master the lesson behind it, he will also seek to master the event itself and not be content to endure it helplessly. Thus, when all happenings become serviceable to him and when he knows that his own reaction to them will be dictated by wisdom and virtue, the future can no more frighten him than the present can intimidate him. He cannot go amiss whatever happens. For he knows too, whether it be a defeat or a sorrow in the world's eyes, whether it be a triumph or a joy, the experience will leave him better, wiser, and stronger than it found him, more prepared for the next one to come. The philosophic student knows that he is here to face, understand, and master precisely those events, conditions, and situations which others wish to flee and evade, that to make a detour around life's obstacles and to escape meeting its problems is, in the end, unprofitable. He knows that his wisdom must arise out of the fullness and not out of the poverty of experience and that it is no use non-cooperatively shirking the world's struggle, for it is largely through such struggle that he can bring forth his own latent resources. Philosophy does not refuse to face life, however tragic or however frightful it may be, and uses such experiences to profit its own higher purpose.(P)

176

The mastery of philosophy will produce a supreme self-confidence within him throughout his dealings with life. The man who knows nothing of philosophy will declare that it has nothing to do with practical affairs and that it will not help you to rise in your chosen career, for instance. He is wrong. Philosophy gives its votary a thoroughly scientific and practical outlook whilst it enables him to solve his problems unemotionally and by the clear light of reason. He will, however, be under certain ethical limitations from which other men are exempt, for he takes the game of living as a sacred trust and not as a means for personal aggrandizement at the expense of others.(P)

177

Those who would assign philosophy the role of a leisurely pastime for a few people who have nothing better to do, are greatly mistaken. Philosophy, correctly understood, involves living as well as being. Its value is not merely intellectual, not merely to stimulate thought, but also to guide action. Its ideas and ideals are not left suspended in mid-air, as it were, unable to come down to earth in practical and practicable forms. It can be put to the test in daily living. It can be applied to all personal and social problems without exception. It shows us how to achieve a balanced existence in an unbalanced society. It is truth made workable. The study of and practice of philosophy are particularly valuable to men and women who follow certain professions, such as physicians, lawyers, and teachers, or who hold a certain social status, such as business executives, political administrators, and leaders of organizations. Those who have been placed by character or destiny or by both where their authority touches the lives of numerous others, or where their influence affects the minds of many more, who occupy positions of responsibility or superior status, will find in its principles that which will enable them to direct others wisely and in a manner conducive to the ultimate happiness of all. In the end it can only justify its name if it dynamically inspires its votaries to a wise altruistic and untiring activity, both in self-development and in social development. (P)

178

If philosophy begins with doubt and wonder, it ends by taking away whatever doubts are left in the mind and converting the wonder into holy reverence.

179

It precisely states and positively affirms the spiritual destiny which awaits man.

180

A time eventually comes when this inner life blooms vigorously and richly within him, when the revelatory whispers of truth are heard clearly and unequivocally, when the joy of liberation from desires and passions shines constantly in his heart, and when deepest reverence suffuses his whole world outlook.

181

What is the worth of the philosophic attainment? Perhaps one of the best answers would be: suppose all men and women possessed it, what would civilized society be like then? It would certainly be freer of its present defects and fuller of realized virtues. War would be unknown, destitution would vanish; peace, knowledge, beauty, joy, and goodness would flourish.

182

Because one thought minted from the mind of a man who has searched long and far for truth is worth a thousand from the mind of one who has never searched for it at all, it would be time well spent to take up a few of these ideas. Each of them thus becomes a diamond with which to scratch the glass of ignorance.

183

Whoever wishes to endure life rather than enjoy it, to walk with saints or fly with angels, must look elsewhere. But whoever wishes to become an inspired, intelligent, brave, and good human being must look to philosophy. For it will make him acquainted with his divine soul, endow him with the power of right reasoning, fortify him against the chagrins and reverses of life, train him never to be hurtful and always to be helpful, and teach him the knowledge of true values.

184

Philosophy is a way of thought not merely for scholars but for everyone who wants to understand truth. It is a way of life not merely for monks but for everyone who is engaged in the world's activity. It offers the best in doctrine, the wisest in conduct.

185

Philosophy teaches men to trust and use their own powers, inspires them to develop the infinite possibilities latent within them. This is true self-reliance.

186

However subtle its doctrines may be, they are so solidly based and so all-comprehensive that the man who has once made them his own has gained a light for the rest of his lifetime.

187

The primary use of philosophy is not to console the suffering and give refuge to the unhappy. Religion can do that. People ought not come to it because they are tired of life and joyless. They should come because it can inspire their life and because they appreciate the beauty of its silent contemplations, the truth of its sublime ideas.

188

The aim of philosophy is not to desert activity but to inspire and illumine it, not to neglect meditation but to bring back its gains of peace and power to transform external life, not to give up reason but to warm and round it out by devotion. Only the neurotic, the dissociated, and the ignorant do otherwise. The wiser ones, better balanced, will let them actively collaborate with one another.

189

It is not a study which fulfils the expectation of personal profit in some form with which other studies are begun. It offers the truth for its own sake: because it is what it is, not for the rewards it does indirectly bring.

190

When a man who has developed an unwavering will and a concentrated mind, a serene contemplativeness and a magnificent dynamism, sets out to remake his external life for the better, surely he will accomplish not less but more than the man who has failed to develop these things.

191

The philosophic procedure leads not only to perpetual inner peace for the man himself but also to spontaneous action for humanity.

192

It teaches patience, confers wisdom, and instills magnanimity. It brings the human creature to full maturity. It liberates him from the conventional attitude of so many persons which covers, through real fear and supposed necessity, what they really are.

193

The immediate effects of this ascent in consciousness to the Overself are wide and varied. Torn emotions are healed and base ones purified. A flaccid will is brought to adamantine strength.

194

The divine character of his inmost being will become plain to him, and that not as a matter of wishful thinking or suggested belief but as firsthand personal experience.

195

Philosophy imposes charity—in Saint Paul's sense—on the heart, and bestows clarity—in Spinoza's sense—on the mind.

196

The worth of philosophy must be estimated not only by its intellectual truth or personal usefulness or social service alone, but by all three. Its unique merit lies not only in its transcendental reach but also in its balanced integrality.

197

Only at the end of a course in these studies can their intellectual, ethical, and practical importance to mankind be adequately assessed. If they do no more than rationally establish without reliance on any supernatural revelation the existence of a Deific Principle and thus confirm the profoundest yearnings of the human heart; if they do no more than dispel the current orthodox errors and unorthodox illusions about the Supreme Mind and reveal a new and truer way of thinking about it; if they provide a proper basis for the belief that death cannot really touch us; if they trace out the secret significance of all the struggle and sorrow in this life and proffer the hope of a new and better one here and now, they will surely have done enough. But the world view which is developed here can do very much more than that. For the theoretical worth of man, the personal happiness of his existence, and the practical contribution of his citizenship depend partly upon his discovery of a world conception which not only satisfies his own head and heart alike, but also serves the social interest.

198

Action should be soundly based so as to render the chance of failure as necessarily impossible as human capacity can render it. This means it should be based on philosophical principles. The mental mastery of these principles will help to give a right direction to the whole of one's life, just as the correct focusing of a camera will help to ensure satisfactory results in the finished photograph. Every man has worked out the basic ideas by which he lives but only the philosophic man has worked them out consciously. Because of the soundness and impartiality and penetrativeness of its approach, his judgements in the most perplexing matters of practical conduct will therefore be more reliable than those passed by so-called practical men themselves.

199

Such teaching arouses man to knowledge of his relationship to the divine, gives solace to his heart and peace to his mind.

200

Each person who brings more truth and goodness, more consciousness and balance into his own small circle, brings it into the whole world at the same time. A single individual may be helpless in the face of global events, but the echoes of the echoes of his inspired words and deeds, presence and thoughts, may be heard far from him in place and time.

201

The man who boasts that he can manage very well in life without studying philosophy, forgets that to possess no philosophy merely means to possess bad philosophy. For it merely means that like an animal he holds an unexamined, unanalysed, and uncriticized view of life. The need of philosophical study is simply the need of understanding our existence.

202

Philosophy ennobles human character and dignifies human personality.

203

But if there is nothing weakly sentimental in philosophy, it kindles the most delicate feeling and the deepest felicity that its votary could ever have as a human being.

204

The philosophic discipline balances a man's mind and stabilizes his feelings. It enhances his sense of values to the point of fastidiousness in responding to the world around him. For him life is full of interest, meaning, and benefit.

205

With more understanding *of* life, there comes more interest *in* life.

206

It may be shattering to the preconceptions and misconceptions of those who believe that Enlightenment is *only* for the dreamer and the escapist to hear it affirmed that this is not so, that it is equally attainable by the person who is at home in the world and by the lover of beautiful forms, sounds, and colours. But clearly such a person would need to be exceptionally well balanced or he would soon lose his way. This is another reason why philosophy holds the quality of balance in such high estimation.

207

Even the glimpse is so dazzling that it can never be forgotten and will tend gradually to reorientate the whole life. Henceforth this new element with all the immense assurance it conveys will characterize his inner life. Thus his outward life becomes a consecrated one. He feels safely held by a power higher than his own. He becomes strong enough to meet life face to face, not suborned by its hardships any more than by its happinesses. "The life of that person is beautiful and blessed who has properly and adequately known the Mind which exists within the mind," says an old text, *The Yoga of the Sage Vasistha*. The quest is not a coldly intellectual affair nor a vaguely dream-life one. He who has adequately comprehended its significance is stirred to his innermost depths with a devotion to it, a reverence for the Real which spreads outward and in time comes to animate both his feelings and his activities. If the Supreme escapes all definition, it does not escape life.

208

The undivided mind, the single vision, the unified life—these are final offerings of philosophical activity.

209

The first awakening to intellectual and artistic values in a young person is an important event, as the first awakening at puberty to sex is a dynamic one. But the first awakening to the vision of what philosophy has to offer transcends them all.

210

If philosophy gives a man nothing more than a loftier conception of himself than he otherwise would have, it would still be a worthwhile study. Yet it is not a conception which makes self-conceit, vanity, and pride grow bigger. On the contrary, it is more likely to be accompanied by a sacred humility.

211

Philosophy has brought refinement to art, truth to metaphysics, a higher level to science, nobility to ethics, and wisdom to living.

212

The philosopher cannot expect to be entirely exempt from disabilities which the whole race suffers. But he can expect to be exempt from avoidable sufferings caused by egoism, unruly passions, lack of will, and lack of foresight. He finds the universe is good and friendly and trustworthy but this is true only because he has established harmony with the Mind behind it. All others who live in discord with it will have to suffer until they learn to amend their ways and eradicate within themselves the causes of this discord. Inevitably Nature will hurt them and Fortune oppose them until they do.

213

To have no other goals than physical excellencies, however good and necessary these may be, keeps a man less than he could become. Even to set intellectual and artistic goals is still not enough, however admirable they may be. All these can find their place if they are crowned by the highest excellence of all, which is the spiritual.

214

Do not ask philosophy to tell you how to make a success of your career or business but only how to make a success of yourself. It is possible that the first will follow as a consequence of the second, but it is not inevitable. Therefore do not believe, as certain American cults have led their followers to believe, that prosperity is the necessary accompaniment of spirituality.

215

It is one of philosophy's best services to show its votaries that there is a higher relation between men and the earth and a hidden connection between them and the Infinite Power.

216

It is the duty of philosophy to supply principles, not to work out programs. But whoever has thoroughly grasped those principles should be able to apply them in most imaginable situations, although the success of his application will depend upon the extent of his equipment and the quality of his knowledge of the technical factors involved in them.

217

Philosophy is not for the entertainment of idle lives but for the enrichment of eager ones.

218

Philosophy bears the most distinctive and most significant mission in the contemporary world. It brings a great light to the service of mankind and confers a joyful blessing on those who accept it. Yet few perceive this.

219

It brings the everyday events of life into a broader perspective. This calms fears, quietens nerves, and creates detachment.

220

Philosophy can help us to attach correct values in our activities as a human being, both physical and cultural. It can provide the base for a code of conduct which will discipline yet benefit us and certainly not harm others.

221

To pass on this philosophical knowledge is as necessary as to pass on essential forms of agricultural or industrial knowledge.

222

Philosophy sees the whole route and therefore can correctly point out the next step forward to those who are still groping their way along it.

223

Only when there will be genuine *inner* acceptance of these ideas will there also be an outer expression of them in spontaneous activity.

224

Philosophy brings a man to serenity, it is often said. But it also brings him to the capacity for gentle laughter, for the humanist power of enjoying life.

225

Philosophy cannot give any man complete happiness, because it cannot make him completely oblivious of every tragedy which is happening around him. But it can give him the greatest possible happiness that life on this earth can yield. And this will not have the fragility and transiency of every other kind but will rest upon a rocklike, lasting base.

226

When a man sticks to unshakeable principles and abides by unalterable ethics, he derives an inner strength which not only is protective but also makes him feel secure.

227

If philosophy disciplines his desires, it also consoles his sufferings. If it chastens him in rapture, it also sustains him in frustration.

228

As he grows in wisdom, he automatically gains in strength.

229

A mind freed from its weaknesses and illuminated by the Overself, a life guided from within and ruled by truth—these are some of the rewards the quest offers him.

230

Such a life, purged of grossness, freed from littleness and stripped of low desires, honest in action and truthful in thought, will expel many useless fears.

231

One of the first fruits of this obedience to philosophic ideals will be his liberation from that narrow provincialism of outlook which fosters national prejudice and harbours racial hatred.

232

It guides him toward intellectual integrity; it encourages him in emotional purity; it elevates him into moral tranquillity.

233

Another consequence of this study and these practices will be such self-command, such serenity in the midst of adversity, such unruffled poise amidst outward disturbances, so sure a centre for ethical life, that the unusual contour of his character might well be envied by lesser men.

234

There is a deep joy in this growing perception of life's larger meaning, a profound comfort in the ever increasing knowledge of its beneficent purpose.

235

That satisfaction which fate so often denies man in the outer world, he may find through philosophic effort in the inner world.

236

The power of philosophy begins to show itself when it begins to vibrate in us as a new inner life.

237

Whoever has confirmed through a lifetime the truth of philosophy, felt its power and obeyed its counsel, will know its worth.

238

In its tenets he can find confirmation of his loftiest feelings.

239

In their enthusiasm, the younger advocates and eager defenders of this doctrine may outrun their facts, but that does not invalidate the doctrine itself.

240

No one who sincerely and intelligently follows philosophy for even a few years could fail to become a better man as a direct result. If anyone does fail to do so, be sure he is unintelligent even if sincere, or insincere even if intelligent, that he has followed only his own ego-prompted imagination and miscalled it philosophy.

241

It teaches us to profess and inspires us to practise the noblest of ideals.

242

It teaches us what to do in the dilemmas of conscience wherever they arise in the art of living.

243

We need these truths to fortify us against ourselves and to nerve us against our enemies within.

244

It is of great value alike to those who are practising self-help and self-improvement techniques as to those who are striving to develop a more spiritual life.

245

Our reward arises in an exaltation of soul.

246

Its wisdom born out of marmoreal calm, its moral code enframed in gracious compassion, philosophy stands peerless above all other offerings.

247

Coleridge: "It is folly to think of making the many, philosophers. . . . But the existence of a true philosophy, or the power and habit of contemplating particulars in the unity and mirror of the idea—this in the rulers and teachers of a nation is indispensable to a sound state of religion in all classes."

248

Because the philosophical approach to the soul is the most comprehensive of all, it is the best of all. For it alone satisfies the needs of the whole man and does not starve any of them. Other ways may suit the primitive or even medieval type of seeker but they will not suit the modern, with his complex nature and richer experience, so well as the philosophical one. Indeed all these others converge in it in the end.

249

The achievements of true philosophy are immensely inspiring. They break down limitations which would otherwise seem insuperable.

250

The worth of this teaching does not depend upon the numbers of people who espouse it. The weaker the response which it receives from the world in general, the stronger should be the effort put forth by the few, if they really believe in it, to keep it alive.

251

Philosophy, with its balanced scheme of living, its recognition of both higher and lower needs, its enrichment and not negation of human existence, has more to offer us than anything else.

252

The philosophic movement is a loose and free one. Its strength cannot be measured by numbers or institutions, for externality and rigidity are out of harmony with its teaching and character. Yet, unorganized and unadvertised though it be, it is not less vital and not less significant than more visible movements.

253

Those who are impressed by numbers, who associate the bigness of a movement with the truth or worth of its teachings, will fail to understand that the smallness of philosophy's following is entirely disproportionate to its quality, its truth, and its worth.

254

Does it matter so much that they are numerically small if they are spiritually great? Is it not better to be with God in a tiny group than to be with pseudo-God in a large majority?

255

This system is not a hobby for the diversion of tea-table gossips; on the contrary, it constitutes a completely adequate answer to the problem of living. It is more relevant to life than anything else imaginable. It satisfies the spiritual hunger of our times.

256

Philosophy alone has the most to offer the man of thought and feeling and action, for its truths are final, its ethics unsurpassable and its wisdom impeccable, its serenity unique.

257

Philosophy provides a standard of human excellence.

258

He will find in philosophy a support which is enduring, because its first principles can never change.

259

Its strength will carry him through every crisis, whether it be a personal or a national one. Its wisdom will guide him in every situation and vindicate itself later in the result.

260

If philosophy has commanded the allegiance of brilliant minds and noble characters, it is because no other teaching could suit their natures and meet their needs so well.

261

Here, in philosophy, he has at last reached what is fundamental and essential for the understanding of life's general purposes and for the proper conduct of his personal ones.

262

The sense of liberation which comes with the advent of philosophy derives not only from its manifold theoretical and practical merits but also from the release it confers from the narrow particularism of attitude which besets most men. One is no longer a religionist only, a mystic only, an ascetic only, a metaphysician only but, within reasonable limits, all these and more. There is a wholeness of outlook, a wholesomeness of feeling which is even greater than their mere sum.

263

In philosophy a man can find everything he needs for his spiritual guidance throughout life. His religious, mystical, metaphysical, and ethical requirements are all provided for. If he faithfully follows its teaching, no other system will ever attract him again.

264

Philosophy can become effective in society only after it has become effective in the individual.

265

When our eyes have been opened to the true meaning of man, when we know that this is not to be found in his transient personality but in his enduring essence, life will possess a quality it never had before.

266

The adept who is an adept in truth and not merely in yoga can and will prove to be a thoroughly practical man of the world. I have some friends who, while not being so far advanced as such adeptship, have nevertheless progressed to some degree on its path, and in every case they occupy positions requiring expert administrative capacity in business or professional worlds, and they possess adequate knowledge and ability to deal with concrete problems of life and affairs.

267

Whoever thinks wills and acts by the light of, and in harmony with, these truths attains goodness free from mere sentimentality, wisdom unmarred by intellectual arrogance, and strength purified from low egoism.

268

The inner life made worthwhile, made beautiful wise and virtuous, the consequence is an outer life made worthwhile.

269

These teachings do in the end help one to live more effectively and even more successfully, but this can only happen after they have been fully studied and comprehended. But that is a process which takes quite a long time.

270

When wisdom comes into a man's mind, wasted effort goes out of his life. For when he understands men and events, he understands how to put himself into a proper relation to them.

271

The man who can combine the serenity and concentration of the yogi with the practicality and activity of a worldling is the man this world needs.

272

Even if such a man fails to win successes in the business or professional arena, he will grandly win his own self-respect.

273

Whoever truly catches the spirit of philosophy in his heart will find his creative intelligence stirred up to new expressions, his aesthetic feelings refined to new appreciations, and his moral purposes tuned to new resolutions.

274

The worth of what he has learned and practised will show itself in his adjustments to adverse situations, equally as in his reactions to joyous ones.

275

If philosophy cannot show a way out of any particular distress, it can show how to refresh the heart's endurance of it and renew the mind's facing towards it.

276

If a man can accept the teachings of philosophy but cannot bring himself to obey the precepts of philosophy, let him stop at this point. Let him shut himself up inside both the necessary and imagined limitations of his character and his circumstances. Even such a theoretical knowledge will not be devoid of value. It constitutes a first step.

277

We may get more wisdom from a single philosophical maxim than from whole pages of prolix, diffused, and long-winded writings.

278

Those who want to disentangle the meaning of dark mysterious symbolisms, such as those of the Hindu tantrik texts and the European medieval alchemists, and who have the years to spend on such time-wasting procedures, will not find the less obscure and more direct statements of philosophy to their taste. But it is certain that they will be able to extract from those chaotic masses of unintelligible verbiage nothing more, and nothing more valuable, than what they can find ready to understand with tremendously less effort and time in the modern philosophical writings.

279

The great virtue of expressing propositions in the clearest possible terms is that it helps to expose in all their nakedness both the errors and the truths thus stated. When a philosopher enters a public forum and elucidates the controversial issues in politics, economics, or ethics, he helps both sides to see what is sound and what is weak in their positions. Thus he helps them more truly than by taking sides himself.

280

These truths, being everlasting and world-wide, give us shelter in periods of violent storm, provide us with refuge in times of distress, and protect us with prudence in years of smiling fortune.

281

When foundational principles are wrong, practical errors will not only remain but go on multiplying themselves.

282

There is nothing in life to which philosophy cannot be related nor the philosophic attitude applied. It is in critical moments that he will display the fruits of his philosophic progress as unsuspected power and unexpected initiative, as unruffled calm and unwavering fortitude.

283

The harsh critic who rejects philosophy finds it nothing more than a bundle of words. But the sincere practitioner of many years experience finds it life-giving and soul-refreshing.

284

A teaching which helps men and women to meet adversity with courage, opposition with serenity, and temptation with insight can surely render a real service to the modern world.

285

Philosophy teaches its votaries to aspire towards the best that is in them.

286

Those who know nothing, or next to nothing, of true philosophy brush the mention of it aside as "fantastic" or dismiss the results of its mystic practices as being "beyond the range of credibility." It is just as logical to brush aside the best in religion and dismiss the best in art.

287

When philosophy applies its full wisdom to any question of human conduct, faith, or purpose, it immediately separates itself from other approaches because they are partisan, limited, partial, and in bondage to the ego.

288

To bring a well-informed and well-educated mind to bear upon all questions, to keep feeling in proper balance with reasoning, to deny the ego its insatiable demand for rulership—this gives a man poise, frees him from lamentable prejudice, and imparts perspective to his conclusions.

289

The contact with philosophy leaves him in time elevated in feeling, stimulated in ideas, and cultivated in aesthetic taste.

290

Philosophy engages the entire being and should develop a balanced, useful, happy, and wise individual who has attained inner poise.

291

If someone were to compile a list of the famous ones who found in philosophy the truth they could find nowhere else, the names would stretch from the Far East to the Far West, from pre-Greek antiquity to postwar modernity.

292

To those who can see, this is the truest way of improving humanity, for it treats both first causes and final effects.

293

The first feeling is one of astonishment that such a large area of knowledge and experience should exist among us humans and yet be almost unknown to most of us.

294

The living proof of these benefits will be himself, possibly on the surface but surely inside himself.

295

If philosophy can provide us with correct principles for thought and behaviour it has done enough; but of course it can do very much more, for it can help to find explanations of our own existence and the universal existence.

296

It is the difference between living on the instinctual level of animals and on the celestial one of the Enlightened Minds.

297

We may call that ideal worth following which brings people closer to knowing the truth about life, which offers them what is real, not illusory, which improves and refines character, and which can be tested by practicable action.

298

In the end all students will become philosophers in the ancient sense of this term—that is, "lovers of wisdom"—and therefore not only feel the Divine but also understand it. Not only this, but they will be able to help others to attain like understanding and be desirous of doing so. The greater their knowledge, the greater their power to help others. Moreover, knowledge of how the Divine works is a safeguard against the pitfalls, pseudo-teachers, and evil ones, for they can then be perceived instantly. Philosophers will not then be deceived by face values. Jesus said, "Be ye harmless as doves but shrewd as serpents."

299

It is at the critical moments of life that philosophy proves its worth, but only to the degree to which it has previously been followed and applied.

300

He who has ascended to these higher levels of being, reflects the changed point of view in all his personal relationships. Resentment collapses, forgiveness arises.

301

If he applies philosophy as much to himself as to his situations, he will be always in command of them.

302

By following the philosophic life, he will be spared some of the troubles and trials of human life, but he cannot expect to be spared all of them. He may even get new ones, but in that case there will be adequate compensations.

303

How many persons have told me that it was the help and support got from these philosophic ideas, truths, and principles which enabled them to endure periods of public terror or private distress without nervous breakdown!

304

The knowledge of philosophy takes the bitterness out of tragedy and the frustration out of adversity.

305

He should not only seek the highest quality of consciousness within himself and try to realize it constantly, but also seek the highest quality of his life in the world—so as to have a fit channel through which to express this realization.

306

Philosophy reduces a man's emotional tensions and increases his mental tolerances. In this sense it is quite serviceable to human beings, but of course it does far more than that.

307

It is in the hour of tribulation that the practice of philosophy proves its worth. In every human life there are critical situations when external resources and loving consolation are simply not enough to meet the emotional need. It is then that we must draw on inner resources and tap our spiritual reserves.

308

The larger outlook resulting from these studies, the long horizon of ever-developing stages which it puts before us, tends to reduce the haste and strain of day-to-day living. It relaxes and stabilizes the human disposition.

309

I recall the experience of shipwreck which happened to me in the Red Sea many years ago when I was travelling on a 5,000 ton cargo steamer which happened to be the only ship sailing at around that time from a certain port. Our ship was smashed in two during the darkness of the night by another steamer four times as large. It rammed us, crushed and broke our steamer into two halves. We sank because we were carrying a cargo heavier than the ship was designed for which consisted of uranium-rich sand, black sand. Luckily the process of sinking took some time, enough to let the few passengers (only a dozen of us) get off safely in a small boat. What I wish to say about this little episode is that when I became aware of what had happened a great calm descended on me together with a great faith and a great patience, and I had to laugh at my travelling companion, a Portuguese bishop who shared the cabin with me. He was highly excited, waved his arms and muttered his prayers. I take this as an illustration of the contrast between the value of philosophy and the value of dogmatic religion.

310

The more he understands life, the more contented he will become.

311

When he is led by metaphysical studies and mystical experiences to realize the vastness and tracklessness of what still lies before the human adventure, he becomes not terrified, as Pascal was, but awed and humbled.

312

Philosophy alone can show a way out of the dilemmas in which science, religion, metaphysics, politics, and economics have unnecessarily involved themselves. But it can do this only if one is prepared either to undergo the philosophic discipline, which creates the correct insight into these dilemmas, or else to accept the findings of those who have already undergone it.

313

No price can be put on what it means to a man to be in possession of an entirely trustworthy system of principles, laws, and truths for the understanding and conduct of life. No situation exists in which he cannot make use of them to his advantage.

314

When the philosopher enters the arena of public affairs with his calm unbiased judgement, his contributions towards the public good have a lasting value commensurate with his freedom from the small personal incentives which actuate the work of those who have not achieved the philosophic attitude of mind.

315

The social value of philosophy is its ennoblement of human relations.

316

The study of philosophy will free men from extreme attitudes, and especially from violent fanaticisms. It can show them that other points of view may have their place too.

317

The philosopher's capacity for historical anticipations is not only the consequence of his broad impartiality, profound penetration, and patient acquisition of all the essential facts, but primarily it is the consequence of his ability to discern the working of karmic causes and effects.

318

It is not likely that the limited little human mind can understand the cosmos. But philosophy can give us clues which make all the difference between blundering in utter blackness and groping in twilight.

319

It develops into a wisdom that is never priggish, a goodwill that is never sentimental.

320

Such a teaching could not turn a man into a fanciful visionary—as the world, confusing philosophical mysticism with the wild aberrations that it mostly knows, may think—but only into a valuable citizen.

321

When a man or woman comes into fuller awareness of the True Self he arrives at the same time at the discovery of his true work, together with the capacity to perform it. Such an individual usually has innate ability—but the development of this ability depends upon his struggles to achieve it. Also, its sphere of activity may not necessarily be what he at first believes. In this case, disappointments and frustrations will arise to serve as indications that he has yet to find the right road. The appearance of talents and capacities can be hastened if one acquires better balance.

322

All this said, we may now say that in this bewildering world and its bewildering activities there is a place for each man and if he has not found it, it is primarily because he has not found himself.

323

We must hold to the value of wisdom, which gives to man so much dignity and goodness, so much honour and usefulness, but we must hold to it above all because it is part of that goal which God has set before us for attainment on this earth.

324

"God hath not created anything better than wisdom," wrote Muhammed. Also the prophet declared that his followers would be rewarded ultimately, not according to their performance of prayer, fasting, charity, or pilgrimage, but only according to the degree of their wisdom.

Its inspired practicality

325

PRACTICAL PHILOSOPHY

Definitions

Bradley defined philosophy as the finding of bad reasons for what one believes by instinct but Aldous Huxley has endeavoured to improve on this. He says, "finding bad reasons for what one believes for other bad reasons—that's philosophy."

In India, popular ignorance gradually identified philosophy with those monks and anchorites who had fled from the world and its woes to monasteries or mountains.

It was once the fashion of many people to sneer at philosophy and to regard philosophers as a ridiculous compound of foolishness and fatuity, but time has begun to change all that.

The notion that there is something futile about philosophy is quite correct when applied to what passes under that name very often, but quite incorrect when applied to genuine philosophy; and it is genuine philosophy which is here presented.

The value of knowing truth lies in its potency for making clear the art of fine living. A philosophy which is not strong enough to vivify personal life is no more than a dry dusty intellectualism, and when philosophy becomes a mode of intellectual wrestling, contributing little or nothing to action, it falls rightly into neglect. Its proper business is to rescue man from mechanical and unintelligent activity and put him on the path to a deliberately wise existence. It should be an insurance against making ethical errors or undertaking stupid enterprises, and its study is the premium to be paid for this valuable insurance.

Here then is a teaching, very old and very wise, which summarizes all human knowledge, actual and possible, and which shows man how best to shape his personal and practical life. I am not its originator. I can but try to re-present it to a troubled, broken, and blinded world which waits for this knowledge in modern form, as a benighted traveller waits for the dawn.

This philosophy rightly understood and rightly used will make men who make history. It calls for people who are ready and able to raise it above the status of a tea table topic, and to devote to its study and practice not merely an occasional free evening, but their whole lives; who will not only understand these great truths intellectually, but feel their transforming power in their hearts, and courageously live them in everyday life. For whoever masters this philosophy will soon feel its invigorating influence in every sphere of his activity, and in its light he will walk life's ways with calm assurance.

The Need

Once I stood on the wide pavement of Broadway. All around flashed and reflashed the electric advertising signs of "The Great White Way." A ragged young man bearing a bundle of newspapers came up to me, thrust a paper close to my face, and shouted raucously, "Man and woman shot." The never ending roar of motor traffic dinned in my ears. Crowds of people pressed by me: expectant faces intent on snatching an evening's pleasure, tired faces eager to get home after a day's toil, painted faces striving to retain a semblance of beauty, hard ominous faces emerging from New York's underworld with sinister intent. There was the stir of exultant activity. I looked around at the crowd which jostled me, and peered questioningly into the faces which moved like a cinema film before my eyes. Which one seemed to express the attainment of inward happiness? Which one revealed a serene detachment from its destructive environment? I turned away, sadly disappointed in my quest. Nearly all had been suborned by the temptations that form such an alluring accompaniment to modern existence. They did not understand that the transitory is true but trivial, the eternal is true and great. They did not understand that baronets cannot escape broken hearts, nor millionaires the miseries of disappointment. They did not know that once a man has taken measure of the suffering which is inherent in life, the wrinkled demon of reflection will pursue him into the very haunts of revelry. He may view with pleasure a hundred happy figures dancing in gay abandon, when lo! its sneer sounds abruptly in his ear, "and even these are but dream figures dancing towards their silent graves." And so they wander through the years alternating between the red flames of passion and the grey coolness of calculation, until the little candles of their lives have guttered out.

They who think that the purpose of human incarnation is to increase pleasures and accumulate property have learned nothing from the instability of life and insecurity of possessions which have marked the period now passing.

The greatest evils of our age are not in its outward materialism but in its inward ignorance, and not in its practical inventiveness but in its mental unbalance.

When we mistake transient sense gratifications for true happiness we suffer later for our error. When we fail to discriminate between what is perishable in our lives and what is truly enduring we rely upon illusory values. The future tempts or torments us; the past keeps us half-buried in its memories; while the truth which could lift us into a region that liberates us from all temporal tyrannies is disdained. Yet peace, sublime and ego-free, can exist for us only when we learn to live, as it were, upon the pinpoint of a moment where all hopes for the future are not allowed to imprison us, and where equally all memories of the past are merely held and do not hold us.

We attain peace, as Buddha pointed out, when we are free from all desires.

Inspired Action

Inspired action is the means of reconciliation between seclusion and society, the service of the noisy crowd with the silence of lofty thought. Spirituality ceases to be a monopoly of the cloister, comes out of the confinement of church, temple, monastery, or mosque, and walks in the marketplace among busy men.

For philosophy teaches us that there is no sharp division between the world of surrounding things and the world of internal aspirations, that both are of the same ultimate essence of mind. Therefore the philosopher will despise nothing because it is supposed to be material, just as he will discard nothing because it is supposed to be anti-spiritual. He has glimpsed the great mystery of all existence, and knows that all things are within and participate in the Overself. Philosophy is identical with action and not with inertia. To make it anything less is to abuse words, for as the "love of wisdom" it must include the application of wisdom.

"Love cannot be idle," says Ruysbroeck.

"I preach you the truth, O monks, for deliverance and not for keeping idle," says Buddha.

The hidden teaching affirms that the universal manifested existence is a Becoming, a change from one condition to another. It is absurd to suggest that a truly spiritual life must be a static one. A static human existence is impossible, and whoever seeks it seeks in vain.

Life in the active world is simply expression, and the divine life can be lived everywhere.

No defense need be made to the fanatics who decry and denounce our desire to get some comfort and convenience from the earth's resources. Western civilization, so condemned by Oriental critics, possesses much that is admirable, despite its obvious faults.

Man is not called upon to renounce his great discoveries and works, but to renounce selfish usage of them.

There can be no salvation in the attitude of mind which denounces the West as wicked and material Occidentalism and upholds an ascetic disdain of material things.

The God Who is to be found within ourselves must also exist equally outside ourselves in the phenomenal universe, else how would He be Infinite?

No, we must rebut the accusation of materialism as stupid, and point out that a better name would be realism. Life in activity is as real as life in repose; expression is no less divine than meditation; and they who have discovered the divinity within themselves will forthwith recognize it throughout the universe.

The Balanced Life

We need to achieve a balanced life with a wise alternation between action and repose, work and meditation, being positive and being passive.

Only the philosopher has the orientation of outlook which enables a man to take his political, social, and economic bearings correctly.

It may not be often that the floors of city offices are trodden by the feet of those who also wander in the caves of mystic contemplation; nor the hubbub of the stock exchange heard by those who also hear the sweet silence of the inner self. The combination in one personality of the two opposite characteristics of meditation and action may be infrequent, but there are those who have achieved it, and who realize that work is not only to make a living, but a life.

When there are more such men and women in towns and cities, when they walk in the hard metropolitan streets and the busy bartering places revealing a serene state of mind which is held and maintained no less among crowds than in solitary places, the soulless character of so much of modern life will be redeemed. The philosophy of inspired action of such persons brings blessings on mankind. Such persons have accepted their lot in worldly life and seek to do their duty; they turn occasion into opportunity and bring the sense of sublimity into their prosaic hours. Their own diviner peace and spiritual poise is blessing to their neighbours like fresh dew on a parched land.

Another name for inspired action is unselfish work. The spiritual man will work no less hard than the average man; his work will be done well, with understanding, calmly, with detachment. His aspiration is towards Perfection, the Supreme Divinity, and this attitude will be seen in all his work, even in the meanest task. He works without the fever of ambition or greed, and he does not allow any pains or pleasures, difficulties or problems to move him from the ideal he has set before him. With calm and equable spirit he does his best. More he cannot do.

A man who is attuned to cosmic harmonies cannot fail to express harmony in all his worldly activities.

This is a quest to be undertaken by those who have suffered and smiled and are still ardently alive, not for those heavy humourless persons who are ascetically dead. Therefore let those of us who are condemned to toil for our daily bread not forget to toil for the spiritual Bread of Life. The notion that a spiritual man may not work vigorously in the world of business and industry is as nonsensical as the notion that a man who can compose perfect music may not eat a hearty dinner.

There is nothing to prevent the sage from being a successful businessman, and nothing wrong in practical activities, for the simple reason that he will not cease being a sage nor lose himself in his activities, and he will remain rooted in Reality amid the world of thoughts and things.

Voltaire wrote of Marlborough that he had a calmness in the midst of tumult and danger "which is the greatest gift of nature for command." Thus even a soldier can derive great benefit from yoga.

Daily meditation will overcome the materializing effect of constant contact with worldly influences, by bringing together the inner and outer selves in communion with each other: one giving strength and light to the other, and the latter expressing this inspiration in active life.

We are able to live a complete and creative existence only after we have arrived at a true attitude towards life through spiritual unfoldment. Only then can we walk the world's ways in safety.

In the end we may learn whether our feelings were wise or deceptive, our thinking sound or unsound, by the experience which comes from our consequent acts. Dreamers, escapists, and ascetics who shy away from activity deprive themselves of this valuable test.

We shall find we must have the strength to say "No" to a thing before we have the inner right to take it. We must learn how to renounce a thing before we can possess it.

We must learn to remain ultramystically *aware* always, even while we are externally occupied with any matter in hand. Our work will not suffer, but be all the better for the poised emotion and peaceful mind which this brings.

326

Philosophy combines a lofty idealism with an intense practicality.

327

This teaching can be understood only by those who try to live it: all others merely *think* they understand it. Only those who have incorporated it in their lives for a number of years can know how intensely practical philosophy is.

328

The practicality of the philosophical quest is something few men discover until they are far advanced on the quest. If the dreamers, the fanatics, the visionaries, the lethargic, the feckless, and the failures seem to be the ones most vocal about the quest, that is merely because they are hardly on the quest at all but only stand around its entrance.

329

Practical philosophy is the art of living so as to fulfil life's higher purpose.

330

It is a grave mistake to regard these matters as having no more than a theoretical interest, to be played with or not according to one's taste. Whoever finds the answers to the questions, whoever knows what man really is, what his prenatal and post-mortem destinies are, what his highest good is, will necessarily find that his practical everyday living is much affected by them.

331

The notion that illumination must turn a man into a mere dreamer, unfit for practical life and incapable of coping with practical situations, is true only when it is of an imperfect kind, or when the man is not properly prepared to receive it, or when it is too short to be full yet deep enough to unsettle him. Illumination in the philosophic sense, however, need not deprive a man of the capacity for energetic action, although it will deprive him of the feeling of hurried action. He will do his necessary work in the world, not with slovenly weakness but with quiet calm.

332

Wisdom begins only when you apply in practice what you absorb in theory.

333

He must use the teaching in his daily life to know its practical value and to prove its practical truth. As he progresses he will discover that the more he uses it, the more he gains in power and strength.

334

It is uncommon to find an individual who, in a single personality, combines a highly spiritual outlook with a truly practical character. He who succeeds in effecting this combination is rare, but he is the type that the coming age needs and demands. For he can prove and demonstrate convincingly to all the world that loftiness of philosophic ethics will not be a weakness in practical life. On the contrary, because it is informed by knowledge and based upon wisdom, it will be a source of strength.

335

The effect of his studies and meditations will slowly but surely reveal itself in his life. His world outlook will sparkle with vitality, his speech will form itself with precision, his deeds will be wise and more virtuous. For philosophy, unlike metaphysics, is not only a theory to be learned from books but even more an integral way of life to be practised in society.

336

The common misconception that philosophy bears no practical relation to ordinary life is due to ignorance. The proper understanding of philosophy would greatly reduce human sin and suffering, would discipline brutal men and selfish women, would dissolve fanatical strife and creedal conflict, would inspire us to put into concrete shape the loftiest ideals of our imagination, would bring a beautiful solace to offset the disappointments bred in homes, offices, fields, and factories. These are tangible things and refute the allegation that the philosopher shuts his eyes to the harassments and activities of common life. The misconception has arisen, however, because so many misguided theologians and so many fantastic dreamers have passed themselves off as philosophers.

337

Philosophy will show a man how to find his better self, will lead him to cultivate intuition, will guide him to acquire sounder values and stronger will, will train him in right thinking and wise reflection, and, lastly, will give him correct standards of ethical rightness or wrongness. If its theoretical pursuit is so satisfying that it can be an end and a reward in itself, its practical application to current living is immeasurably *useful*, valuable, and helpful.

338

It is not that truth has to be made practical, for it is the most practical thing which exists. It is that men have to become better instructed in it, as well as in the higher laws which reflect it, and then live out what they have learned.

339

It is quite proper to seek personal advantage even when embracing a religious cult or a spiritual teaching. If men thought they would get nothing at all from it, few would ever embrace one. But this is not the spirit in which to embrace philosophy. That is to be sought in utter purity of motive, because truth is to be sought for its own sake, whether its face is ugly or pleasant. Nevertheless, personal advantages accrue. Philosophy teaches how to be well and live well, how to avoid misery and attract happiness, how to bear suffering and achieve peace of mind. Its values and results are as related to practical living as anything could be, but eyes are needed to see them.

340

Not to escape life, but to articulate it, is philosophy's practical goal. Not to take the aspirant out of circulation, but to give him something worth doing is philosophy's sensible ideal.(P)

341

If leadership and guidance, inspiration and light are ever to come to humanity from mystical circles during this colossal upheaval, be sure that they will come only from those who have wedded head to heart and contemplation to practical service.

342

It is a false ethic which would tell us that material things are valueless, that worldly prosperity is worthless. Philosophy is full of common sense along with its rare uncommon sense. Therefore it teaches giving the proper value to material things, appraising worldly prosperity properly by pointing out that inward quality and inner life must support it for genuine happiness.

343

The philosopher may walk unfalteringly and surefootedly because he sees reality and understands the truth of life.

344

To bring the divine presence into the midst of one's work and one's work continually into the divine presence—this is an inspired and worthwhile active life.

345

There is a direct relation between the abstract concepts of metaphysics and the concrete problems of individuals, between the ultimate principles of the one and the immediate needs of the other. But most people are too short-sighted to observe this relation, too blurred mentally to comprehend. They regard metaphysical truth as a dispensable luxury, or a leisure hour hobby, without which they can get along quite well if called upon to do so. On the contrary, it is basic for character, foundational for behaviour, solutional for problems, and prophylactic for troubles. If at first it seems intangible, in the end it becomes invaluable. Yes, Philosophy is tremendously practical but only those who know it from the inside, who have felt its power in trying circumstances and followed its guidance in perplexing ones, know this. In good and bad periods, through long spells of ordinary routine and sudden turning points at critical times, it shows its practical benefits, its everyday applicability. Its ability to steady the emotions during times of perplexing crisis and to quieten the nerves in places of distracting noises proved itself during the war.

346

The time has gone when the philosophic and the practical, the religious and the realistic, the spiritual and the material are to be regarded as being mutually antagonistic; today we must regard them as working to a common end and purpose, as reconcilable in ultimate unity. Thus our actions should come to be visible emblems of the invisible inner life in which we must take our roots.

347

Philosophy says he has to bring his scheming mind, his rational mind, his concrete mind to bear upon solutions to his practical problems; but he must work them out under the inspiration of the soul, else they are solutions that solve little.

348

Those same capacities, applied to worldly careers, professions, or businesses, are more likely to bring a man success than failure. We often hear that philosophy is useless to hungry men or poor men. This is false. For the quality of intelligence and character developed by it is higher than the average and therefore its possessor will know better how to rid himself of hunger or poverty than will the possessor of an inferior quality of intelligence and character.

349

How shall I act rightly and wisely? This is the problem which faces every man. Hence philosophy not only teaches a way of thought but also a way of action. This is inevitably so because, unlike mysticism, it is concerned not merely with a segment of life but with the whole of it. There is something defective about a teaching if it forgets the ultimate purpose for which it itself exists, if it leaves its followers in the air, and therefore cannot be successfully applied in practical action. We may understand the value of our intellectual formulations only when they are put to the test in actual practice. In putting an idea, a theory, or a doctrine to the practical test or in bringing a way of living into practical operation, we enable it to reveal its truth or falsity, its scope or limitations, its merits or demerits. A doctrine must be tested not only by its intellectual soundness but also by its practical results. The first test can be instantly applied but the second only after a certain time has elapsed. Thus the good is separated from the bad, the right is distinguished from the wrong, the true is divided from the false, either by intelligence in the sphere of abstract ideas or by time in the sphere of spatial things. The first shoots of wheat and weeds cannot be distinguished by ordinary sight or knowledge, but give them time to grow up to maturity and everybody can distinguish them. The barrenness or fruitfulness of any teaching is in the end inexorably ascertained by applying the test of historical results, that is, the test of time.

350

Nothing could be more practical than applied philosophy. The student will find his will strengthened by its definite affirmations, so that he will bring a bolder heart to the troubles and duties of everyday living. He will find his feelings less disturbed by the evil in other men's characters and deeds. He will find his thoughts inspired by its declaration of the benevolent purpose and supreme intelligence behind his life.

351

The philosophic way is neither to live a crippled ascetic life out of touch with the times nor to give itself up totally to the foolishness of the times.

352

When knowledge is worked out in action, reflected in attitude, and formed in the entire life, then only does it become real.

353

Even as the narrow ascetic seeks to deny life, so the more tolerant philosopher seeks to affirm it. It is true that the materialist does the same, but he does it in ignorance of what life really is, and he does it for the benefit of the little fragment of his own personality alone. The philosopher, on the contrary, works in the light of higher knowledge and works for the benefit of the All.

354

When these thoughts pass down from his head to his heart and from his heart to his will, only then will he really be a student of philosophy. The heart must be opened to them, the will must be directed by them. With that his life will change, at first little by little, into a blessed one.

355

It is not enough to convert thoughts into deeds. The latter must also be done in the right place and at the right time, if they are to achieve their object.

356

The effects of the discipline show themselves in his handling of worldly affairs, in his swift resourcefulness during urgent situations, his calm balance during critical ones, and his practical wisdom during puzzling ones.

357

Philosophy demands that we actualize our ideals. Wisdom must flower in deeds that accord with it or it is not wisdom. Action is the decisive factor, the acid test of all mystical, metaphysical, and religious pretensions to a superior ethic. Therefore the ethical values, such as compassion and integrity, which arise from the interior experience of metaphysical and mystical meditation must also be upheld in the exterior space-time world.

358

The practical contact of life will supply a test of the worth of his dominant ideas, a means of verifying the truth of his holiest beliefs, and an indicator of the grade or strength of his moral character.

359

He does not and cannot separate life from philosophy. Those who assert that it is a study for mere dreamers are wrong.

360

The artist, working through the medium of imagination—whether he imagines scenes or sounds—creates a beautiful piece. The philosopher, working through the same medium but seeking self-improvement, creates a beautiful life.

361

Being a philosopher is being alive, not denying life. Philosophy is bought at a price, nothing less than a man's whole life, which is to be directed thereafter by a blend of intuition, intellect, and revelation. If therefore anything is thrown away, it can only be because it is not worth keeping.

362

Although it is far better to read philosophy than to ignore it altogether, it is immeasurably better to feel the emotional urge and inner drive which are needed to bring about its application to day-by-day living. If they are lacking but the wish for them is present, two things can be done that will help to attract them. First, begin to pray to the higher power for such a grace. Second, establish contact, fellowship, or discipleship with those who are themselves impregnated with such resolve, fervour, and deep yearning.

363

Although philosophy is eminently practical, it does not, like materialism, lose itself wholly in such practicality. It does not throw away its fine intuitions, noble dreams, and wise thoughts while planting its feet firmly on earth. Rather does it seek to hold a reconciling balance between its dreams and its deeds, between the inner life and the outer world.

364

The philosopher is a practical man. He understands quite well—as much as any materialist—that he has to live out this physical life to which he was born in the physical world of which he is a part. Therefore, although it is metaphysically graded as being like a dream, it must be dealt with properly, adequately, efficiently, and attentively.

365

Philosophy must have an interest for men of flesh and blood, must be of service to those who live in a practical ordinary world, must have bridges to religion and art and science, must not be isolated from lesser forms of inquiry even though it seeks the higher ones.

366

If it were not in closest contact with the facts of human life, it could not be philosophy. But the real reason why it is charged by critics with promoting dreaminess and with being unpractical is that they are interested only in some of the facts whereas philosophy is interested in all of them.

367

His basic values may become firmer and more positive as his understanding of philosophy becomes fuller. They support him during the difficult periods of adjustment to the world in which he has to live and work. They guide him ethically and protect his character.

368

The ascetic who wants to keep his life "simple" does not want the "burden" of possessions. The hedonist sees no burden in them, but rather beauty and comfort. He welcomes them. The philosopher, able to absorb both views, reconciles and accepts them, for he recognizes the play of Yin and Yang through all life, including his own.

369

By pointing out the way of development immediately ahead of the aspirant, as well as the goal remotely distant, philosophy shows its practicality.

370

The materialist says he can enjoy peace of mind only if all his material needs and satisfactions are obtained. The idealist says he is indifferent to such material things because peace of mind can only follow spiritual satisfaction. The one is stating a quarter of the truth, the other three-quarters, because both are looking at different aspects of life. Neither one is looking at the whole of life. This requires man to secure a varying minimum of money, clothes, shelter, food, fuel, and so on, whoever he is and whatever his outlook. His inner needs will still have to be met, but these depend on his evolutionary stage as to their nature and quality.

371

Philosophy does not approve of deterioration in the quality of human welfare and its justification in the name of so-called spirituality.

372

The philosophic mode of life coheres with the metaphysical system behind it. The one is a practical expression of the thorough thinking of the other. The confidence which fills the first harmonizes with the certitude which stamps the second.

373

The philosophical life is a simple life, partly because it seeks to escape unnecessary anxieties, partly because it wants to save time and energy for what seems more desirable.

374

Those who regard it as a disincarnate entity hovering in the air have not understood philosophy. It does not separate action from thought, conduct from consciousness, nor society from self. But neither does it commit the materialist error of making action, conduct, and society end in themselves, any more than it commits the mystical error of making ecstasy, feeling, and visions end in themselves.

375

It is an ironic fact that the philosophic way of living, far from being suitable for dreamers, misfits, and escapists only, is in the long view the most practical way of all ways of living.

376

Philosophy is intensely practical; yet, because it is also well balanced, it judges neither by results alone nor by intention alone, but by both.

377

This teaching recognizes that Mind is the primary element in life, but it recognizes also the contributions of the physical and the intellectual. Its aim is to enable the student to maintain all effort in correct proportionate balance.

378

The last test of what intellect, intuition, or feeling offers as the truth must be provided by the will. In the realm of *doing*, we discover its rightness or wrongness.

379

It is not enough to grasp spiritual realization intellectually. We have to embody it physically.

380

Pragmatism is of the adolescent stage of mental development. It is crude realism directed towards utility and satisfaction only. Its weakness lies in its acceptance of satisfaction and utility as the test of truth. Each man may have a different definition of what satisfies and is most useful, hence contradictions arise. Pragmatism can see truth only in the fruits of effort, which is only partially correct. Philosophy also sees truth in its fruits of practice, but it tests theories also. Pragmatism only tests practice. It deals only with one aspect of philosophy, what man can do; it forgets to take the world as it is. The world is forever changing, partly due to Nature and partly due to man. The two aspects taken together form the basis of philosophical thought and study. In favouring the one aspect only, pragmatism is one-sided and imperfect philosophically.

381

It does not agree with either the fools who are infatuated with worldly life or the fanatics who condemn it, but finds a reasonable equilibrium of attitude between them.

382

We may hopefully expect to find, and we shall not be disappointed, that the noble principles of philosophy are visible in the noble results of philosophy.

383

Is it a merely theoretic, vaguely academic matter? No! For those who rule states or pass laws are guided in their actions and decisions by their outlook on life generally as by their ability to rule themselves. This is most often half-conscious or instinctual. Philosophy brings both the lower and the higher sources into clear consciousness.

384

Power will tread on the heels of knowledge only if we apply it.

385

If its disciples fail to put philosophy into practice, their failure does not invalidate its truth nor derogate its worth but does show that they are only half-disciples.

386

The only education worth the name is that which prepares a pupil for life, that which teaches him how to live.

387

It is here, in a simple, common situation that one finds oneself, that philosophy has its place, just as much as in the profoundest movement of thought.

388

Only those who know some of the secret laws of the universe know that this is not a teaching for mere dreamers and irresponsible escapists. They know that the ultimate peace, safety, and health of a people depend on the extent to which the principles of living under these laws are understood.

389

The man who faithfully obeys the injunctions and practices the regimes of philosophy can never be a failure, whatever the world says. Nor can he be unemployed, for he understands that his real employer is the Overself and that the work he is doing will not end while life does not end.

390

Even a limited amount of the *practice* of philosophy produces disproportionately larger gains.

391

He believes, intuits, perhaps even knows that the Real, the True, the

Good, and the Beautiful are the best things in life and the most worth seeking, that their quest will lead him through mystical regions and ethereal experience. But that is no excuse for deserting critical judgement and practical sense.

392

Philosophy affects the whole of life: not only thought but also action, not only consciousness but also diet.

393

The philosopher knows just as well as anyone else the importance of money. He does not, like the ascetic, take a vow of poverty nor, like the fanatic, decry its power to bring happiness. But neither does he give it the value which the materialist gives it. He is balanced.

394

The need is for a combination of practical self-interest with idealistic soul-interest.

395

With wisdom in temptation and fortitude in tribulation, guided by noble principles rather than by momentary impulses, he will expound the nature of philosophic ethics by the nature of his everyday living.

396

Practical life will benefit in every way if the inner life is inspired by philosophy. There is no danger of the man becoming a vain futile dreamer or of his brain becoming deranged. Look for such dangers in the cults, psychic and occult, not here. The philosopher may sit on his mountaintop if he elects to, but he will not consider that this is the best way to live, the ideal. It may serve a special and temporary purpose, or satisfy his temperament, but he will be just as ready to descend into the valleys and cities if the Overself bids him.

397

What did it mean to the American destiny and to the human channel through which that destiny was being formulated in the last century that the most illumined mind in the country, Ralph Waldo Emerson, twice talked to Abraham Lincoln in the White House at Washington during a dark year of the Civil War? What did it mean to Lincoln that the one man in America who could do so brought him a spiritual gift of hope, light, and fortitude? It is significant that a few months after Emerson's visit, Abraham Lincoln issued the preliminary proclamation of the Emancipation of the Slaves, an act which made the fighting of the war to the bitter end inevitable. To Emerson the war was an inescapable crusade. It was something holy in its resolve to remove the foulness of slavery from the land. Therefore he firmly opposed any end to the war which would not achieve this goal, or, in his own words, "Any peace restoring the old rottenness."

Philosophy aims at producing a group of men and women trained in mind control, accustomed to subordinate immediate interests to ultimate ends, sincerely desirous of serving humanity in fundamental ways, and possessed of philosophic knowledge which will make them valuable citizens. They will have balanced characters, based on refined feeling and exercised reason. It will be their constant endeavour to maintain a clear and definite outlook on the personal and public issues of the moment. Philosophy does not sit in helpless passivity when confronted with the spectacle of hustling cities and busy factories. Its supreme value to mankind lies in the solid ground it affords for a life devoted to the unremitting service of humanity.

In the magazine *Lucifer*, H.P. Blavatsky says, "If the voice of the mysteries has become silent for many ages in the West, if Eleusis, Memphis, Antium, Delphi have long ago been made the tombs of a science once as colossal in the West as it is yet in the East, there are successors now being prepared for them. We are in 1887 and the nineteenth century is close to its death. The twentieth century has strange developments in store for humanity."

The time has come to develop the knowledge and extend the understanding of a teaching which few know and fewer still understand. Occupied principally, as it is, with matters of eternal rather than ephemeral life, it finds today a larger opportunity for service than it could have found at any earlier period in consequence of the evolutionary forces which have been working on man's history, ideas, attitudes, communications, and productions. It is the most important knowledge which any human being could study.

398

There is no such thing as a merely theoretical philosopher. If anyone is not a practising philosopher, he has not understood correctly nor theorized properly.

399

Neither mysticism nor metaphysics is sufficient by itself. We need not only the union of what is best in both, but also the disinterested driving force of moral activity. Only when our metaphysical understanding and meditational exercises begin to interpret themselves in active life do we begin to justify both. The Word must become flesh. It is not enough to accumulate knowledge. We must also apply it. We must act as well as meditate. We cannot afford like the ascetical hermit to exclude the world. Philosophy, which quite definitely has an activist outlook, demands that intuition and intelligence be harmoniously conjoined, and that this united couple be compassionately inserted into social life. Like the heat and light in a flame, so thought and action are united in philosophy. It does not lead to a dreamy quietism, but to a virile activity. Philosophic thought fulfils itself in philosophic action. This is so and this must be so because mentalism affirms that the two are really one. Thus the quest begins by a mystical turning inwards, but it ends by a philosophic returning outwards.

400

This is the final test. Philosophy works. Whatever you do, wherever you go, it can be put to practical use. It cannot be isolated from life, for it is always intimate with life.

Its "worldliness"

401

It is quite true that the full preparation for, and practice of, mysticism takes us away from life in the world. But its work need not stop there. The very same forces which activate it can later become the inspiration of a new life in the world, the foundation of an effective practicality.

402

Philosophy leaves the physical plane only to return to it, lets go of activities only to take them up again. For the physical world is as much its proper concern as any other. Everything is reverenced, every act turned into a religious rite.

403

Worldly life, which is either a trap or a hindrance to the unphilosophical, is a school of instruction and an avenue of service to the philosophical.

404

The self and the world are linked closely together: to understand the resulting combination both must be studied, and side by side. Otherwise the end of the road is half-truth, not the full truth.

405

Faced with the mystery of his own existence, man finally finds an answer in religion or mysticism. If he adds the mystery of the world's existence, he must look for his complete answer in philosophy.

406

The immature spirituality and incomplete enlightenment which sneers at life in the world and idolizes life in the monastery, which furthermore confuses defeat in the external struggle for existence with triumph in the internal struggle for God, is unphilosophical. We may strive for a place in society and the gains that go with it as strenuously and as determinedly as any ambitious man, so long as we remember to keep our earthly ambitions subordinate to our celestial ones, so long as we do not forget to strive also for a more abiding inner status and rustless wealth. We may aim at effective accomplishment and successful outcome of the work we are doing, whether it be banking or bricklaying. There is no harm in that and God will not hold it against us in the higher reckoning. The harm begins when we lose our sense of proportion and let the success itself become a supreme value of life, when we become blind to anything higher and insensitive to anything nobler, when we disregard ethical laws and social responsibilities in our thirst to attain it, when we are broken in spirit by failure and weakened in fibre by disappointment.

407

The philosophic aspirant is not asked, like the yogic aspirant, to quit the world. But he is asked to quit the world view which has kept him spiritually ignorant. Hence, outwardly he may live as full a life as he pleases if only inwardly he will live according to the higher laws of philosophic knowledge and ethics.

408

We are sent to this world to learn its useful lessons, and were we to succeed in blotting out consciousness of what is going on around us in it, we would merely be blotting out an opportunity to learn them. This is what happens if trance is prematurely achieved.

409

Let the metaphysical dreamers assert that the body is nothing, the world unimportant or even non-existent. To the philosopher both are significant, meaningful, and life in them purposive. Are they not, in the end, devices to extract the divinity within us?

410

The situations which develop from day to day afford a field for enquiry, analysis, reflection, intuition, and ultimate understanding in themselves, quite apart from the application of principles already learned.

411

However far from philosophy these matters and events seem to be, in reality they illustrate or exemplify some part of the teaching.

412

The philosopher seeks to live in his century. He is not so immersed in the ideas of antique centuries that he is unable to interest himself in the ideas of his own.

413

It would be a mistake to believe that the philosophic attitude does exclusively seek to enter into the world's life any more than it seeks to escape from that life. It uses and includes each of these movements but it does so only at the right time.

414

The practice of philosophy does not preclude one from living normally in the world, from marrying and begetting children, from acquiring possessions and dwelling in comfort, or from building a successful business or professional career. It does not regard the normal human life as inferior and illusory, nor the abnormal ascetic life as high and holy. It takes both in its stride and looks on both as correct in their own places because both are needed there, but it seeks to achieve at the earliest moment a sane balance which shall free the individual from the tyranny of both.

415

Philosophy does not ask the mystically minded to give up their mysticism but to expand it, to take a realistic view of the world situation and to adjust themselves to the century in which they live.

416

If he can combine and balance a practical attitude towards the world with a transcendental detachment from the world, he will fulfil man's higher purpose.

417

The rules which are laid down for monks should not be confused with the codes for non-monks. The latter need a realistic respect for financial values counterbalanced by an idealistic indifference to them. This makes necessary the finding of equilibrium between the two poles, a kind of inner bicycle riding.

418

Philosophy does not want to escape life but to fulfil it.

419

The ascetic aspirant seeks salvation *from* the world. The philosophic one seeks salvation *in* the world.

420

The world will not be overcome by running away from it nor by shutting our eyes to it, but by comprehending its significance and bringing it into co-operative, side-by-side association with our spiritual quest.

421

The worldly side of things must be included with the spiritual side, related to it, balanced by it, purified through it. This is the sane view of philosophy.

422

Mystical practice, religious devotion, and metaphysical reflection are not, with him, an escape from unpleasant and inconvenient facts or awkward and difficult situations, but contributions toward the proper and effectual way of dealing with them.

423

Not by moving further and further away from reality, blindly and obstinately, can the seeker discover truth. He must face the facts of common life before he can unveil those of the uncommon life.

424

The refusal to be realistic, the persistent looking aside from facts as they are, the being naïve under the delusion of having faith—this is not spirituality; it is simply mental adolescence.

425

The message for our times is: "The day of professional spirituality is past. It has bred religious hypocrisy and mystical futility. The day of a spiritualized mundane existence is here. We are to live in the world but not be of it. We are to set aside an hour a day for meditation and reflection but to attend to all other duties the rest of the day. Thus we shall have the chance which ascetics and monks lack, of translating spiritual ideas into spiritual deeds. The attraction toward the divine need not mean repulsion from the world. There is room in human life for both the heavenly and the earthly. To deepen knowledge and increase beauty, to spread compassion and to uplift man—this is our work today."

426

True spirituality for this age is to be found outside the cloister. Character is to find its needed testing ground *in* the world. Contemplation is to be practised as a preface or an epilogue to the day's work.

427

The orientation of modern spirituality, under the changed conditions of today, is not towards retreat from the world but towards a spiritualizing effort in the world.

428

The philosophic student cultivates correct attitudes towards life, fortune, men, and events until they are built into his character. In this way he is practising philosophy all the time, not merely during his reading hours.

429

The varied character of daily experience and the confirmation of summed-up total experience ought to enrich his understanding of philosophy as well as provide opportunities to apply it constantly.

430

To say that the inner activity of mystical life is quite compatible with the outer activity of worldly life is to deceive oneself. The mystic may—and in these times usually must—come to terms with the world, but it is not his inner guidance that bids him arrive at this compromise. It is outer compulsion that bids him do so.

431

We moderns have to learn how to pursue truth and practise meditation, how to worship God and overcome ego while in the very midst of active affairs, for no other way is open to us.

432

One man may find his way to the Overself by guardedly living in the world whereas another may find it through turning his back on the world. But before the first can complete his search he will have to retire temporarily and occasionally from the world, and before the second man can do the same he will have to test his inner life by temporary and occasional returns to the world.

433

It is one of the contributions of philosophy that it elevates useful work to the status of a component of spiritual activity, instead of degrading it, as mysticism does, as being detrimental to such activity. Hence, insofar as the philosophic student is striving to carry out his daily task honestly, efficiently, perfectly, and in the spirit of service, he is improving his own character for philosophic purposes too.

434

The philosophic student will not make the mistake of using the quest as an excuse for inefficiency when attending to duties. There is nothing spiritual in being a muddler. The performance of worldly duties in a dreamy, casual, uninterested, and slovenly manner is often self-excused by the mystically minded because they feel superior to such duties. This arises out of the false opposition which they set up between Matter and Spirit. Such an attitude is not the philosophical one. The mystic is supposed to be apathetic in worldly matters, if he is to be a good mystic. The philosophical student, on the contrary, keeps what is most worthwhile in mysticism and yet manages to keep alert in worldly matters too. If he has understood the teaching and trained himself aright, his practical work will be better done and not worse because he has taken to this quest. He knows it is perfectly possible to balance mystical tendencies with a robust efficiency. He will put as much thought and heart into his work as it demands.(P)

435

Religion's prayer and mystical meditation can be, and are, used to forget grinding troubles and escape hard duties. The peace of mind thus felt is pleasant, but not of lasting benefit. For the meaning of the trouble or duty is missed, and its place in the man's development, lost. Philosophy, while not disdaining the use of prayer and meditation, does not allow them to become escapist and obscure the need of practical attitudes also.

436

During the moments of meditation he will find the wonderful possibility of what he can become, but during the hours of action he will find the wonderful opportunity of realizing it.

437

But life must not end in meditation or else it will become extremely, if not entirely, self-centered. Meditation itself must bear fruit in active expressions.

438

Henry Suso acquired a reputation for mystical wisdom and ascetic piety when he remained secluded inside a monastery for twenty years. He lost it in less than half that time when he emerged to live and act in the outside world. For there was the testing-ground which measured his real achievement, as well as the evil forces which would destroy such a man's good work.

439

The effectiveness of action is raised immensely when it is inspired by mystical means. The fruitlessness of meditation is widened immensely when it is kept aloof from action.

440

It is not only in meditation's deep well that the divine has to be found, but also in the daily routine. It has to be naturalized.

441

In the end, the art of life can only be learned by living. Reverie and meditations, thinking and study, mystical raptures and inner visions are only means to this end, not the end in itself.

442

To think out an ideal, a way of conduct, is only a part of the battle a man will have to fight with himself over himself. The other part is to *do* it. Only when the ideal is applied in action does it become wholly realized. This is why the monk's existence is not enough, any more than the worldling's is enough. We need the world of action and experience to draw out our latent resources, to give us the chance to develop in the whole of our being and not merely in thought alone.

Relation to religion and mysticism

443

Philosophy does not seek to displace religion but to deepen it.

444

Religion is not the final utterance of the Holy Ghost. That privilege belongs to philosophy.

445

Philosophy includes religion but not "a" religion. It is universal, not sectarian.

446

If religion is man's first gesture toward the Infinite Being, philosophy is his full commitment toward it.

447

Philosophy seeks to bring him into full consciousness of what religion only partly prepares him for.

448

In religion man gropes in the dark night for his higher self. In mysticism he moves less haltingly toward it in the breaking dawn. In philosophy he walks straight to its realization under the high noon.

449

Let him keep everything that religion has given him, provided it be real religion and not the pretense of it, but let him also seek everything that mysticism and philosophy can offer him. He cannot come to the second except through the first, nor to the third except through the second. If he combines them, greater reward will come to him.

450

Our personal concern is not with exoteric religions, which are all without exception in their period of decay and dissolution; it is with esoteric knowledge, the knowledge which was possessed by Jesus, Buddha, and Krishna alike and secretly taught to their closest disciples.

451

Philosophy is religion, is mysticism, but only when they have come to maturity. It has been reached by the best minds of the other two and by the best minds among the sceptics and atheists, but again only on their attaining maturity.

452

Any account of the philosophic life which left the impression that it had no place for religious veneration and personal prayer would be misleading. Practical philosophy calls for the regular pursuit of devotional exercises just as much as it calls for the regular pursuit of mystical ones. The four genuflections and associated prayers are the means to this. To neglect the duty of daily worship on the plea that one has risen above it is an excuse which is manufactured by the lower self to perpetuate its own sovereignty. The higher philosophic experiences are not open to the man who is too proud to go down on bent knees in humble reverence or spiritual pleading. The student's religious fervours and exercises will not be rendered obsolete and consequently rejected, but they will be assimilated to and made use of in the larger philosophic life. Philosophy would indeed be foolish if it were to kick away the ladders of religion and mysticism by which people may ascend to it. Just as food can never displace drink for the sustenance of a healthy body, so meditation can never displace prayer for the sustenance of a healthy spiritual life, any more than study can displace meditation. Worship and prayer are essential philosophic duties.

453

We must retain as philosophers whatever worthwhile things we possessed as religious believers. We must retain the principles even if we will have to vary the forms of religious worship, prayer, devotion, aspiration, and communion.

454

The faith in and the practice of reverential worship into which he was initiated by religion must not be dropped. It is required by philosophy also. Only, he is to correct, purify, and refine it. He is to worship the divine presence in his heart, not some distant remote being, and he is to do so more by an act of concentrated thought and unwavering feeling than by resort to external indirect and physical methods. With the philosopher, as with the devotee, the habit of prayer is a daily one. But whereas he prays with light and heat, the other prays with heat alone. The heart finds in such worship a means of pouring out its deepest feelings of devotion, reverence, humility, and communion before its divine source. Thus we see that philosophy does not annul religious worship, but purifies and preserves what is best in it. It does annul the superstitions, exploitations, and futilities connected with conventional religious worship. In the end philosophy brings the seeker back to religion but not to *a* religion: to the reverence for a supreme power which he had discarded when he discarded the superstitions which had entwined themselves around it. Philosophy is naturally religious and inevitably mystical. Hence it keeps intact and does not break to pieces that which it receives from religion and yoga. It will, of course, receive only their sound fruits, not their bad ones. Philosophic endeavour does not, for instance, disdain religious worship and humble prayer merely because its higher elements transcend them. They are indeed part of such endeavour. But they are not, as with religionists, the whole of it. The mystic must not give up being religious merely because he has become a mystic. In the same way, the philosopher must not give up being both mystical and religious merely because he has become a philosopher. It is vitally important to know this. Philosophy does not supersede religion but keeps it and enlarges it.(P)

455

Just as science and religion meet and must meet in metaphysical philosophy, so religion and theology meet in mystical philosophy.

456

If it be true that the hidden teaching effectually reconciles religion science mysticism and philosophy, it does so in the only way in which they can be reconciled, by dropping them into their proper places and not by placing them all on an equal level. For it treats religion as an infant; mysticism, science, and metaphysics as youths; and philosophy alone as an adult.

457

Religion is man's quest of reality on its elementary level. Metaphysics is the same quest on its lower-intermediate level, and mysticism is the higher-intermediate one. In philosophy, the quest is completed on the highest plane.

458

There is something beyond mysticism. Peace is not the final goal of man. It is good but it is not enough. Just as religion must finally find its culmination in mysticism, so mysticism must find it in philosophy, and so metaphysics must find it in philosophic mysticism.

459

This is a special worth and admirable feature of true philosophy, that it does not leave behind and supersede earlier spheres of development but rather lets the later ones include and penetrate them. They are all necessary.

460

Man's fundamental need of the quest is first somewhat superficially assuaged by religion; growing stronger, it is next more deeply satisfied by mysticism. But only when the precious waters of philosophy are fully drunk is it finally and perfectly met.

461

Philosophy repudiates nothing in yoga, nothing in religion, nothing in mysticism that is correct or necessary. How could it when it draws its own lifeblood from the mystical intuition and the devotional attitude? But it does *complete* them by introducing what is further necessary and it does *equilibrate* them by shifts of emphasis and keeping them in place.

462

To pass from religion to philosophy is not to reject religion but rather to absorb its best elements and then integrate them into higher ones.

463

Philosophy carries us upward from lower to higher conceptions of the Deity.

464

We may understand how this movement from one standpoint to another becomes possible when we remember that we begin to learn astronomy on the assumption that the geocentric system—which is based on the belief that the earth is the centre of our universe—is valid, for this renders much easier the explanation of such unfamiliar themes as the poles, the equator, and the ecliptic. Later however we are told that this standpoint is only preliminary and that it was adopted for the sake of convenience in dealing with beginners so as to render their studies easier. The heliocentric system—which is based on the belief that the sun is the centre of our universe—is then put forward as being valid and the other is dropped. The instructional method used in the hidden teaching is similar. Here *religion* represents a preliminary standpoint for beginners in the study of life. After its values have been thoroughly absorbed, the latter gradually advance to the next standpoint, the *mystical*. When the students have won the fruits of meditation and reflection, they travel still further until they reach the third and final standpoint of *philosophy*, which develops ultramystical insight and practises disinterested activity. Thus each standpoint is a characteristic feature of a certain stage of inner evolution.

465

Philosophy can understand, and sympathize with, atheism as an expression of man's effort to free himself from superstition—albeit a clumsy, groping, and dangerous effort. But its own practice leads it to discover the godlike soul as man's real self, so it cannot help rejecting the materialism which would deny that along with the denial of God.

466

The voice of philosophy is necessarily more restrained, less shrill, than the voice of religion or cultism. But if this makes it quieter and less heard by the crowd, it also makes it better heard by the sensitive and more enduring in the result.

467

Where religion converts a man, philosophy transforms him. Where religion affects a part of a man, philosophy affects the whole.

Living synthesis, not anemic eclecticism

468

Philosophy is not one teaching among many others, to be chosen in rivalry amongst all. It is fundamentally different from them in kind and nature.

469

Just as Religion is larger than the religions, so is Philosophy larger than the philosophies.

470

Although philosophy is unique it is also all-inclusive.

471

The philosophic outlook rises above all sectarian controversy. It finds its own position not only by appreciating and synthesizing what is solidly based in the rival sects but also by capping them all with the keystone of nonduality.

472

The mystic who sees no utility and no purpose in breaking his own tranquillity to descend into the suffering world and serve or save its inhabitants, justifies his attitude by declaring that the sufferings are illusory and the inhabitants non-existent! Where is the incentive to altruistic action in this doctrine of nonduality, where the inspiration for art, where the impetus to science? The answer may not be obvious but nevertheless it lies enshrined in the very nature of these tenets.

473

It is not quite correct to state, as has been done, that this teaching represents the essence of the Indian Vedanta philosophy. Its sources have included it but they have also been many and varied. And, in the doctrine of higher individuality, for instance, there is an actual divergence between the two teachings.

474

Vedanta is superb, the most logical of all metaphysics; but because it is a metaphysic and a mystique, it is for me inconclusive. We need more a guide to how to live in the body and keep it well. We need to gather up a synthesis of knowledge—a key to the World-Idea, a practical guide to healthy living, a devotional and mystical system of prayer and meditation. The philosopher is unable to follow the Vedantin in ignoring the outer conditions of life to the extent that he does. Their proper handling is ignored only by paying a proportionate price in trouble of some kind. Let the Vedantin talk much and often of the non-existence of the body; you will find that in one way or another, in illness or in lack, he cannot help being aware of the body.

475

The thoughtful man is too much of a Buddhist to limit himself to Advaita. But counter to that, the intuitive man is too much of an Advaitin to limit himself to Buddhism. The wise man balances and blends the two in philosophy.

476

The absolutist metaphysics of Subramanya Iyer in the East and Lilian de Waters in the West declares only the One Reality; it would reject the whole universe as non-existent and the whole human race along with it. The dualist metaphysics declares that this Reality reveals and manifests itself in the time-space finite world. The integral metaphysics of philosophy says, however, that it is unwise and unbalanced to separate these two solutions of the mystery of life and then to oppose one against the other. They are to be fitted together, for only in such completeness can the full solution be found. Dualism answers the intellect's questions and satisfies the heart's yearnings but monism responds to the intuition's highest revelations. Both standpoints are necessary, for man is both a thinking and a feeling being; it is not enough to regard him only as an intuiting one. But this does not mean they are all on the same level. What is silently revealed to us by inner stillness must always be loftier than what is noisily told us by intellectual activity.

477

Philosophy does not dwell on the subject of nonduality. There are metaphysicians aplenty who will discuss or teach it for those who want to learn or listen. Philosophers neither support nor deny the doctrine. Here they are closer to Buddhism than to Hinduism.

478

The Advaitin who declares that as such he has no point of view, has already adopted one by calling himself an Advaitin and by rejecting every other point of view as being dualistic. A human philosophy is neither dualistic alone nor nondualistic alone. It perceives the connection between the dream and the dreamer, the Real and the unreal, the consciousness and the thought. It accepts Advaita, but refuses to stop with it; it accepts duality, but refuses to remain limited to it; therefore it alone is free from a dogmatic point of view. But in attempting to bring into harmony that which forever is and that which is bound by time and space, it becomes a truly human philosophy of Truth.

479

The comparative study of religion, mysticism, and metaphysics, as they have appeared in different centuries and in different parts of the world, will have a liberating effect on those who approach it in a thoroughly scientific independent and prejudice-free spirit. A comparative view of all the different spiritual cultures leads to a broader understanding of each particular one.

480

Where others present one with a statement of an issue or a description of a situation that is limited to a pair of opposites, the philosopher will either reconcile them or look for the third factor.

481

It is the joyous duty of philosophy to bring into systematic harmony the various views which mankind has held and will ever hold, however conflicting they seem on the surface, by assigning the different types to their proper levels and by providing a total view of the possible heights and depths of human thought. Thus and thus alone the most opposite tendencies of belief and the most striking contrasts of outlook are brought within a single scheme. All become aspects, more or less limited, only. None ever achieves metaphysical finality and need ever again be mistaken for the whole truth. All become clear as organic phases of mankind's mental development. Philosophy alone can bring logically opposite doctrines into harmonious relation with each other by assigning them to their proper places under a single sheltering canopy. Thus out of the medley of voices within us philosophy creates a melody.(P)

482

Philosophy can be true to itself, to its highest purpose and clearest perception, only by discarding all bias and prejudice, narrowness and polemics, and accepting the visitations of grace through whatever mode it chooses to manifest. Philosophy must and does welcome the old and traditional but refuses to confine itself to that alone. It must and does greet the new and original if the holy spirit is therein too. It cannot be tied by time or place, group or race, celebrity or anonymity.

483

To attempt to construct a synthesis of truths drawn from different quarters is laudable, although in the end it depends on the judgement of the person making it. To attempt to mix the unmixable, to force oil and water into unity, is a different matter.

484

Philosophy does not indulge in a superficial, anaemic eclecticism but in a large and living synthesis. Thus, it wholeheartedly advocates the study of Indian spiritual culture if made from an independent standpoint and included in a comparative view, but it unhesitatingly refuses to swallow wholesale the same study from a convert's standpoint and as the follower of some guru.

485

There are fragments of this teaching to be found in ancient Rome amongst the Stoics, in ancient Greece amongst the Platonists, and in ancient India amongst the Buddhists. But they are fragments only. If you want the complete system, you must go to philosophy.

486

The intimate association of Eastern thought with Western culture, of ancient wisdom with modern knowledge, will give to each element a new and broader meaning while blending and harmonizing all of them. Philosophy combines in a truly catholic manner those elements of truth which are present in all these teachings but without any of their errors, absurdities, and archaic limitations.

487

The hidden philosophy is not something with which mankind at large is acquainted today. Many fragments of it have certainly found their way into the world, but the complete pattern of this philosophy has not.

488

Philosophy promotes the fullest intellectual independence, but not the freest intellectual anarchy. Therefore it adjures the student at the same time to gather up the harvest of the whole world's best thought from the earliest times to the latest.

489

The time has come to take in all the best of these currents and rise above narrowing loyalties. Only by such a synthesis can we arrive at Truth.

490

When this loftier standpoint is reached, these different schools and techniques are seen not as contrary but as complementary to one another.

491

The history of truth is an international one. It is from and for all the peoples of the world.

492

Each science can only deal in a limited range of facts. Philosophy takes up the results of all the separate sciences and puts them together. Then it takes up the results of all the arts, all the religions, all the yogas, and all the other branches of human activity. Finally it combines the lot. None of these branches can authoritatively pronounce on the meaning of universal existence, for this is beyond its sphere of reference. It may indeed talk foolishly when it ventures to do so. This is why philosophy is unique.

493

Philosophy is unique in this respect: no other teaching views life so broadly and yet so penetratingly.

494

Whereas most other forms of culture are mere branches of it and consequently emphasize one particular aspect of life, philosophy embraces its whole field.

495

Anything that concerns human life is grist for the mill of philosophic reflection and action. For philosophy does not merely concern itself with interpreting life but also with remolding it.

496

It is here that the beautiful balance of philosophy rejects at one and the same time two opposing ways which appear in the history of mysticism. The one would, through oversystematization and burdensome detail, turn its methods into rigid frozen complicated mechanisms, as if the inner being were a piece of engineering rather than a living thing to be nourished and warmed. The other would, through vague foundations, the pretext of freedom, and excessive individualism, turn its teachings into an anarchy of conflicting ideas and personal phantasies or an arena for contending personal ambitions.

497

Philosophy rises above sects and is therefore free from sectarian dispute, friction, and hostility. It is naturally tolerant, knowing that as men rise in cultural and moral development, their beliefs will rise in truthfulness and nobility.

498

As broad an investigation as the records of knowledge allow, and as deep a reflection upon the facts elucidated—this is the aim of the serious philosopher. He will be careful to take all the facts and all the evidence—so far as he can get them—into account, and not disregard such portion of it as is distasteful to him, not neglect those findings which are unknown to or unwanted by the kind of society in which he is brought up and lives.

499

Philosophy is free. It is both for those who seek an ideal or guidance from the leaders inside institutions and for those who will have nothing to do with institutions.

500

There is no room for a fixed and finished sectarianism here. The unfoldment of inner life must not be cramped into an arrested form.

501

The philosopher cannot take a one-sided view. He must stand on a higher level above such narrowness, and thus get a larger picture. It may not be possible for humans to be totally unbiased but it is possible to *try* to be fair and just. This requires an awareness of the other aspects. It does not require the fusion of differences, the mixing of the unmixable. They can be left where they are, each in its own place, contributing what it alone can contribute. Each can be reconciled into acceptance of the other's right to exist separately without invasion. A forced synthesis is pseudo-unity.

502

If philosophy accepts all viewpoints as being valid, it does not fall into the error of accepting them as being equally valid. It says that they are progressively valid and rest on lower or higher levels.

503

It readily grants the utility of these progressive stages at their time and in their place, but it rejects them as ends in themselves. Philosophy recognizes only one end to be attained—the Real.

504

Philosophy recognizes the all-importance of points of view. It knows that no results are tenable unless they are ultimate ones—that is to say, unless they are got by adopting the ultimate point of view.

505

Let the various insights and revelations out of which the well-established faiths and teachings have grown flourish as they find themselves, reformed and purified today if their needs so dictate, but why attempt to mix them all together? What would the result be but a kind of stew? If a synthesis is sought, say of the Buddhist and the Christian, let those who like one have it. But for others does not diversity, as in a garden, give more picturesque, interesting, and richer results?

506

Those who have not taken the precaution to study other teachings, other ideas, other experiences, and other revelations, but only the views of their own favoured teacher, may have learned the worst and not the best. And those who know only their own religion, their own nation's history and form of government may pay in some way or other for their ignorance. Comparative study will be part of the education of a better world. It will not only bring less prejudice and more tolerance, but also—what is more important—help to establish truth.

507

Each seer gets hold of some facet of truth and contributes that to the world-stock. Let us be tolerant.

508

None of these teachers tells, or seems able to tell, the whole story. Each gives out all he can—a fragment of it. The hour is at hand when they should be joined together, when a synthesis of truth should be made from all of them.

509

Whoever advocates a particular view usually produces plenty of evidence on its behalf but withholds some or all of the evidence on behalf of opposing views. It is only the philosopher who tries to get a complete picture of the situation from different sides. It needs more than a little imaginative effort to understand the other and unfamiliar ways of looking at a question. But the results are usually worthwhile.

510

We may fully sympathize with a standpoint and yet we need not hesitate to utter certain criticisms of it. How else can a just view be got?

511

It teaches men not to limit both the field and the freedom of their search by limiting themselves to a single teaching or a single teacher in the restricted and dependent tie of discipleship.

512

Physics, metaphysics, religion, and mysticism must unite before each can speak truth, which is a unique whole and not a particular fragment as they individually are.

513

But we shall not arrive at such a higher standpoint unless we arrive at clear thought about the matter. One of the trickiest obstacles in the way of correct thinking about these problems is the partisan habit of propounding a dilemma which presents one with the choice between two alternatives. Thus *either* one must accept materialism and reject religion *or* vice versa. The proper course to be travelled will not only lie between these two extremes but also take us into lands beyond them.

514

The Greek love of balance and sense of proportion are incorporated in philosophy as much as the Roman-Stoic love of self-mastery and sense of mental values.

515

Philosophical study welcomes lofty, wise, and inspired ideas "from every side," from every religion, from every century. Such width of outlook breeds tolerance, enlarges knowledge, promotes goodwill.

516

The dogmatism which vehemently asserts that only in its particular sect or creed lies final salvation has nothing to do with philosophy and is alien to the discovery of truth. This must be so, for the philosopher seeks balance and uses counterbalance whenever necessary.

517

Details are significant, but only in their relation to the whole, to the greater purpose of all life.

518

Philosophy criticizes any approach to truth which arrogates to itself the privilege of being the only path to enlightenment. For in practice philosophy makes use of any and every one needful. It is too spontaneous to limit its efforts to purely ancient or merely Oriental forms.

519

By refusing to join philosophy to any built-up structure, social or cultural organization, or particular group of people, this approach keeps its own freedom and bestows that same freedom on those who study it.

520

It is too time-wasting, muddling, negative, and one-sided to look for error in every other doctrine and then magnify it enormously. The atmosphere of criticism becomes habitual and leads to no constructive result. It is better to gather the flowers of wisdom and the fruits of peace.

521

The profit of a full and explicit picture of the universe is immense. It provides the seeker with a safe course and a correct destination. Otherwise his undirected efforts may spend themselves in a lifetime of groping wandering and haphazard movements. The greatest advantage can come only from a world-picture of the greatest completeness. Only with one that presents all principal aspects of the human entity, and of its place in this picture, can that entity understand how best to live out its incarnation.

522

We may try to take not a bird's-eye view of the world but a God's-eye view of it.

523

The wisdom embedded in philosophy belongs to all the ages, and not to any particular time.

524

As one reflects upon the majestic grandeur of this teaching, its amplitude and height, one feels like a traveller who stands for the first time at a vantage point of the Himalayas, where loftier and ever loftier snowy summits fill the whole horizon to his left and right, as far as his eyes can see.

525

Philosophy stretches itself out on all sides. It is limited only by the limits of man's capacity to comprehend it.

2

ITS CONTEMPORARY INFLUENCE

Response to a vital need

These teachings have appeared in the world in their present form and at the present time because they correspond to a genuine need of a certain section of humanity.

2

These teachings have been released, not to gain proselytes—although they will come—but primarily to help seekers who are already familiar with the first principles of mysticism.

3

The age of esotericism has come to an end and the age of open teaching is upon us. The hierophants of ancient Egypt were very cunning in the methods they adopted to hide their knowledge and even invented two kinds of symbolic alphabets, the hieroglyphic and the hieratic, for the use of themselves, their students, and initiated members of the aristocracy, leaving the common demotic alphabet for the use of the masses. The Brahmins of India severely punished any one among them who revealed their teachings to the multitude. Most of the lama masters of Tibet made candidates for instruction undergo a long probation before the higher teachings were communicated to them. The necessity of reserve was strongly impressed upon his followers by Pythagoras, so that his own and their writings are involved in obscurity, covered with symbolism, and often misleading if taken literally. But times have changed since those ancient days. Brahmin writers have revealed their own religious system to the world. The ashrams of great Yogis publish, in books accessible to all who can read, the sayings and teachings of the Yogi masters. The Tibetan adepts sent Blavatsky to the West to disseminate a part of their teaching through Theosophy. From these and other instances it should be clear that the old policy of secrecy has been abandoned. There are not only intellectual reasons for this change in policy—such as the general diffusion of learning and literacy as masses who could not formerly read or write are everywhere acquiring or have acquired these abilities—but also a much more important one: humanity itself is faced with such a tremendous peril that the peril of divulging the divine mysteries is small by comparison. The discovery of atomic power has placed in its hands a weapon with which it threatens to destroy itself, to eradicate its society, and to eliminate its civilization from the face of this planet. In these tragic and unprecedented circumstances, it is a duty laid upon philosophy to come to the help of those individuals, however few, who are sufficiently impressed by the gravity of their situation, whether before or after the great destruction has taken place, to seek for the true sources of life, guidance, strength, and grace as their only refuge, their only salvation.

4

These truths, which were formerly kept wholly esoteric and narrowly confined to an intellectually privileged elite, must now be given to the widest possible audience because humanity's position is so precarious. The old secrecy has outlived its usefulness.

5

If the truth in all its fullness is given out indiscriminately and promiscuously, we may expect results of a mixed good and bad character. Some of the bad sort we are already seeing in the strange stew which associated Zen Buddhistic enlightenments with liquor, drugs, sexual promiscuity, and antisocial rejection of responsibility. If the times in which we live were not so critical as they are, it would not be right or wise to let everyone, even the deformed in character and the deficient in capacity, come into knowledge of the truth. But the times being what they are, this is a risk that must be taken, a price that must be paid for the service that will thus be rendered to the ready and the worthy who seek the real salvation.

6

Whatever misinterpretation or misuse will be made by unready persons of the teachings thus disclosed, enough compensation will be achieved by the benefit conferred on those who are ready.

7

It is the business of philosophy to cast out error and establish truth. This takes it away from the popular conceptions of religion. Philosophy by its very nature must be unpopular; hence it does not ordinarily go out of its way to spread its ideas in the world. Only at special periods, like our own, when history and evolution have prepared enough individuals to make a modest audience, does philosophy promulgate such of its tenets as are best suited to the mind of that period.(P)

8

Whatever were the motives which dictated the exclusive reservation of ultimate wisdom in former centuries and the extraordinary precautions which were taken to keep it from the larger world, we must now reckon on the dominant fact that humanity lives today in a cultural environment which has changed tremendously. The old ideas have lost their weight among educated folk—except for individuals here and there—and this general decay has passed by reflex action among the masses, albeit to a lesser extent. Whether in religion or science, politics or society, economics or ethics, the story of prodigious storm which has shaken the thoughts of men to their foundations is the same. The time indeed is transitional. In this momentous period when the ethical fate of mankind is at stake because the religious sanctions of morality have broken down, it is essential that something should arise to take their place. This is the supreme and significant fact which has forced the hands of those who hold this wisdom in their possession, which has compelled them to begin this historically unique disclosure of it, and which illustrates the saying that the night is darkest just before dawn. This is the dangerous situation which broke down an age-old policy and necessitated a new one whose sublime consequences to future generations we can now but dimly envisage.(P)

9

This is a period when esoteric pretensions are out of joint with the times, when direct communication is to be the rule or else none at all, if anything of value is really to be given to the world. Those zealous protectors of the truth who surround it with enigma and riddle, who hide it under out-of-date symbols and unnecessary jargon, forget that they live now in an age of science, not an age of medievalism.

10

It is claimed that esotericism is essential to protect truth from adulteration and mankind from bewilderment and miscomprehension. This is true. But it is not true for all time—not for our own time.

11

The work done by science and rationalism has been a necessary one, but it was destructive of religious codes and consequently of moralities based on those codes. Mankind must now perform a piece of constructive work in the sphere of ethics or it may experience a social collapse of colossal magnitude. It is here that the hidden teaching can step in and offer a valuable contribution.

12

When this secrecy was overdone, either for selfish monopolizing reasons or through rigid inherited traditions, the masses were permanently excluded not only from the knowledge for which they are unfit but also from that for which they have, by the processes of evolution, become ready. The end result was to keep them permanently ignorant, to prevent them from growing as quickly as, with encouragement, they could have grown, and to confuse their minds.

13

The inborn potential of fitness for this knowledge may be larger than appears on the surface, where family, surroundings, circumstances, and false religion may prevent its liberation and development. The concept of reincarnation explains why this is possible, but it also explains why all reserves and potentials are not equal, nor equally liberated, and therefore why some discrimination must be practised. But this should be tentative, not final—flexible, not rigid. For it is not so easy as most believe to predict the course of future inner growth for a person. If he is unable or unwilling to absorb this knowledge now, he might be able to do so in ten years' time. The essential thing is to shut no one out from its offering, not to hide its very existence from people, as certain religious circles have done in the past.

14

Philosophy cannot escape being as affected by our iconoclastic times as any other form of culture. It does not and cannot live in a history-tight compartment. Consequently when it witnesses the spectacle of the common people more and more taking the future in their own hands, more and more being liberated from patriarchal modes of ecclesiastical government, more and more having to stand on their own spiritual feet, it cannot waste its time in deploring the inevitable. Instead, it must set about reducing the causes which have hitherto prevented it from having a popular appeal and simplifying the presentation which has hitherto made it the monopoly of a superior few. It must ally itself with the people and sincerely strive to bring out their finer potentialities and assist them to rise to a level where they can better understand it. This it must do if it is to be true to itself, to its own noble ideals and divine mission.

15

It is a Brahminical notion that because minds young in evolution cannot grasp the higher intellectual truths, they should therefore be taught nothing but intellectual falsehoods. This has been their practice, and the degradation of the masses is a living witness to the unwisdom of this extreme practice. Philosophical verities have been carefully hidden from the millions and made the preserve of a mere few. The others have been given a grossly materialistic religion and an ethical code based on utter superstition. The consequence is that now Western ideas and modern education are beginning to spread their ripples beyond the cities to the villages and beyond the better classes to the illiterates. The moral power of religion is breaking down and the miserable masses are being left without anything better than incipient hopelessness and the educated classes without anything better than bitter cynicism. How much wiser would it have been to make the fruits of philosophy available to those who sought them, how much wiser to have carefully taught at least some of the truth about life to these younger minds instead of hiding all truth from them so completely that when the more intelligent ones wake up and discover how they have been deceived, the sudden shock of disillusionment unbalances them utterly and leaves them without ideals and with revolutionary destructive instincts. Too much concealment of the truth has led to the disaster of Bolshevik and Nazi reactions. Too much shielding of undeveloped minds from the facts of existence has left them prey to the worst superstitions and the most harmful charlatanry in the fields of thought and action. The doctrine of secrecy must not be pushed to foolish limits. Let us face the fact that man's mentality has grown and let us give it nourishment suited to its age. If the easier principles of philosophic truth are taught gradually and led up to from the superstitious dogmas which merely symbolize them, the slow revelation will not unsettle the minds of people but on the contrary will strengthen them against wrong-doing and nurture their own self-reliance.

16

The duty to which we are called is not to propagate ideas but to offer them, not to convert reluctant minds but to satisfy hungry ones, not to trap the bodies of men into external organizations but to set their souls free to find truth. There are individuals today to whom these teachings are unknown but who possess in the deeper levels of their mind latent tendencies and beliefs, acquired in former lives, which will leap into forceful activity as soon as the teaching is presented to them.

17

In the twentieth century such secrecy has become superfluous. The deepest truths of man's inner nature have already been published to the whole world. The most recondite teachings have been publicly proclaimed in nearly every modern language.

18

The age of esotericism is past. With the world-menace darkening every year, Truth can no longer hide herself in an obscure corner. She must now speak forth challengingly and boldly to the public consciousness.

19

It is true that the differences of evolutionary grades must be respected. It is true that the mass of people are children spiritually. But it is also true that children can be taught something and led a few steps onward however low their grade. Moreover, we live in times when the old evil forces are so active only because they feel the approach of new and good ones.

20

The evolutionary trend wins out whether we like it or not. Plato in Greece, the Brahmins in India, wanted to keep knowledge and therefore education within the ranks of a few. Their reasons were solid enough *at the time*. But in this epoch the trend is different, for we do not live in a static universe. It is in the direction of more knowledge and more education for more men, women, and children. This applies on every level from the most physical and technical to the most spiritual.

21

Will the masses ever come of cultural and spiritual age? Can the common man ever find enough nourishment in true philosophic ideas? Yes, this can happen if those at the top accept truth, for sooner or later their ideas filter downward, even if somewhat thinned by the process of popularization.

22

The thinking of the toiling masses is perhaps beyond its influence, but the thinking of those who rule, lead, teach, and direct those masses is not. Therefore it aims primarily at penetrating the minds of those few.

23

In the end philosophy is not only for the minority of well-educated minds or for the elite of the persons refined by culture, upbringing, innate sensitivity, but also for the majority who can take it in *partially*; here and there some points can be grasped and accepted. Properly presented with psychological perception of the audience's disposition, nature, capacities, knowledge, and faith, it can be linked up with what they already hold, dovetailed in, and built up further.

24

In an era when the turn of the karmic wheel brought democracy to the ascendant, we had to expect and must accept that philosophy would be brought within the reach of the masses. The old days when a tiny elite of cultured persons of high character and high capacity were alone teaching and learning it have passed. It is public culture and not private. Just as television and radio have brought sports and races into the homes of everybody, so they will bring philosophy to those who are willing to listen to talks about it—whether fit or not. In an attempt to make it more understandable to the masses, it will have to suffer some measure of adulteration, perhaps even falsification; but the instincts of the masses will of course keep them listening to what is appropriate for them—sports and the races—rather than to explanations and expositions of philosophy. The point, however, is simply this: that there is nothing secret today about philosophy and those who attempt to turn it into a system of occult secrets for the few are out of tune with the times. They will be swept aside by the Aquarian Age which is only just now beginning, the age when knowledge will be freely dispensed to all and when the mind of man will measurably grow and develop in rising to this new opportunity.

25

The world's need today is not really for more new ideas, which means more thoughts, but for more wisdom, which means how to manage the thoughts which humanity has already accumulated through the centuries.

26

It is only if the level of public feeling and intelligence is raised that the basic truths of philosophy could come into wider acceptance.

27

The mass-intellect was not yet then developed enough, nor educated enough, and hence not yet capable enough, to understand a teaching so universal, so impersonal, and so utterly nonmaterialistic. But is it able to do so now? The answer is that it still cannot understand fully and properly; it is, however, better able to do so partially.

28

What was right in the medieval days of religious persecution and in the antique days of popular illiteracy, is no longer right in twentieth-century days of religious freedom and popular education. Mysticism must not continue to seclude itself. It must find outer expression and emanate inner influence.

29

The old rule that a teaching must be limited to the spiritual and intellectual measure of those to whom it is addressed cannot be discarded but it may be expanded and liberalized.

30

If it is to be popularized, this must be done under some reserves, to protect its own purity and integrity. But these reserves need not and ought not be as large and forbidding as they often have been in the past. The extraordinary times in which we live, the world-wide area of the crisis, and the nature of the crisis itself require this liberalization.

31

If these thoughts are to carry any value they ought to be in rhythm with the World-Idea; their theme ought to celebrate what it is giving out to all the denizens of this globe.

32

Although it is primarily a teaching for those who are somewhat advanced in the cultural scale, it has many points which are simple enough for anyone to grasp.

33

The worth of philosophy can be rightly appraised and appreciated only by mentalities that are equal to it in intelligence morality and subtlety. No others are really competent to judge it. Then is it solely for a mere handful? No, for what we are unable to take hold of by full sight we may still take hold of by well-placed faith.

34

That a proportion of the masses, if only given the chance, would rise to an acceptance of the higher truth—a larger proportion than is generally believed, even though it would still be a minority—is a situation which the history of the past few centuries, the contemporary invention and menace of the atomic bomb and nuclear missile, and the ferment in religious circles and religious ideas have combined to create. It is a new era, yes, but the seekers and the awakeners enter it to their own danger. For they lack the moral preparation and correct mental instruction; it is easy to enter by the wrong door: then confusion, folly, fanaticism, or hallucination mix well into whatever bit of truth is found. The risk is there. We see it plainly enough today, when the drug-takers are also taking over the truth.

35

In this age of plain speaking, universal education, religious tolerance, and popular uplift, secrecy has not only become irrelevant but even sinful.

36

The hidden teaching can no longer afford to be deprecated by religionists and despised by rationalists. It can no longer be confined to a few intelligentsia but must be brought to them, even if it be necessary to placate popular opinion by over-emphasizing personal benefits and to make concessions to contemporary knowledge by over-emphasizing the scientific standpoint. For more people are ready to discard antiquated doctrines than would seem likely. And the dangers which formerly attended the promiscuous disclosure of such information have largely vanished. The days when Krishna could speak of having taught this wisdom, which goes beyond ordinary knowledge, as a secret to kings only, or when the high priests of Egypt could initiate Pharaohs and nobles alone, have gone, not to be recalled.

37

The fact that the principles of the hidden teaching are now given out publicly and openly, whereas in former centuries they had to be given out secretly and privately, must be carefully appraised. If it indicates progression in one sense, it also indicates retrogression in another. It shows that greater opportunities for intellectual and spiritual freedom exist today, but it also shows that the power of religious institutions and faith in religious truth have waned.

38

We do not need to persuade or convert others to philosophy but we ought to offer them the material which they can investigate as and when they feel inclined to do so.

39

If these truths are too solemn to be made the subject of cheap publicity, too profound to be comprehensible to everyone alike, they can at least be introduced unobtrusively.

40

Philosophy was formerly the esoteric possession of a select elite. No attempt was made to popularize it. The reasons given for this were serious and convincing. But in some respects the situation has changed so largely that a reconsideration of this attitude has become necessary. The literacy and the leisure needed for its study have appeared. The confusion in the minds of religious believers and the weakening of ecclesiastical authority which it could easily have caused, are conditions which have already appeared of themselves through other causes.

41

From the moment that these teachings were printed and circulated, they became public property and lost their esoteric character.

42

If the millions have no taste for truth, it is partly because they have never been offered the chance to acquire it. If they prefer the debased and debauched, it is partly because they have been schooled to appreciate them.

43

The great advances in human intellect and scientific knowledge, the great collapses of religious institutions, the widespread propaganda for political and economic movements which have captured the faith and following that earlier went into religion—these things have by themselves made the self-revealing of the hidden philosophy most necessary. But the grave moral and physical perils which surround us today make it still more necessary.

44

The teaching is not usually or at first comprehensible to the multitude. But given time and some systematic and purposeful training, it *could* be made comprehensible to them. They have in the past been underrated, their potentialities neglected. The duty of guiding and elevating these supposed morons has been selfishly unperceived. Responsibility ought to accompany privilege.

45

Those who do not like philosophy and cannot understand it are simply not ready for it. We cannot compel them to take it up. But we can keep it available for them, whenever the time comes that they do feel a need for it.

46

Its message must not only be made clear for the unfamiliar but also vivid for the insensitive.

47

To treat the masses as feeble-minded, incapable of understanding truth and fit only to be nourished on falsehood, is to disregard two facts: first, their evolutionary character; second, their inner identity with truth's divine source. Why disguise or dilute? Why appeal only to their lowest and dullest? If you reach their highest and best once out of twenty tries, this is much better and more important than never reaching it at all. This was Emerson's way.

48

The time has come when it is dangerous not to divulge these straight truths to everybody but to keep them back from everybody. The lack of spiritual reverence and the lowness of moral tone, the ignorance of karmic consequences and the violence of greed and hatred—these are the things today which are immensely dangerous to humanity—not the divulgements of philosophy.

49

The whole of philosophy cannot be disseminated quickly and easily to the masses. But this is not to be used as an excuse to do nothing at all for them.

50

The time has come to bring these truths out into the open, to declare them publicly, to remember that the periods for esotericism are past, and to cease playing the game of concealment. Otherwise a third world war remains a menace.

51

Today every seeker is welcome to philosophy's ranks provided he or she be sincere and qualified.

A more timely formulation

52

A fresh spiritual impulse, a fresh revelation of the Eternal Truth which inheres in the very nature of the world's essence, must be given shape and form.

53

A portion of what was formerly the possession of a small exclusive elite is now ripe to become the possession of the common people themselves. A fragment of what was exceptional wisdom in antiquity is ready to be regarded as ordinary knowledge in modernity.

54

The message of philosophy has never been appropriate to any particular time, because it has always been above all historic times. Nevertheless modern man will find more in it than ancient or medieval man could ever find or get.

55

Metaphysics in its finest form of presentation could never have confronted us before this twentieth century. All knowledge and all history have been moving towards this grand cultural climax. We have had foregleams and approximations, summaries and condensations of the hidden metaphysics ever since man began to record his thoughts; but we have never had the opportunity of a detailed working-out of its every point until science appeared to provide the data which now render this possible. Magnificent indeed are the vistas now opened up to us.

56

It was as fitting as it was inevitable that such a picture of the universe should have been created in the West and that the rejection of all pictures in favour of merging in the nothingness of Nirvana should have dominated the East. Now, with the perspective of both hemispheres' histories behind us, and with the opportunity to become adequately and accurately familiar with both hemispheres' knowledge—an opportunity which could not arise before this twentieth century—the time has come for a balanced attitude towards them and for an integral union of what is complementary in them.

57

The mystic must not be averse to modern culture, which he often naturally despises as materialistic or abhors as atheistic. He must draw on the resources of twentieth-century knowledge to reinforce, develop, explain, expand, and restate the dusty traditional inheritance of mysticism. He ought not to exalt the mighty illuminated past at the expense of a so-called degenerated benighted present.

To deny that our wits have been sharpened and our interpretive methods improved during the thousands of years which have disappeared into the waters that flow down the Ganges would be to libel the human mind and to turn it into a helpless stone. And when, as so often happened in the Orient, the static custodians of traditional culture were so bemused by their bookshelves that they refused to adapt their doctrines to the needs of the time, they were carrying conservatism to the point of plain silliness. On the other hand, service of the present need not be accompanied by a funeral dirge on the past. Ancient culture and modern science ought to be wedded together if we are to unlock the higher wisdom. Is not modern research unconsciously already beginning to furnish new proofs of ancient tenets? We need the old *truths*, not the old *follies*. A thought which is ten minutes old might be truer than a thought which is ten thousand years old. What has truth to do with time?

During the whole of my literary activity I have tried to develop this idea of a close collaboration between the rational and emotional sides of man's nature. This notion arose not merely because I have witnessed at first hand the tragic disasters of human lives wrecked through foolish and wholesale rejection of the claims of reason, but also because I perceive the immense importance of entering into an alliance with the trend towards science which has come to dominate modern existence.

58

Humanity has not stood still during all these thousands of years. It has decisively changed in most ways, evolved in some ways, and degenerated in others. This is clear when we consider its outer life, but not so clear when we consider its inner life. It will be better grasped if we pause to note that a twentieth-century teaching in its fullness would have been unsuitable for an ancient seeker. Indeed, it would be something which he could assimilate only in part; the rest would be beyond his capacity. When men and women have been brought up only to obey blindly the dead teachers of vanished centuries and never to think anything out for themselves, their true development is hampered. Hence the ancient ideas and practices, which were excellent for the ancient peoples, are not adequate to the needs of today's historical situation.

59

Philosophy of today must be based upon the bedrock of scientific facts.

60

Where else can philosophy get its proper start except in experienced data?

61

We have to create an intellectual world-view which can be adequate enough to meet criticism or defend itself against all the other intellectual world-views of our time. But whereas the philosophic one is spiritual in the truest sense, these others are either frankly materialistic or superstitiously mystical. Those adherents of religio-mystic doctrines who have failed to appreciate the importance of such work, as well as those who have even sharply criticized it, reveal by their attitude a narrowness which is surely not the mark of authentic spirituality.

62

There has not been so far any school whose outlook was broad enough to take in the philosophical one, nor whose inspiration was deep enough. The time will come when to provide for this deficiency will be laid as a duty on someone's mind, nor can it be far off.

63

The immediate task today is for philosophy to deliver its message. The secondary task is to assist those who accept this message to come to a proper and adequate understanding of it. The first is for the multitude and hence public. The second is for the individual and hence private.

64

A jealously guarded hidden teaching far more advanced and complicated than the present one will be revealed by its custodians before this century closes. But when this does occur, the revelation will only extend and not displace the foundation for it which is given in these pages.

65

As a necessary result of all that has gone before, someone will have to face this task of establishing a school of thought that will synthesize the Oriental teachings with the scientific Occidental discoveries. The teaching will have to be delivered impersonally, as it is in schools of chemistry and physics, without establishing that personal dependence of which Indians are so enamoured but of which a philosopher is unable to approve.

66

The spiritual seekers who followed René Guénon and the poets who followed T.S. Eliot fell into the same trap as their leaders. For in protesting, and rightly, against the anarchy of undisciplined and unlimited freedom, both Guénon and Eliot retreated backwards into formal tradition and fixed myth. Both had served their historic purpose and were being left behind. Both men were brilliant intellectuals and naturally attracted a corresponding type of reader. Their influence is understandable. But it is not on the coming wave of the Aquarian Age. New forms will be needed to satisfy the new knowledge, the new outlook, the new feelings. The classical may be respected, even admired; but the creative will be followed.(P)

67

This is a pioneer work, this making of a fresh synthesis which draws from, but does not solely depend upon, the knowledge of colleagues scattered in different continents as well as the initiations of masters belonging to the most different traditions.(P)

68

Today the seeker finds offered to him the culture of the whole world. The wisdom of many civilizations has been bequeathed to him from the past, from long-gone eras as also those more recent in time or distant in space. How fortunate is his position in these ways!

69

This grand synthesis could have come into being only in this twentieth century—that is, after science had been brought by facts to destroy its own fetish of "matter" and only after the secret philosophic book of the Brahmins had been wrested from their grasp.

70

Wisdom requires that we throw emphasis on those aspects of the teaching which will make most appeal to the contemporary mind. It also requires that we bring forward those features which are most pertinent to modern needs. For this reason it is desirable that Truth should be restated.

71

Our beliefs must assume a clearer form in this rational age. Whatever is true in them need not fear such remodelling. Modern science hints at confirmation of the age-old intuitions of religion and mysticism. During the past hundred years man has accumulated enough scientific detail to make a worthy system of knowledge, but he still lacks the guiding principle of putting the details together. Only the higher philosophy offers this principle.

72

When we think of the tremendous alteration which has taken place in the educated man's conception of the world and when we think of the tremendous social economic and political changes which have followed as a consequence, we may begin to grasp something of the significance which should be assigned to this first public Western and modern presentation of the hidden teaching.

73

The needs of this age emphatically demand action in the outer world. Quite a few people of talent, position, vision, or influence have adopted these views, and will take their place in the forefront of things when the destined hour of the New Age sweeps down.

74

So many today are busy studying the ancient and medieval systems of mysticism that it might be prudent to pause for a moment and consider whether we, today, in the altered conditions under which we now live, do not need a more timely formulation of mystical practice and theory and training—something which still keeps what really matters and what really *must* matter in all such systems, but discards the accretions, the non-essentials, the obsolete, and which even invents new forms to suit the modern demands upon us.

75

The correct attitude is neither anti-Indian nor pro-Western. It is universalist. It considers that both cultures have valuable contributions to make. But it also considers that the time is ripe for a thoroughly universal attitude which refuses to identify itself with either of these two standpoints but rather takes a third which is superior to both, because creatively formed to suit the new present-day needs.

76

In the days when racial cultures were isolated from each other, a world-wide synthesis of mystical teachings was impossible.

77

The time has come for creative rather than interpretative endeavour, for something appropriate to the twentieth century and shaped to the lives of modern peoples.

78

It is well attuned to the twentieth century for it reflects the individualization of human thinking which is one immediate goal which confronts the race now.

79

To stand aside from the general movement of world thought and to decry the great intellectual trends of today, is folly; to utilize it for the furtherance of enduring aims and to ally ourselves with modern culture, is wisdom.

80

No reasonable being will now prefer to accept vague uncertainty to solid certitude. Modern scientific outlook is rightly impatient of contentions which cannot be upheld with any show of fact. The sciences have now placed at the disposal of philosophy so much valuable material that the era of superstitious belief need never return.

81

The esoteric tradition has come down to its present state of shreds and patches but even so it is of the utmost value to the seeker after truth. The eighteenth and nineteenth centuries produced situations and created circumstances which began to force its disclosure. The twentieth century has continued this activity and yielded new materials.

82

From being not even a name to the masses, from being either a chimera or an enigma to those for whom it is a name, philosophy will become a respected fact, even though its practice will, as always, be a matter for the few.

83

The studies in comparative religion, the research in the psychology of religious experience, the implications of atomic physics—all these are bringing in a new atmosphere, wherein truth becomes clearer.

84

Beliefs which suited the days when men lived in a forest clearing will not suit the days when he lives in a scientific civilization. Consequently the hidden teaching, which in former times would have dashed in vain against the mass dullness, may now make a remarkable impact on the group of matured minds.

85

To expect a complete and world-wide acceptance of such an advanced teaching is to expect the impossible, for there are great gaps in comprehension and fitness between the simple and the elite. But the vast spread of education and the hunger for knowledge have created larger audiences who want to move forward more quickly.

86

Medieval or Oriental mystical statements which are quite true but which fail to move us today will lose nothing if their essence is put into topical terms.

87

When history has given our own times their proper perspective, the re-entry of philosophy into its rightful place in human thinking, and especially of its picture of the evolutionary World-Idea, will take its place along with such far-reaching innovations as jet propulsion.

88

With the coming of this twentieth century, scientific thought has moved up startlingly near to philosophical metaphysics, while popular thought is really less distant from philosophical religion than it appears to be.

89

The ideology of such an advanced philosophy cannot be successfully and quickly spread by lip or pen. It can spread slowly but steadily by the force of evolutionary experience alone. Men must *grow* into its acceptance; they cannot be converted. Such has hitherto been the historic generalization. But the twentieth century is outstanding for the rushing tempo of its ideological development. We may rightly expect therefore that more are ready for this philosophy than ever before.

90

These ideas are not really new, but they have been half-forgotten or wholly overlooked. Anyway, the time is ripe to restate them. But they must be restated with electrical sparkle and spring freshness. The old forms simply will not suit us.

91

The age permits and demands heterodox independent thought given out with courageous frankness. It has forced us to face repressed or half-repressed thoughts and instincts and, so to speak, we have to come to terms with them. It has seen through the hollow mummery of much so-called religion.

92

Long-revealed truths that have only a feeble influence must be reaffirmed by inspired individuals or proven by scientific ones. Poets must celebrate them anew and religionists fit them into their credos.

93

Modern civilization must unite somehow the hitherto non-mixable currents of scientific thinking and social action on the one hand with the mystical and individual path of self-development on the other.

94

Philosophy may be—indeed must be—written afresh for every fresh generation but its principles are imperishable. They cannot change. Only the methods of expounding them, only the phraseology of expressing them can change.

95

It is not enough to preserve this old knowledge; we must also promote its adaptation to the new science.

96

Insofar as it is possible to do so, why not put some of this traditional knowledge in a modern dress? And why not let it be enriched by culture, by art, even by science, so long as its great truths remain untouched and unharmed? Finally, why not humanize its practical disciplines and ethical demands, in particular its required sacrifices and worldly renunciations, and thus learn to look on them as they were among the wiser Greeks—*trainings* to make perceptions clearer and reactions healthier so that the mind serves truth and the animal existence is kept in its place?

97

Each people must find its own meaning for its own self in these teachings to suit its own conditions and experiences. None can alter the essentials which are firmly fixed, but the way in which they are presented can, and usually must, be reshaped by those conditions and experiences when the old form is obviously no longer appropriate to its changed needs.

98

It would be a miscomprehension to believe that because we say that a modern version of philosophy must rest on science, we mean that science *alone* is to be its foundation. That would be quite wrong. For it must not, need not, and cannot desert its other traditional bases such as mysticism, religion, art, and the teaching of bygone sages.

99

The truths which were known by Lao Tzu, Buddha, and Jesus are still valid in the conditions of today—which are so different—otherwise they would not be true. But the form of expressing them may well be different.

100

The essential truth of things being always the same, its restatements can never alter, its principles never become obsolete, its revelations never become false. Nevertheless, the presentation of truth must be evolutionary in its development if it is to keep pace with the development of human mentality.

101

The ideological presentation of the teaching will become more complex as the human mind evolves and as human knowledge itself becomes more complex.

102

Philosophy can give nothing original to the present-day world, but it can make alive for, and usable by, the world, truths which were faded through neglect or even discarded through ignorance.

103

We do not claim that an entirely new teaching has been given to the world. But we do claim that a teaching and a praxis which we found in a primitive antique form have been brought up-to-date and given a scientific modern expression, that some parts of it which were formerly half-hidden, and others wholly so, have been completely revealed and made accessible to everyone who cares for such things.(P)

104

We do not claim finality in the absolute sense for this exposition. History holds in her bag many "latest" forms of philosophy but no "last" form.

105

So long as human minds are active in this search, so long will it be true that the last word has not been spoken or written. Nor ever will it be until thinking comes to an end, the silence is entered, and being replaces it.

106

The wider intellectual awareness of modern man cannot comfortably accept teachings based on narrower awareness of ancient man. Yet those teachings were fundamentally correct, because both teacher and taught were closer to the heart of Nature. Moreover, because they were not so intellectually extroverted, they were closer to faith in God.

107

These are old truths but there is a need of making them vivid to the feeling and reasonable to the mind of twentieth-century man.

108

There are no schools in the higher philosophy because there are no speculations. It is not truer today than it was in Greek times for it is not the result of an evolutionary process.

109

Since, in the field of basic spiritual teaching, as those who have made a comparative study of it well know, there is nothing new at any time, we may only expect nothing more startling than new teachers. Let us not criticize the staleness of their revelations, but rather welcome the newness of these revelators. For each, being a different personality, set apart from all the others, necessarily individualizes what he brings us, making its form different from the form of all offerings that have come before his; it is an expression of his own unique self.

110

Truth can speak afresh; its terminology need not copy itself again and again: indeed if it is truly creative and inspired it could not do so.

111

There is room to bring a fresh understanding, a free original approach, and a personal realization of philosophy, and thus see the teaching for oneself.

112

Even if we do borrow as much wisdom as we can find from antiquity, we should not—when bringing it forward—forget or mistake the time in which we live, and, if possible, we should bring the old to cohere with the new. If this is not possible, accept the best wisdom.

113

Old teachings may have to be formulated afresh to meet new conditions. This can be done by honest, unself-seeking, unbiased persons, without any disloyalty to the teachings.

114

We cannot modernize truth: it would be senseless and futile to try to do so. It would also be an insult to ancient sages. But reinterpret—yes!

Whom it best serves

115

There are some who, by reason of innate tendencies acquired from previous existences, can find their way to spiritual peace only through Oriental paths, especially Indian ones. This is understandable and ought to be respected except when it becomes an unreasonable and unbalanced adulation. But there are others who, although largely interested in and greatly attracted by Oriental mysticism, perceive nevertheless that a more universal attitude is safer and better, and who perceive in such independence a closer approximation to the liberating effect of truth. Philosophy is for them.

116

Philosophy's daring religious concepts attract the young while its reflective metaphysical ones attract the middle-aged and elderly.

117

The number of those who devote themselves to philosophic thought and practice is not a significant one. It is indeed quite a small one. But as life on this earth will get more and more intolerable (as it is doing in this twentieth century), people will get more and more to realize that there is something wrong or lacking in the faith by which they live—be it faith in simple materialism or in orthodox religion. After they have thus started a'questioning some of them will pass to the ultimate stage and go a'questing. In the end they will arrive at philosophy because all other teachings are merely on the approach to it. In the end the number of its votaries will continually increase. But they will not, say within the next thousand years, be in any danger of becoming quite a crowd. They shall have to go on living in loneliness. They will remain a tiny minority, with the satisfaction of being less tiny than it is now. The only choice which is usually presented to us is a vicious and false one. We are asked to choose between materialism and orthodox religion, thus dividing us into the supposition that these are the only possible spiritual views which mankind can adopt. This supposition is an unjustified one. We are moving beyond them. We are no longer limited to such a narrow choice. There is a third road open to us—that of the philosophic view. Out of the clash between two such opposite attitudes, there has been born for independent thinkers a third attitude which is truer than both.

118

Philosophy is for those who feel this desire to understand spiritual processes and find the study quite interesting.

119

Such abstract mystical or metaphysical thinking is a luxury which only those who have income-producing property or funds can afford: this is a statement often heard but seldom questioned. It is one of those statements which, because they are partly true and partly false, require closer examination than others.

120

The theory of philosophy is suited and available to everyone who has the intelligence to grasp it, the faith to accept it, the intuition to recognize its supreme pre-eminence. The practice of philosophy is more restricted, being for those who have been sufficiently prepared by previous inner growth and outer experience to be willing to impose its higher ethical standards, mental training, and emotional discipline upon themselves. To come unprepared for the individual effort demanded, unfit for the intellectual and meditational exertions needed, unready for the teacher or the teaching, is to find bewilderment and to leave disappointed. A premature attempt to enter the school of philosophy will meet with the painful revelation of the dismaying shortcomings within oneself, which must be remedied before the attempt can be successful.(P)

121

Philosophy is for those who do not find enough nourishment in orthodox religion yet shrink from the emptiness of orthodox atheism as well as from the silliness of unbalanced mysticism; it is for those who have felt in the presence of Nature's grandeur or beauty intimations of a higher life and remembered the momentary exaltations induced by art, literature, or deep repose, and who aspire to further and more prolonged contact with that kind of life.

122

One may come under the influence of philosophy through intellectual conviction, emotional expansion, or intuitional cultivation, through mystical ecstasy or deep suffering.

123

It is a teaching for the person of large mind and larger heart, who is no longer satisfied with creeds or systems that are only fragmentarily true.

124

Philosophy is not a physically-organized sect but a movement of thought. It is for those who insist on finding a relationship with God through their own experience.

125

Philosophy is for those who are not satisfied with hearing an echo of echoes but who want the music of heaven directly.

126

Philosophy is for those who prefer to face realities free of myths, veils, and distortions; who prefer to be mentally mature and want to understand life as it is and not make a pretense of what it is not. Hence ideas which religion presents under thick incrustations of mythopoetic pictures, philosophy explains by rational thinking which leads later to intuitive understanding.

127

A man is not usually ready for the wisdom of philosophy until years of faith and its disappointment, hope and its frustration, desire and its satisfaction, culture and its ripening, and most of the phases which richness of experience brings with it form the mind to receive such a revelation. The middle-aged appreciate it more than the young. This does not necessarily mean, however, that all the young are barred from it. Some may have gone through these phases in former reincarnations so completely as to be well enough prepared. Even so, Nature usually sets the age of thirty or thereabouts as *her* requirement for initiation into philosophy.

128

The adherents to philosophy become so by virtue of accepting its teachings, following its practices, and cherishing its ideals. There exists no organization which they could join, no order of which they could become members. For the philosophic way is a solitary one and its traveller must venture it alone with his higher self.

129

One does not come into philosophy by horizontal conversion, as with religious and mystical changes of allegiance, but by upward progression. Philosophy takes no one away from any other organization for the simple reason that it is only for those who have seen through the limitations and have exhausted the usefulness of all organizations.

130

If a life of inward beauty and emotional serenity appeals to a man, he is ready for philosophy.

131

As said in *The Hidden Teaching Beyond Yoga*, such a teaching will at first appeal to the more educated persons and only later filter down to the less educated masses who will take from it what they can or what is of more interest to them. Whoever feels a need for some clue to life's meaning can satisfy it by philosophy whatever class he belongs to.

132

It is for those only who are searching for a clear light that, while revealing the inner meaning of their own life, will not obstruct the free exercise of their reasoning mind. It is for those who are busily engaged in the world's work yet feel and must satisfy a hunger for truth, a need of peace, and an aspiration toward the Overself.

133

Truth is for those who keep their minds at least free and independent, whatever they may have to do through the compulsion of circumstances in the outer world.

134

Those who cannot assimilate themselves with the materialistic civilization of today but who cannot turn back to the self-deception of orthodox religion or go forward into the fantasies of contemporary mysticism, will be able to find no refuge except in philosophy.

135

Its appeal is to those who, already religious, are looking for greater depths to their present belief and to those who, now unreligious, are looking for something more positive than scepticism, yet still based on reason and experience.

136

Philosophy is for those who seek to look well below the surface of existence; it is not for the shallow or the complacent; their egos could not bear the implacable truth which such deep search reveals.

137

Only the matured and prepared can gain the most from philosophy: the pathological and criminal, the unbalanced and disturbed can get more *of what they need* by looking elsewhere.

138

It is emotion which is the real and effective cause of conversion from one religion or non-religion to another, but it is inner growth which brings anyone to philosophy.

139

Philosophy, with such serious aims, cannot expect discriminative appreciation from those who are ever ready to pronounce judgement freely on stupendous subjects which divide studious thinkers all over the world, nor can it be useful to the light-minded who, over a cup of tea, dispose permanently of the fate of philosophical problems which have baffled the intelligentsia for centuries.

140

Whoever has felt in his own experience the awakening of mind, hope, perception, and faith may be ready to learn a little more about philosophy.

141

The religio-mystical-emotional occult-imaginative approach is for tense frustrated neurotics, whereas philosophy is for sensible sane people who have some hold of themselves and who don't forget the realities.

142

The undiscriminating multitude are usually satisfied with orthodox religion; the more sensitive need mysticism, but only the intelligent and determined handful want TRUTH, cost what it may. Such alone will be willing to make the effort needed to comprehend the higher message contained in the book.

143

If embittered heretics in orthodox religion and frustrated sufferers in personal life come to philosophy for negative reasons, hopeful seekers after truth and intelligent appraisers of value come to it for positive ones.

144

It is not just for academic students—although they, as human beings equipped with minds, need it too—but for all life-meaning students, all truth-seekers, all would-be reality-experiencers.

145

Philosophy offers itself to men of the world, although monks may take to it if they wish. It ends in inspired action, not in dull reverie.

146

If there is any future for a teaching it belongs to the present one. It does not have to stand on the defensive just as it does not have to use loud-speaking propagandists. Its existence is justified by humanity's essential need of knowing what it is, what the world is, and what to make of its own life. If humanity finds such needs satisfied by its orthodox religions, mysticisms, and metaphysics—why then, that is as it should be. For only when it has tried and tested them all, only when it has noted their insufficiencies and failures, only when its own mind and heart have adequately matured is it likely to appreciate our teaching. The great intellectual width of this teaching, the grand compassion which it inculcates, and the sane balance which it advocates must commend it to those enquiring minds who not only seek but are ready for the best.

147

Philosophy is simply mysticism grown up and become fully mature. The completeness and sanity of its tenets commend themselves therefore to the proficient rather than the novice.

148

The philosophic world-view will be satisfactory to those few only who do not scorn mysticism because they esteem science and who do not scorn science because they esteem mysticism.

149

At whatever point in the world of human knowledge we start from, if we push our investigation deeply enough, and if we try to correlate it with the general body of knowledge, we shall be brought to the consideration of philosophy.

150

Philosophy is not for those to whom the search for Truth does not appeal. It is not for those to whom worship is merely a conventional and respectable act. It is not for those to whom the aspiration for self-improvement is an unprofitable enterprise. It is not for those who are afraid to depart along little-travelled tracks or thoughts, thereby risking the label of being eccentric or peculiar.

151

The educated classes are expected to stand in the forefront of this struggle for world-enlightenment and therefore it is for the more thoughtful among them to absorb the hidden teaching.

152

The man who is intellectually ripe and morally ready for philosophy's explanations will not be able to hold out against them, provided he examines them carefully.

153

Philosophy does not have to defend itself, nor even to explain itself. It is only for those who have grown and grown until they are ready for it. They will appreciate its worth and perceive its truth without argument.

154

Those who like to be just and tolerant will appreciate the perfect fairness with which philosophy regards every view, doctrine, and belief.

155

H.G. Wells believed, and I agree with him, that few human beings are adult before the age of thirty-five, and it must be remembered that philosophy is a study for the mentally mature adult. Also philosophy is a study for the mentally strong, and the common and agreeable notion that lunatics constitute only a small part of the population is not confirmed by recent history.

156

Philosophy draws some of its students from the orthodox religionists but more from the unorthodox and the irreligious.

157

Beginners who feel they need a standpoint, a guru, and a group to provide support, guidance, comfort, and instruction may or may not profit by them. They will then find the independence of philosophy less attractive.

158

There are cults for all human varieties, for the infantile emotions, for the adolescent ego, for the adult animal. The developed human, who outgrows such pabulum and needs something for a higher intelligence and higher character, will inevitably and naturally look elsewhere—in science, art, literature, music, and mysticism. In the end, when he is ready for it, he will recognize the worth of a fuller philosophy and let the Overself take over.

159

Philosophy is not for fools, not for those who prefer the appearance of things to their reality.

160

The interest in philosophy develops out of different motives. The need of finding inner peace is one man's motive; the wish to understand life is another's.

161

Religion (and to a lesser extent mysticism) is for troubled persons, deprived persons, helping them bear their destiny. Philosophy does the same but is primarily for truth-searchers, as is mysticism to a lesser extent.

162

They come to philosophy when they have exhausted other sources, paths, and directions, only when their search is prolonged enough and intelligent enough to show, with time, that the truth is not findable elsewhere.

163

Philosophy is not for kindergarten minds: therefore it cannot offer the spurious solace of mere phrases nor substitute the imaginary for the real.

164

This teaching will only be of interest to those who have long felt an aspiration towards higher-than-ordinary experience.

165

Philosophy will have little interest for those who are eager only for animal satisfactions and human selfishnesses. It is for more evolved types, who understand that a higher life is possible and worth working for.

166

Those who are looking for emotional or occult thrills may find the philosophic way too dull or too barren, perhaps even too demanding. But what they are seeking is not the same as the living presence of the Spirit.

167

There is no room on the philosophic path for self-deceptions, no space in the philosophic mind for illusions. Those who want them—and they are many—soon turn away from the sharp disciplines which are so destructive of these enemies of truth.

168

The sanity and balance, the inspiration and practicality of philosophy commend it to those select individuals who are seeking a mode of thought and a way of life suited to a century which is both the heir of such a long stretch of human striving and the parent of a new cycle of human history.

Some esotericism is still unavoidable

169

It is a gross error to believe that this knowledge is reserved by the Higher

Power for an elect few. It is reserved by people themselves by their own lack of interest in the subject, lack of willingness to submit to the necessary self-discipline, or inability to meet the qualifications for the work and study involved.

170

The mystic would gladly give all that he has gained to all whom he meets, gladly share his revelations and his ecstasies with all beings; but he soon finds that the minds and hearts and wills of others are totally unprepared to receive what he would like to give, and so he soon retreats after painful experiences. In short, he does not have to form or join any esoteric cult. Esotericism is imposed upon him by the facts of human nature.

171

If it be true that the hour is ripe to unveil the tenets of philosophic mysticism to many people, it is also true that this unveiling must be cautiously, discriminatingly, and guardedly done.

172

The teaching was mantled in secrecy not as an anti-democratic device to preserve it for the exclusive benefit of the ruling classes—although that is how it worked out in practice—but as a necessity forced upon its custodians by a realization of the limitations on the mind of the multitude.

173

A teaching so rarefied that it can engage the interest of only one person in several thousands, and a practice so rigorous that it makes the extinction of egoism an indispensable condition of attaining truth—these two factors alone without the others, like ever present persecution by official established orthodoxy, would explain why the teachers shrouded themselves in secrecy.

174

If formerly the hidden teaching was kept strictly secret, there were excellent reasons for this prohibition. But today these reasons have lost a part of their validity. Therefore a part of the ban has been broken and some of it revealed, but not the most important part. This latter remains as before, to be communicated only orally and only privately to the tested few.

175

The reader will naturally ask why, if the higher wisdom is of such importance to mankind, it has not been made generally available for the benefit of mankind. I can reply only that this knowledge has been rarely attained and even then more frequently in remote lands than in Europe or America and more frequently in antiquity than during modern times. Whenever it has been alluded to and wherever it has been written about, it has been generally expressed in language which was either cryptic or obscure, or in terminology which was either symbolic or technical. Consequently even those statements of it which have appeared in book, Bible, or palm-leaf text have been largely misunderstood where they were not completely ignored. Moreover, there was always the overt or open antagonism of religious heads who feared for their own influence or power. However, the rapid advances made by science mysticism and philosophy in our own generation betoken possibilities of a brighter welcome for the advent of truth. These advances encourage hope for a wider friendlier reception.

176

Few have fully grasped the nature of these ideas and fewer still have thought out their full implications.

177

If people are so determined to become the victims of their own egos that no words, no sage counsel, can stop them, there is no other course left except to leave them to suffer the consequences of their actions and thus learn the hard way.

178

Philosophy is an exclusive cult not by its own choice, but by the compulsion of circumstances.

179

It is only a few who can comprehend the far-reaching significance of this teaching. They alone will remain utterly loyal to it.

180

The need for secrecy must be treated with respect. It does not mean that the truth is to be suppressed for all time or for all men. It means that one must not speak of it to men whose mentality cannot receive it or whose character cannot be touched by it. It means that one ought not to put forward ideas whose ultimate destiny will be the same as their immediate one—to be resisted or rejected.

181

However useful religion is for the masses, it does not speak very clearly to the few who want the Truth and nothing but the Truth. From the small number of seekers interested in these teachings it is obvious that more than three-quarters of the people are not ready for philosophy.

182

We have also to remember that every light throws a shadow, that the light of truth is opposed by the adverse element in Nature, that it finds its first barricade against the enemy in the curtain of complete secrecy with which it must be kept shrouded. The hostile forces of ignorance jealousy hatred and malice have to be fought by such secrecy. The task before the sages of keeping truth alive is too important and the opposition to it too strong to permit us to expose it unnecessarily to the danger of failure through the defection of traitors, the indiscretions of fools, and the babbling of gossips.

183

All seekers inevitably gravitate to the kind of teaching that suits their grade; the better the stuff they are made of, the better the quality of teaching they are likely to accept. Thus their different spiritual requirements are provided for, and thus we find in existence a medley of cults and a variety of sects. Nine-carat truth may hope to achieve some popularity, but twenty-four carat may not. Consequently philosophy does not lend itself to propaganda and can have no large-scale appeal. Its expectation of finding students will necessarily be qualified by its realization of limited appeal. It is too tough for the multitude, too subtle for the prosaic, too remote for those preoccupied wholly with personal cares and fears. It must perforce remain to a considerable extent an esoteric doctrine to be communicated only to those who have first made themselves fit to receive it by maturing their intelligence and disciplining their character. Hence it is not enough to be a seeker. That by itself does not entitle anyone to initiation into the highest truth. He must also be fit to receive it. Such a select few will be completely outnumbered by the gross multitude. We must thrust wishful thinking aside and resignedly accept this bare fact.

184

Frank Lloyd Wright, the distinguished architect, says that when a true master in the arts appears, he is at first suspected, then he is denied and ridiculed. "Genius is a sin again the mob," Wright adds. How often is this tragic situation true in public activities of spiritual pioneers.

185

The willingness to communicate spiritual knowledge is conditioned by how much or how little desire there is for it, by the presence or absence of the passive receptivity of it, and by the degree of development in the receiving person.

186

The real bar to access to this knowledge is put up by people themselves, by their lack of intelligence or intuition, or by their unmovable attachment to selfishness or sensuality. The actuality of reincarnation makes nonsense of the assertion that all persons ought to be given truth, all the truth; for it shows that not all are fit or prepared to receive the entire truth.

187

The custodians of esoteric truth do not pursue a spendthrift policy. They do not give it away indiscriminately. They are not satisfied with its value being recognized by few people outside themselves. But there is nothing much they can do about it. The upward development of mankind can no more be forced than can the upward growth of an oak tree.

188

It was written in the opening pages of *The Hidden Teaching Beyond Yoga* that the higher truth would be proclaimed in our era more publicly than in the past. This was misread to mean that every esoteric piece of knowledge would be proclaimed. This is not what was meant. The whole truth cannot be given to the whole of mankind. This is because of possible breakdowns in religious relations or misunderstandings in moral connections. But much larger portions can now safely be revealed, or traditional teaching translated, with only the most necessary restraints.

189

Although more men are ready to receive it than ever before, philosophy's time has not yet come. There is still only a tiny minority which can recognize its truth, appreciate its worth, and practise its ethic.

190

The truth should be told to all mankind, but we know well enough that all mankind will not care to listen. Idealism must be balanced by realistic sense.

191

It must be said that in these days and under the modern sky, the medieval obsession with secrecy no longer applies, except as regards certain knowledge which could be misused by those who lack scruples.

192

The higher truths are not necessarily too hard to explain to most people; however, most people are either unfit for them or uninterested in them. Why wonder if some enlightened man withheld part of what he knew at a certain level or time?

193

It would be a lunatic's dream to look forward to a widespread favourable result of our humble effort at making these teachings more readily available than in the past. We shall respect our responsibilities and opportunities in this matter and not betray them. But at the same time we shall insist on seeing things as they are and shall recognize that only a select few are already attuned to receive such ideas. The others will have to be taught, slow step by slow step, by life and time.

194

Few are willing to look at the face of truth; illusion is more attractive. Most see only what they want to see; thus their minds remain shut and undisturbed.

195

Philosophy by its very nature can only appeal to the adult intelligences among us. And, unfortunately, the possession of an adult body does not give a man the possession of an adult intelligence.

196

It will not appeal to the cynical and supercilious intelligentsia asking for harsh realities nor to the pious and sentimental religionists asking only for soothing syrup.

197

The labouring classes have seldom been allowed, owing to the conditions under which they have laboured and lived, to gain the emotional detachment, the physical leisure, and the intellectual reflectiveness which philosophy requires.

198

If these truths prove arrestive to some minds, even dazzling in their effect, they stir no interest at all in other minds, for there are varying degrees of inner ripeness.

199

If it is too far above people's heads, or too idealistic in its demands, it may not be suitable for general publication. To present truth to those not yet ready for it is largely to waste it.

200

Its truth sears the ego like a red-hot iron. Hence philosophy repels men.

201

It is too subtle for popular appeal, too selfless for popular emotion, too honest for popular thought.

202

A strong minority is bitterly opposed to this teaching, the great majority of people are both ignorant of and indifferent towards it, while only a few eagerly adopt it.

203

A few men, gifted with deep insight, have attained this knowledge and guard it closely. They fear more harm than good would be done by revealing it to the unready and unprepared masses. So they cautiously keep this property a secret. Only the candidate who proves his character and fitness by long probation is taught.

204

It is not to be expected that the hidden teaching, which has been the accepted thought of the world's master minds, can quickly become the accepted thought of inferior minds.

205

It is a firm conviction with the adepts that it is better to have two or three in a community who are earnestly and indefatigably striving to conquer their lower selves and unite with their higher selves than to have two or three thousand public followers who are largely nominal only. They are interested in, and appreciative of, quality rather than quantity. Nor do they consider it sensible to propagate their wisdom among men whose minds are too undeveloped, whose intuition is too uncultivated, and whose hearts are too unprepared to receive it readily and sympathetically.

206

Those who come out publicly to help mankind free itself from false ideas sustained by selfish vested interest, or who give out teachings which dissipate the ignorance sustained by powerful forces that are insensitive to the Spirit's voice, may earn the gratitude of some people but may have a penalty inflicted on them by these others.

207

To explain philosophy and advocate its doctrines to those who are unready for and unsympathetic toward it is to commit a kind of desecration.

208

It is useless to talk of these higher matters to those who are not even wishful to reform their character and reorient their tendencies. The result would not only be either incomprehension or miscomprehension, but also antagonism.

209

The ethical qualifications needed for this study are lofty; the intellectual attainments required for it are high. These and these only constitute the reasons why it has been in a closed circle, because few have been those fit enough or who cared enough for it.

210

It is unwise for the adepts and unhelpful to the masses to place advanced truths in the latter's unprepared hands when they have not mastered the elementary ones.

211

So many seekers are looking for occult "experiences," so few are looking for the understanding of truth, that philosophy could not, on this ground alone, become popular.

212

Philosophy is for the few. This is and must be so for several reasons. Its way of disciplined living is hard, its rejection of false emotional solaces is unpopular, its search for factual reality rather than personal fancy is bothersome.

213

The belief that if people can be taught truth they will respond to it spontaneously collides with the facts.

214

To believe that truth should be confined to a few is a belief that may easily be misunderstood and therefore unjustly criticized.

215

The mastery of any subject moves through a series of steps and the higher the step the fewer the number of those capable of understanding it.

216

He would be a foolish man indeed who let the unready take the time he could put into more fruitful service.

217

The philosopher hopes to educate the mind and train the temperament only of his disciples, for with them he needs the minimum of energy and effort. If he were to set out to educate and train the masses, both he and they would be dead before much could be done.

218

It is as hard to get a brutal, materialistic egotist to understand and accept philosophy as it is to get an uneducated, illiterate, and semi-savage Amazon forest-native to understand and accept the quantum theory.

219

Great truths and small minds go ill together.

220

The loftier standards of the philosopher—which apply as much to his eating as to his thinking—are enough to keep most people out of philosophy.

221

Is the world ripe for such a single all-enclosing system? We must ruefully answer that it is not although it ought to be.

222

Philosophy finds its opposition from the bigoted sectarian on the one hand, and the sense-bound materialist on the other.

223

Most men are more body than mind, a few more mind than body. Philosophy cannot, by its very nature, appeal to those in the first group and can only appeal to a limited number in the second one.

224

When we remember that a magnet repels as well as attracts, we may see how, and understand why, if philosophy draws to itself those mentally intuitively and morally equipped to accept it, it also leaves uninterested those not so equipped.

225

Philosophy does not look for any other results upon the contemporary world from its teaching than are to be expected from the inherent nature of the men in that world. It measures those expectations by cool, intelligent observation, not by wishful enthusiastic emotion.

226

Because we are a minority does not mean that we are to be a discouraged minority. We understand the very good reasons why this must be so, and why it has always been so. We have set our standards and we must serenely accept the consequences.

227

When a man finds out the truth about philosophy, he cannot help becoming its friend; if he is strong enough, he cannot help becoming its follower. But since the facts which lead to recognition of its truth must be personally experienced, and this is not easily come by, few are its friends, fewer still its followers.

228

While he is driven by sensual instincts, unpractised and unwilling to control them, the disciplines of philosophy would alone drive him away. Add the deep level on which its studies are conducted, and his complete indifference to such teachings is explained.

229

Small sectarian minds are not confined to religion: they appear in mystical circles too. But in the large free air of philosophy, they feel uneasy, uncomfortable, and soon retreat.

230

If there is any concealment in his attitude, then it is called for both by the needs of his personal situation in a non-comprehending community and by the sacredness in which he holds philosophy.

231

A certain statement by Lao Tzu might have the salutary effect of a cold bath, metaphorically, on certain naïve people who do not know the difference between religio-mysticism and philosophical mysticism. He said, "If the Tao could be offered to men, there is no one who would not willingly offer it; if it could be handed down to men, who would not wish to transmit it to his children?"

232

If much has been given out, much has also been kept back.

233

Those sunk in paralysing vices or stupefied by the glare of modern commercialism will regard it as something to scoff at, if not to scorn.

234

The program for spiritualizing life which it offers could be carried out only by a small number of people who are endowed by nature with the right temperament and by fortune with the right circumstances for it.

235

It would doubtless be pleasant to congratulate ourselves that men and women are to be found today attracted to reading these books, ready to attend these lectures, and willing to practise these exercises. But the same situation existed in the closing years of Rome. It is necessary to contrast the number of those who feel these impulses with the number of those who do not. It will be found that the difference is too wide to allow any complacency. It is also necessary to examine and measure the depth of this interest. Here too we shall find that much of it is too shallow to allow any illusions, an intellectual playing with what ought to be seriously held things.

236

There is this about philosophy which could be frightening to those unready for it—which means most persons. It is the complete impersonality which it commends in its practice and demands in its learning.

237

They think there is something inhuman in being impersonal.

238

Even many of those who have had the good fortune to come into contact with philosophy have either misunderstood it and so missed their opportunity, or neglected it because its disciplines seemed too troublesome.

239

There is no need to lament the fact that so few persons agree with our beliefs. So long as human beings continue to be born different from each other, so long must we expect them to hold different opinions. And when some of them have climbed into the rarefied atmosphere which philosophy breathes, their opinions will not only be different but also rare.

240

It is not a question of selfishly withholding truth, or of sentimentally sharing it, but of acting with wisdom.

Dangers to be recognized

241

The danger of misunderstanding this subtle teaching is not only the likelihood of going wrong metaphysically and psychologically, but also of going wrong morally.

242

Let us admit at once that in the hands of the unprepared and undisciplined and uninformed, the doctrine of "God in me" may prove dangerous to its follower. The danger is not in the doctrine itself, for it is a perfectly true one, but in him, in his conceit and lust. These may cause him to misapply the doctrine to suit the desires of his ego or the passions of his body. They may give him false licence under the pretext that he is expressing unbridled the authentic freedom of Spirit when, in fact, he is expressing the freedom of an animal. Thus truth can be misapplied distorted or caricatured by its supposed friends.

243

Unless a man has the requisite mental ability and moral inclination to benefit by philosophical study, it is useless to offer it to him. The masters therefore seek to restrict their personal tuition to those who are fit to embark on a course of philosophy. The mentally immature, the experientially ill-equipped, and the emotionally unfit people will only be bewildered by or rendered antagonistic by such an offering. The standards must be maintained and enforced if philosophy is not to degenerate, as it has so often done in the past, into scholasticism or mysticism.

244

Although systematic concealment of its doctrines has been abandoned, some items of practical knowledge are still withheld because of the danger of their misuse for evil ends.

245

The danger is of a fall into psychism, mediumship, sorcery, and black magic—above all the danger of stimulating the personal ego—which accompanies the abuse and misuse of mystical knowledge by those unready or unworthy of it. It was awareness of these dangers both by the official heads of certain religions and by its solitary adepts which kept mysticism a secret hidden and guarded from the public for centuries and left them with the relatively harmless dogmas and theatrical parades of public religion. But continued silence would have been even worse than these evils while the waves of materialistic belief washed over humanity. Because humanity has been losing its religious faith and growing worse in its moral character, even though it has been gaining in technical skill and scientific knowledge, much knowledge has been given out that was formerly kept esoteric. The practical teachings about meditation especially have been given out for the benefit of those intuitive enough to heed them.

246

Why do not those who know the higher mystical truths give more generously from their store of knowledge? They do not withhold it from anyone who is ripe to receive it. The others who are still unripe could not benefit by it because they would not understand it or, understanding, would be shocked and frightened by its terrifying impersonality. Nor is this all. The old saying, "Knowledge is power," applies here also. Knowledge of the dynamic forces and subconscious operations of the human mind can easily be abused by ignorant persons or misused by selfish ones. Because, through the soul, we are linked with God, something of the creative magic of the divine comes into possession of a man with the knowledge of certain truths concerning the soul. It would be as dangerous to give this knowledge to unprepared and unpurified masses as it would be to give a box of dynamite to a child as a plaything. The history of the destruction of Atlantis, and of another continent which preceded it, is in part the history of the premature use by humanity of forces which it is not morally entitled to use. Our own civilization today is faced by a related danger unless humanity stops looking for guidance and salvation in the wrong direction; unless the blind following of blind leaders comes to an end, the major portion of civilization will come to an end and this planet will be largely depopulated. Those who seek protection from God against this menace of the future will find it only as they come into harmony with God or insofar as they entrust themselves to the guidance of leaders who have come into that harmony. Those who protest against these impending terrors, or pray to be saved from them, are alike walking in ignorance. Nature, which is God Active, governs man by her own laws, which bring him the results of his own doing.

247

Ordinarily it has been assumed that if philosophy in its fullness is taught too soon, the results will be as bad as if the teaching were delayed too long. It has long been the custom to wait until a person is ready for it, otherwise he will receive it incorrectly, misuse its practices, and drop his moral values.

248

The moral dangers resulting from a promiscuous dissemination of philosophy, the confusion of public ethics arising from its indiscriminate advocacy, were other reasons which kept its custodians from revealing it to the masses, from all whose minds were still immature and whose characters were not sufficiently formed. For such people tend to make it a support for their own weaknesses and a pretense for their own sins. Its idea of the relativity of morality would be taken advantage of for immoral ends. Since philosophy advocates a far higher ethic than is commonly followed, how great would be the horror of its custodians at such a lamentable result? Since it advocates the highest kind of personal responsibility for one's actions, how great would be their consternation at the personal irresponsibility which might be shown by those who could only pick up one or two of its truths at best, and that without rightly understanding them? The extreme effect of the highest revelations upon the lowest mind was seen in cases like that secret fraternity of the "Assassins" whom the Crusaders discovered in the Near East, a fraternity of insane and criminal mystics whose motto was "Nothing is true: everything is permitted."

249

No philosopher will go out of his way to deprive others of a faith which is important to their life or destroy their trust in the teaching of a religion which gives them moral support. To do so would be to harm them, and weaken their higher purposes: it would lead directly to cynicism or materialism or even despair.

250

The deeper truths of philosophy are idol-smashing, and that reason, among others, has rendered it advisable to keep them hidden away like the most precious gems. To the undeveloped, unprepared mind they are at least disturbing, at most, alarming.

251

The bare naked truth—whether it be that of man's essential loneliness or of matter's essential emptiness—would, if suddenly and bluntly revealed, only frighten those who are unready for it.

252

There is danger for the unprepared in philosophy. Being out of their depth intellectually, emotionally, and morally might upset their faith and create uncertainties, doubts, uneasiness. They might then withdraw altogether. They might then flee for refuge back to the simpler creed, or accept conversion to another kind of exoteric religion, or become total sceptics.

253

It would be of little use to take such a teaching as mentalism to the masses, for it would make them feel out of their depth intellectually.

254

For to teach the masses that the world of their experiences is only an idea, is to tell them something which may be easily misconstrued. It may then become a means of destroying their entire mental stability and of plunging their entire practical life into chaos.

255

These doctrines that the world is only an idea and that the personality is only a wave are likely to terrify the populace.

256

It is not only the needs of public religion and private safety which have compelled this secrecy about philosophy, not only its intellectual hardness and mystical subtlety. There have also been the dangers involved in its meditational exercises. These bring eventually the powers of a concentrated mind and of a concentrated dynamism to bear upon life. If selfishness or ambition, passion or desire, greed or appetite be strong and ungratified, then it is likely that these powers will be made to serve ignoble ends or, worse, to injure others in the process.

257

How many were those who, being unable to rise to the level from which Jesus spoke, were unable to understand him? He, a mystic, so far removed from interest in this world, was charged with political crime!

258

No hierophant will divulge his secret knowledge of the way to, or the working of, these powers to those who are likely to abuse them through weakness or wickedness.

259

Undeveloped minds, unintuitive hearts, or unevolved characters are not ready for truth. They can receive it only at the cost of reducing its largeness and sullying its purity.

260

So widespread is the intellectualization of the present generation that any mystical or religious teaching which presented falsehoods in smooth plausible logical and literate language could more easily find acceptance than one which presented truths in simple statements.

261

It is understandable why the medieval Talmudic scholars of southern France and their outstanding leaders prohibited anyone under the age of thirty from reading philosophy and metaphysics: they perceived the dangers to the young unfortified minds of falling into heresy or, worse, into atheism. As for the actual practice of mystical exercises, other European rabbis limited it to those who were over forty because of the mental perils, particularly madness, involved in it. The Godhead, "The Most Hidden of the Hidden" in the Hebrew phrase, is utterly beyond human reach.

262

Why was it believed so necessary in former times to keep so secret the true nature of the Godhead? Why did Hindu religious laws threaten the Brahmin priests with death if they revealed it, or punish the darker-skinned lower castes with burning oil poured into their ears for listening to any reading aloud of the holy books holding this and other revelations? Why were the Hebrews warned never to utter the real Name of God? Because the common mind would soon confound the philosophic conception of the Deity with the atheistic one, would destroy religion and substitute a soulless materialism for it. This fear, misapplied by selfish vested interests, led authority to poison Socrates, crucify Jesus, decapitate al-Hallaj, murder Hypatia, and put Molinos to rot and die in a prison dungeon. If caution counselled the survivors to refrain from telling the whole truth, there was sufficient justification. But times are now different. There is a ferment of questioning, discussion, experimentation, rebellion, seeking, writing, reading, and publishing in the religious world, weaker in some places, stronger in others.

263

The advocacy of truth in a truthless world is fraught with considerable danger. It must be done cautiously, discreetly, quietly, unobtrusively, and it must be limited only to those who are ready for it. Not only must it not be discussed with the unready—a futile self-deceptive procedure at best and a trouble-causing one too often—but they must definitely be avoided. Otherwise their hostility will sooner or later be aroused.

How philosophy presents itself

264

But when we say that philosophy must today make itself available to the public we do not mean obtrude itself upon the public. It is too conscious of the inequalities of character, intelligence, aspiration, and intuition to delude itself into the belief that it could ever become popular or attractive to the multitude.

265

The popularization of an esoteric doctrine has its dangers, as recent history has testified. But the maintenance of ignorance also has its dangers, which the same history corroborates. Is there a dilemma here? For clearly it is a disservice to throw immature mentalities into bewilderment by teaching what is beyond their grasp. But it is also a failure in service to keep quite silent. So the middle way must be taken: to tell neither everything nor nothing.

266

The wise man will not take other men as being better than they really are or more intelligent than their powers of understanding permit them to be. He will, on the contrary, take a scientific rather than a sentimental view, see clearly what precise possibilities they possess for immediate improvement of character and what ideas they can immediately grasp.

267

The incapacity of some persons to receive the teaching is illusory. The fault lies really in the inefficiency of those who present it—in their failure to make it clear enough, vivid enough, logical enough, to render it intelligible. And if it be true that there are those who come to the teaching with duller natural faculties than others, then they ought not be denied its benefits, as the Brahmins with their secrecy denied the lower castes in India, but given more help than the others and taught more skilfully.

268

Much depends on the way these teachings are presented. If the author understands them well enough and clearly enough, and if he has the gift of transmitting his understanding just as much, the reader will gain the benefit of this straight thinking. The mysteries involved in teachings will begin to vanish.

269

The great defect in the ancient Indian and medieval European writers on mysticism is that they failed to put their thoughts into the logical form of a scientific demonstration. They did not reason the matter out as the modern mind does, but began by taking a scriptural text and ended by writing a verse-by-verse commentary on that. And as scriptures themselves usually began and ended with a dogma, the modern reader does not know whether he is being led to truth or to its opposite. Philosophy fails if it fails to produce in us the powerful conviction that we are moving from fact to fact along a path of rigorous reasoned truth.

270

The multitude of seekers after happiness, which means in the end seekers after their own sacred source, live on widely different levels of understanding and exhibit very diverse kinds of character. Why then should the whole of truth be presented all at once at a single time straightway to all of them, the young and the mature alike? No, it must be revealed gradually and slowly or, if abruptly, by stages.

271

The teaching will always be adapted to the intellectual and moral capacities of its hearers. Hence the teachers will speak differently to different men or groups of men. Only at the highest level of in-take will there be absolute identity and purity of teaching.

272

The modern philosopher gives out his knowledge with a wide generosity, which contrasts markedly with the niggardly secrecy of certain "occult" teachers.

273

The principles of chemistry have no individual's name attached to them. We accept them not because so-and-so discovered them, but because they can be tested and proven by anyone anywhere. So it is with principles and teachings. Because they are really factual, no names or personalities should be put forward as the guarantee of their correctness. They must be presented impersonally. This is a teaching which can and will be expanded; which is open to change, correction, and improvement—like every science. It asks us to look at the facts of life and see how they support it. The teachings are to be presented impersonally. They should be examined as actual facts found in Nature. The emphasis will be on these facts, and the personality of the teacher pushed into the background.

274

The truth must appeal as such to a man by the light of his everyday experience, and by a competent knower and expert communicator it can be explained in the same light. But whether the man's receptivity and understanding can stretch the whole way that truth extends is another matter.

275

Discretion tells only what it is necessary to tell, for it knows that more will obstruct or bewilder and not help. And it tells even that only when the proper time has come.

276

Such knowledge is the property of a few. It is their responsibility to keep the torch of philosophy alight.

277

The philosophic attitude does not hoard truth like a miser in complete secrecy, yet it does not proclaim it openly like a town crier. It gladly feeds those who are hungry for it, but no others.

278

Fired by this noble ideal and seeking its realization though he is, nevertheless he will not waste his energies in trying to convey to the undeveloped mind more than it can take in. This is not spiritual obscurantism.

279

We can best form public opinion by first forming private conviction.

280

Such was the primitive intellectual condition of the masses in former times that spiritual truth was best conveyed and easiest understood through parables, myths, allegories, and personifications. In our own day, improvement of the intellectual condition permits of straightforward statement and scientific precision in conveying the same truth. Thus the appeal to imagination is displaced by the appeal to reason.

281

To have used such obscurities as a mask in the days when plain writing would have endangered the writer's life is defensible; to use them today, when free thought and free speech are common democratic privileges, is not.

282

There is excellent reason why the communication of such teachings should be made with good taste, with artistic form, and with some refinement.

283

If the philosophical few realize that their doctrines have little appeal to the masses, they need not feel disturbed. They must acquire something of the patience which Nature herself possesses. Truth must be their hope and its ultimate power must be their reliance.

284

Philosophy can afford, as nothing else can, to await the ages for the vindication of its truth.

285

To tell everything and imply nothing is as undesirable as to tell nothing and imply everything. This is the general rule concerning the disclosure of such knowledge. But at times there will be special cases where it should not be applied, where either full disclosure or full reticence is necessary.

286

It is our duty to spread this teaching but not our duty to spread it among those who cannot profit by it.

287

Whoever takes it upon himself to preach and promulgate a system of thought needs to remember that those who need Truth most like it least.

288

Because the philosopher has freed himself from the intense attachment to personality which is so common, he feels no desire to impose *his* beliefs, ways, views, or practices on other people. And this remains just as true in political matters as in religious ones.

289

Philosophy is faced with the problem of educating each individual seeker who aspires to understand it. There is no such thing as mass education in philosophy.(P)

290

Such a teaching cannot indulge in propagandist methods or militant sectarianism. It must live quietly and offer itself only to those who are intellectually prepared and emotionally willing to receive it.(P)

291

If philosophical mysticism must inevitably remain denied to most by reason of innate incapacity to believe or practise it, philosophical concepts may yet be rendered most accessible by presenting them in the plainest of popular language.

292

It is perfectly possible for every person to rise into the high planes of spiritual realization, but it is probable only for one in ten thousand. That one is born gifted, selfless, determined, or fated. But what of the other 9,999? Religion must help them, since they are unable to help themselves. If we preach the gospel of philosophy, it is for the sake of that one, not for the multitude who we know will not heed it, since they lack the inborn power to obey it; and likewise for the sake of finding out that one in ten thousand we reckon it is worth the trouble of preaching.

293

The advanced mystic has little value for the masses, who can neither understand his attainment nor profit by his example. He may be willing to give them his grace but how can they receive it? Sensitivity of mind and conscious search for the Divine must exist as prerequisite conditions before this can happen. If he is to teach at all, he must teach ripe individuals. He must leave all others to the tuition of institutional religion. Nor can he wisely engage himself in forming groups and organizing societies. These at best are for the half-ripe. The best work of a mystical leader calls for personal attention and individual guidance.

294

It is the worship of outer formal success and ignorance of the inner spiritual reality in religion which has led so often to the triumph of error and defeat of truth, to officialdom, organization, and worldliness. It is the same worship which, in a different sphere, is applied in history to the same unworthy objects with the same deceptive results. The belief that the nations like the religions go from bad to good to better is as falsely but frequently taught as is the belief that power and progress travel together. The same suffocation which overcame the original purity of Christianity overcame many of the finer elements who were crushed by the power of arms, cunning, or treachery. It is this worship of material splendour and military force—so far distant from true heroism—which has made the Roman Empire a subject for so much praise in so many books. Yet the ruthless brutality and vast bloodshed which accompanied both the growth and maintenance of that empire receive little denunciation. Writers and readers are impressed by the splendid buildings and straight roads but know little or nothing about the destroyed spiritual culture of the conquered "barbarians." The official history of religions is as much a mixture of the false with the true as the official history of nations. Those who are capable of independent thought, and who are willing to make the required research among the mutilated records salvaged from deliberate destruction, may hope to find out some part of what really happened and what was originally and really taught by the prophets. All others will have to be satisfied—and generally are—with substitutions, frauds, and perversions among which a remnant of the pure truth shines out the more brilliantly by contrast with its setting. For it was impossible to exclude all the truth from the teaching and the records, nor—let it be said in justice to the official teachers and historians—was it desired to do so.

He who is fully aware of this state of affairs, because he has explored the neglected by-currents of religious history and discovered things which can bring no reward of position, promotion, honour, or money, who has also devoted his time and life to learning the secret of time and understanding the meaning of life—such a lone individual will not be so imprudent as to oppose his forces against this universal current of admiration for what is spurious but successful, false but powerful, dishonest but accepted. If he does not seek martyrdom, he will prefer to remain withdrawn, obscure, retired, and dispense his knowledge or grace to the few who really seek Truth. As for the others, the multitude, who must attend throughout the day to their physical wants and have neither the leisure nor facilities nor inclination to probe such matters—what are they to do? Knowing no better, what else can they do than accept the lies along with the truths, the impostures along with the authenticities, the whole dubious mixture of good and bad. Until quite recently this lone individual could not help them even if he wished, for the attempt would at once call down official persecution and extinction. All that he could do was what in fact he did do, pass the truth to a closed circle and thence let it be transmitted in the same secret way to other closed circles through the centuries.

If today so much has been publicly released as to constitute a veritable revelation, we must thank these pioneers and initiates who both in Europe and in the Near-East and India kept the teachings intact during earlier times. And although nothing can still equal the personal initiation by a master in effectiveness, nevertheless the wider intellectual initiation of our times is itself an immense advance on the secrecy formerly imposed by harsh necessity and makes most of the teaching available to the multitude.

295

Such an exalted teaching is never to be forced on others; they must first feel the desire for truth, and that strongly enough to begin to seek for it. Each man therefore obtains the truths to which he is entitled. It is all a matter of ripeness.

296

Plotinus warned his disciples against trying to argue doctrines or discuss tenets or explain philosophy to "those people with whom we can make no way," as he called them. The books containing his own teaching were not circulated publicly but secretly, and only he who was deemed fit to study them could lay hands on a copy.

297

Philosophy can only silently spread its internal influence rather than noisily build up any external institution. It can only lead the way to a new consciousness rather than into an old organization.

298

Because it respects the fact that evolutionary fitness brings to all persons what is truly their own, philosophy never seeks to make proselytes. Only when they are ready to be led to its own higher position does it bring its truth to them. And even then such truth will be dropped quietly like a seed into their minds, to grow by its own mysterious power and in its own hidden way.

299

For philosophy to attempt propaganda on its own behalf among the millions of people unready to receive it would be to enter into competition with religions which seek power, wealth, prestige, and followings. In the end philosophy would have to measure its success by these things, instead of by its capacity to lead a man into thinking and living in the truth. Further, the temptation to make itself more acceptable and more popular would finally bring about the undesirable result of enfeebling, diluting, or even falsifying the truth.

300

It prefers to let, not the pressure of propaganda, but the experience of life and the conclusions of reason, the guidance of intuition and the endorsement of sages persuade men to accept these doctrines.

301

The occultist's attempts to introduce mystification are completely remote from the philosopher's caution in phrasing his teaching to fit the receptivity of his hearers.

302

Its reticence grows not from an aristocratic pride but from a sensitive humility. Philosophy does not go out of its way to seek recruits.

303

The teaching does not have to go forth to meet people. They will find their own way to meet it as they develop through science, religion, art, and life.

304

Philosophy can have no missionary arrogance since, unlike religion, it does not seek to displace one set of beliefs by another. Nor can it have any propagandist aggressiveness, since it tolerantly holds that all men find the degree of truth for which they are ready, and that a higher degree would be useless because beyond their capacity to absorb.

305

It has been a traditional view of philosophy that people should be left undisturbed in their faith, even though it is recognized by superior minds as faulty or erroneous. Only when their own minds become troubled about it should its defectiveness be admitted and a truer faith be placed before them.

306

He may say nothing to disturb those who desire to rest in the preliminary stage of spiritual understanding, which is the religious stage. It is better to leave them to the tutoring of life, to the processes of evolution.

307

No one favours philosophy in official circles; no one spreads it. Slowly, gently it must spread itself. As men become better, more intuitive and more intelligent, they respond to its fine doctrines and precepts. To let them know that it exists is all one can do. After that they will come to it, if they wish.

308

They are afraid of popularizing the teaching because this leads, first, to diluting it and, finally, to falsifying it. They are correct. But this is not enough reason for clothing it in such obscurity and expressing it in so much verbosity that the ideas become even more difficult to grasp than need be.

309

A truth which lies buried in myth or enshrined in allegory is not a truth fully and clearly understood. To make it so, and to present it in a connected reasonable statement, is the special task of our own century.

310

Because they sought to help the multitude for whom they came, rather than the elite, sages used the popular language to deliver their teachings. Hence Buddha spoke in Prakrit rather than in Sanskrit, Jesus in Aramaic rather than Hebrew.

311

By the single fact of its refusal to proselytize, philosophy is taken out of the ranks of conventional teaching; but by its daring thought it is taken out even more. And it is distinguished even more by the calm tolerance of its attitude towards other teachings, by the measured fairness with which it appraises them, and by its refusal to degenerate into personal offensiveness or bitter animosity. It knows quite well that truth cannot be elucidated in an atmosphere of angry feelings and personal polemics.

312

He would be untrue to philosophy if he were to seek a single proselyte. Nevertheless, when through his work anybody does accept this teaching he rejoices with and for him. But this jubilation is mostly on the other's account. The gain is the proselyte's, not the philosopher's.

313

The philosophic movement must spread itself by teaching, not by propaganda.

314

There is no room in philosophy for the exhibitionism which tries to attract attention to itself.

315

Useless would it be to thrust these truths on unprepared people and to get them to take up a way of spiritual growth unsuited to their taste and temperament. Persuasion should arise of its own accord through inner attraction.

316

Without relaxing the scholarly requirements of accurate presentation, it is still possible to put before laymen in more familiar forms and terms this higher truth to some extent, leaving the fuller presentation for better prepared students.

317

That a long and persistent course of intellectual striving is the coin to be tendered for the full understanding of its metaphysical side is undeniable. That this—not less than the unorthodox character of its conceptions, with their likelihood of giving a shock to the mind—has tended to make the whole system esoteric is also undeniable. But that the few leading ideas could be presented in a greatly simplified manner, and so made easier for popular taste, is not less undeniable. If most people show indifference towards this teaching, that is not altogether their fault.

318

Philosophy has no wish to argue these points with sceptics, no urge to triumph in the debate over opponents.

319

Philosophy does not seek a popular following. It does not even set out to win friends and influence people.

320

It is not necessary to decorate this doctrine with the red embroideries of prejudice-pandering in order to induce men to accept it. The propositions it contains establish themselves within intuitional minds by the inherent force of their truth.

321

In the end the truth is its own best propaganda and does its own proselytizing.

322

Philosophy would not be itself if it sought to stage theoretical debates: those who find it satisfying grow or come into it of themselves. But it does seek to show that materialism serves its adherents less while mentalism enlightens them more, that narrow sectarian versions of religion catch less of the divine atmosphere than mentalism does.

323

These over-optimistic enthusiasts show an imperfect acquaintance with human nature when they imagine revivals and proselytizations can spread philosophic truth. What can be spread by such means is speculation, fancy, and opinion.

324

Adherence to philosophy is the most fundamental act of a man's life. He cannot be emotionally rushed into it, as he can into adherence to a religious cult. It is the result of growth.

325

The time has come to teach the masses principles which formerly they were taught in parables.

326

If we wish to serve the many with this truth-offering, then the terminology which bewilders and irritates them must be absent from our speaking and writing, whether it be the jargon of metaphysics, the exoticism of Sanskrit, or the abracadabra of occultism; let us say plainly what we mean.

3

ITS REQUIREMENTS

Basic qualifications

To become a seeker in intention is admirable as the first step but it is only the first one. To qualify as a seeker in fact is the second. What are the required qualifications?

2

Philosophy expects nothing from its votaries that is beyond their power to give. Hence it makes different demands on different people, graduating its ethic and instruction, its injunctions and duties, its precepts and counsels, to their strengths capacities and circumstances. But nevertheless it sacrifices nothing of enduring value, for at the same time it reminds them not to forget the final ideal, the ultimate end toward which all their lesser efforts are moving. Thus it accommodates itself to those who want an easier and longer route, making itself accessible to ordinary people, yet it does not separate itself from the rarer souls who are so circumstanced and so formed by nature as to gladly give themselves to the shortest and hardest route.

3

Just as a physically immature baby could not take a half-mile walk, however much it wished or even willed to do so, so a spiritually immature man could not take in the higher philosophy, however much he wished or willed it. The intuition and intelligence, the character and capacity needed for this latter purpose must be present in him, and used, before the teachings can really reach him.

4

If philosophy hides its truth from mental unreadiness and its votaries from social persecution, it is, nevertheless, always ready when it is needed by any sincere seeker who has evolved to the requisite degree. If he has got enough religious prejudice and mystical superstition out of his mind to be free to think for himself, if he has lifted his character somewhat above the common weaknesses, if his sense of values is such that the Truth appears desirable above all things, then philosophy is the only thing to which he can turn for guidance and enlightenment—and philosophy will surely welcome him.

5

To learn is to receive knowledge; but he who seeks to learn this Truth which is both behind and beyond all other truths must come with his mind, his heart, his body, and his will. With his mind because his thought must be pushed to its deepest measure. With his heart because his love is demanded more than he now knows. With his body because it is to be the temple of the holy spirit. And with his will because he may not stop this enterprise until he is through.

6

He has to learn discrimination if he wishes to become a philosopher. This is not merely that moral quality which separates right from wrong for the religious man, but that psychological act which separates the perceiver from the objects of his perception, the experiencer from the objects of his experience, in its elementary operation. Although it will have to reunite them again in its later operation on a higher plane, as the unenlightened man unites them on a lower one, that plane cannot be reached abidingly by jumping, only by climbing.

7

The acceptance of such a teaching as philosophy implies an unusual degree of intelligence—which is not the same as education or even intellect, although it may include these things. For the recognition that there is a world of being beyond that registered by the five senses, a world of consciousness not limited to that reported by the thinking ego, a divine soul hidden within that ego itself, a superior power involving us all in its cosmic order—such a recognition can come only to those with unusual intelligence. Faith is good but not enough, for one day it may change through circumstances or be confused through lack of knowledge. Such intelligence is best for it includes and guides faith but goes farther than it.

8

Philosophical intelligence combines the intellectual faculty with the intuitive.

9

Without pure philosophy, there is no possibility of ascending the higher peaks of truth. In the highest esoteric school of Asia no one is admitted before first having been taken through a course of the essentials of this subject. In this school there is no progress without the full use of intelligence and sharpened reason. The lack of this quality has helped to contribute to the downfall of organized mystical movements known to us all.

10

The study of philosophy educates the mind in deep thinking. It must be approached in the spirit of scientific detachment.

11

Something of the impersonality and detachment of the mathematician are necessary to the beginning philosopher.

12

He is to be concerned solely with the reality, with that which Is, and not with the presentation of it which others have invented.

13

At this stage he is finished with compromises: he can accept nothing less—and wants nothing else—than the pure Truth.

14

Unless men possess the right intuitional calibre, they cannot grasp this teaching, for it stands at an altitude beyond the reach of the gross and the materialistic.

15

The courage to become independent of his own past beliefs is needed. The strength to set aside the patterns of thought imposed on his mind by long habit is required. These qualities may not necessarily have to come into action but they must be there.

16

The hysteric, the neurotic, or the paranoic is unready for philosophy's guidance, unfit for mysticism's meditation. It is useless for such a one to apply as a candidate for initiation. Let him get rid of his self-centered mania first.

17

Philosophy demands the purity and experience of a sage, not the purity and ignorance of a child.

18

Philosophy does not compete with any religion, any mystical or metaphysical system, for it does not consider itself as existing on the same level as any of them. It can only be grasped by those who bring the necessary intuitive, mystical, intellectual, moral, and devotional qualifications to it, and it can only be appreciated by those who can grasp it.

19

Philosophy is for those who demand the ultimate, who are satisfied with nothing less and who have enough discernment to discriminate between it and its many substitutes.

20

Those only will appreciate this point of view who have awakened to the need of penetrating through illusion to reality and who understand how important this is to humanity's future.

21

Philosophy calls for some leisure to study it and for some capacity to understand what is being studied. It is not enough to be an amateur in philosophy: one must become an expert.

22

The first lessons of the higher philosophy cannot be usefully taught to those who have not learned the last lessons of religion. But for those who have gone a little way into mysticism or metaphysics, such instruction need not be deferred.

23

People of all religious faiths can come to the study of philosophy. They will not be able to keep their faith after such study, however, without profoundly deepening it. Nor will they be able to keep with it the enthusiastic arrogance or intolerant ignorance which accompanies so much sectarianism.

24

Oriental wisdom enjoins in general withholding truth from the unready, and in particular from those who do not want or seek it, from inebriated or agitated persons, from those in whom lust or greed, wrath or impatience predominates, and, understandably, from lunatics.

25

Philosophy gains recruits only from those whose values are so lofty that they regard the finding of truth a satisfying end in itself, and whose minds are so tolerant that they make their search for it in the widespread field of comparative and universal cultures.

26

The independent mind, which seeks all the facts and not merely some of them, which does its own thinking about those facts, is naturally better suited to philosophy than the dependent mind, which accepts without demur inherited creeds and established sects.

27

His intellectual integrity must be such that even if his search for truth ends in ideas which upset much of what he has hitherto accepted, he will not flinch from making the change.

28

Swedenborg: "Without the utmost devotion to the Supreme Being, the Origin of all things, no one can be a complete and truly erudite philosopher. Veneration for the Infinite Being can never be separated from philosophy."

29

Philosophy is for those who can think closely and who are willing to abide by the results of their thinking. It is not for those who settle everything by the evidence of their senses. That is why it has never been a necessity to those who must see reality with their eyes and touch it with their hands, as it has been to those who were content to know with their minds.

30

In the study of modern science, in all laboratory analysis or examination of natural phenomena, great stress is laid upon the necessity for strict impersonality and freedom from every trace of wishful thinking, personal emotion, and prejudice. This is of equal necessity to the student of philosophy.

31

He is ready to learn philosophy when he is ready to strip himself of all prejudice, or at least to allow philosophy itself to do this to him.

32

Uninformed seekers have to learn various lessons before they find their way to this path, to philosophy. They are attracted to ancient ideas and outworked methods of which only a portion really suit today's humanity. What has happened to the races and to the globe on which they dwell has affected their character and mind, their tendencies, capacities, and faculties. Those who look back nostalgically to teachings and texts, lands and names so honoured—and quite worthily too—do not know or understand this. The fact that there are certain basic eternal truths is certainly irrefragable. That Mind always was, is, and will be, is one of them. That the human soul is linked with it (through the World-Mind) is another. But the methods by which this link may be vivified and the men who are to use them and the circumstances under which they live have all been modified.

33

After he has had the courage, freedom, intelligence, aspiration, and discrimination to work through all the cults—especially the personality-worship cults—and creeds, persistently, calmly, and survived the temptation of idolatry, he may be fitter to revere the noble impersonal Godhead.

34

If you wish to know the Truth, you must accept its disconcerting revelations along with the pleasant ones. You must be willing to practise inner detachment from everything and everyone as well as to enjoy the beautiful moments of rapture.

35

If people come to mysticism with unbalanced or diseased minds, as a number certainly do, and if they permeate their mystical acquisitions with their own defects, they cannot do the same to philosophy. For the end result would be either that they flee from it on deeper acquaintance or that its demands and disciplines would begin to permeate them. This in turn would equilibrate or heal their minds.

36

Those who belong by natural affinity to this teaching stay with it. All others eventually find their proper level elsewhere.

37

I took the trouble of looking up the meaning given to the Sanskrit word *shraddha*, which is one of the six subsidiary qualifications required of the aspirant to the knowledge of higher Vedantic philosophy. Here are the results: (1) Monier Williams' massive Sanskrit dictionary laconically defines it as to have "trust"; (2) Govindananda, in his work the *Ratna-Prabha*, defines it as meaning "a respectful trust in all higher things"; (3) Venkatramiah, in his version of the *Aitareyopanishad*, says it means "faith in the Vedantic verities as inculcated by the preceptor"; (4) Vasudeva, the ascetic, gives its significance as "the strong faith in the words of one's teacher," in his *Meditations*; (5) Professor Girindra N. Mallik, M.A., defines it as "faith in the contents of the scriptures." But what is the esoteric and therefore the truest meaning of *shraddha*? My own interpretation is: "that faith in the existence of truth, that determination to get at truth, come what may, which would make one a hero even in the face of God's wrath."

38

He who would become a philosopher must keep away from partisanship, must cultivate an independent state of mind so as to be free to receive ideas from any source. In this way he can really learn what others have thought or found long ago or in his own epoch, whether they lived in the East or West. Such detachment is not easy to acquire or to maintain without self-discipline.

39

His attitude should be: "Take the truth, whether or not it be useful to practical life. Take it for its own sake, disinterestedly and enthusiastically, whether it be close to personal needs or far from them."

40

It needs for its study an enlarged outlook and gives in return a still larger one. This is true philosophy, universal, wide-horizoned, inclusive, and reconciliatory.

41

It needs some courage to face facts as they are and the world as it really is, but this is better than harbouring illusions which are going to be relentlessly and painfully dispelled.

42

There is another side to this demand that an aspirant be at the stage where he has been prepared for, and is ready to imbibe, the higher truth. The demand must not be pushed to the extent that those who have not had any opportunity for such prior preparation will be shut out altogether. Something can and ought to be given them to the utmost possible degree.

43

Few persons are at the required level of full intellectual, intuitive, moral, and metaphysical development for philosophy but many persons are capable of benefitting by its practical applications.

44

If some of its tenets are admittedly unfamiliar and provocative, this is not to say that they are outside the reach of anyone with moderate capacity who will approach them with a will to understand.

45

The mind which has not yet been properly prepared by the philosophical discipline to receive truth directly through intuition, must meanwhile receive it indirectly through faith and reason.

46

Philosophy is not for him whose mind is so riddled with race prejudice as to think nothing good can come out of Asia, or whose own attitude is so steeped in violent bias as to judge people solely by their appearance, or whose ideas are lit only by his own little guttering candle of limited experience.

47

It does not admit the popular delusion that every member of the human race is fit to pass proper judgement on any issue merely by consulting his opinion or feeling about it—much less about religion and mysticism.

48

The hidden teaching is only for those who prefer to travel freely on a road rather than crawl slavishly in a rut. Only the strong can submit to this mental isolation.

49

It is comforting only to the few who are prepared to part with their egoism, their pride, their sensuality, and their inertia for the sake of truth.

50

Error will creep into his finite apprehension of the infinite truth if he has not previously made himself ready, pure, balanced, and mature.

51

If only because philosophy was not there for anyone to pick up casually if he wished, but only there for anyone who could think and intuit, its possible adherents were well limited in number. Such a man would inevitably think and intuit himself more and more into its great teachings to the degree that he wished to seek truth and was able to abandon ego.

52

Philosophy is primarily for the fairly advanced mentality; for the person who is familiar with the chief spiritual conceptions and practices; for the aspirant who is experienced and mature.

53

Only one who has spent his life in religious, mystical, and philosophic investigations can appreciate the universal, the timeless, and the placeless character of this teaching.

54

No man who has totally failed to use his intuitional faculty will have the capacity to receive philosophy.

55

Every child must pass through a proper training in elementary and intermediate mathematics before the principles of higher calculus can be explained to it. So those who wish to grasp the advanced portion of philosophy must likewise prepare the mind and heart, the will and character.

56

A high level of general education is a distinct advantage for those who would take up such a study, but it is not an absolute essential.

57

It is for all classes, all types of mind, and all kinds of character. It is for the simple as well as the astute, the sinful as well as the good. But alas! personal histories show that it is the astute and the good who mostly accept philosophy. The others who need it because they too are human beings accept it less frequently.

58

Those who prefer the pleasant to the true will naturally fear to enter the kingdom of philosophy.

59

Only those who can follow philosophy wherever it leads them and practice its tenets with unflinching courage will ever become philosophers. It is not enough to affirm principles; they must also be applied and given tangible form.

60

Those who are cultivated, educated, and intelligent enough to appreciate what philosophy offers them may yet be blinded by prejudice or selfishness or be too stupefied from gorging the passions to do so.

61

Sensitive and introspective minds will more quickly find their way to these truths than dull and extroverted ones.

62

If he is to reach this pure well of truth, its water untainted by bias or prejudice, he will do best by keeping independent.

63

Both a properly disciplined body and a philosophically-strengthened mind should be our reliance.

64

One should seek for knowledge of the Higher Laws governing life, for true purity of character, and for humility if he wishes to reach the Highest Truth.

65

Seekers who are not satisfied with conventional doctrines or mystical experiences must be willing to do some difficult but profitable reasoning.

66

The truth cannot be found by those who cannot protect themselves against deception, and especially self-deception.

67

Philosophy carries good tidings to the human race, but they will be regarded as "good" only by those members of the race who are able and willing to take an impersonal and impartial view of things.

68

Not everyone is ready for the truth when it comes to him.

69

The kind of mind which likes to keep everything neatly labelled (good or bad) and everyone neatly classified (atheist, believer, Christian, Hindu) will be somewhat puzzled, slightly uneasy, and partly derisory when confronted by philosophy or philosophers.

70

One who is ripe to receive truth will respond to its presentation at once, convinced that it must be so.

71

One who is ready will feel the power in these written truths and will follow their injunctions obediently.

72

That everyone and anyone should be taught philosophy is an unreasonable demand. Only those who consciously seek truth and deliberately practise self-discipline are entitled to such teaching.

Philosophic discipline

73

Truth is a many-sided unity. It cannot be found by a narrow single-track mind. To take a fragment of truth and call it all of the truth, to stand on one point of view and ignore all other points entirely, is easier for lazy minds. But this is not philosophical. This is why some kind of preparatory self-training to broaden and deepen oneself mentally is required by philosophy and why it cannot be handed over on a plate.

74

That some restraint and discipline are needed is implied by the very notion of a quest for higher goals. That some portion must be set by the teaching itself but another must be self-imposed arises out of the balanced, sensible nature of philosophy. It has no place for fanaticism or tyranny.

75

Without requiring the ambition for sainthood, it does require the capacity to recognize the need of a discipline and the willingness to undergo it.

76

Truth already exists within man. He has to bring it from the centre to the circumference of his consciousness. If it is hidden from his view, that is only because he has not looked deep enough or has not cleared away the obstructions to his view. Those obstructions are entirely within his lower self, and may be removed by practice of the philosophic discipline.

77

He has first to find out what it is that keeps him from the higher self. And, this known, he will see the need and value of the philosophic discipline as a means of eliminating these obstacles.

78

Philosophy requires every acolyte to submit to a self-imposed discipline. That he shall not knowingly cherish an untruth in his feeling is the first and easier requirement; that he shall not unknowingly cherish an untruth in his thinking is the second and harder.

79

This path is a master stroke. This method of destroying the illusion of the self by means of the intellectual function which is its primary activity stands supreme and almost alone. That very function automatically ceases when directed upon itself in the way that is herein taught. And with its cessation, the self is dissolved, appropriated by the Universal.

80

The most striking point in this simple technique is that he uses the very ego itself—for so long indicated by all mystics as the greatest enemy on the

Path—as the means of divine attainment. These words may sound like pure paradox, but they happen to be true. The strength of his enemy is drawn upon for his help, while that which was the supreme hindrance transforms into a pathway to the goal.

81

The ability to discriminate between appearance and reality, between the false "I" and the true "I," is developed by subjecting the reports of the senses to the criticism of the intellect, by checking emotion with reason, by standing aside from all of these faculties with the intuition, and by diving deeper and deeper into one's essence in meditation.

82

The enigmatic questions which have long haunted the human mind and will long continue to haunt it and which will rise insistent in the mind of the aspirant are: What is he to seek? How is he to gain the objects of his search? What are the prospects of the fulfilment of such an aspiration and the hindrances likely to attend it? The answers to them are a gradual revealing which follows on the heels of the cultivation of certain attitudes to truth and to persons and things.

"What is he to seek?" He should seek reality and the knowledge of it which is truth. This is the ideal which is set before him. This is to realize his spiritual nature and thus achieve his higher destiny. Because truth is so subtle and so hard to find, his search after it should be well guided, his knowledge of it properly tested, and his adventures in meditation morally and intellectually safeguarded. Truer ideas are needed; nobler standards are called for. Such ideals, truthfully formed, deeply held, and wholeheartedly applied, can only benefit man and not hurt him. He who has been given a glimpse of the Ideal will not be able to lie always asleep in the sensual. The finer part of his nature will revolt against it again and again.

The Ideal serves more than one useful purpose. It is not only a peak to whose summit he tries to raise himself by slow degrees. It is also a focus for meditation exercises, a guide for practical conduct in certain situations, and a compass to give general direction to his trend of thought, feeling, and doing. It causes the aspirant to feel that he has been led through varying events to the new path which now opens up before him, that a spiritual meaning must be given to the period of his life just closed. The sequence of events and the accumulation of experience will force him to face his problems in the end. If he can do this honestly, analyse them intelligently, and intuit them adequately, he may acquire a valuable new point of view.

"How is he to gain the objects of his search?" The truth-seeker will begin to turn inward in quest of unity with his own soul and outward in quest of unity with mankind. Life is the guide that is bringing him home to himself and to kindlier relation to his fellows. Life itself teaches and disciplines towards these great ends. The following of the integral philosophic quest, with life as the guide and teacher, will involve the re-education of moral character—which is done in part by constant reflection and special meditations on the one hand and discipline of the senses on the other, and in part by prayer, aspiration, and worship. In addition, if a man cultivates the habit of barring entrance to negative thoughts and of instantly throwing weakening ones out of his mind, his character will strengthen itself more quickly. The outcome will be certain relationships to oneself, to others, and to situations and things.

The ascent toward truth proceeds by steps. If at first the merits of a particular teaching or teacher impress the emotions unduly, it is also likely that a more critical study of the one and a more thorough experience of the other will show up unsuspected defects. The philosophic student tries to avoid undergoing these unpleasant changes by getting a balanced view of the pros and cons from the start. He ought not to be so swept off his feet by the great admiration felt for a genius or a doctrine that he has no clear perception of the former's defects or the latter's faults. He must maintain balance not only in the face of lower emotions but also of nobler ones.

83

All human knowledge is conditioned by the fact of human relativity. Human nature, human intellect, and human egoism impose their limitations not only in material experience but also in mystical experience. Statements of divine truth made by mortal men should be read in the light of the fact that they are subject to such relativity. None is infallible, none eternally authoritative. Such seems to be the unhopeful situation. Is there then no way of disengaging the human agency from the divine message which manifests through it? The answer is that this way does exist and that its method is an intellectual as well as emotional purification, a moral and practical discipline, an intuitional and mystical preparation, and above all an elimination of the personal reference carried on incessantly through a long period.

84

Philosophy can be understood only by the actual process of philosophizing, by passing through the whole course of emotional and mental discipline which philosophy involves.

85

The student should seek clear ideas and warm feelings in his spiritual studies and devotional aspirations.

86

The pure revelation comes only to those who can bring themselves at the bidding of truth to sacrifice ruthlessly their previous beliefs, if necessary. All others get a partial or mixed revelation.

87

The goal is to obtain a higher consciousness which flashes across the mind with blinding light. All his effort, all his training is really for this.

88

The philosophic training will show its result in his capacity to separate the actual operation of the Overself in him from any admixture by his own personal thoughts, feelings, and expectations.

89

The thing that passes for illumination with most mystics is generally a mixture of genuine mystical experience with an interpretation of it furnished by the intellect, the emotions, tradition, education, teachers, suggestion, and so on. The medium through which the experience is brought down into conscious communication or understanding often interferes with it and reshapes it. The philosophic discipline, with its self-criticizing, keen rationality and its ego-subordination, purification, and illumination, is intended to prevent this interference from happening.

90

The advanced section of the philosophic discipline represents an endeavour to reduce the number and thickness of these coloured windows through which the mystic receives revelations and delivers messages. But this is only its first endeavour. In the end, it strives to force him from them altogether, to rescue his illumination from everything that might limit its pure transparent universality.

91

Is it not possible to free mystical reception from these egoistic interferences, misrepresentations, exaggerations, distortions, and falsifications? Yes, it is possible. With the philosophic discipline the mystic may discipline his ego, train his feelings, guide his intellect, and check his intuition so that the truth breaks into space and time through his human personality in faultless purity.

92

Man's imperfect nature must be rendered utterly passive, its distorting interference utterly eliminated, before the divine truth can manifest itself in all its authoritative purity.

93

He will train himself to distinguish between the fancies of the ego and the certainties of the Soul. And it is one purpose of the philosophic discipline to assist him to do so. For the rest he must depend on self-critical observation and careful checking of results.

94

The knowledge of self which philosophy can give is unique. But it can be got only by turning the whole of the psyche's force inwards in steady penetration and sustained meditation. The hidden doors of our mental being must be opened, the delicate sources of our emotional being must be traced, the gossamer thread of our deepest consciousness must be followed. All this calls for the exercise of will, the effort of concentration, the refinement of attention, and surrender to patience.

95

It is impossible for any aspirant to attain the full and equilibrated illumination if he does not have this preliminary preparation of the philosophic discipline. He can get results, he can get striking experiences, but the supreme result is beyond his own powers of receptivity.

96

Philosophy imposes a severe mental discipline upon those who would pursue its truths.

97

He who knows and feels the divine power in his inmost being will be set free in the most literal sense of the word from anxieties and cares. He who has not yet arrived at this stage but is on the way to it can approach the same desirable result by the intensity of his faith in that being. But such a one must really have the faith and not merely say so. The proof that he possesses it would lie in the measure with which he refuses to accept negative thoughts, fearful thoughts, despondent thoughts. In the measure that he does not fail in his faith and hence in his thinking, in that measure, the higher power will not fail to support him in his hour of need. This is why Jesus told his disciples, "Take no anxious thought for the morrow." In the case of the adept, having given up the ego, there is no one left to take care of him, so the higher Self does so for him. In the case of the believer, although he has not yet given up the ego, nevertheless, he is trying to do so, and his unfaltering trust in the higher Self is rewarded proportionately in the same way. In both cases the biblical phrase, "The Lord will provide," is not merely a pious hope but a practical fact.(P)

98

The philosophic discipline shows us how we are to treat ourselves. The philosophic morality teaches us how we are to treat others. It provides both abstract principle for theory and concrete rules for conduct.

99

He may make use of adverse periods to test the worth of philosophy and the merit of its teaching, instead of letting them become a source of depression.

100

The inexperienced and the unbalanced may measure spiritual progress in terms of emotional ecstasy or meditational vision, but the mature and wise will measure it in terms of character—its nobility, its rounded development, and its purity.

101

The philosophic training will help him to stop inserting the ego into his experience and to cease imposing its bias on his reading of it.

102

Philosophy begins its instruction to the neophyte by the startling assertion that neither he nor any other candidate is ready or qualified to receive truth. It declares that this qualification, this readiness, must first be developed in the candidate himself. This work of development is called the philosophic discipline. He should study himself and examine his experiences in the most critical light. Alibis, pretenses, and excuses should be mercilessly rejected. The dice of doubtful cases should be loaded against it, and he should begin with the premise that he is either faulty in judgement or guilty in conduct.

103

Those who want philosophy without accepting its discipline get only a fragment of it.

104

The philosopher's research is a disinterested one. There is no particular body of doctrines which he sets out to support, no religious institution whose power or prestige he seeks to increase. He deliberately controls his predilections, trains his thoughts, and disciplines his feelings so as to make himself capable of that intellectual detachment which is a necessary prerequisite to getting at the truth.

105

The philosophic discipline aims to shock the aspirant out of the complacency with which he views himself into a more critical view. He may feel chagrin and mortification at what he sees.

106

Philosophic life in our sense is not a matter of reading practical maxims. It is giving assent in action and offering wholehearted belief in feeling to the best values, goals, and purposes.

107

The philosopher develops the principal sides of his human nature, that is, his intelligence by reasoning, his knowledge by study, his piety by devotions, his mystical intuitiveness by meditation, and his wisdom by association with those more evolved than himself.

108

The first aim therefore is to know Truth as it is and not merely as it is to us.

109

Its aim is to produce a man who shall be humanly mature and spiritually secure, who shall be flesh and mind put to the service of spirit.

110

The study of philosophy must be no desultory pursuit; it must follow a consecutive and sequential course if its principles are to be mastered and its problems solved.

111

Thought, feeling, and will are the three sides of a human being which must find their respective functions in this quest. Thought must be directed to the discrimination of truth from error, reality from appearance. Feeling must be elevated in loving devotion towards the Overself. Will must be turned towards wise action and altruistic service. And all three must move in effective unison and mutual balance.

112

He should always remember that the mere reading about philosophy will not make him a philosopher. Nor will even the thinking about philosophy itself transform him into one. Both these activities are certainly necessary but they need one more to complete them. And that is the *practice* of philosophy in conduct, the expression of it in daily living.

113

Meditation, rightly done, is indispensable to the philosophic quest, but it must be accompanied by other practices or endeavours which are not less indispensable to the success of this quest.

114

Meditation must predominate in the beginner's stage. It is the most important effort then required of him. But the other requirements need not therefore be neglected. It will not only be greatly to his advantage to develop metaphysical reasoning and wise action, but the combination of all three will yield results far in advance of those which their separate and subsequent development could possibly yield.

115

Only he who lives from moment to moment by the clear light of its teaching, by the deepest faith in its tenets, and by the ardent feeling of its worth is a true disciple of philosophy.

116

Three tasks are required of him for this integral culture. The four elements of the psyche are to be purified, developed, and balanced.

117

Everyone in some way, blindly or consciously, slavishly or independently, wrongly or correctly, necessarily and always believes in a particular decipherment of the enigma of life. But only he who has brought the best mental equipment to bear upon it is likely to make the best decipherment. And only the philosophical discipline gives this.

118

The cravings of the senses are to be brought under control. The soul is to be their master; the mind is no longer to be their slave.

119

An external asceticism of a sensible kind is also called for. If, on the specious advice of those who say repression is worse, he yields to sexual passion every time it solicits him, he makes harder the internal battle against it. For temptation is not removed by yielding to it if the removal is merely temporary, and the recurrence is certain and swift.

120

He has to reject the appeal of sensuous things for a time and retreat from their pursuit. This is intended to free him from their tyranny over him.

121

The disinclination to start practising meditation and the inability to sustain it for long when started are due in part to the mind's strong habit of being preoccupied with worldly matters or being attached to personal desires. This is why the study of wholly abstract metaphysical and impersonal topics is part of the Philosophic Path.

122

A sense of sacredness should enter his philosophical studies if they are to bear more fruit.

123

Some essentials are: purification of character, discipline of emotion, ennoblement of motive, practice of meditation, study of the metaphysics of truth, elevation of conduct, and a constant heartfelt aspiration towards the Divine. Prayer, too, of the *right* kind, is helpful because ego-humbling. And the right kind is the philosophic kind.

124

The various branches of philosophical study and practice include the preparatory stages of the ascetic life and then the further fuller stages of being, thinking, feeling, meditating, intuiting, and discriminating. There are two levels of reference: the Absolute and the Relative, equivalent to the Metaphysical and the Physical-Practical, the Reality and the Appearance.

125

In one's search for the Higher Self, it is necessary to cultivate impersonality and objectivity along with reason, emotion, and balance. These should always be present in one's analyses of experiences, since inaccurate conclusions would be reached without them.

126

The striving for impersonality is uncommon; however approved in theory, actual practice is unpleasant and unwilling.

127

The earnest seeker who has already achieved a certain degree of awareness and understanding has the beginnings of what may be a splendid opportunity to make phenomenal progress in his present incarnation. But everything in this world must be paid for; the greatest treasures are attained only at the greatest cost. The aspirant must now embark on a do-or-die endeavour to lift his character onto a higher plane altogether; to purify his motives; and to be prepared to sacrifice all worldly objects first inwardly and, finally, outwardly—if called upon to do so. The spiritual returns are correspondingly great, however. They are: serenity, understanding, liberation, satisfaction, and the delight of perpetual communion with the divine Overself—while being always in Its blissful Presence.

There must also be the dedication to service. Here, more often than not, the spiritual returns are a terrible sadness which must be borne alone and unshared.

Such is the philosophic life—the only conceivable way of life for many, now, and for many more, later on—forever motivated and sustained by the unchanging living Reality, Mind.

128

The mental tendencies which he has brought over from previous births, the effects of physical heredity and environment, the influence of society, and the suggestions of education—all of these have to be disciplined and purified, if he is to acquire truth without unconsciously deforming it.

129

This discipline frees his mentality from the tendency to place merely temporary and local influences above the truly universal and eternal elements. Thus, it clears a pathway for the real revelations.

130

Another of the practical applications of philosophy is the injunction to waste nothing. The usefulness of anything is entirely a matter of relativity. That which is useless to you in a certain connection may become useful in a different connection or at a later time. Again, it may still be useless even when considered under these two aspects but yet it may be most useful to another person. Therefore if there is some thing you don't want to keep, give it away to someone who needs it. Don't throw it away and destroy it. You are only a steward. If you take a purely personal standpoint or if you live merely for the present moment, such counsel may make no appeal to you. If, however, you have risen to the philosophic and universal standpoint and consider everything not merely relative to your own ego but also to the All, then you will see your responsibility in this matter. This does not mean you are to become miserly. On the contrary you are to become generous. For in the last counting everything belongs to Mother Nature. We are only her stewards and our task is to use her possessions wisely and co-operatively.

131

Philosophy tells us that it is the business of everybody, nations as well as individuals, to look behind their sufferings and thus ascertain the causes of which these sufferings are merely effects. If men wish to start a better and happier life, it is needful that they should understand the lessons of their own past. If this happier existence is to be a reality, it cannot come about unless they break inwardly and outwardly with this past.

132

A fully ripened mind comes more easily and more naturally into the truth. The labours of reflective thought joined to the stillness of suspended thought, the emotion of reverential worship balanced by the independence of self-reliance, are only different aspects of the process of ripening: there are others. The large outlook which follows minimizes the ego and pushes out blocks. Slowly or suddenly the Spirit is let in, fills, and takes over. Consciousness *literally* comes into its own—itself.

133

A brave insistence on facing his inarguable prejudgements will be required of him.

134

The philosophic ethics must be applied not only in his well-studied understanding but also in the depths of his personal relations.

135

The old idea was that a spiritually minded person should sport a long beard, indulge in ascetic self-denials, and be portentously solemn. The new idea is that he should keep his spiritual-mindedness but be more human, more like one of ourselves.

136

Philosophic training tries to produce in its votaries a lofty personal character and a wide social outlook. It shames narrow attitudes and releases beneficent feelings.

137

We must see things in their proper proportions. This is why the philosophic student must consider all available aspects of a situation, all sides of a question, and both the past causes and future outcome of an event.

138

There is a danger to his pilgrimage towards truth if he lets a fixed and finalized statement of it become dominant. It is the danger of arrested growth, or spiritual constriction.

139

The conflict with himself, with ill will and evil will, with false thought and mistaken thought, can end only when the quest itself ends.

140

Since most people come to the same subject with personal preconceptions, they leave with different conclusions! Only those who have undergone the purifying discipline of philosophy are likely to have the same conclusions.

141

This further implies the eliminating of all prejudices and the purging of all preconceptions from one's outlook. The mind must be open, not attached unduly to anything, not the victim of contemporary external influences, but ever ready to *enquire*.

142

He must not be afraid to disparage his own past thought and work, values and techniques, if need be.

143

"The Buddhist discipline or exercise (*yoga*) as is told by the Buddha consists of two parts, philosophical and practical. The philosophical discipline is to train the mind to absolute idealism and see that the world is Mind, and that there is in reality no becoming such as birth and death, and that no external things really exist; while the practical side is to attain an inner perception by means of supreme wisdom. To be great in the exercise that makes up Bodhisattvahood (*mahayagayogin*) one has to be an expert in four things (three of which are intellectual and the last one practical): 1) to perceive clearly that this visible world is no more than Mind itself; 2) to abandon the notion that birth, abiding, and passing-away really took place; 3) to look into the nature of things external and realize that they have no reality (*abhava*); 4) to train oneself towards the realization of the truth in the inmost consciousness by means of supreme wisdom."—Suzuki's *Lankavatara Sutra* Studies

144

There are truths in the philosophic doctrine which man's heart cannot easily, or at first, accept. This is because they are distasteful. Only after sufficient education by teacher, study, life, or reflection can he bring himself to believe what he does not like.

145

The history of religious and mystical ideas should be investigated and studied from an impartial independent standpoint, without bias for, or prejudice against, with enough critical ability to sift facts from opinion yet with enough sympathetic interest in the subject to collect materials widely from time and place. This is not work for a dried-up pedantic scholar without inner experience of his own, nor for a gullible excitable enthusiast, nor for a self-limited committed scientist, nor for a tradition-bound, excessively past-worshipping, anti-modern, religio-scholar-mystic. With this work should be conjoined a comparative study of those ideas, which requires not only historical talent and learning but deeper inner knowledge, advanced and personal experience, and skill in communicating the higher yields of intellect, feeling, mystical intuition—in short, some philosophical equipment. There would be no place in such teaching for rigid dogma, no division into "official" monopolized truth and unenlightened unblessed invention, certainly no denunciation of heresy.

146

Ignoramuses and blockheads find it easy and pleasant to criticize the backwardness and darkness of the Middle Ages and the periods of antiquity. Such criticism gives them the feeling of being on a superior plane altogether, of having truth where these earlier, and consequently unluckier, forebears had error.

I personally do not take such a silly attitude. I criticize the past without denying its possession of spiritual treasures. The modern student should revere the teachers and study the teachings of antiquity. He will honour the lives and treasure the words of Jesus and Buddha, Krishna and Confucius, Muhammed, Plato, and Plotinus alike. But he should not confine himself to any single one of them alone nor limit himself within any single traditional fold. He must also lift himself out of the past into the present. He must reserve his principal thought, time, and strength for living teachers and contemporary teaching.

147

To be unattached is also to be unattached intellectually, to take up no intellectual position as against all the others and to refuse partisanship, sectarianism, group joining, one-sidedness, and exclusion of all other ideas and teachings. By refusing to join a sect the candidate for philosophy refuses to put himself in the position which regards all those outside the sect as being the unchosen race.

148

Dr. Johnson understood the philosophical attitude rightly when he said that we have both to enjoy life and to endure life.

149

The great sacrifice which every aspirant is called on to make is the sacrifice of that ignorance which separates him from his Divine Source. This ignorance cannot be removed by the intellect alone, however, or by Yoga alone.

150

The pleasant and painful vicissitudes of human life are common to all, but a correct viewpoint regarding them is not. So the philosophical discipline aims to provide it.

151

He must come on this quest not for a few years but for all his life.

152

It is necessary for the student to make a combined effort of will, analytic reflection, prayer, and study to understand and dissolve the obstacles created by the ego.

153

It is vital to see clearly the difference between teachings that spring from and serve only the ego, and those that spring from and lead to the Overself.

154

There are no initiatory rites, no disciplinary rules and vows.

155

If you ask what reality is, in philosophy's view, the answer must be consciousness. If you further ask what man's work in this life is, the answer must be to become conscious of consciousness as such. But because, ordinarily, consciousness never discloses itself to him but only its varying states, he can accomplish this work only by adopting extraordinary means. He will have to steel his feelings and still his mind. In short, he will have to deny himself.

156

Plutarch pointed out that if anybody could easily fulfil the injunction "Know thyself," it would not have been considered a divine precept.

157

Its searching and searing truth will draw out all his vanity and leave him feeling quite hollow inside.

158

If he makes worship a preparation for meditation, and if he accompanies investigation of the inspired texts by application of the knowledge gleaned; if he joins purification of his body to purification of his mind; he may expect to gain a balanced state of illumination in return for this balanced approach.

159

No single path will suffice. All must intertwine with each other, help each other, balance and regulate each other. It is the totalized and equalized effort which counts most.

160

Life asks from him something more than spiritual aspiration, more than prayer, more than meditation. He needs to offer all these, but he must also be intelligent and practical, kind, and controlled.

161

Wisdom lies in combining the three chief yogas, not in separating them. For instance, low vitality does not promote high intelligence but rather hinders it, hence some physical disciplines are as needful as mental ones. The three yoga groups are not only not antagonistic to each other but actually complementary. Whoever ignores any single one can make only one-sided progress.

162

A path which requires so much from the traveller will inevitably be a slower path than the religious and mystical ways. But it will also be a surer one.

163

These critics of philosophy should closely question themselves whether the real reason for their dislike of it is that it humiliates them into secretly acknowledging their lack of the courage to follow the philosophic Quest.

164

His special need is to unite intellectual breadth and emotional balance with this inner attainment.

165

We have deeply felt the force of Epictetus' outcry: "Show me a man modelled after the doctrines that are ever upon his lips. So help me, Heaven; I long to see one Stoic!" It is not less easy to preach than to practise in our own time. But here is the acid test which will reveal what is and what is not pure gold. On the basis of such a test, mankind seems to cry in vain for a single Illuminate.

166

It is possible by depth of thought or by persevering over the years to so impregnate the mind with these implacable truths that it automatically reacts philosophically to its varied experiences and situations.

167

These truths must become so vivid in his mind that he cannot help acting upon them.

168

The promises of religion are mild efforts to console weaker people, but the rewards of philosophy are truths that have to be heroically borne.

169

The basis of this philosophic discipline is a well-developed reason, a sound character, and a cultivated mystical intuition.

170

Not by harsh outrages on the body but by the simple growth of higher value through deeper penetration of the truth, is the philosophic way. "The purity which cometh from knowledge is the best." says the *Mahabharata*.

171

In the end he should seek to gain confirmation of the teaching and practical knowledge of its working by firsthand personal experience. This achievement is possible, but at the cost of living out in action what he learns in thought.

172

The practice of philosophy is not easy, but it is the only way to gain its advantages. When it takes firm root in day-to-day life, experience, behaviour, and activity, its truth is tested and survives, solidly confirmed.

173

We must examine current concepts of the world with the greatest care, and then have the courage to accept all the consequences of such examination. We must question life in the profoundest possible manner, never hesitating to probe deeper and deeper, and truth will come when the answer comes.

174

The quadrangle of religious devotion, metaphysical study, mystical meditation, and inspired action makes the tool for philosophic work.

175

His is no narrow one-sided quest. All through life he will be seeking wisdom for his mind, goodwill for his heart, and health for his body.

176

Although it is necessary to differentiate these lines of approach to the Overself in the study stage of growth, it would be wrong at any time to regard them as being mutually exclusive. Actually metaphysics and mysticism must, at the last, meet and intermingle. From the first the sensible student will perceive this and use each, in turn as well as together, to broaden his outlook and balance and understanding.

177

Philosophy attends to each side of this five-sided creature man and thus gives him a training that is broad enough to meet life's demand.

178

He has to take the subtle thoughts of philosophy, the deep emotions of religion, the sensible practicality of modernism, and the whisperings of his own intuition to form a composite systematic credo.

179

If he is to take on the label of philosopher, he will try to bear his troubles with fortitude and endeavour to keep hold of the great eternal truths in support of it.

180

The way is long and hard. It involves developing all the different sides of the personality. Prayer and meditation lead to the cultivation of intuition and aspiration—and these, at the same time, must be accompanied by the strengthening of will, plus study and reflection. All efforts should be made side by side, so to speak, to lead to a balanced psyche—the philosophic ideal.

181

The philosophic approach to a problem is first to look at it and then to look away from it.

182

In the turmoil of daily events it is easy to lose philosophic perspective. He should not let this happen but instead strive constantly to gain such a perspective.

183

Without this discipline they will be unable to distinguish the authentic communion with an inspiring source from their own personal thoughts and feelings.

184

The ego is so bound up with the thoughts his mind produces and his intuition yields, with the experience his meditation practice and prayerful worship invoke, that it is most essential for him to undergo a course of purificatory discipline to obtain ego-free results.

185

How successfully he perceives the truth will depend partly on how successfully he overcomes the limitations and escapes the associations of his own personality.

186

It is, in a sense, one long experience of becoming impervious to desires, ambitions, and, last of all, even to aspirations for growth. It is a dying to the lesser, personal self as one awakens and surrenders to the greater Over-Self.

187

He divides into two persons, the onlooker and the player, a feat beyond ordinary capacity and possible only when the philosophic quest has trained mind and re-educated feeling.

188

If, as some think, the philosophic way of life is a hard one, it still remains the right one. All other ways are mere compromises, just concessions to human weakness.

189

The philosophically minded student thinks clearly in advance of the probable consequences—both good and bad—of a contemplated line of action. For he does not want to walk blindly or negligently or rashly.

190

The slow gradual enlightenment of views will finish his development.

191

First he believes in it vaguely, then he understands it precisely, next he practises it daily, and in the end he becomes one with it utterly.

192

A time comes when the seeker is so thoroughly penetrated with philosophic ideals that the higher life will become the everyday life.

193

The initiation into wisdom—if it is to be lasting—is not suddenly given by any master; it is slowly grown by the experiences and reflection of life. Thought is gradually converted into habit, and habit is gradually merged into high character. The philosophic attitude, if it is to be genuine, will pass into the student's nerves and move his muscles.

194

If he cannot by his natural power achieve this, he can at least prepare himself for it and await the grant of grace.

Wholeness, completeness, integrality

195

When the principle of true development is understood, it will be seen that no side of human nature is really hostile to any of the others and that all sides are complementary partners.

196

The philosophic goal is to be spiritually aware in all parts of the psyche, with the complete life as the final result. To give one's life a philosophical basis is to give it the quality of impregnable stability. To give one's knowledge a philosophical foundation is to give it the quality of intellectual soundness. To confine attention exclusively to some particular aspect of truth, ignoring the other aspects which balance or complete it, can only lead to a misleading result. That the approach is different but the goal is the same may be quite true of all ordinary systems of religion and mysticism. It is not quite true of philosophy. Here the approach is many-sided while the goal is integral.

197

It is not enough to clear the egoistic, passional, and emotional colourings from the psyche. If he sees the truth from a very limited point of view, he will still fail to receive or transmit it rightly. Therefore the psyche's different sides must be fully developed: his thinking capacity, intuitional receptivity, emotional sensitivity, and active will must themselves be brought to an adequate degree before his view of truth will be adequate enough.

198

Each part of the human psyche fulfils a separate and necessary function. None is a substitute for or a rival to any of the others; it does not displace but only complements them. Each has its own special work which could not be done by them. A full view of truth calls for a full technique. Only philosophy provides for it.

199

For he has to regenerate the *whole* of his nature, and not merely one side of it, if he is not only to perceive the whole truth but also to perceive it unspoiled and undisturbed.

200

The path is fourfold and not threefold. For it consists of (1) the development of intelligence through both concrete and abstract reasoning, (2) the development of mystical consciousness through cultivation of intuition and practice of meditation, (3) the re-education of moral character, (4) practical service.

201

The fourfold path calls for action, intuition, devotion, and knowledge.

202

He should seek to develop on all four sides of his nature—the intellectual, the emotional, the practical, and the intuitional. The entire endeavour should be directed towards discovering his weaknesses of character and remedying them, strengthening his capacity to think abstractly and metaphysically, refining and ennobling his feelings, disciplining and understanding his passions, cultivating and responding to his intuitions. Thus the philosophic quest is an integral one. It aims at a total illumination of the mind and transformation of the character.

203

Philosophy demands so complete a training only because it offers so perfect a goal.

204

The smoothly rounded symmetry of this fourfold development makes not only for the fullest acceptance of truth but also for the maturest kind of living. Because philosophy considers and improves the human personality as a whole, it is nothing less than inspired practicality. There is indeed no new situation which it cannot meet and negotiate for the best, no old one for which it has failed to offer guidance and in which it has failed to give support.

205

In leading men toward a higher life and a truer world view, it is as justifiable to cajole their feelings as it is to convince their reason; it is as right to stimulate in them the warm aspiration of a mystical devotee as it is to harden the cold precision of a metaphysical scholar; it is as needful to inspire them to compassionate service as it is to exalt their moral outlook. All these are needed for an adequate result. All these qualities are a necessity for a fuller and better-poised life. Each supplements the others and supplies what they, by reason of their own nature and limitations, cannot supply. All these separate things can take an aspirant some way along the quest, but none will take him all the way. Most efforts are aimed only at one or the other, for they often contradict each other, whereas philosophy not only aims at all together but also seeks to achieve something more. For on the one hand it seeks to unfold the transcendent faculty of insight and on the other it seeks to test all its teachings against the opposition of actual experience in the active world.

206

If the change in character and outlook, understanding and conduct is to be a deep and lasting one, then it will have to proceed out of all sides of a man's nature, out of his thinking and feeling, experience and intuition, study and belief—which means that it must proceed out of the knowledge and practice of philosophy. His change must be based on rational ideas as well as emotional movements, on practical results as well as theoretical formulations, on the experiences of other men as well as his own.

207

We have to bring the cosmic experience to the living human organism as a *whole*, not merely to just a part of it. For man is a unity and can fulfil his higher purpose only as he does so with all his being and does not try to separate it into parts.

208

He not only has to receive this illumination in all the parts of his being rather than any one part, but also to receive it equally. It is the obstruction arising in the undeveloped or unpurified parts which is the further cause of his inability to sustain the illumination.

209

It may surprise people to learn that wholeness is a spiritual quality, that all parts of the man must receive and share in the light.

210

We must bring our whole personality to this quest and not merely a part of it. All sides are valuable to each other, hence all are needed by ourselves and all must be embraced. The rich fullness of philosophic life appreciates beauty, aspires to knowledge, activates the will, is suffused by feeling, and cultivates intuition. All these activities—emotional, mental, physical, mystical, metaphysical, and ethical—are to be inseparably consolidated in one and the same character. There must be a total response of our total nature to this call from the Overself. For it is not something which can penetrate our reasoning alone, for example, and leave the rest of our being cold. The quest cannot be limited to any single way alone. It must be wide enough and comprehensive enough to enable us to throw all the forces of our being into such a supreme enterprise. How far is this generous ideal from the narrow ideal of asceticism!

211

That man is truly civilized who has unfolded the possibilities of his physical nature and his spiritual nature both, who has refined his feelings and tastes and developed his thought and intelligence, who rejects the sterility of ascetic living standards based on poverty but welcomes those of aesthetic and functional value based on beauty and comfort.

212

That the goal is nothing short of completeness is what so few understand or want, for it demands more from them than the goal of merely experiencing pleasant feelings. It demands the whole man.

213

Make wholeness a theme for your thoughts and meditations, a focus for your studies and aspirations.

214

When all parts of his psyche concur in an attitude, when each function or faculty is coordinated with the others in the reception and deliverance of truth, then there will be harmony and unity within his inner being and outer life.

215

Yes, we need to know the truth, to discover what *is* in the world around us and in life within us, but we also need to feel and intuit it by experience. This coming-together makes for its realization.

216

The four sides of the pyramid of being—thinking, feeling, doing, and intuiting—must be drawn together, properly developed, and held together in proper balance. The inclination to fragment the self is the inclination to follow the easiest path, not the needed path. The whole person needs both developing and balancing; part of it cannot be left safely in neglect while the other part is intensively cultivated.

The philosophic goal is to be spiritually aware in all parts of the psyche, with the complete life as the final result. The aspirant must engage the whole of his person in the work of self-illumination, and not merely a part of it. If only a piece of it is active in this work, only a piece can get illumined or inspired. Even meditation itself—so important for the awakening of intuition—is only a part, and a limited part, of the Quest. Wholeness must be the ideal, if the whole of the Overself's light is to be brought forth and shone down into every day's living, thinking, feeling, and being. Anything less yields a lesser result. And if the whole is not held properly, is unbalanced, it yields a distorted result.

217

The teaching that the Quest cannot and should not be separated from life in the world is a sound one. Therefore, it is part of philosophy and is not some eccentric enterprise to be undertaken by those who wish to escape from the world, or who, being unable to escape, consider themselves as belonging to a class apart from others in their environment—superior to them, different from them, and holier than them. They also come to consider the Quest as an artificial system of living, devoid of spontaneity and naturalness—something to be laboured at by making themselves abnormal and inhuman. One of the consequences of this attitude is that they tend to overlook their everyday responsibilities and thus get into difficulties. Philosophy has consistently opposed this tendency. Unfortunately, in the reaction from it, there has arisen a fresh confusion in the minds of another group of students who do not understand the beautiful and adequate balance which true philosophy advocates. These students, swayed by such teachers as Krishnamurti, become so enthused by the notion of making spiritual progress through learning from experiences and action alone that they follow Krishnamurti's advice and throw away prayer, meditation, and moral striving, as well as study under personal teachers. This limits them to a one-sided progress and therefore an unbalanced one. Total truth can only be got by a total approach; as *Light on the Path* points out, each of these forms of approach is but one of the steps and all steps are needed to reach the goal.

The whole of his being must be involved in the effort if the whole of truth is to be found. Otherwise the result will be emotional alone, or intellectual alone, or adulterated with egoistic ideas and feelings.

218

It is not enough to be a philosopher because the mind sees the teaching is true; the heart also must be engaged in the matter and love it. Nor are these two enough. The whole person must be lifted up also into it and himself experience the truth.

219

It enters into the fullness of philosophy only when it is felt in the heart, understood in the mind, intuited in the soul, absorbed by the stillness, and actualized in the world.

220

Body and mind depend upon one another, act upon one another. The dualism which would separate them entirely, which would even put them against each other as antagonists, is erroneous. The biological view of man, the psychological view, and the spiritual view of man are complementary.

221

It is not enough to be a good person. One must also be a wise person. It is insufficient to be self-disciplined. One should also be self-illumined.

222

We must be able to reason remorselessly without becoming imprisoned in reason, because we must do justice to every part of our being; but only as a part of the whole must we do justice to the intellect.

223

Those who assert that inner spiritual change can come only from outer physical change and those who assert the opposite are both alike—extremists and fanatics. The two procedures are needed together and should accompany each other.

224

He will be able to manifest more of the Divine when he is developed to the point of being complete in himself than when he is not.

225

There is no other way for man to grow in his fullness than the way which covers the whole of human life and uses the whole of human faculty. There is no other way to make himself fit for the next stage of evolution, which will make him more than man.

226

The foolish man acts at random; the intellectual man plays off his reasons against each other and so may find his power to decide paralysed; the emotional man rejects every guide except personal feeling; the philosophic man uses reason, feeling, and intuition alike.

227

All sides of the psyche are so intertwined that only an integral development will be enough. A balanced mind cannot be got unless the ethic of renunciation has been accepted, for instance, for the vicissitudes of fortune bring disturbing emotions in their wake.

228

Not a one-sided, not even a many-sided, but only an all-sided progress will suit philosophy.

229

When the light of truth enters it will then shine into all parts of his being, not into the intellect alone. It thus becomes a living power, not merely something to be talked or written about.

230

The extraordinary completeness of philosophy, the fusion and equilibrium of being and doing, thinking and feeling, introverted stillness and extroverted living, egolessness and egoity, make it rare and precious.

231

Thus, striving and studying, praying and willing, meditating and aspiring, he uses all the self to reach to the All-Self.

232

The logical mind can take him only part of the way. The imaginative mind can take him where the other cannot. If he leaves out either the first or the second, he will suffer loss.

233

If we are to come to truth at all, we must come to it with all our being, not with a half or a quarter of our being.

234

If he is to be made whole, his everyday personality must put itself into perfect harmony with, and under the rule of, his super-personal Overself.

235

It may not be possible for many persons to achieve such wholeness altogether, but as far as it is possible it should certainly be sought.

236

Specialization in the search after knowledge leads inevitably to an unbalanced picture of the whole. The expert usually knows more about one single thing but less about everything else. He loses the art of putting all these bits of knowledge together in a just and undistorted way.

237

Religion adores God from a distance, mysticism feels God's ray within itself, metaphysics knows the certitude of God's existence only in the intellect. Philosophy alone makes a many-sided approach to God.

238

An idealism which is sincere but naïve and a detachment which is earnest but frigid are not enough.

239

His mind cannot easily take hold of the many-sidedness of truth in its entirety. Yet only by so doing can he bring its seeming contradictions together and reconcile them.

240

The whole self must seek truth if the whole truth is to be found.

241

No one faculty of human nature is the whole of it. The body's wills, the heart's feeling, the intellect's reasoning, and the soul's intuiting must all be considered and brought into play.

242

If the inner life is cultivated in part of one's being only, the illumination when it comes will light that part only. But if the intellect worships as well as thinks and if the emotions move with it, both develop together in wholeness.

243

A total effort to purify all areas is needed if there is to be a total removal of the blockages, the compulsions, the distortions and the superstitions rather than a temporary suppression of them.

244

The satisfaction of one part of his nature may be sufficient for him but it is not sufficient for Life. Sooner or later in this or in another birth, he will have to nurture what has been neglected.

245

Philosophy is not limited to work in meditation, although that is perhaps its most notable dramatic form. It is also applied in the area of everyday living routines and relationships. It is also active in work on character, emotions, and attitudes. It takes in the body and its diet.

246

To recognize that the paths down which the ego has led him are illusory is admirable and necessary, but it is only a first step. It will not stop him from continuing to go down them unless he has acquired something more than his merely intellectual knowledge. Other things are equally indispensable to complete his approach.

247

What the Chinese vividly call "walking on both legs"—that is, joining and using two or more of our faculties instead of a single one—avoids narrow-mindedness and leads to better results.

248

If the truth is sought for with every faculty of a man's being, its illumination when found will enter every faculty too.

249

If he brings only a part of his ego into the Quest, then only a part of it will become enlightened and only a part of his activities will show the effects of enlightenment.

250

If active intelligence will stop him from making one kind of blunder, active intuition will save him from a different kind. He cannot afford to neglect any part of his psyche. There must be an integral and total development of it.

251

We must find truth with our intellect and feel it with our emotion, surrender to it with our intuition and apply it with our will.

252

If the illumination is to complete itself, it must be passed through the intellect as well as the emotions, the will as well as the imagination, until it lives in every part of his being.

253

So many seekers find a little calm from their meditation, but quite soon when they are back in the world's turmoil they lose it again. This is inevitable if they depend on the short meditations alone, which is as much as most Westerners can perform. If, however, they would support these attempts with the cultivation of the higher knowledge which philosophy offers they would be less likely to lose those calm moods.

254

One must not be premature in demanding final union with the Overself. That comes only after years of all-round development. One must first prepare himself inwardly to receive it; only then may he expect the ultimate union. This preparation affects the whole personality—intellect, emotion, will, and intuition.

255

Because his whole nature is involved in the search for truth, it is his whole nature that in the end finds and receives it. Consequently he gains a certitude, a surety that is complete, unshakeable, and stable.

256

Plato's teaching that the three great ideals of truth virtue and beauty are reflected down to and through all levels of existence—however obscured and diminished and feebler they become with each descent—is one of the grandest offerings of the Western world.

257

When devotion stands on knowledge, it stands on a rock which nothing and nobody can move, nor hardships weaken.

258

We may yield intellectual assent and yet remain emotionally unconvinced, just as we may yield emotional assent and yet remain intellectually unconvinced. Philosophy harmonizes both these sides of our nature and thus dissolves the disharmony.

259

The ardour of his devotion and the fervour of his aspiration will not be lessened because he has begun to get rid of his metaphysical poverty and social sterility. On the contrary, they will be supported by the one effort and confirmed by the other.

260

Faith may carry a man through crises but faith plus knowledge will carry him all the better.

261

His loyalty to the teaching must penetrate through all the levels of thought and feeling and faith.

262

The work of self-integration is the taking up of the whole physical and emotional and intellectual nature into the intuitive higher one.

263

The proper way to solve his problems is to bring to bear upon them not only all that his own experience and reason and other persons' counsel and knowledge can command, but also all the intuitive leading he can obtain from an ego-freed heart and a thought-quieted mind. This is the total approach to them.

264

A balanced development will not stimulate the intellect and starve the feelings, nor do the opposite. It will give the intuition the highest place, making it the ruler of reason, the check on emotion.

265

The thinking, feeling and willing faculties of human nature have to be developed and refined before they can give some measure of the higher satisfaction and happiness—but by themselves and left to their competing selves they cannot give the full measure and perfect quality of these twin rewards. They need to be integrated to be brought harmoniously together, put in their proper place and ruled by another faculty operating on a level above them. Such a one is the intuition.

266

It is needful on the philosophic path that he understand as well as feel. But if now he begins to try to understand this wonderful consciousness with his thinking intellect alone, he will necessarily limit it. The effort to comprehend which he is called upon to make must therefore be much more an intuitive one.

267

Thus, and thus alone, can a man become entire and integrated, using all his nature and all his being for the most desired and desirable end.

268

To isolate some detail and make it a whole unto itself is always imprudent but it would be much less so in this case if it were the intuition.

Balance

269

The principle of balance is one of the most important of philosophic principles.(P)

270

Balance has a unique place, for it is not only needed as a qualification to be cultivated but also as a regulator of all the other qualifications. This is because it is an effect of which the activity of intuition is a cause. Thoughts, feelings, and actions which are in alignment with intuitive direction are balanced in nature, whereas those which are not are unbalanced ones. In the universe we find balance present with the same uniqueness attached to it. For not only does it appear there as the Law of Recompense to balance all actions with reactions but also as the Moral Law in the human entity to balance his right deeds with satisfying results and his wrong ones with painful results.

271

The philosophic life is essentially a balanced one. Therefore it is condemned by extreme Western materialists, who would extrovert human energies for sensuous ends, and by extreme Eastern mystics, who would introvert them for supersensuous ends. It does not arrive at its balance by compromising these two views but by combining them.

272

All that is needful to a man's happiness must come from *both* these sources—the spiritual and the physical—from the ability to rest in the still centre, in the developed intellectual and aesthetic natures, in the good health and vigour of the body.

273

In the world of today there are signs of mental disorder and emotional upset everywhere. In the world of mystic and occult studies there are similar signs, although of a different kind. In the postbag of a writer whose subject borders the fringe of these subjects there is also ample evidence for the existence of such maladies. People should first free themselves to a sufficient extent and recover their sanity before they get immersed in ideas which will only aggravate this malady. When we come to the world of students of philosophy, insanity disappears—because it is a subject which regards the sage, the fully developed philosopher, as the sanest of men because he is the best balanced of men. We may perhaps find a percentage of dreamers among them, as the metaphysical flights and subtle analyses which it calls for may lift them a little too high above practical concerns; but philosophy is automatically self-adjusting and soon brings them down again to these concerns, whereas the other subjects, the mystic and the occult, leave them up there in hazy clouds where, if they are not careful, they may lose their bearings.

274

The quest does not stop with yoga. We have also to achieve a wise balance between feeling for inner peace and thinking for ultimate truth. Reason must be cultivated because we have not only to feel the presence of God but also to discern true from false gods—that is, true from false ideas of God.

275

Clear thinking has nothing to fear from a warm heart, so long as the two co-operate but do not melt into one another, so long as they walk hand in hand and do not tumble over each other, for so long can we call upon their help with equal freedom. Our personal problems cannot be solved by slushy sentiments alone; but neither can they be satisfactorily adjusted by steely logic alone; we need a balanced wisdom in dealing with them. Only such a wisdom can best explain these problems and explode our delusions about them.

276

The reasoned thoughts of man must be confronted by the delicate feelings of man, balanced and mingled to produce a better person than either alone would produce.

277

Even our understanding of balance has to be corrected. It is not, for philosophic purposes, the mean point between two extremes but the compensatory union of two qualities or elements that need one another.(P)

278

The required condition of balance as the price of illumination refers also to correcting the lopsidedness of letting the conscious ego direct the whole man while resisting the super-conscious spiritual forces. In other words, balance is demanded between the intellect which seeks deliberate control of the psyche and the intuition which must be invited by passivity and allowed to manifest in spontaneity. When a man has trained himself to turn equally from the desire to possess to the aspiration to being possessed, when he can pass from the solely personal attitude to the one beyond it, when the will to manage his being and his life for himself and by himself is compensated by the willingness to let himself and his life be quiescent, then his being and his life are worked upon by higher forces. This is the kind of balance and completeness which the philosophic discipline must lead to so that the philosophic illumination may give him his second birth.(P)

279

The basis of the universe is its equilibrium. Only so can the planets revolve in harmony and without collision. The man who would likewise put himself in tune with Nature, God, must establish equilibrium as the basis of his own nature.(P)

280

It is most important to get rid of an unbalanced condition. Most people are in such a condition although few know it. For example, intellectuality without spirituality is human paralysis. Spirituality without intellectuality is mental paralysis. No man should submit to such suicidal conditions. All men should seek and achieve integrality. To be wrapped up in a single side of life or to be overactive in a single direction ends by making a man mildly insane in the true and not technical sense of this word. The remedy is to tone down here and build up there, to cultivate the neglected sides, and especially to cultivate the opposite side. Admittedly, it is extremely difficult for most of us, circumstanced as we usually are, to achieve a perfect development and equal balance of all the sides. But this is no excuse for accepting conditions completely as they are and making no effort at all to remedy them. The difficulty for many aspirants in attaining such an admirably balanced character lies in their tendency to be obsessed by a particular technique which they followed in former births but which cannot by itself meet the very different conditions of today. We must counterbalance the habit of living only in a part of our being. When we have become harmoniously balanced in the philosophic sense, heart and head will work together to answer the same question, the unhurrying sense of eternity and the pressing urge of the hour will combine to make decisions as wise as they are practical, and the transcendental intuitions will suggest or confirm the workings of reason. In this completed integral life, thought and action, devotion and knowledge do not wrestle against each other but become one. Such is the triune quest of intelligence, aspiration, and action.(P)

281

It is not only balance inside the ego itself that is to be sought, not only between reason and emotion, thought and action, but also and much more important, outside the ego: between it and the Overself.(P)

282

But it is not enough that all these varied elements of his being should be harmonized and balanced. It is also needful that they should be balanced upon a spiritual centre of gravity.

283

A well-balanced person is not necessarily one who takes the measured midpoint between two extremes but one who *lets* himself be taken over by the inner calm. The needed adjustment is then made by itself. Although this avoids his falling into lopsided acts or exaggerated views, a merely moderate character is not the best result. More important is the *surrender* to the higher power which is implicit in the whole process of becoming truly balanced.(P)

284

Balance is the perfect control and mutual harmony of thought, feeling, and action.

285

Sanctity needs the balance of sanity.

286

Greece's greatest contribution to the quest was the idea of Balance. Those who lack it, lack the proper capacity to receive truth *as it is*. And among them those who are narrow and fanatical, who make a special claim to supremacy for *their* way, cult, or doctrine, end by becoming the victims of their own exaggeration. A single glimpse is announced as a permanent illumination; a perception of metaphysical truth is announced as total illumination.

287

What most modern seekers need is to attain equilibrium in themselves and to achieve harmony in their lives. From the first, they will be able to enjoy inner peace; from the second, outer peace.

288

There are two poles in all activity. To get a true picture of life both must be recognized, and neither denied. But since these poles are opposite extremes, it is an unfortunate human tendency precisely to deny one or the other.

289

To avoid this imbalance, look for both poles in each case and establish them. Do not be satisfied with a one-sided view which excludes all others, nor with sectarian smugness which knows only one way to live rightly—its own.

290

Little minds are dismayed or baffled by this truth. They would like the universe to bear a single face, and life to have a single direction. But then the growth for which they are here would not be possible. Larger minds are given enough vision to reconcile the contradictions and to write the opposites. They see life whole, not in fragments.

291

The fanatics, the extremists, the exclusivists, and the intolerant never find truth. This is in part because they persistently reject the pole which opposes the one on which they have taken their stand. They refuse to see that it is needed to do justice, to complete the picture, and to explain the tension between both. It is needed to give a deeper and clearer view of their own experience. This is why philosophy teaches the need and value of achieving balance between opposites.

292

How shall a person balance himself? The word means a lot more than its seeming simplicity suggests. He can start by not letting any one part of himself carry the whole person away, off his feet. But balance is not only a matter of making nature and character, activity and living, better proportioned. It is also a matter of mental calm, by whose light proper values may be seen and each thing put where it ought to be. The philosopher's body-consciousness, for instance, is part of his whole consciousness and now no longer fills all the space. It is where it belongs, in its own place.

293

He should cultivate those aspects of his psyche which need further stature and he should deliberately neglect those which have already been over-cultivated. In this way he will bring about a better equilibrium, a sounder harmony within his own being.

294

The virtue of this balanced approach shows itself in every department of the Quest. For instance, in the relationship between disciple and master, he will avoid the one-sided emphasis upon the latter's personality which certain circles in the Orient and Occident foster through their own immaturity.

295

One of the chief symbols of this law of balance is the cross.

296

A man is able to balance a pair of scales if he holds them at their centre. He is able to balance the various human functions if he finds his true centre. From that point he can see where one has been neglected and where another has been overused. From that source he can get the strength and guidance to make the necessary adjustments.

297

He ought not to become so saturated with his metaphysical studies or so strained by his mystical contemplations that everything else, and especially everything human, has lost interest for him. When this happens, when he is no longer capable of enjoying himself, or relaxing, his mental equilibrium is upset.

298

Wisdom requires balance and hence the wise man rejects extremes and reconciles opposites.

299

The philosopher seeks to attain a proper equilibrium which will enable him to move within the world of turmoil, conflict, egocentric men, and materialistic aims and yet keep in continuous contact with the consciousness of his Overself.

300

In the sense of proportion, balance, and measure we find a gift from philosophy, as also a path to philosophy.

301

If a seeker lacks sufficient practical experience, he must learn to "do" more and to "dream" less; if he is highly intuitive and idealistic, he must learn also to be physically active and constructive in a down-to-earth fashion.

302

I have often insisted on the need of keeping the personality to a well-balanced form. This insistence arises principally out of the nature of true philosophy itself. It must be lived. But it also arises out of the need for self-protection against the perils which oppose the quest: internally, the wanderings of fancy into hallucination and the self-engrossment which breeds neuroticism; externally, the negative passions and blind materialism of a deteriorating society.

303

A metaphysical truth ought not be treated in a dry arid manner as if it stood quite alone, apart from its connections with the rest of philosophy. If the devotional, the active, and the aesthetic sides are left out from the wholeness, the union with these other aspects, metaphysics can easily become lifeless and monotonous. Philosophy lives in the heart no less than in the head, in its glorious beauty no less than in its sturdy support for the life of action.

304

Buddhism is a religion founded on disillusionment with life. But philosophy, being more than a religion, cannot rest solidly balanced on such a slender foundation. If with Buddhism it sees the ugliness, the transiency, and the suffering in life, it also sees the beauty in Nature and art, the Eternal behind life and the satisfaction in it. Why should philosophy pretend to see no bright places because it can see the dark ones? Why should it deny the thrill of music in human existence because it can hear the wail of misery? This is why it is as quietly happy as it is gravely resigned.

305

It is common enough to see aspirants become one-sided and, to this extent, unbalanced. Because they are attracted or helped by some particular way—a special method, attribute, teaching, or doctrine—this is no reason to ignore all the others or to make it the central pivot on which the whole of life rests. Light ought to broaden his outlook, not narrow it.

306

Half-right, half-wrong, many theories and judgements need to be paired in order to compensate and balance one another.

307

In the Masonry of ancient times, the initiate was given the symbol of two pillars in his course of instruction. The meaning was that a true balance should sustain his progress.

308

Another reason for the great importance of achieving a balanced personality is that the dangers of neuroticism, inertia, fantasy, and psychism are thereby avoided.

309

It is rare to find a man whose mind is evenly balanced, rarer still to find one whose mind and life are so.

310

In a wisely balanced life, neither contemplation nor activity will be auxiliary to the other. Each will be useful, even necessary, to the other.

311

It is laudable to practise optimism to a justifiable degree, but it is reprehensible to practise it to an absurd degree. Balance is needed.

312

The unbalanced genius is not to be admired for his unbalance but in spite of it.

313

It is natural that the endeavour to follow this ideal of Balance will spill over into his judgements and opinions. He will want to see all sides of a matter, and especially all the weaknesses in his own views, all the sound points in opponent's views.

314

Balance requires the businessman to live for something more than his office. It requires the artist to live for something more than his studio. Both may be giving a useful service to many people. Still this is not enough. They need also to serve the ideal of their own higher integration.

315

To achieve proper balance it may be necessary to over-emphasize some particular attribute, quality, or capacity.

316

A balance may be established between opposites or between complements.

317

Man not only needs intelligence to find his way to the truth, he needs balanced intelligence.

318

To attain balance is good but not enough; to sustain it is also called for.

319

This principle of Balance operates throughout the universe. The growth of plant and animal forms is balanced by their decay, their life by their death. If this principle failed to operate for only fifty years, the seas would be packed with fish to such an extent that their waters would spill over and flood most lands, submerging their cities.

320

Few have symmetrical faces; few stand equally upon both feet.

321

To gain better balance he needs also the virtues opposite to his own virtues.

322

When the imbalanced person becomes a nonconformist, he becomes an extreme nonconformist. If he does the right thing, he usually does it in the wrong way.

323

It is not easy to cultivate sensitivity without cultivating softness at the same time.

324

Balance is always needed. A good stretched too far may become an evil, virtue grown unbalanced may become a vice, a truth pushed to extremes may become a grotesque parody of itself.

325

A well-balanced, well-developed man will habitually function in all parts of his being, regularly draw on all his resources, and live in harmony with his whole psyche.

326

In our time even more than in other times, world history has produced political, religious, racial, economic, and other kinds of fanatics, some of them quite frenzied ones. But no philosophic fanatic has been produced. For how could the balance, the discipline, the intelligence, and the impartiality so often and so rightly inculcated by philosophy ever let that happen?

327

Humour can be used to restore a lost sense of proportion or to show up a deplorable lapse from sanity.

328

Some have been pushed off balance by certain happenings in their lives but most were born with the tendency, which was either latent, and needed time to show itself, or patent, and was displayed from childhood.

329

The body's senses, if unexamined, unanalysed, and left uncontrolled, lead him into an animalized existence. But understood and ruled by reason with aspiration, they serve him.

330

The pleasures of life may be taken—he need not become morose and gloomy—but balance and discipline are needed to take them wisely.

331

When there is no collision between intellect and emotion, or between intuition and egoism, or between imagination and will, it may be said that one's inner harmony has been fully attained.

332

He may well study in different schools of thought and experiment with different views of life. But this is advisable only if he takes care to do so with a balanced approach, tempering enthusiasms with analysis, acceptances with discrimination, acclamations with criticisms.

333

Let us welcome the offerings of art and culture, of applied intellect and civilized living, without hostility or belittlement, even while remembering the mocking futility of an existence which does not go beyond them to the deeper values of the Overself.

334

The cases of Krishnamurti and D.H. Lawrence are very illustrative of the need and value of balance. Here are two men of unquestioned genius and independent thought who have influenced the currents of their time. Krishnamurti aroused people to the fact that they were really captives and invited them to leave their cages. Lawrence denied the conventional denial of sex. What both these men had to say was important, and needed to be said. But Krishnamurti was so rigidly uncompromising and Lawrence so passionately rebellious that their very necessary contributions have themselves become fresh sources of misunderstanding. What is sound in their teaching is a part of philosophy, and quite acceptable: but the exaggeration and over-emphasis which accompany it are not. They are the consequences of the teachers' temperamental imbalance. Again and again seekers after truth have been counselled to practise the art of bringing together and balancing the different elements of their nature, the different factors of the quest, the different demands of everyday living. Philosophy is able to give us peace because it incorporates this art.

335

Whenever religion becomes and remains an obsessional activity, it is time to call a halt. The need of keeping mental equilibrium is supreme with the philosophy of truth as it was with the philosophy of Greece.

336

A well-balanced man cannot be thrown down. He may be pushed about by circumstances but he will always keep, or return to, his centre.

337

The best Greek minds rejected superstition and refused to give metaphysics and religion and science any place beyond that which was their due. They avoided the excessive religiosity of the Indian minds, which Buddha tried to correct.

338

The Delphi Temple inscription carved on the wall was not only, "Know Thyself," but continued, "Nothing in excess."

339

Our schools teach many subjects to the young to prepare them for life, to train them for a career, to show them how to discipline the mind, or merely to instill information. But none teaches them the much-needed subject of balance. Where there is too much of one thing, or too little of it, there is unbalance. Where certain attributes preponderate and others are deficient, there is the same result. It is not only extremists and fanatics who suffer from this trouble, but millions who pass as ordinary citizens, for it takes widely different forms.

340

With this beautiful ideal of balance ever before him, he will be able to avoid falling into anarchy's abyss, on one side, or becoming a mere copy of his teacher, on the other.

341

The Ideal Balance may be impossible to attain but we can get nearer to it and establish a useful working balance.

342

If it be asked why all this bother to equilibrate the ego, why all this talk about the necessity of balance, the answer is that what the *Bhagavad Gita* calls "evenness of mind" is an inescapable precondition to the accurate reception of the philosophic enlightenment.

343

All of Rudyard Kipling's famous poem *If* is a preachment upon the virtues of balance.

344

When thought and feeling grow purer together, when knowledge and aspiration wax stronger side by side, when idea and action progress mutually, he will come to know this truth about the virtues and values of balance by his own self-experience.

345

Impulsiveness can be a help toward moving more quickly to the goal, but by itself, without the check and balance of intuitive and rational development, it becomes fanaticism and is harmful.

346

Enthusiasm is a helpful emotion when new ideas have to be put forward against inertia or opposition. But when it loses its inner balance and proper measure, becomes incautious and exaggerated, then it renders a disservice to its own cause.

347

He should realize the wisdom of setting up for himself the ideal of a balanced, integral development. If he needs to develop along other lines in order to balance up, the abstention from meditation for periods will do him no harm.

348

The heart must *feel* the truth; the head must *know* it; both activities must unite in equilibrium. Without such a result there is only bubbling enthusiasm or dry studiousness but not philosophy.

349

It is also a matter of bringing the self into equilibrium, first within its own little range and second with the larger existence of the universal being.

350

It is important to bring about a measure of balance within his own person: otherwise he finds only an incomplete or fanatic or distorted truth. To avoid the first he must supply what is lacking. To remedy the second he must withdraw into equipoise. To correct the third he must get knowledge from a reliable source, be it man or book.

351

Pericles claimed, in the Funeral Oration, that Athens had found a golden mean, a sober balance, in its institutions. And in golden letters was inscribed on the temple at Delphi: "Nothing too much. The modest Mean is best." Although the dictionary defines the Mean as "midway between extremes" and although a good principle may defeat its own purpose if carried too far, the philosophic Mean is only sometimes the midpoint; at other times it is not. For where there is a deficiency on one side, or an over-emphasis on the other, it may be necessary to move the point nearer or farther, according to the situation.

352

It is an error to believe that finding a balance between two extremes, Confucius' Golden Mean, is another form of compromising with truth. Rather is it giving both units in the inescapable pairs of opposites which constitute life, universe, and being, their proper due as determined by the particular circumstances and time. The result is an interweaving of the two rather than a forced unnatural division of them. But their proportions will naturally vary in each case, in every situation, and not at all necessarily be equal.

353

The proportion of development needed by each part of his being will differ with every individual. Only a correct ratio will lead to a correct balance of all the parts.

354

The philosopher seeks to make a balance between the inner and outer life. But it would be a mistake to believe this means fifty-fifty measure. Each individual must find his *own* measure.

355

Philosophic balance is not to be defined as the middle point between two extremes, nor as the compromise of them. It is determined on a higher level altogether, since it is determined and regulated by the intuition.

356

Aristotle used the word "proportionate" when advocating correct balance (his doctrine of the mean), by which he made clear that balance is "relative to us": it is a variable depending on each individual.

357

Such balancing does not mean an equal measure of each element; it means the necessary and sufficient measure.

358

What is often overlooked is that the middle way, the point between extremes, varies in position with each person. It is not the same for all.

359

Balance does not mean achieving equality between pulls from different forces or between the activities of different faculties.

360

This is not to be mistaken for the static balance of a lower level, of a neutral, middle-ground position. It is a dynamic balance.

361

Balance is not reached by choosing a point half-way between two opposite conditions, but by choosing one that is just right, that accords to each condition just what the individual particularly needs for his well-being and development.

362

To the question "What is the relative importance of the constituents of the threefold path?" there can be no stereotyped answer. Each man will find that one to be most important to him which he most lacks. Whoever, for example, has practised little meditation in the past will probably feel within himself—and feel rightly—that meditation is the most important member of the tribe. But this will be true only for himself and not necessarily for others. The improvement of concentration and the tranquillization of a troubled mind are essential. He must have experience in yoga before he can have expertness in philosophy, but if he wants to overdo it, if he becomes excessively preoccupied with this single facet of life, then he is to that extent unbalanced. The aim must always be to bring each element not only to maturity, but also into balance with the other elements. Whatever is needful to achieve these aims becomes important to an individual. He must not let one member of the self walk too far ahead of the others without stepping back to bring them up too. He must tread a middle path and keep away from extremes.

The philosopher cannot afford to take only a selfish or sectional view; he must take a balanced all-embracing one, if only because he knows that his duty towards truth calls for it. This is why the man who has no philosophic aim in life cannot achieve balance in life.

363

Balance cannot be reached if completeness has not previously been reached.

364

The balanced life must be a balance of fullness, not emptiness. The aspirant's day should contain earnest self-humbling prayer and warm heartfelt devotion as well as calm contemplation and studious reflection. The one should express the tearful anguish of unsatisfied aspirations as the other should express the determined exercise of a mind intent upon truth and reality.

365

All the different sides of his nature have to find their equilibrium in this ultimate condition. Every part of him has to finish its growth before that can fully happen.

366

Not only is he to integrate all his human functions but he is also to do this on the highest level of their development. Nor is he to stop there. He must equilibrate as well as integrate.

367

The inner equilibrium which, the *Gita* says, is yoga's goal is not only a state of even-mindedness but also a state of equalized development. It is a delicate state and cannot be retained if the yogi is deficient in certain sides of his being.

368

As we traverse different ranges of experience so we acquire different qualities, capacities, perceptions, and ideas, which all contribute toward the ultimate end of balance, of perfecting our character and developing our mentality.

369

It is a paradoxical demand: that we enrich our individuality at the same time that we purify it.

370

The student's task does not end and cannot end with metaphysical study alone, nor with ultra-mystical contemplation alone. Action is also needed. Indeed, the illumination thus gained will of itself eventually compel him to add this factor spontaneously by an inward compulsion, if he has not already begun to do so by an external instruction. This is true of all the qualifications which philosophy demands of the aspirant: mystical feeling, metaphysical thinking, and altruistic action. Each of the trio, when a certain ripe degree of its own development has been reached, will spontaneously impel him to seek after whichever of the others he has neglected. For himself this means that he can claim to understand a truth when he feels and knows it so profoundly and acts up to it so faithfully that it has become a part of himself—not before. There is then not merely understanding alone, not merely mystic experience alone, but also a transformation of contemplation into action. Life thereafter is not merely thought out in the truest way but also lived out in the loftiest way.

371

With knowledge, wisdom, and understanding developing in him along with devotion, aspiration, and reverence, and with the two trends culminating in appropriate action, his quest will be properly balanced, sane, and productive.

372

It is better, less hazardous, and more gratifying to unfold the spiritual side of the psyche's different parts simultaneously rather than successively.

373

No balance other than an illusory one can be established in the individual if development has not been completed in the individual.

374

The balance will establish itself automatically when these elements are fully developed and these qualities are brought together in our own consciousness.

375

The ideal is not to achieve this inner balance with scanty materials but to achieve it with the amplest ones.

376

A proper balance between two needs must be found by satisfying both, not by only partially satisfying each of them.

377

Only a great nature can take a great illumination and not become unbalanced by it. That is why the full cultivation, all-around development, and healthy equilibrium of the man is required in Philosophy.

378

It seeks to give him a personality which is richly developed and not ascetically starved, which is sensibly balanced and not fantastically lopsided.

379

To hold the balance between these various faculties, and not to exaggerate one at the cost of the others, is as difficult as it is desirable.

380

The admirable balance of Chinese temperament enabled it, until unsettled by the recent madness, to admire individuality, originality, and at the same time to respect past genius and the achievement of tradition.

381

The lines of evolution will not be fully worked out by a partial entry into truth. Man must bring the full measure of his wholeness into it. In this way he will not only completely realize himself as a spiritual entity, but will also achieve harmony and balance within the realization itself. Nothing less will satisfy his profoundest needs.

382

Philosophy seeks harmony. It brings thinking and feeling not only into a working relationship with each other, but also into one that helps, corrects, and completes the duty of the other.

383

It is of great importance to develop balance, reason, and emotional awareness simultaneously. Exercises should include intellectual analysis of oneself and one's experiences, increased efforts in self-control and outward expression, and an intensified attitude of love and loyalty.

384

He may keep out the ego's interference and yet not reach the pure truth because he cannot keep out his evolutionary insufficiency.

385

Those who talk or write truth, but do not live it because they cannot, have glimpsed its meaning but not realized its power. They have not the dynamic balance which follows when the will is raised to the level of the intellect and the feelings. It is this balance which spontaneously ignites mystic forces within us, and produces the state called "born again." This is the second birth, which takes place in our consciousness as our first took place in our flesh.(P)

386

The danger of a lopsided character is seen when humility reverence and piety are largely absent whilst criticism logicality and realism are largely present. The intellect then becomes imperiously proud, arrogantly self-assured, and harshly intolerant. The consequence is that its power to glean subtler truths rather than merely external data is largely lost.(P)

387

The student must hold the picture of his personal life as a whole. He must not see it only as it is at some particular moment or period. If he can succeed in doing this, he will also succeed in banishing the constant oscillation between over-depression on one side and over-elation on the other, between being subjugated by the pain of today and by the pleasure of tomorrow. He will have attained peace.

388

So long as he is living exclusively in one side of his being, so long as there is no balance in him, what else can his view of life be but an unbalanced one? Nor will the coming of illumination completely set right and restore his balance. It will certainly initiate a movement which will ultimately do this, but the interval between its initiation and its consummation may be a whole lifetime.

389

The preliminary requisites to a lasting illumination are development and balance. If part of his nature is still undeveloped in relation to the finished goal and if all parts are off balance in relation to one another, the illumination will go soon after it comes. This balance of mind and life are essential.

390

If he does not understand that balance between inner being and outer nature must be sought and found, he may find that meditation or even abstract reflection may leave him inapt for the ordinary affairs of men who have to live in activities of earning their livelihood or who have to discharge their responsibilities to self, family, and community.

391

Without balance in the recipient there can be no proper transmission or perfect reception of truth. The different parts of his being will absorb and, in consequence, express it unequally. But, granted that the development of these parts is sufficient, where equilibrium is accomplished, there will be the best conditions for the experience of enlightenment to be really what it should be.

392

The separatist spirit which would erect the pediment of truth on the single pillar of yoga alone or of metaphysics alone ends always in failure or, worse, in disaster. When each sphere of activity whose integral union is needed for the successful completion of the structure asserts its self-sufficiency, it begins to suffer what in the individual human being is called an enlarged ego. The student of metaphysics who despises mysticism and the student of mysticism who despises metaphysics will pay the penalty of neurosis for this unhealthy and unbalanced state of his mental life.

393

Without this balance of character he may lose his wisdom while engaged in the very enterprise of desperately seeking to improve it!

394

Those who, like Krishnamurti, will recognize none but the highest level and have no use even for the steps leading up to it become extremists and fanatics.

395

He who has heavily overbalanced his psyche, whose capacity for critical thinking has been gorged with food while his capacity for reverential worship has been starved to death, is to be pitied. For the unhealthier his condition becomes, the healthier he actually believes himself to be!

396

When a particular part of a man's being is thrown out of balance, it is not only that part which is affected but the whole man himself.

397

The value of achieving this delicate balance of faith and reason, of fact and imagination, is shown by what happens to those who, lacking it, put all their trust in predictions and make hopes for the future depend wholly on them. They find themselves betrayed.

398

If his whole approach to truth is lopsided, his discovery of truth will be disfigured.

399

When a single aspect of truth is allowed to obscure or cover, displace or swallow all the other aspects of it, then its balance—one of the most precious of its features—is lost.

400

An attitude of studied indifference to the lesser matters of life simply because one takes the philosophic goal as being of high importance may lead to serious neglect of practical affairs and everyday living. The results could well be deplorable. Such an attitude is not acceptable philosophically.

401

Whoever reaches this point and fails to establish a good equilibrium between heaven and earth, will have to hang suspended between them, no longer on earth but not at all near heaven.

402

Small minds or narrow ones give no validity or little importance to any side of life or culture which does not interest them. Thus they unbalance themselves.

403

Even though he may see the need of correcting his imbalance, he may not be able to see how to achieve it. For the full and correct recognition of his deficiencies may need outside help.

404

Too little intuiting and too much intellectualizing create an unsymmetrical personality. Too little thinking and too much feeling provide a disequilibrated equipment for truth-seeking. In both cases, the man finds half-truths, one-sided truths, but not the grand, great truth.

405

Unbalance leads to unsound judgements and extremist decisions.

406

Whoever gets too much taken up with a single aspect of a subject is liable to exaggerate its importance and upset his balance of mind about it.

407

With an improper balance of these sides of his being, the result of his efforts to communicate his revelation may be another of those inspired insanities which make mystical literature an object of severe criticism.

408

Only by accepting the existence of "the pairs of opposites" in all phases of life, and hence in his spiritual life too, and by establishing this connection in his thoughts, can he develop spiritually in a healthy safe and successful way.

409

When we attain balance, it forces us to note the presence of interconnected opposites in every case. It is only the unbalanced who ignore, deny, neglect, or seek to escape from one or another of these opposites. Proper consideration will try to bring them together, accepting the tension between them as a necessary part of truth about the subject, the person, the situation, or the event.

410

The balance needed by faith is understanding; by peacefulness, energy; by intuition, reason; by feeling, intellect; by aspiration, humility; and by zeal, discretion.(P)

411

Neither the Buddhistic emphasis on suffering nor the hedonistic emphasis on joy is proper to a truly philosophical outlook. Both have to be understood and accepted, since life compels us to experience both.(P)

412

Inner balance is not established by setting two polar opposites against each other, as miserliness against extravagance, but by combining two necessary qualities together such as bravery with caution.(P)

413

Man must seek and find the feminine side of his dual nature; woman must seek and find the masculine. In this way a balanced relation will be established, although the physical body will naturally establish the dominant side.

414

By bringing into a fusion the masculine and feminine temperaments within himself, he also fuses knowledge and feeling, wisdom and reverence.

415

One of the first requisites is to cultivate a sense of balance, a healthy poise between thinking and doing, believing and doubting, feeling and reasoning, between the ideal and the actual.

416

When these two—the positive and negative currents—come together, the electric lamp lights up of its own accord. When these two—intellect and feeling—are properly coordinated, and the character is both properly developed and purified, the Overself in a person begins to shine of its own accord.

417

Let him remember that there are dangers in both optimism and pessimism, that the proper course is to try to see things just as they are, and that nothing in life is all black-shadowed or all rosy-hued.

418

If we seek to become philosophical it is not at all necessary to lose practicality and ignore actuality. We ought to become sufficiently equilibrated to create conditions, make things, and devise arrangements which are visible *here* and serviceable *now*. This should not stop us from mentally training ourselves to follow abstract ideas or metaphysical systems by which lofty levels are attained.

419

The practical wisdom of keeping anchored to earth must balance the spiritual wisdom of seeking flights above it.

420

The idealist should listen to the more responsible cautious voice of practical experience, just as the practical man should take some of the risks of idealism.

421

An independent research will necessarily be a critical one, but the criticism must be balanced by sympathy or it will fail in doing justice and judging accurately.

422

It is not enough for anyone to be a success in integrity if he is a failure in judgement.

423

Here faith and knowledge counterbalance one another, here a solid practicality in dealing with the world is redeemed by a noble morality, here the secrets of meditation are made lucid while the questions of intellect are satisfied.

424

Why must he oppose the pleasurable feelings of the body to the pleasurable feelings of the mind, as if they must always be enemies? Is it not saner to reconcile them in happy combination, to balance them in reasonable proportion, to establish a Chinese "golden mean" between them?

425

Such a balance requires warmth in the heart as well as coolness in the head.

426

Reason must walk side by side with emotion, science with mysticism, compassion with self-interest, action with thought. This balanced life and no other is the truly philosophic one.

427

Thinking and feeling must first balance one another and then only may they, and should they, blend with one another.

428

They have a mutual service to render. Devotion should guide reason and reason should guide devotion.

429

Thus reason and emotion no longer wrestle with each other and no longer oppose one another as antinomies, but find abruptly a point of common fulfilment.

430

Such is the all-round development of the human psyche offered by philosophy. It balances mystical intuiting by logical thinking, religious belief by critical reflection, idealistic devotion by practical service.

431

The Balance required preceding enlightenment is not only between intellect and emotion, thought and will, but also and mainly between the lower and the higher wills, between ego's desires and Overself's self-contentment.

432

When the two wills, higher and lower, are brought into balance and perpetually held there, he has secured the necessary conditions for enlightenment.

433

Our need is to achieve a balance between these two demands of human nature, between useful activity and mental serenity.

434

He who wants society all the time is as unbalanced as he who wants solitude all the time.

435

He has to become expert in keeping both feet firmly on hard ground while keeping his head in this lofty pure atmosphere. This is what sound balance means.

436

He who has gone deeply into himself without abandoning his hold on external reality has kept the balance of his mind.

437

The need today is for harmonious balance between the inner and the outer being, between divine spirit and earthly body, so that the one faithfully reflects the other.

438

When he establishes an equilibrium between the two poles of life, his inner experience fits into the outer, operates with it, and does not contradict it.

439

This is the strength of philosophy, that if it is analytical or critical on one side, it is synthetical or reconciliatory on the other; if it is occupied with the highest possible metaphysical flights, it is grounded on the most solid scientific facts and attentive to the most practical of details; if intellect and feeling are in it, so are intuition and inspiration.

440

A proper balance has no room either for stubborn conservatism or for uncurbed iconoclasm—although, if circumstances are extreme, it may use the one to offset the other.

441

He who can unite self-effort with dependence on grace in a constant balance is able to gain peace. The key to success lies in maintaining balance.

442

Just as in practical life we harmonize and balance two opposing facts to arrive at adequate decisions, as, for instance, between the need of prudence and the need of enterprise, so too in spiritual life it is essential to reconcile apparent incompatibles.

443

Imaginative vision is to be checked by respect for facts, balanced by meticulous reasoning.

444

When the wisdom of experience is married to the drive of youth, tempering it but not paralysing it; when dreams are fulfilled in actions and ideals are reflected in emotions; when intuition reigns over intellect and guides will, man has achieved a worthy balance.

445

The active side of his personality must be properly balanced by the passive side.

446

When they are at the point of just ripening into middle age, the two opposing forces in man or in the universe achieve perfect balance of their polarities.

447

We need this state balanced between mere faith and prudent scrutiny.

448

What philosophy seeks—and what most "systems" do not—is an all-around understanding and development, and an equilibrium between the body and the higher individuality.

449

External activity may be likened to life at the circumference of a wheel; internal meditation may be likened to life at the centre of the wheel.

450

Stillness at the Centre, activity on the circumference—this is equilibrium that is set by Nature (God) as the human ideal.

451

We find that even so serene and enlightened a mind as Emerson's was liable to fall into error like any other mystic's, except that since his mind was unusually perspicuous and intelligent—bordering on the philosophic—this liability was much smaller with him. He suffered from an excess of optimism, which to that extent threw him out of balance at times. A single yet striking instance occurs in his *Lecture on War*. "Trade, as all men know, is the antagonist of war," he said. Yet it was the greed to secure a larger share of the world's growing trade which led in the last hundred and fifty years to several wars. "History is the record of the mitigation and decline of war," he continued. How little its horror has been mitigated since Emerson delivered that sentence in the year 1853, the slain civilian victims of mass air-raids (30,000 in Rotterdam alone) silently inform us. "The art of war, what with gunpowder and tactics, has made battles less murderous," he concluded. The enormous destructiveness of modern weapons, and especially the fiendish murderousness of atom bombs, flatly and fully contradict this statement. How could so honest a thinker, so lovable a man as Emerson fail so grievously in judgement? It was because his balance was not adequately and correctly established.

452

What we have to do is to take only so much of each important factor in life as is really necessary for a balanced life. We must beware of taking too little or too much. Thus a man may have dinner every day but should not live solely for the eating of dinners. So he may practise mysticism but need not make it the sole element of his existence. He should live not for mysticism alone but for the whole of life itself. He may be a practising mystic but should not stop with that.

453

If allowed to absorb too much of his attention, the fascination which mystical teachings and meditation have for the student will render it very difficult for him to cope with the struggles of commonplace existence. If this happens, he should deliberately drop his study of abstract teachings, together with meditation exercises, and concentrate all of his attention on personal matters—at least until he regains balance.

454

He who shuts himself up within the narrow confines of religion alone, or mysticism alone, or metaphysics alone, shuts himself off from the great stream of Life. The way must embrace many apparently antithetical things yet it is really one. Hence the wise man will first evoke within the self those diverse elements which are next to be coordinated into the rounded entirety of a splendid harmony. Hence too it is foolishness for the imprudent mystic to abandon his critical faculties on the threshold of his quest and to scorn the guidance of reasoned knowledge; he wanders haphazard along a path not without its dangers for it skirts at times the very edge of the precipices of madness, delirium, deception, and error. For such scientific and metaphysical knowledge acts as both pilot for the journey and check against its dangers. Without it a man gropes alone and blindfolded through the world-darkness. He does not know the proper meaning, place, and purpose of his multiform experiences. He does not understand that the ecstasies, the visions, and the devotions which have consumed his heart must later give place to the calm, formless, and abstract insight of philosophy. And it was because Ramakrishna was divinely led, in the deepest sense of the term, that he eventually accepted this fact and submitted to the philosophical initiation at the hands of Tota Puri and thus set out to make the ascent from being a visionary to becoming a sage. The lesson of this is that man, like all else, must be viewed in his entirety. Perhaps Hegel's greatest contribution was his discovery of the Dialectical Principle. For it showed the imperative need of surveying *all* around a matter and of understanding it in the fullness of its entire being rather than in the narrowness of a single facet. Ignorance of this important principle is one of the several factors responsible for the birth of fanatical fads, crankish cults, and futile revolutions. In the application of this principle, reason rises to its highest.

455

Wisdom lies in looking into and recognizing the proper limits of both metaphysics and yoga and coordinating them harmoniously. Each is essential and admirable within certain limits; each becomes a dangerous drug beyond them, for then its strength becomes a weakness. We must welcome it so long as it remains where it belongs; we must judge it harshly as soon as it usurps another's place.

456

To obtain a balanced result it is necessary to make a balanced approach and not to rely on a single kind of effort only. The moral character must become involved in the quest of upliftment; the intellectual faculty must work at the study, as well as reflect upon the lessons of, life itself; the intuition must be unfolded by persistent daily practice of meditation; and the everyday practical life must try to express the ideals learned.

4

ITS REALIZATION BEYOND ECSTASY

Mysticism and mystical philosophy compared

Philosophy clears away all the unnecessary mystery from mysticism, while preserving a proper attitude of awe and reverence to whatever is worthy of it.

2

Whereas not a few mystics in the past have been gullible votaries of superstition also, philosophical mystics seek to be entirely free of it. They want their mysticism to be worthy of a rational man.

3

The difference between the two is that one is partially inspired whereas the other is fully inspired.

4

It is not enough to measure the grade of a mystic by his emotional feelings. We must also concern ourselves with his egolessness, his intellectual expression, his aesthetic sensitivity, and his effective practicality. These things make up the difference between an infantile mysticism and a philosophical mysticism.

5

There is this important difference of approach between the would-be mystic and the would-be philosopher. The first is often actuated by emotional conflicts or frustrations for which he seeks some kind of compensation. The second is motivated by a deep love of truth for its own sake.

6

There is much more under judgement here than a merely verbal distinction. The matter is not so simple but far more complex than it seems. For philosophical mysticism introduces some new principles into mysticism which make a profound difference in results and values.

7

Whereas mysticism alone acquaints a man with his true Self, philosophical mysticism does this and also acquaints him with his connection with universal life. It not only tells him of the great laws of evolution and compensation, but also affiliates him with the great soul of the world.

8

All yoga and mystic methods, as well as certain religious practices, although of the highest value as preliminary disciplines, are not the ultimate ends in themselves. If one has sufficient sharpness of mind—that is, sustained concentration on abstract themes—and sufficient freedom from any kind of egoistic preconception whatever, one can instantly grasp the truth and realize it. But who has that? Hence, these various methods of developing ourselves, these yogas, have been prescribed to assist us. Their practice takes a long time, it is true, but the actual realization is a matter of a moment. Nor can it ever be lost again, as can the feeling-ecstasies of the mystics. All these doctrines have their place for people of different degrees of understanding, and it is our duty not to destroy the faith of those who cling to them. But for those who want the highest Truth, and who are prepared to part with their illusions for its sake, there is only "the straight and narrow way, and few there be that find it." It is narrow only because the ego must be left outside the gate; it is straight because it goes direct to the final truth.

9

The mystic may get his union with the higher self as the reward for his reverent devotion to it. But its light will shine down only into those parts of his being which were themselves active in the search for union. Although the union may be a permanent one, its consummation may still be only a partial one. If his intellect, for example, was inactive before the event, it will be unillumined after the event. This is why many mystics have attained their goal without a search for truth before it or a full knowledge of truth after it. The simple love for spiritual being brought them to it through their sheer intensity of ardour earning the divine Grace. He only gets the complete light, however, who is completely fitted for it with the whole of his being. If he is only partially fit, because only a part of his psyche has worked for the goal, then the utmost result will be a partial but permanent union with the soul, or else it will be marred by the inability to keep the union for longer than temporary periods.

10

The philosophic mystic seeks to rise from what is sense-tied to what is sense-free, from the appearance of reality to the pure reality itself. The perceptual symbols and optical phenomena which are so often labelled "mystical" are, therefore, a degree less sensuous to him than their physical counterparts. They are helps at first on the upward way, but they become hindrances in the end. To live permanently in the midst of a psychic mirage, however pleasant or dazzling it seems at the time, is not going to help his true advancement in this path. He should be warned by their appearance not to dally too long with them, but to pass them by unheeded and seek the true insight ahead. This rule is pushed to such an extent in the highest mystical circles of Tibet that the lama-student who has emerged from his novitiate is even warned against accepting as the goal the visions of an enveloping universal light—which is the supreme clairvoyant vision possible for man—and told that this is merely a test of his fixed purpose and a trap for his metaphysical knowledge. He is warned that they will pass as they come. They are useful as *steps* to the Truth, but they are not the *permanent* realization of truth itself. Those who are babes just emerging from the wood of ignorance may *see* the mystic light in a temporary clairvoyant vision, but those who are grown adults will *know* it always as the principle of pure consciousness which makes all vision, whether clairvoyant or physiological, possible. The divine reality being the ultimate and undisclosed basis of all existences, if we externalize it in spectacular visions and phenomenal experiences, we miss its pure being and mix it up with mere appearance. Thus the very experiences which are considered signs of favourable progress in meditation on the mystic's path become signs of hindrance on the philosopher's path.

11

Another difference between a Philosopher and a Mystic is the following: the Mystic may be illiterate, uneducated, simple-minded, but yet may attain the Overself. Thus he finds his Inner Peace. It is easier for him because he is less intellectual, hence has fewer thoughts to give up and to still. But Nature does not absolve him from finishing his further development. He has still to complete his horizontal growth as well as balance it. He has obtained depth of illumination but not breadth of experience where the undeveloped state of faculties which prevents his light from being perfect may be fully developed. This can happen either by returning to earth again or continuing in other spheres of existence; he does all this *inside his peace* instead of, as with ordinary man, outside it. When his growth is complete, he becomes a philosopher.

12

He who has attained illumination, but not philosophic illumination, must come back to earth for further improvement of those faculties whose undeveloped state prevents the light from being perfect.

13

The need of predetermining at the beginning of the path whether to be a philosopher or a mystic arises only for the particular reincarnation where attainment is made. Thereafter, whether on this earth or another, the need of fulfilling the philosophic evolution will be impressed on him by Nature.

14

It will be noticed that some of the meditation exercises given in *The Wisdom of the Overself* concern the re-education of character and involve the use of mental images and logical thoughts. The aim of ordinary yoga being to suppress such images and thoughts, it is clear that the philosophic yoga does not limit itself to such aims. It certainly includes and uses them when and where necessary, as in some of the other exercises, but it does not make them its ultimate ones. On the other hand, the images and thoughts which it uses are not quite the ordinary kind. Brought into being within the atmosphere of detached contemplation or intense concentration as they are, inspired at certain moments by the light and power of the Overself and directed towards the purest impersonal goal as they should be, they do not interfere with the philosophic student's quest, but, on the contrary, actually advance it further.

15

Whatever creative abilities he possesses will, in the end, be vivified and not nullified by the effects of philosophic experience. This is not always the case with mystical experience. Here is another important difference between the two.

16

"Mystical philosophy" is a better term than "philosophical mysticism."

17

Philosophy constructively trains the mystic in securing a correct transmission of his supernormal experience through his normal mentality.

18

The relativity of all man's earthly experience is a limitation which is carried into the realm of his mystical experience too. But here he has the advantage that he may escape from it under certain conditions. The demand for an absolute authoritative and unvarying spiritual truth can then be satisfied.

19

The fantasies which are often produced by beginners as the valued fruits of their meditation will be regarded with repugnance when they have shifted their standpoint to a higher plane. When they follow the philosophic discipline, visions and messages which are the result of an intoxicated imagination or luxuriant fancy will then no longer be able to impose upon them and pretend to be other than what they really are. The temptation to implant our egoistic motives and to project our human feelings into the interpretations of these phenomena is so strong that only the curb of such a discipline can save us. All the psychic experiences are the ephemeral and accidental by-products of the mystical path, not abiding and essential results. They are signs of a passage through the imaginative part of the inner being. When students are so fortunate as to enter the truest deepest part of being, such experiences will vanish forever or for a time. Hence they are not to be regarded as worthwhile in themselves. The philosopher like the mystic may and often does see visions, but unlike him he also sees through them. He possesses true vision and does not merely experience a vision. But it takes time and experience to separate what elements are essential and what are merely incidental, what is enduring from what is transient, and the interpretation built up out of the original experiences from the experience itself.

20

No mystic experience is continuous and permanent. All mystic experiences come to man in broken fragments. It is therefore the task of philosophy to turn them into a coherent and systematic correlation with the rest of man's experience. And it can do this successfully only by examining mysticism with as much criticism as sympathy; it should neither take trance-reports at their face value nor dismiss them as being of less importance than ordinary sense reports.

21

What has come so accidentally may likewise depart accidentally. What he has stumbled into he may also stumble out of. Therefore the philosophic mystic tries to remove as much of the unconsciousness of the whole process as he can by making use of the intelligence to complete it even as, paradoxically, he begs for Grace at the same time and for the same purpose.

22

Were the glorious realization of the Overself devoid of any feeling, then the realization itself would be a palpable absurdity. It would not be worth having. The grand insight into reality is certainly not stripped of fervent delight and is surely not an arid intellectual concept. It is rightly saturated with exalted emotion but it is not this emotion alone. The beatific feeling of what is real is quite compatible with precise knowledge of what is real; there is no contradiction between them. Indeed they must coexist. Nay, there is a point on the philosophic path where they even run into each other. Such a point marks the beginning of a stable wisdom which will not be the victim of merciless alternation between the ebb and the flow of a rapturous emotionalism but will know that it dwells in timelessness here and now; therefore it will not be subject to such fluctuations of mood. Better than the exuberant upsurges and emotional depressions of the mystical temperament is the mental evenness which is without rise or fall and which should be the aim of the far-seeing students. The fitful flashes of enlightenment pertaining to the mystic stage are replaced by a steady light only when the philosophic stage is reached and passed through. The philosophic aim is to overcome the difference between sporadic intuitions and steady knowledge, between spasmodic ecstasies and controlled perception, and thus achieve a permanent state of enlightenment, abiding unshakeably and at all times in the Overself.

23

To view the inferior mystical experiences or the ratiocinative metaphysical findings otherwise than as passing phases, to set them up as finally representative of reality in the one case or of truth in the other, is to place them on a level to which they do not properly belong. Those who fall into the second error do so because they ascribe excessive importance to the thinking faculty. The mystic is too attached to one faculty, as the metaphysician is to the other, and neither can conduct a human being beyond the bounds of his enchained ego to that region where Being alone reigns. It is not that the mystic does not enter into contact with the Overself. He does. But his experience of the Overself is limited to glimpses which are partial, because he finds the Overself only within himself, not in the world outside. It is temporary because he has to take it when it comes at its own sweet will or when he can find it in meditation. It is a glimpse because it tells him about his own "I" but not about the "Not-I." On the other hand, the sage finds reality in the world without as his own self, at all times and not at special occasions, and wholly rather than in glimpses. The mystic's light comes in glimpses, but the sage's is perennial. Whereas the first is like a flickering unsteady and uneven flame, the second is like a lamp that never goes out. Whereas the mystic comes into awareness of the Overself through feeling alone, the sage comes into it through knowledge plus feeling. Hence, the superiority of his realization.

The average mystic is devoid of sufficient critical sense. He delights in preventing his intellect from being active in such a definite direction. He has yet to learn that philosophical discipline has a steadying influence on the vagaries of mystical emotion, opinion, fancy, and experience. He refuses to judge the goal he has set up as to whether it be indeed man's ultimate goal. Consequently he is unable to apply correct standards whereby his own achievements or his own aspirations may be measured. Having shut himself up in a little heaven of his own, he does not attempt to distinguish it from other heavens or to discover if it be heaven indeed. He clings as stubbornly to his self-righteousness as does the religionist whom he criticizes for clinging to his dogma. He does not comprehend that he has transferred to himself that narrowness of outlook which he condemns in the materialistic. His position would be preposterous were it not so perilous.

Mysticism must not rest so smugly satisfied with its own obscurity that it refuses even to make the effort to come out into the light of critical self-examination, clear self-determination, and rational self-understanding. To complain helplessly that it cannot explain itself, to sit admiringly before its own self-proclaimed impalpability, or to stand aristocratically in the rarefied air of its own indefinability—as it usually does—is to fall into a kind of subtle quackery. Magnificent eulogy is no substitute for needed explanation.(P)

24

The crucial point of our criticism must not be missed. Our words are directed against the belief which equates the criterion of truth with the unchecked and unpurified feeling of it—however mystical it be. We do not demand that feeling itself shall be ignored, or that its contribution—which is most important—toward truth shall be despised. Our criticism is not directed against emotion, but against that unbalanced attitude which sets up emotion almost as a religion in itself. We ask only that the reaction of personal feeling shall not be set up as the *sole* and sufficient standard of what is or is not reality and truth. When we speak of the unsatisfactory validity of feeling as providing sufficient proof by itself of having experienced the Overself, we mean primarily, of course, the kind of passionate feeling which throws the mystic into transports of joy, and secondarily, any strong emotion which sweeps him off his feet into refusal to analyse his experience coldly and scientifically. Three points may be here noted. First, mere feeling alone may easily be egoistic and distort the truth or be inflamed and exaggerate it or put forward a wanted fancy in place of an unwanted fact. Second, there is here no means of attaining certainty. Its validity, being only personal, is only as acceptable as are the offerings of poets and artists who can also talk in terms of psychological, but not metaphysical, reality. For instance, the mystic may gaze at and see what he *thinks* to be reality, but someone else may not think it to be so. Third, the path of the philosophical objection to appraising feeling *alone* as a criterion of truth and of our insistence on checking its intimations with critical reasoning may be put in the briefest way by an analogy. We *feel* that the earth is stable and motionless, but we *know* that it traces a curve of movement in space. We *feel* that it is fixed in the firmament, but we *know* that the whole heliocentric system has its own motion in space. The reader should ponder upon the implications of these facts. Are not the annals of mysticism stained by many instances of megalomaniacs who falsely set themselves up as messiahs merely because they *felt* that God had commissioned them to do so? This is why the philosopher is concerned not only with the emotional effects of inner experience, as is the mystic, but also with the *truth* about these effects.(P)

25

I have not swung overnight into the criticism of yoga but rather have gradually matured into criticism of wrong weighings on the scale of yoga. Yoga is as profoundly necessary to my own life as before. Only I want it at its very best and do not want to mistake its intermediate stage for its final one.

26

I realize that this explanation alters the statement in *The Quest of the Overself* materially and I must explain that that book was written, like most of my earlier books, for those who have not yet reached the level of philosophy but are seeking peace through mysticism. The quest of truth is another and higher matter for which mysticism and yoga are preparatory stages.

27

"By whatever form a man worships Me, in that form I reveal Myself to him," is the gist of a statement made by Krishna in the *Bhagavad Gita*. This is his way of saying what philosophy teaches, that the idea of God which a Man holds is not necessarily altered when he has a Glimpse or feels an inspiration, since these occur on the mystical level. Only philosophic enlightenment gives the double experience of raising man to the higher consciousness and correcting his intellectual idea of God at the same time.

28

The mystically inclined who glory in their anti-rationality and impracticality may play the part of intellectual babes and worldly boobs if they wish to do so. But the philosophically inclined, realizing that they live in an era where the evil forces against which they must struggle have reached unparalleled intensity and revealed the most diabolic cunning, realize that they cannot afford such a luxury. They will consequently foster all the practical shrewdness, the critical intelligence, observance, and alertness they can summon up.

29

What they do not perceive is that inward contemplation is only a technique, not an end in itself. The proper end of contemplation is the attainment of a higher consciousness. That consciousness is not, as they erroneously suppose, incommensurable with outward activity. But contemplation, as a practical exercise, certainly is. Here, then, is where they confuse a method with the goal of that method. It is perfectly possible to sustain both the higher consciousness and physical and intellectual activity at the same time. The latter need not necessarily imperil the former. Mystics who complain that it does do so are really complaining that it imperils the formal practice of contemplation—which is a different matter.

30

There are many who say that this attempt to unite contemplation with activity is a self-contradictory one and foredoomed to failure. Answer: with the narrow preparation of ordinary religious mysticism, it certainly seems an impossible feat; but with the fuller preparation of philosophic mysticism, it is a balance that can be learned in the same way that a skilful tightrope walker learns his art, even though it seems just as impossible at first.

31

Because the over-eager quest of mystical experiences has been criticized in these books, it would be a mistake to believe that the philosopher never has them because he has outgrown them. He may have them. Their appearance is not improper and it is unlikely that anyone who consistently meditates will not have a few or many. But whether he has them or not, he is inwardly detached from them—free of them.

32

It is a great advance for him when he begins really to seek truth instead of personal bliss alone, however mystical that may be. Indeed, where there is true knowledge there is bliss, but Truth is not limited to it. It is far wider than that.

33

In the Buddhist's deeper meditational training—minutely described in the *Abhidhamma* collected and recorded by the Buddha's disciples—it is noteworthy that ecstasies first, and bliss next, cease about halfway along the path, to be succeeded by intense inner quiet for the advanced and terminal stages. Yet the texts on yoga which go beyond this halfway stage are few, and are studied by few. For it is at this point that mysticism ends, and real philosophy begins.

34

Texts might prove misleading if studied alone; they must be personally expounded by a competent teacher. Moreover, if but two books, for instance, out of thirty, were taken alone they would give a one-sided and inaccurate picture. But the book by Sri Krishna Prem, *Yoga of the Bhagavad*

Gita, can be quite helpful. The aim of *The Hidden Teaching Beyond Yoga* is to prepare a basis, to create an atmosphere, but it does not go farther than that. There is a lower mysticism and a higher mysticism and the two are separated in time by the philosophic discipline. Nothing of the higher mysticism has been revealed in *The Hidden Teaching Beyond Yoga*. That is given in *The Wisdom of the Overself* together with several practices or exercises which develop the supramystic insight hinted at as being the final source of knowledge. Neither mysticism as ordinarily known—that is, the lower mysticism and yoga—nor philosophy of a purely intellectual-rational kind can ever lead to this goal. Nevertheless they are essential stages on the way thereto. One must not make the mistake either of discarding meditation (as recommended by Ashtavakra) and resorting only to ratiocination, or of despising ratiocination (as ordinary mystics and yogis do) and trusting solely to meditation. Both are needed. But both are only preliminary disciplines. Only the supramystic exercises can lead to the final revelation and these were given to the West for the first time in *The Wisdom of the Overself*. They were formerly kept esoteric in every sense of the word, but times have changed.

35

Such misunderstandings as that reasoning alone leads to realization, that it can replace meditation, and that metaphysics is superior to mysticism could not possibly arise, as can be seen from the second volume [*The Wisdom of the Overself*]. For in this final volume the old gods are restored but placed in new shrines; it shows that the earlier preparatory chapters were really leading up to it. These misconceptions are likely to occur because in the first volume [*The Hidden Teaching Beyond Yoga*] I deliberately criticized certain things in order to stress what, it seemed to me, the time had come to stress. For I wanted to clear the ground of all this debris, thus preparing the way for the higher mysticism unfolded in *The Wisdom of the Overself*. The essential principles of mysticism and yoga have remained intact but are explained from a new angle of approach, the scientific-philosophic, so as to clarify the real issues. As the angle of approach differs, so does what is seen appear differently too. I am fully prepared to accept the blame for whatever mistakes I have made in the past, but I consider it is more important to learn how they have constituted stepping-stones to my present-day higher knowledge. I have been engaged in a widespread mystical research for most of my lifetime, so that the conclusions which I have formulated are at least worthy of consideration, if not more. I consider it a sacred duty to free that which is so precious to me from the large falsifications, extravagant claims, ancient distortions, and degraded doctrines from which it is suffering. I cannot remain silent and indifferent while its treasures are caricatured by the unscientific and unphilosophical or while its truths are deformed and shamelessly cheapened by the egoistic, the hyper-emotional, and the foolish. We must view this subject as a whole, not merely in its bright or dark patches. This means that we must be bent on realistically seeing both. Our morals must be tough enough to do so and exalted enough to accept the consequences of facing unpleasant facts without losing a far-sighted confidence in the essential worth of mysticism. For so far as I am aware nobody within the ranks of the mystically minded capable of speaking with sufficient authority has heretofore ventured to explain the existence amongst them of large-scale gullibility, notorious charlatanry, and failure to beneficially affect public life by frankly exposing the limitations, defects, errors, and misunderstandings prevalent in mysticism itself in a scientific and philosophic manner.

36

The philosopher enjoys a continuous inner peace. He has no particular wish at any time to exchange it for the mystic's bliss although through his capacity for meditation he may be able to do so.

37

The mystic touches the serenity and light of the Overself but falls away from them soon. The philosopher does not merely touch them but attains their fullness forever. The first is partial and provisional whereas the second is final and complete.

38

Philosophy stands aligned with mysticism so far as this aim of achieving the profoundest inward self-absorption through meditation is in question, but it stands aloof from mysticism so far as rational, moral, practical, and social issues are in question. A correct appraisal of mysticism can only be formed by examining its ideology against the wider background of philosophic doctrine.

39

The yogic viewpoint still embraces the phenomena of causation, however refined.

40

Philosophy prescribes just enough meditation to make its votaries mystically conscious but not enough to make them forget the philosophic goal amidst its pleasures.

41

The philosophic goal when entering into mystical experience of the higher kind or when viewing one's relation to anyone else or to any situation, is to see the truth correctly and understand it rightly, to add nothing to it out of personal associations or habitual tendencies.

42

The next point of difference is the active nature of philosophic realization as compared to the passive nature of mystical realization. This is the result of the holding-up of compassion as part of the philosophic aspirant's ideal from the beginning to the end of his course.

43

The philosophic experience is a becalmed mystical rapture.

44

The line of demarcation between the lower and the higher mysticism is clearly shown. For the lower mystic has sublime experiences and makes inspired utterances but does not understand profoundly, clearly, and fully what these experiences are nor what these utterances mean. Neither his attainments nor his knowledge has arrived at adequate self-consciousness. He is in the position of poets like Tennyson, who confessed that his *In Memoriam*, which was written to proclaim human immortality, was wiser than he himself knew. (See Plato's *The Apology of Socrates* 7, regarding this.)

45

The end of philosophic seeking is not a fleeting mystic ecstasy but a durable mystic consciousness inlaying every thought, word, feeling, and deed.

46

That which the mystic *feels* is what the metaphysician *thinks*. The philosopher *knows* and *acts* it, as well as feels and thinks it.

47

So long as his attainment depends on a contemplative stage which in its turn depends on inactivity and solitude, so long will it be only a half-attainment.

48

A mysticism which does not take into account all the chief functions which make a being human—will, feeling, reason, and intuition—leaves some of his evolutionary possibilities undeveloped and cannot give a *finished* result but only a partly finished one. It fails to do justice to the glorious ideal set before him by the World-Idea.

49

He must continue to probe for himself into the recesses of his own mind. This requires much patience. He is quite correct in wanting to be aware of every step of the path and in refusing to move blindly. On this path he needs to balance the claims of reason and feeling and to understand accurately what it is that he is trying to do. He cannot go back to the unconscious beliefs of spiritual childhood. This is the difference between ordinary mysticism and philosophical mysticism.

50

The mystic is usually satisfied in enjoying this inner stillness whereas the philosopher needs also to know where it emanates from.

Discriminating analysis, mystical depth

51

What the mystic seeks through love and self-purification alone, the philosopher seeks through love and self-purification and knowledge as well.

52

Philosophy offers the same meditational experience as mysticism, but it carries this experience to a wider and deeper level and at the same time integrates it with moral social and rational elements.

53

Philosophical mysticism keeps and contains all that is best in ordinary mysticism but reinforces and balances it with reason, culture, shrewdness, and practicality, expresses it through service or art.

54

When the mind withdraws from its creations *after* understanding their mentalness and looks into *itself*, it discovers the final truth. But when it does this prematurely—that is, before such enquiry into the world's nature—it discovers a half-truth: the nature of the "I."

55

The virtue of philosophic yoga is that it makes reason an accomplice and not, as with the other yogas, an enemy of the quest of spiritual realization.

56

The philosophical mystic has no use for such vagueness and precariousness. He must know what he is about, must be self-conscious and self-possessed. But all this on the intellectual level only. He will be the personification of humility, the incarnation of self-surrender, on the emotional level.

57

Mysticism requires the unreserved surrender of the ego to the soul. From this quite correct requirement, unphilosophic mystics draw the quite incorrect conclusions that the ego's faculty of reasoning and use of will are to be banished from the domain of practical affairs. It should not, for instance, provide for its worldly future, because God is to provide for it. Belief in mysticism is no excuse for such illogical and inaccurate thinking, much less for the paralysis of willing. The mystic may give himself unto the soul and yet render unto thought and action that which is rightly theirs.

58

Both the technique of meditation and the study of metaphysics must be brought into satisfactory adjustment.

59

Philosophical understanding can bloom within him only after he has cultivated his metaphysical intelligence as well as his mystical intuition.

60

How can science and mysticism meet when each uses a different faculty, the one intellect and the other intuition? They *can* meet by following two steps: first, by each one understanding its own and the other's place, function, and limitation, and second, by amalgamating their viewpoints, thus rising into the domain of philosophy.

61

Truth will not insult intelligence, although it soars beyond intellect. Let the religionists talk nonsense, as they do at times; but holiness is not incompatible with the use of brains, the acquisition of knowledge, and the rational faculties.(P)

62

It is not enough to negate thinking; this may yield a mental blank without content. We have also to transcend it. The first is the way of ordinary yoga; the second is the way of philosophic yoga. In the second way, therefore, we seek strenuously to carry thought to its most abstract and rarefied point, to a critical culminating whereby its whole character changes and it merges of its own accord in the higher source whence it arises. If successful, this produces a pleasant, sometimes ecstatic state—but the ecstasy is not our aim, as with ordinary mysticism. With us the reflection must keep loyally to a loftier aim, that of dissolving the ego in its divine source. The metaphysical thinking must work its way, first upwards to a more and more abstract concept and second inwards to a more and more complete absorption from the external world. The consequence is that when illumination results, whether it comes in the form of a mystical trance, ecstasy, or intuition, its character will be unquestionably different and immeasurably superior to that which comes from the mere sterilization of the thinking process which is the method of ordinary yoga.(P)

63

There is a little confusion in some minds as to the precise differences between philosophic meditations and ordinary meditation. The following note is intended to help clear up this matter. There are five stages in the philosophic method. The first four of these stages cover the same ground as those in traditional mysticism. It is in the last stage that a vital difference appears. In stage one, the student learns to concentrate his faculties, thoughts, and power of attention. He must fix beforehand any object for his gaze, or any subject for his thoughts, or any theme for his feelings. This provides a post, as it were, to which the horse of his mind can be tethered and to which it can be made to return again and again each time it strays away. In stage two, he must definitely drop the use of his bodily senses and external objects, withdraw his attention entirely within himself and devote it exclusively to considered thinking about and devotional aspiration to his spiritual quest, making use only of an elevating idea or ideal as a tethering post. In stage three, he is to reverse this method, for he is not to fix beforehand any theme for thought, not even to predetermine the way in which his contemplation shall develop itself. His conscious mind is to be thoroughly free from any and every suggestion from the thinking self, even if it be of the purest kind. For everything must here be left entirely to the higher power. In stage four, the student unites completely with his higher self and its infinite universality, drops all personal thinking, even all personal being. In stage five, it might be said that he returns to the first two and recapitulates them, for he reintroduces thinking and therefore ego. But there is a notable difference. The thinking will be, first, illumined by the higher self's light, and second, directed towards the understanding of Reality.

64

The use of metaphysical thinking as part of the philosophic system is a feature which few yogis of the ordinary type are likely to appreciate. This is both understandable and pardonable. They are thoroughly imbued with the futility of a merely rational and intellectual approach to reality, a futility which has also been felt and expressed in these pages. So far there is agreement with them. But when they proceed to deduce that the only way left is to crush reason and stop the working of intellect altogether, our paths diverge. For what metaphysics admittedly cannot accomplish by itself may be accomplished by a combination of metaphysics and mysticism far better than by mysticism alone. The metaphysics of truth, which is here meant, however, must never be confused with the many historical speculative systems which exist.(P)

65

The activity of analytic thinking has been banned in most mystical schools. They regard it as an obstacle to the attainment of spiritual consciousness. And ordinarily it is indeed so. For until the intellect can lie perfectly still, such consciousness cannot make itself apparent. The difficulty of making intellect quite passive is however an enormous one. Consequently different concentration techniques have been devised to overcome it. Nearly all of them involve the banishment of thinking and the cessation of reasoning. The philosophical school uses any or all of them where advisable but it also uses a technique peculiarly its own. It makes use of abstract concepts which are concerned with the nature of the mind itself and which are furnished by seers who have developed a deep insight into such nature. It permits the student to work out these concepts in a rational way but leading to subtler and subtler moods until they automatically vanish and thinking ceases as the transcendental state is induced to come of itself. This method is particularly suited either to those who have already got over the elementary difficulties of concentration or to those who regard reasoning power as an asset to be conserved rather than rejected. The conventional mystic, being the victim of external suggestion, will cling to the traditional view of his own school, which usually sees no good at all in reasoned thinking, and aver that spiritual attainment through such a path is psychologically impossible. Never having been instructed in it and never having tried it, he is not really in a position to judge.(P)

66

Continued and constant pondering over the ideas presented herein is itself a part of the yoga of philosophical discernment. Such reflection will as naturally lead the student towards realization of his goal as will the companion and equally necessary activity of suppressing all ideas altogether in mental quiet. This is because these ideas are not mere speculations but are themselves the outcome of a translation from inner experience. While such ideas as are here presented grow under the water of their reflection and the sunshine of their love into fruitful branches of thought, they gradually begin to foster intuition.(P)

67

The logical movement of intellect must come to a dead stop before the threshold of reality. But we are not to bring about this pause deliberately or in response to the bidding of some man or some doctrine. It must come of its own accord as the final maturation of long and precise reasoning and as the culmination of the intellectual and personal *discovery* that the apprehension of mind as essence will come only when we let go of the idea-forms it takes and direct our attention to it.(P)

68

This is the paradox: that *both* the capacity to think deeply and the capacity to withdraw from thinking are needed to attain this goal.(P)

69

The mistake of the mystics is to negate reasoning *prematurely*. Only after reasoning has completed its own task to the uttermost will it be psychologically right and philosophically fruitful to still it in the mystic silence.(P)

70

He must seek in metaphysics for the secret of the universe and in mysticism for the secret of his own self. This is a balanced approach.

71

Philosophy is not hostile to yoga; the latter leads to steadiness of mind; with this one can then exercise discrimination. The combination of concentration and enquiry leads to fitful glimpses of truth. These glimpses must then be stabilized by constant effort and remembrance throughout the day until they become second nature.

72

The mystic who refuses to use his brains is displaying not a virtue, as he believes, but a failing. Yet such a man has become stereotyped in the thought of most people as a type of man possessed of a flabby intellect. What they have not known is that there is another kind, the philosophic mystic, who seeks to develop his brain-power alongside of his mystical intuitions. Philosophy silences thought when it wants to feel inner peace or enter spiritual ecstasy, but it stimulates thought when it wants to understand this peace and that ecstasy.

73

The typically medieval mystical school of thought taught the utter necessity of restricting the powers of will and intellect, dissolving them in single-minded devotion to prayer, meditation, and ascetic life. Philosophy teaches the contrary and urges the full development of these powers but safeguards this development by, first, dedicating it to mystical purposes and impersonal aims and, second, controlling it by mystical intuition.

74

Philosophy does not ask us, as mysticism does, to stifle the intellect, but to illumine it. It demands effective thinking and not mere daydreaming, intellectual self-discipline and not misty vagueness. Its journey lies through meditation reinforced by reason.

75

The mystic is content to be carried away by his feelings. The philosopher wants to understand both the nature of their movement and the character of the destination.

76

The lower mystic uses his mystical experiences as an alibi to justify his mental slothfulness. He knows nothing of that organized systematic effort to answer every question and clear every doubt which the higher mystic had to pass through before he attained the superior grade.

77

Metaphysics is a discipline in rationalization while yoga is a discipline in detachment and concentration.

78

Our aim must be all-round development—a sane, healthy, balanced life. Meditation is not enough, albeit essential in its place. The cultivation of a sharp keen intelligence for philosophical reflection is just as essential. The two must work hand in hand, with a perfect development of each ideal as the goal. The kingdom of heaven is in the head as well as the heart.

79

We can understand the attempt of metaphysics to know the supreme reality and know the attempt of mysticism to feel in God's presence. But the first depends on filling the mind with the subtlest thoughts whereas the last depends partly on emptying the mind of thoughts.

80

If he thinks for himself and feels for others, he will appreciate the superiority of the philosophic form of mysticism.

81

That keen rationality could and indeed should accompany sensitive spirituality is both practical wisdom and evolutionary necessity. A tendency to act the fool in worldly and intellectual matters is not a sign of mystical strength, as some aver, but a sign of mystical weakness.

82

My final ancient authority that this combination of *yoga* and *vichara* is essential is Buddha. He said: "The man discreet, on virtue firmly set, in intellect and intuition trained. The man with keen discrimination blessed may from this tangle liberate himself."

Keys to the ultimate path

83

The student travels through the different stages on the journey to supreme truth. But without competent guidance he may fall into the error of mistaking one of the stages for the truth itself. He does not usually understand that there is a graded series of developments, each one of which looks like the truth itself, and that only after all these have been passed through can he reach the glorious culminating goal.

84

There is only one truth, hence only one true illumination. But there are various degrees of its reception.

85

The journey from preoccupation with the intellectual forms of truth to living in the truth itself, is a long and arduous one. Even the start is harder than it seems, for those very forms which have been so helpful in the past must be increasingly regarded as traps and less and less as guides.

86

Such an attainment as philosophy proposes cannot be reached all at once. It must be approached through a series of preparatory steps. They will be slow in pace at first, but quicker later and sudden towards the end.

87

It is quite true that the attainment of this higher consciousness is an attainment of wholeness, as some modern mystics claim. For then only is the conscious ego forced to relinquish to the Overself its hold upon the rest of the psyche. Nevertheless, when this is felt and said, it must be stated that the pattern of wholeness is still not finished by its first attainment, for that is only the first stage—albeit an immensely dynamic and memorable one—of a process.

88

It is a long journey from the condition of seeker to that of sage. But this is true only so far as we ascribe reality to time. To those who know that our human existence is a movement through events, but that the human being in its essence transcends all events and dwells in timelessness, this journey may be considerably shortened or swiftly brought to its destination. For that, the thorough understanding of philosophy and its incessant application to oneself is required.

89

The truth may not always burst on its votary in a sudden brief and total flash. It may also come so slowly that he will hardly know its movement. But in both cases this progress will be measured by his abandonment of a purely personal and self-centered attitude towards life.

90

For the ordinary mystic it is very very hard to live in the world, in the way that ordinary men do, after he has experienced the world around him as mere illusion and its activities as vain. Only the philosophically trained mystic can find sufficient motive in his knowledge and sufficient urge in his feeling to take part in these activities if needed or desirable.

91

The same mystical experience which detaches others from action inspires him to it. This difference of result springs from a difference of approach.

92

If a man sinks in this contemplation without bringing it into reciprocal balance with reason and compassion, he will soon fall into a state in which, quite clearly, it will be difficult for him to demand active usefulness from himself. He will set up immobility of thought and body as his chief goal, indifference of feeling and desire as his ultimate beatitude. The consequence of this disequilibrium may be gratifying to the man himself, but cannot be gratifying to society also. Nevertheless, however high such a mystic may soar like the skylark, he must then be faced by the problem of reconciling the two existences. There are yogis who assert that the one blots out the other. How then, we must ask them, if the man is no longer aware of any other mind than the Divine Mind or any other life than God's life, can he be aware of the personal business to which he is called and to which he does attend from hour to hour?

93

To the fearful, uninstructed seeker everything connected with a worldly life is a stop on his upward way. To the philosophically enlightened student, it is actually a step on his upward way. He redeems the earthly environment by thinking rightly about it, turns every earthly deed into a sacrament because he views it under a divine light, and sees a fellow pilgrim in the worst sinner.

94

The mystic must live a double existence, one during meditation and the other during work. The philosopher is released from such an awkward duality. He knows only one existence—the philosophic life. The divine quality permeates his whole activity as much as it permeates his meditative cessation from activity. Work too is worship for him.

95

There are three things man needs to know to make him a spiritually educated man: the truth about himself, his world, and his God. The mystic who thinks it is enough to know the first alone and to leave out the last two, is satisfied to be half-educated.(P)

96

It is not enough to know the internal self as the mystics know it. We must also know the *real nature* of the external world before we can realize Truth. This means that one will see oneself in the All and possess a perfect comprehension with the All.

97

Suffused with pious feeling as a man might be, uplifted in heart and bettered in character as this may leave him, it is still not enough to fulfil the higher purpose of his existence. He needs also to understand what is the Idea behind his particular life, and all other lives.

98

The ecstatic feelings which come to the mystics are emotional and personal albeit they pertain to the higher emotion and they are a most exalted part of the personality. On the other hand, the feeling which comes to the sage is not ecstatic but serene. It is not emotional and not limited to the personality alone. The centre of the psychological gravity differs in the two cases. Whereas the mystic revels in the ecstatic comprehension of his interior "I," but is doomed to revel brokenly and intermittently, the sage is concerned with what lies behind that "I"—that is, the Universal Self, the realization of which does not depend upon meditation or trance alone and therefore need not be broken when meditation or trance is suspended.

99

Reality is to be found neither by thinking alone nor by not thinking at all. This high path which opens to the philosophic student is one of unwavering deeply abstract concentration of the mind in the real, whether the mind be thinking or not thinking, and whether the individual be acting or not acting.

100

If mysticism reveals the nature of man, philosophy reveals the nature of the universe.

101

If he has started thinking in a philosophic manner about his own life, he will have done enough. But if he seeks also to wrest the universe's own secret from it, he will have done more.

102

The mystic seeks God by forsaking the world physically or else by renouncing it emotionally. His happiest moment is when he can withdraw from it intellectually so completely that it is lost from his consciousness in an abnormal trance state, a rapturous ecstatic union with God alone. The philosopher passes through all these stages, too, but does not stop there. He follows an opposite movement too. He finds God in the world as well as in himself.

103

The first great event full of wonder will be this discovery of what is within himself; the second will be his discovery of what is within the world. For within himself he will find the soul and within the world he will find the working of God. He will discover that it is literal fact that everything happens under the laws and forces of the Higher Power, and that this is as true of human life as it is of plant life and animal life. He will find that the infinite wisdom is, everywhere and everywhen, taking care of every human being; that this includes himself and those who are near and dear to him; and that therefore he has no need to worry weakly or despairingly over them, for the experiences which they get are those which they need or earn. When he is no longer anxious about himself, how can he be anxious about other people? When he has committed his own life to God, what else can he do about other people's lives than commit theirs to God also? He finds that everyone is here not for the body's sake but for the soul's sake, and that this is the real criterion wherewith to measure all happenings and all experiences. He will no longer let himself be deceived by appearances, no longer let events rob him of his inward peace. He will remain passive to the Higher Power, obedient to its leading, and receptive to its prompting. It will carry him serenely and sustain him adequately.

104

Is it possible to unite both ways, the active life in the world outside and the quiet life in the stillness within, and find no break, no essential difference, no falsification of the oft-stated idea, "God is everywhere"? The answer is Yes! and has been tested in ancient and modern experience. "What is the World?" gives the same reply as "Who am I?" Withdrawing from the physical sense-world as the mystic does or going into physical action with the senses engaged need not break the union, the awareness of divine presence.

105

Of course it is quite true to say that the truth is inside man, that he must search there. But it is also true that the truth is outside man and in the cosmos itself *because he is a part of it*. Why be one-sided and reject the second direction in favour of the first or reject the first in favour of the second? Both are necessary to the full perception of truth.

106

There are mystics who experience the Overself in its glow of love and joy of freedom, but without receiving knowledge of the cosmic laws, principles, and secrets. There are other mystics who are not satisfied with the one alone but seek to unite and complete it with the other. They are the philosophical mystics for whom the meaning of the self and the meaning of the world have become two sides of the same coin.

107

To arrive at a simultaneous consciousness of both states—the personal ego and the impersonal Overself—is possible, and has been done intermittently by some people such as mystics and artists—or permanently by philosophers.

108

The philosopher cannot set the spirit apart from the body, nor the spiritual life from the worldly life—for him, they penetrate one another.

109

The materialist sees plurality alone and sees superficially. The mystic in his deepest contemplation sees Spirit (or Mind alone) without seeing Plurality, and sees incompletely. The philosopher sees both Mind and its manifold world-images as essentially the same and sees rightly and fully.

110

What he knows and what he perceives will harmonize with, illustrate, or complete one another.

111

The thinking of thoughts no longer veils spiritual being from him. Instead it is now an activity which acts as a transparent medium for that being.

112

Others may turn away in despair or disgust from the harshness of the worldly scenes; he must gaze into and beyond them. Others may ignore or escape from its uglinesses; he must take them up into his scheme of things, and, taking, transcend them by philosophic knowledge.

113

Philosophy takes its votaries on a holy pilgrimage from ordinary life in the physical senses through mystical life in the sense-freed spirit to a divinized life back in the same senses.(P)

114

Just as the splendours of the setting sun bathed in fiery, glowing colors may be profoundly appreciated despite one's awareness of the fact that the sciences of life and optics explain these splendours in a bald, prosaic, disenchanting way; just as an excellent dinner may be eaten with keen enjoyment undisturbed by one's knowledge that the constituents of these tempting dishes were really carbon, nitrogen, hydrogen, and so on, so the varied factors which go to make up the picture of our universal existence may be seen and experienced for what they are by the integrally developed man in their material tangibility despite his deeper awareness of the overwhelming difference between their single Basis and their manifold appearances.

115

The highest contribution which mysticism can make is to afford its votaries glimpses of that grand substratum of the universe which we may call the Overself. These glimpses reveal It in the pure unmanifest non-physical essence that It ultimately is. They detach It from the things, creatures, and thoughts which make up this world of ours, and show It as It is in the beginning, before the world-dream made its appearance. Thus mysticism at its farthest stretch, which is Nirvikalpa samadhi, enables man to bring about the temporary disappearance of the world-dream and come into comprehension of the Mind within which, and from which, the dream emerges. The mystic in very truth conducts the funeral service of the physical world as he has hitherto known it, which includes his own ego. But this is as far as mysticism can take him. It is an illuminative and rare experience, but it is not the end. For the next task which he must undertake if he is to advance is to relate his experience of this world as real with his experience of the Overself as real. And this he can do only by studying the world's own nature, laying bare its mentalistic character and thus bringing it within the same circle as its source, the Mind. If he succeeds in doing this and in establishing this relation correctly, he will have finished his apprenticeship, ascended to the ultimate truth, and become a philosopher. Thenceforward he will not deny the world but accept it.

The metaphysician may also perform this task and obtain an intellectual understanding of himself, the world, and the Overself. And he has this advantage over the mystic, that his understanding becomes permanent whereas the mystic's rapt absorption must pass. But if he has not passed through the mystical exercises, it will remain as incomplete as a nut without a kernel. For these exercises, when led to their logical and successful issue in Nirvikalpa samadhi, provide the vivifying principle of experience which alone can make metaphysical tenets real.

From all this we may perceive why it is quite correct for the mystic to look undistractedly within for his goal, why he must shut out the distractions and attractions of earthly life in order to penetrate the sacred precinct, and why solitude, asceticism, meditation, trance, and emotion play the most important roles in his particular experience. What he is doing is right and proper at his stage but is not right and proper as the last stage. For in the end he must turn metaphysician, just as the metaphysician must turn mystic and just as both must turn philosopher—who is alone capable of infusing the thoughts of metaphysics and the feelings of mysticism into the actions of everyday practical life.(P)

116

This mysterious experience seems also to have been known to Dionysius the Areopagite. It is definitely an experience terminating the process of meditation, for the mystic can then go no higher and no deeper. It is variously called "the Nought" in the West and *nirvikalpa samadhi* in the East. Everything in the world vanishes and along with the world goes the personal ego; nothing indeed is left except Consciousness-in-Itself. If anything can burrow under the foundations of the ego and unsettle its present and future stability, it is this awesome event. But, because it is still an experience, it has a coming and a going. Although it is forever after remembered, a memory is not the final settled condition open to man—for that, philosophy must be brought in. Mysticism may remove the ego temporarily after first lulling it, but philosophy understands the ego, puts it in its place, its subservient place, so that the man remains always undeserted by the pure consciousness.

117

He comes by growth of knowledge and width of views, by metaphysical evolution and emotional discipline, to a great calm. From then on he neither seeks eagerly for incarnational experience nor aspires loftily for liberation from it. Argument and discussion, meditation and exercises and spiritual states, labels and categories, teachers and teachings and quests are only for observation, not participation. Others may think he has lapsed and shake their heads in sorrow or pity. This is not to be used as counsel for beginners: if followed it could only hinder them. But to prevent limited views, sectarianism, and fanaticism arising among them, as so often it does, they can well be told occasionally that such a stage exists, and it may be theirs when a patient development brings them to it.

118

The student who has reached this stage is forced to adopt an uncompromising attitude if he is not to stagnate. He shuts up his holiest books and puts them aside, turns away from the traditional instruction of his teacher and flees from the sheltering society of hermitages or fellow students into the rough hard materialistic society which he has hitherto disdained. Henceforth he must look to nothing and nobody outside his own self for final guidance or strength. That which he seeks must now be found within or not at all. He perceives now that all techniques and teachers are like a sundial, which indicates the presence of the sun and measures its relative position, but if one does not at last turn away from the dial and look upward, then one will never see or know the sun in itself. To use the dial for a time is a help; to become preoccupied with it for all time is a hindrance. He is now ready to enter the ultimate path. For there are two paths within the quest.

119

The need of going beyond the ordinary yogas if he is to arrive at a deeper and purer truth, is a perception which will force him to engage in further research as well as independent research.

120

All the processes of creation and dissolution are true only from the scientific or practical standpoint but they disappear when the student inquires deeply into them. It is a matter of getting right understanding and then he sees they are mere thoughts or imaginations. A long training in right—that is, philosophic—thinking is required before the mind becomes habituated to such views. This is *gnana yoga*. After that he has to practise a still higher kind of yoga which goes on in the midst of activity and has nothing to do with meditation as ordinarily known. That ultimate path gives realization. He gets glimpses first, lightning-flashes, which through continued effort gradually become stabilized and finally merge into continuous knowledge of truth.

121

The mystic will not care and may not be able to do so, but the philosopher has to learn the art of combining his inward recognition of the Void with his outward activity amongst things without feeling the slightest conflict between both. Such an art is admittedly difficult but it can be learnt with time and patience and comprehension. Thus he will feel inward unity everywhere in this world of wonderful variety, just as he will experience all the countless mutations of experience as being present in the very midst of this unity.(P)

122

What science calls the "critical temperature," that is, the temperature when a substance shares both the liquid and gaseous states, is symbolic of what philosophical mysticism calls the "philosophic experience," that is, when a man's consciousness shares both the external world of the five senses and the internal world of the empty soul. The ordinary mystic or yogi is unable to hold the two states simultaneously and, quite often, even unwilling to do so, because of the false opposition he has been taught to set up between them.(P)

123

The life of sense and thought veils the life of the soul from the non-mystical extroverted person. The rapture of ecstatic trance veils the external world from the mystical person. Neither man's condition is full, perfect, and complete. The mystic's is higher, but he needs to advance still farther to a continuous balanced state where the activity of sense and thought does not veil the external world from him, but where both are felt as different phases of one divine reality and seen as the same experience from two different points of view. Such is the philosophic achievement. Although it contains the ordinary state it is not limited to it, and although it experiences mystical union it does not need to enter into an abnormal condition like trance to do so. Thus whether the physical world and the thinking intellect reveal or conceal this reality depends upon whether or not the philosophic insight is brought to bear upon them.

124

The Infinite cannot be set against the finite as though they were a pair of opposites. Only things which are on the same level can be opposed to one another. These are not. The Infinite includes and contains within itself all possible finites. The practical import of this truth is that Mind cannot only be experienced in the Void but also in the world. The Reality is not only to be discovered as it is but also beneath its phenomenal disguises.

125

The philosopher is satisfied with a noble peace and does not run after mystical ecstasies. Whereas other paths often depend upon an emotionalism that perishes with the disappearance of the primal momentum that inspired it, or which dissolves with the dissolution of the first enthusiastic ecstasies themselves, here there is a deeper and more dependable process. What must be emphasized is that most mystical aspirants have an initial or occasional ecstasy, and they are so stirred by the event that they naturally want to enjoy it permanently. This is because they live under the common error that a successful and perfect mystic is one who has succeeded in stabilizing ecstasy. That the mystic is content to rest on the level of feeling alone, without making his feeling self-reflective as well, partly accounts for such an error. It also arises because of incompetent teachers or shallow teaching, leading them to strive to perform what is impracticable and to yearn to attain what is impossible. Our warning is that this is not possible, and that however long a mystic may enjoy these "spiritual sweets," they will assuredly come to an end one day. The stern logic of facts calls for stress on this point. Too often he believes that this is the goal, and that he has nothing more about which to trouble himself. Indeed, he would regard any further exertions as a sacrilegious denial of the peace, as a degrading descent from the exaltation of this divine union. He longs for nothing more than the good fortune of being undisturbed by the world and of being able to spend the rest of his life in solitary devotion to his inward ecstasy. For the philosophic mystic, however, this is not the terminus but only the starting point of a further path. What philosophy says is that this is only a preliminary mystical state, however remarkable and blissful it be. There is a more matured state—that of gnosis—beyond it. If the student experiences paroxysms of ecstasy at a certain stage of his inner course, he may enjoy them for a time, but let him not look forward to enjoying them for all time. The true goal lies beyond them, and he should not forget that all-important fact. He will not find final salvation in the mystical experience of ecstasy, but he will find an excellent and essential step towards salvation therein. He who would regard rapturous mystical emotion as being the same as absolute transcendental insight is mistaken. Such a mistake is pardonable. So abrupt and striking is the contrast with his ordinary state that he concludes that this condition of hyper-emotional bliss is the condition in which he is able to experience reality. He surrenders himself to the bliss, the emotional joy which he experiences, well satisfied that he has found God or his soul. But his excited feelings about reality are not the same as the serene experience of reality itself. This is what a mystic finds difficult to comprehend. Yet, until he does comprehend it, he will not make any genuine progress beyond this stage.(P)

126

We may welcome and appreciate the radiant ecstasy of the mystic's triumph, but we ought not to appraise it at other than its proper worth. If we become so completely satisfied with it that we seek no higher goal, then our very satisfaction closes the door to the possibility of realizing the Overself. Only the sage—that is, the master of philosophy, to which metaphysics is but a necessary stage—can appreciate the calm which comes with mystical bliss. The peace which mysticism yields is genuine, but fitful, for it can only thrive in an atmosphere of constant exaltation. And when each exaltation intermittently passes—as it must—our mystic is left very flat. It is philosophy alone that exists in the very antithesis of such an atmosphere of comings and goings; therefore, it alone yields *permanent* peace. The yogi may shut his eyes and pass his time in pleasant meditations, but for large chunks of his day he will be forced to open them again and attend to physical matters. Then the world will confront him, pressing for a place in his scheme of things, and demand rational interpretation. He has got to explain this antithesis between self and not-self, between "I" and the world.

127

The yogi who achieves the capacity to be without thoughts for a certain period of time is still the victim of time, unless he has sought to understand its meaning, its nature, and above all what lies behind it. This latter is a philosophic work. If it is used to support yoga or if yoga is used to prepare the way for it, a proper relationship is established; otherwise we may have the spectacle of Swamis who come to the West after lengthy meditations and begin to betray signs of erratic conduct—signs which I do not need to describe.

128

Philosophy brings the knowledge of the "I" as it really is (in the deepest sense) into the consciousness of a man. Mysticism does the same. How could anything higher be realized by any human, concerning things human, than what is taught in both these fields? Then what more does philosophy offer? It offers a fuller result and completes the work by including the world.

129

It is here that the vital difference between the ultimate and yogic paths becomes apparent. Ramana Maharshi took the stand which nearly all yogis take: that is, we need have nothing to do with the affairs of the world which we have renounced. Let us sit quietly and enjoy our inner peace. But on the ultimate path the goal is quite different. We begin *after* having passed through yoga, and having found peace. Then we seek truth. The latter when found reveals that the Overself is present in all men—nay, all creatures—as their ultimate being. We not only know this but FEEL it. So we cannot remain indifferent to the lives of others. Therefore—and now is revealed a great secret—when we attain liberation from the endless-turning wheel of reincarnation, we voluntarily return again and again to earth solely to help others, mitigate suffering, and reduce ignorance. So long as one creature lives in ignorance and pain, so long a true adept MUST return to earth. But this applies only to the adepts in WISDOM. The adept in yoga does not want to return to earth again, does not feel for others, and is happy in enjoying his exalted peace. He is quite entitled to this because he has worked for it. But he has not attained Truth, which is a higher stage. There is a tremendous difference in the goal we seek. The yogi's aim is a sublime selfishness; the true adept's is a burning desire to serve humanity. The successful yogi dwells in great peace and that suffices for him. Nevertheless yoga is an essential stage through which all must pass, for mind must be controlled, sharpened, and purified and peace must be attained before he is fit to undertake the great inquiry into what is Truth.

130

Through yoga or meditation, one arrives at mind-control. Then he takes his sharpened, concentrated mind and applies it to the understanding of the world. Thus he discovers that the world of matter is ultimately space and that all material forms are merely ideas in his mind. He discovers, also, that his inmost self is one with this space, because it is formless. Then does he perceive the unity of all life, and only then has he found Truth—the whole truth. All this must be discovered by experience, not by intellectual theory, and here his power to control thoughts becomes important . . . first to make the mind absolutely still, then to use this exceedingly sharpened mind to survey and penetrate the truth of things. That is why neither mysticism nor yoga can lead directly to Truth. They are only preparations for the higher path that does lead to Truth.

131

It is the duty of an advanced mystic who wishes to attain greater heights for himself and be of greater service to others to try earnestly to graduate to the ultimate path. This does not demand that he give up any of his mystical practices or beliefs, but merely that he amplify and supplement them. He must first develop the trinity of head, heart, and hand, or reason, intuition, and action, and then bring them all into proper balance. If in addition he is inspired by the ideal of service, he will attract to himself the unseen help of those who are also dedicated to such service.

132

The hidden teaching starts and finishes with experience. Every man must begin his mental life as a seeker by noting the fact that he is conscious of an external environment. He will proceed in time to discover that it is an ordered one, that Nature is the manifestation of an orderly Mind. He discovers in the end that consciousness of this Mind becomes the profoundest fact of his internal experience.(P)

133

The first step is to discover that there is a Presence, a Power, a Life, a Mind, Being, unique, not made or begot, without shape, unseen and unheard, everywhere and always the same. The second step is to discover its relationship to the universe and to oneself.(P)

134

Two things have to be learned in this quest. The first is the art of mind-stilling, of emptying consciousness of every thought and form whatsoever. This is mysticism or Yoga. The disciple's ascent should not stop at the contemplation of anything that has shape or history, name or habitation, however powerfully helpful this may have formerly been to the ascent itself. Only in the mysterious void of Pure Spirit, in the undifferentiated Mind, lies his last goal as a mystic. The second is to grasp the essential nature of the ego and of the universe and to obtain direct perception that both are nothing but a series of ideas which unfold themselves within our minds. This is the metaphysics of Truth. The combination of these two activities brings about the realization of his true Being as the ever beautiful and eternally beneficent Overself. This is philosophy.(P)

135

In the ordinary state, man is conscious of himself as a personal thinking and physical entity. In the mystical trance-like state, he loses this consciousness and is aware of the Divine alone. In the philosophic state, he returns to the ordinary consciousness but without letting go of the diviner one.

136

Whenever I have used the term "the centre of his being," I have referred to a state of meditation, to an experience which is felt at a certain stage. The very art of meditation is a drawing inwards and the finer, the more delicate, the subtler this indrawing becomes, the closer it is to this central point of consciousness. But from the point of view of philosophy, meditation and its experiences are not the ultimate goal—although they may help in preparing one for that goal. In that goal there is no kind of centre to be felt nor any circumference either—one is without being localized anywhere with reference to the body, one is both in the body and in the Overself. There is then no contradiction between the two.(P)

137

The body belongs to our field of consciousness, but we need not limit ourselves solely to it. We can for example bring into experience higher mental states where the body and the memory of it play only a little part. This indeed is one of the purposes of yoga, but it is not necessarily a purpose of philosophy. The philosopher is content to let the body be there, provided he can bring it alongside and within his other consciousness of the Overself.

138

Many complain that they are unable in meditation successfully to bring their active thoughts to an end. In the ancient Indian art of yoga, this cessation—called *nirvikalpa samadhi* in Sanskrit—is placed as the highest stage to be reached by the practitioner. This situation must be viewed from two separate and distinct standpoints: from that of yoga and from that of philosophy. Would-be philosophers seek to become established in that insight into Reality which is called Truth. Intuitive feeling is a higher manifestation of man's faculties. So long as the feeling itself remains unobstructed by illusions, and—after incessant reflection, inquiry, study, remembrance, reverence, aspiration, training of thought, and purification—a man finds the insight dawning in his mind, he may not need to practise meditation. He may do so and he will feel the satisfaction and tranquillity which comes from it. Those who become sufficiently proficient in yoga, even if they achieve the complete cessation of thoughts, should still take up the pursuit of understanding and insight. If they are content with their attainment, they can remain for years enjoying the bliss, the tranquillity, the peace of a meditational state; but this does not mean knowledge in its fullest meaning.

139

The notion, uncritically learned and sedulously taught by several Hindu sects, including a modern one which is actively proselytizing the West, that a criterion for whether a man has attained the highest state is his ability to remain constantly immersed in the trance, is not endorsed by philosophy. These sects, being of a religio-mystic order, have yet to reach a higher standpoint.

140

The philosopher rejects the demand either to accept the world or to renounce it. For him this is unrealistic. He does neither of these things. Only those who are much too ignorant of the real nature of the world can concern themselves with such a demand.

141

The yogi seeks release from the chains of rebirth as his objective. The philosopher knows that this result will follow automatically as a by-product of his own objective—the Real.

142

Carrying in himself whatever he has found in study and meditation and prayer, he returns to the world to gain experience of life and to apply in practice what he has learned.

143

The knowledge got from metaphysics, the intuitive peace gained from meditation, must now be accompanied by practical work done wisely and altruistically in the world to express both. The student must evoke the strength to descend into this sharply contrasting activity. The quest is not a single-track but rather a triple-track affair. He must travel along it with his intelligence, his intuition, and his deeds. "All speak of the Open Path, only rare ones enter the complex path," wrote Shah Latif, the eighteenth-century Sufi poet. When rational thought and mystical feeling and self-alienated action are thus integrated into one, when life becomes a sincere and successful whole, it becomes philosophic. It may be that such a combination of qualities has been rare in the past, but it is certain that it will be necessary in the future. The world will need men and women as leaders who have their roots deep down in the life of the divine self but who have their intellects very much alert, their hands very much alive, and their hearts very much expanded.

144

He has next to submit himself so completely to this experience that its inner light becomes his outer life.

145

It must not be thought that this is a mode of living which is half in the world and half out of it. Rather is it a mode which knows no difference between the world and the Spirit—all is of one piece.

146

It is a natural self-control which comes into play without any willed effort, spontaneously and easily. It is one consequence of achieving the third stage of philosophic questing, completing and applying to active everyday living the fruits of the second stage, contemplation. Ego and animal fall far back in the human to where they belong.

147

Nature is guiding us toward a progressive self-enlargement, not, as some think, toward self-attenuation.

148

Life is not a matter of meditation methods exclusively. Their study and practice is necessary, but let them be put in their proper place. Both mystical union and metaphysical understanding are necessary steps on this quest, because it is only from them that the student can mount to the still higher grade of universal being represented by the sage. For we not only need psychological exercises to train the inner being, but also psychological exercises to train the point of view. But the student must not stay in mysticism as he must not stay in metaphysics. In both cases he should take all that they have to give him but struggle through and come out on the other side. For the mysticism of emotion is not the shrine where Isis dwells but only the vestibule to the shrine, and the metaphysician who can only see in reason the supreme faculty of man has not reflected enough. Let him go farther and he shall find that its own supreme achievement is to point beyond itself to that principle or Mind whence it takes its rise. Mysticism needs the check of philosophic discipline. Metaphysics needs the vivification of mystical meditation. Both must bear fruit in inspired action or they are but half-born. In no other way than through acts can they rise to the lofty status of facts.

The realization of what man is here for is the realization of a fused and unified life wherein all the elements of action, feeling, and thought are vigorously present. It is not, contrary to the belief of mystics, a condition of profound entrancement alone, nor, contrary to the reasonings of metaphysicians, a condition of intellectual clarity alone, and still less, contrary to the opinions of theologians, a condition of complete faith in God alone. We are here to live, which means to think, feel, and act also. We have not only to curb thought in meditation, but also to whip it in reflection. We have not only to control emotion in self-discipline, but also to release it in laughter, relaxation, affection, and pleasure. We have not only to perceive the transiency and illusion of material existence, but also to work, serve, strive, and move strenuously, and thus justify physical existence. We have to learn that when we look at what we really are we stand alone in the awed solitude of the Overself, but when we look at where we now are we see not isolated individuals but members of a thronging human community. The hallmark of a living man, therefore, ought to be an integral and inseparable activity of heart, head, and hand, itself occurring within the mysterious stillness and silence of its inspirer, the Overself.

The mistake of the lower mystic is when he would set up a final goal in meditation itself, when he would stop at the "letting-go" of the external world which is quite properly an essential process of mysticism, and when he would let his reasoning faculty fall into a permanent stupor merely because it is right to do so during the moments of mental quiet. When, however, he learns to understand that the antinomy of meditation and action belongs only to an intermediate stage of this quest, when he comes later to the comprehension that detachment from the world is only to be sought to enable him to move with perfect freedom amid the things of the world and not to flee them, and when he perceives at long last that the reason itself is God-given to safeguard his journey and later to bring his realization into self-consciousness—then he shall have travelled from the second to the third degree in this freemasonry of ultimate wisdom. For that which had earlier hindered his advance now helps it; such is the paradox which he must unravel if he would elevate himself from the satisfactions of mysticism to the perceptions of philosophy. If his meditations once estranged him from the world, now they bring him closer to it! If formerly he could find God only within himself, now he can find nothing else that is not God! He has advanced from the chrysalis-state of X to the butterfly state of Y.

If there be any worth in this teaching, such lies in its equal appeal to experience and to reason. For that inward beatitude which it finally brings is superior to any other that mundane man has felt and, bereft of all violent emotion itself though it be, paradoxically casts all violent emotions of joy in the shade. When we comprehend that this teaching establishes as fact what the subtlest reasoning points to in theory, reveals in man's own life the presence of that Overself which reflection discovers as from a remote distance, we know that here at long last is something fit for a modern man. The agitations of the heart and the troublings of the head take their dying breaths.(P)

Insight

149

The term "insight" has a special application in philosophy. Its results are stamped with a certitude beyond mere belief, better than logical demonstration, superior to limited sense observation.

150

Philosophy seeks not only to know what is best in life but also to love it. It wants to feel as well as think. The truth, being above the common forms of these functions, can be grasped only by a higher function that includes, fuses, and transcends them at one and the same time—insight. In human life at its present stage of development, the nearest activity to this one is the activity of intuition. From its uncommon and infrequent visitations, we may gather some faint echo of what this wonderful insight is.(P)

151

Intuition knows earthly truth without the intervention of reasoning, while insight knows divine truth in the same direct way.

152

"Intuition" had come to lose its pristine value for me. I cast about for a better one and found it in "insight." This term I assigned to the highest knowing-faculty of sages and was thus able to treat the term "intuition" as something inferior which was sometimes amazingly correct but not infrequently hopelessly wrong in its guidance, reports, or premonition. I further endeavoured to state what the old Asiatic sages had long ago stated, that it was possible to unfold a faculty of direct insight into the nature of the Overself, into the supreme reality of the universe, that this was the highest kind of intuition possible to man, and that it did not concern itself with lesser revelations, such as giving the name of a horse likely to win tomorrow's race, a revelation which the kind of intuition we hear so much about is sometimes able to do.(P)

153

There is an irreducible Principle of Being behind all other beings, an Unconditioned Power behind all lesser and limited powers, a final Reality which was never born or put together. Call it what you will, you can neither define nor describe it adequately: men do not perceive it because they do not have the necessary faculty for perceiving it, for that is a faculty which has nothing to do with the affairs of their little ego and its little world. But they can awaken this insight, nurture it, develop it.

154

But if the Ultimate is forever beyond human grasp, some suggestion about its nature is not beyond the grasp of human intuition. He who has developed himself sufficiently to receive unhindered such a suggestion is a man of insight.

155

All metaphysical study and all mystical exercises are but preparations for this flash of reality across the sky of consciousness which is here termed insight. The latter is therefore the most important experience which awaits a human being on this earth. If metaphysics or mysticism is regarded as an end in itself and not as a preliminary, then its follower misses what lies at the core of one's life.

156

Insight may apparently be born suddenly, but it is really the culminating stage of a long previous development.

157

It flashes forth out of the darkness and *must* be seen. Whereas a book containing new and tremendous revelations of truth may be read but its meanings not seen because not understood, here, on the contrary, to see is to understand. Why? Because it is also *to be*.

158

Such is the overwhelming certitude of philosophic insight that it does not need any other support to justify its truth for itself. Its possessor may, if he wishes, for the sake of others, put in such a support when attempting to communicate with them in words: but for himself it is not at all necessary. It is in a class entirely by itself and leaves the possessor with such awe, such a feeling of homage to its reality and truth, that he will be loath to mention it in any ordinary gathering of men.

159

Reason moves continuously around the idea of the Overself whereas insight enters it directly.

160

In *The Hidden Teaching Beyond Yoga* I most unfortunately gave the impression that the higher truth was only to be got as an understanding—in contrast with the mystic's realization, which was only an experience. Within a few weeks of its publication I wrote and issued an "Appendix" to clear up this matter and had it incorporated in the printed text in all further editions. Moreover, in the sequel, *The Wisdom of the Overself* I returned again to the same point, explaining again that the philosophic insight is a fusion of both knowledge and realization, understanding and experience.

161

Insight is the flower of reason and not its negation.(P)

162

Insight can only supervene when thinking consideration has finished its work and relinquished its effort in favour of an ultramystical process.

163

When the form-making activity of the mind is brought to a standstill by the combined twofold process of yoga and enquiry, insight into the mind itself can then be obtained, but not before.

164

What the intellect formulates as opinion, belief, or observation arises out of its own movement in thinking. What the insight experiences as being arises out of the intellect's utter stillness so that it permits itself to be replaced by the higher faculty which alone can know reality.

165

The intellect is not able to get this kind of knowledge, not able to gain access to this higher dimension. But what is denied to it is granted to another of man's faculties—insight. True, this is still only a latent one in nearly all men. But it is there and, with the Overself's grace, can be unfolded.

166

Insight is not a work of the logical reason. Yet the keenest reasoning is present in it. It is not merely a movement of the emotions. Yet the heart element is equally present in it.

167

The philosopher's insight is not only sublime, like every other mystic's: it is also precise.

168

It is not enough to attain knowledge of the soul; any mystic may do that. It is necessary to attain *clear* knowledge. Only the philosophic mystic may do that. This emphasis on clarity is important. It implies a removal of all the obstructions in feeling, the complexes in mind, and obfuscations in ego which prevent it. When this is done, the aspirant beholds truth as it really is.(P)

169

Insight into truth comes from a region which metaphysics cannot enter. Nevertheless his insight should be able to square with the reason and appeal to the heart.

170

He who possesses insight does not have to use arguments and reach conclusions. The truth is there, self-evident, inside himself as himself, for his inner being has become one with it.(P)

171

Insight possesses for the sage the highest degree of that instantaneous certainty of their own existence possessed by other men.

172

The ordinary metaphysician can form no precise and impeccable idea of truth without the guidance of the philosopher's insight, or if he does it is purely a speculative one. Such insight remains the highest norm, the final criterion, open to mankind.

173

Because the philosophic experience is the supreme human experience, it explains and makes understandable all the others.

174

We need not be afraid of deserting reason when it has finally fulfilled its lofty office. For the insight for which we exchange it is not really opposed to it but implements it. That which reason describes as the indefinable and infinite pure nondual mind is actualized by insight.

175

It is out of the interplay of meditation, metaphysics, and altruistic action that insight is unfolded. No single element will alone suffice: the conjunction of all three is needed and then only can insight emerge. We cannot in the end escape from this complexity of life. The metaphysician who has not balanced his overmuch thinking with richer feeling, the yogi who has not brought his contemplative tendency into better equilibrium with altruistic action, suffers eventually from psychic ill health and external failures. For he is only one-third or one-half alive.

176

When this knowledge becomes a fusion of thought and feeling, intuition and meditation, it bursts out as insight. This is extremely clear, finally established, and certainly balanced. When adjusted to everyday living it is naturalized. There is then no higher satisfaction for the self, no nobler ethic which stays inside wisdom, and no more religious way to worship God. In profiting himself he profits humanity also. For what has happened in his mind will and must affect other minds too.

177

If a man is to rise to the philosophic insight, he will find it through intellect and feeling, intelligence and intuition, mystical experience and deep penetration into consciousness—his own and the world's.

178

Such a revolutionary acquisition as insight must necessarily prove to be in a man's life can only be developed by overcoming all the tremendous force of habitual wrong thinking, by neutralizing all the tremendous weight of habitual wrong feeling, and by counteracting all the tremendous strength of habitual wrong-doing. In short, the familiar personal "I" must have the ground cut from under its feet. This is done by the threefold discipline. The combined threefold technique consists of metaphysical reflection, mystical meditation, and constant remembrance in the midst of disinterested active service. The full use and balanced exercise of every function is needful. Although these three elements have here been isolated one by one for the purpose of clearer intellectual study, it must be remembered that in actual life the student should not attempt to isolate them. Such a division is an artificial one. He who takes for his province this whole business of truth-seeking and gains this rounded all-comprehensive view will no longer be so one-sided as to set up a particular path as being the only way to salvation. On the contrary, he will see that salvation is an integral matter. It can no more be attained by mere meditation alone, for example, than by mere impersonal activity alone; it can no more be reached by evading the lessons of everyday external living than by evading the suppression of such externality which meditation requires. Whereas metaphysics seeks to lift us up to the superphysical idea by thinking, whereas meditation seeks to lift us up by intuition, whereas ethics seeks to raise us to it by practical goodness, art seeks to do the same by feeling and appreciating beauty. Philosophy in its wonderful breadth and balance embraces and synthesizes all four and finally adds their coping stone, insight.(P)

179

Right conduct, right meditation, right metaphysics are all essential to the birth of the truest insight and are all involved in realization. They must all pervade and perfectly balance each other.

180

These three efforts—to develop, to balance, and to fuse the qualities—once achieved and perfected, yield insight.

181

When a certain balance of forces is achieved, something happens that can only be properly called "the birth of insight."

182

In the illumination that spontaneously follows the balance that is reached when completeness of development itself is reached, man finds his real love, his most intense gratification.

183

Philosophy must critically absorb the categories of metaphysics, mysticism, and practicality. For it understands that in the quest of truth the co-operation of all three will not only be helpful and profitable to each other but is also necessary to itself. For only after such absorption, only after it has travelled through them all can it attain what is beyond them all. The decisive point of this quest is reached after the co-operation between all three activities attains such a pitch that they become fused into a single all-comprehensive one which itself differs from them in character and qualities. For the whole truth which is then revealed is not merely a composite one. It not only absorbs them all but transcends them all. When water is born out of the union of oxygen and hydrogen, we may say neither that it is the same as the simple sum-total of both nor that it is entirely different from both. It possesses properties which they in themselves do not at all possess. We may only say that it includes and yet transcends them. When philosophic insight is born out of the union of intellectual reasoning, mystical feeling, and altruistic doing, we may say neither that it is only the totalization of these three things nor that it is utterly remote from them. It comprehends them all and yet itself extends far beyond them into a higher order of being. It is not only that the philosopher synthesizes these triple functions, that in one and the same instant his intellect understands the world, his heart feels a tender sympathy towards it, and his will is moved to action for the triumph of good, but also that he is continuously conscious of that infinite reality which, in its purity, no thinking, no emotion, and no action can ever touch.(P)

184

Insight is a function of the entire psyche and not of any single part of it.

185

Insight is not merely the result of wedding intuition with reason, although this is an essential prerequisite to its birth, but actually something that arises of its own accord through the operation of a higher power. Such an operation is called Grace and religious devotees or practising mystics do get an experience of its lower phases.

186

The ordinary mystical insight is also a transcendental one but there is this difference, that it is not pure, it is always mixed up with an emotion or a thought. Philosophical insight is utterly pure.

187

The "natural" philosophic attainment gives insight as a continuity whereas meditation gives it as an interruption. More, its attitudes are so relaxed, its operations so effortless, its outlook so carefree, that those who have to work hard to get the temporary enlightenment know that nothing else in life has the same importance, the same value.

188

Where we speak either metaphysically or meditationally of the experience of pure consciousness, we mean consciousness uncoloured by the ego.

189

Insight reveals the goodness, beauty, power, and stillness of the Inner Reality whence this world of turmoil and strife has emerged, and which cannot be dragged down to that world. However, the ordinary faculties of thought, feeling, and acting can be so profoundly affected by the experience of attaining insight that they will then see all problems in a different light. Thus, practical help follows indirectly in this, as well as in other ways.

190

Misunderstanding about the usefulness of insight regarding mundane affairs is easily cleared. It is like bringing a printed page before a lamp: the lamp's light is not concerned with the individual words, but rather clarifies the whole of what appears on the page. Similarly, although insight is not concerned with the lesser faculties, the illumination it provides enables the latter to deal far more effectively with everyday affairs.

191

When contact between the light and the eye is established, the resultant act of seeing is an instantaneous affair. When contact between the Real and the insight is established, the resultant enlargement of consciousness is equally immediate.

192

Thinking will come to an end, but not consciousness.

193

His understanding becomes extraordinarily lucid, as if a powerful light had been thrown upon the field of Consciousness.

194

It is all like a gigantic dream, with every human inserting his own private dream inside the public one. A double spell has to be broken before reality can be glimpsed—the spell which the world lays upon us and that which self lays upon us. The man who has completely awakened from this spell is the man who has gained complete insight. This faculty is nothing other than such full wakefulness. It is immensely difficult to attain, which is why so few of the dreamers ever wake up at all and why so many will not even listen to the revelations of the awakened ones. However, Nature teaches us here as elsewhere not to let patience break down. There is plenty of time in her bag. Life is an evolutionary process. Men will begin to stir in their sleep erratically but increasingly.

195

On the highest plane all insights are one.

196

See Chapter 55 of Lao Tzu where he defines "insight"; also Chapter 16: "To know the Eternal is called Insight."

197

Even the Southern Buddhist Pali texts admit that truth (*Dharma*) is *attakkavācara*—that is, not attainable by reason alone—but is finally reached by *Samadhi*—that is, right *insight*.

198

A mystic experience is simply something which comes and goes, whereas philosophic insight, once established in a man, cannot possibly leave him. He understands the Truth and cannot lose this understanding any more than an adult can lose his adulthood and become an infant.(P)

199

Because he has worked for his prize, because he has undergone a patient and arduous training, and because he has taken every step on the way with full comprehension and clear sight, his inspiration is not here today and gone tomorrow but, when he acquires it, remains constant and is permanently kept.

200

There are certain signs whereby the nature of insight characterizes itself in its possessor's relations with his fellows. Foremost among these are understanding and sympathy, a reverent regard for the sanctity and needs of another's personal life. A man of insight will never utter recriminatory words; he will be slow in judgement and swift to bless.

201

The signs of genuineness in true insight include (a) conformity to facts of Nature and not merely logic of argumentation or speculation, (b) clear direct understanding of what it sees, (c) freedom from admixture of any kind of personal predilection, aversion, auto-suggestion or motive, (d) indications that the seer has fully overcome his lower self.

202

No racial peculiarity, no geographical limitation, no cultural bias can enter into such universality of insight.

203

The ever changing world-movement is suspended and transcended in the mystical trance so that the mystic may perceive its hidden changeless ground in the One Mind, whereas in the ultramystic insight its activity is restored. For such insight easily penetrates it, and always sees this ground without need to abolish the appearance. Consequently the philosopher is aware that everyday activity is as much and as needful a field for him as mystical passivity. Such expression, however, cannot be less than what he is within himself through the possession of insight. Just as any man cannot express himself as an ant, do what he may, simply because his human consciousness is too large to be narrowed down to such a little field, so the philosopher cannot separate his ultramystic insight from his moment-to-moment activity. In this sense he has no option but to follow and practise the gospel of inspired action.(P)

204

When, as recorded in the *Potthapala Sutra*, the Buddha refused to answer the questions "Is the world eternal? Is the world not eternal? Is the world finite? Is the world infinite?" he expressed something more than mere contempt for the futility of the logical self-torture of the intellect. For in his explanation of this refusal, he affirmed by implication that philosophy stood on a higher rung than mysticism. He said: "These questions are not calculated to profit, they are not concerned with the Dharma, they do not redound to right conduct nor to detachment, nor to purification from lusts, nor to quietude, nor to tranquillization of the heart, nor to real knowledge, nor to the insight of the higher stages of the Path, nor to Nirvana." Observe that these reasons are quite obviously placed in an ascending order according to their importance, because they begin with external conduct and end with Nirvana. And observe further that *insight* is not only placed higher than peace but *actually said to belong to the higher* stages of the Path. And observe finally that insight is placed only one stage below Nirvana, to which in fact it leads.

205

This is the true insight, the permanent illumination that neither comes nor goes but always *is*. While being serious, where the event or situation requires it, he will not be solemn. For behind this seriousness there is detachment. He cannot take the world of Appearances as being Reality's final form. If he is a sharer in this world's experiences, he is also a witness and especially a witness of his own ego—its acts and desires, its thoughts and speech. And because he sees its littleness, he keeps his sense of humour about all things concerning it, a touch of lightness, a basic humility. Others may believe that he stands in the Great Light, but he himself has no particular or ponderous self-importance.(P)

206

If insight is superior to information then the philosopher has something to give mankind which the scientist cannot give.

Service

207

The mystic who gives himself up to solitary struggle to gain a solitary delight is beyond our criticism but also beyond our praise.

208

Our ideal is not the yogi who has secured his own nirvanic satisfaction; it is not the man who is so wrapped up in his own peace as to be indifferent to the woes of others. It is the sage who is ready to sacrifice his own leisure in order to assist others, enlighten others, assuage the sorrows of others.

209

A spiritual exaltation which does not manifest itself in the service of humanity exists for its possessor alone. Him alone do we love who forsakes the seclusion of the solitary places wherein he attained Nirvana and goes back among men to help his frailer brothers. He alone is worthy of our regard who descends to exhort us towards the steps of the higher life and to encourage us in our efforts to climb, who nerves us with his strength, illumines us with his wisdom, and blesses us with his selfless Love.

210

He comes to the service of mankind by an indirect route. For his primary service is to the Overself. But after he makes this inward act of entire dedication to it, the Overself then bids him go forth and work for the welfare of all beings.

211

To be able to contemplate the Overself as an "other" is already an achievement of high order. But because it is, first, an intermittent one, second, an incomplete one, and third, an imperfect one, it is not yet the highest. In the latter there is final, permanent, and perfect immersion in the Overself.

212

His last task is to re-enter the busy world and dwell in it as focus for unworldly forces, to heal the suffering and guide the blinded.

213

The philosopher will fall neither into the cold unfeeling indifference of the recluse nor into the frothy effervescing fussiness of the sentimentalist. He knows that the first attitude is generated by excessive introversion, the second by excessive extroversion. His ideal being the balance between them, he will attend properly to his own self-development but, side by side with it, work helpfully for mankind.

214

He notes that other people's outer sufferings are greater than his own, while their inner understanding of those sufferings is less. He is both willing and ready to disturb his own bliss with their misery and he will do this not in condescension but in compassion. Saint Paul, following the master whom he never saw in the flesh but knew so well in the spirit, put all other virtues beneath compassion. Are the few who try to be true Christians, in this point at least, utterly wasting their time? For so say the yogis who would abolish all effort in service and concentrate on self-realization alone. Yet neither Jesus nor Paul was a mere sentimentalist. They knew the power of compassion in dissolving the ego. It was thus a part of their moral code. They knew, too, another reason why the disciple should practise altruistic conduct and take up noble attitudes. With their help he may bring one visitation of bad karma to an earlier end or even help to prevent the manifestation of another visitation which would otherwise be inevitable.

215

Ancient spirituality thought that what was most important was to cultivate individual soul. Modern materialism thinks it should be social betterment. These two goals have usually been placed in opposition. But modern spirituality refuses to accept such a false dilemma. Let us seek *both* the cultivation of the soul, it declares, and the betterment of social conditions. Why, when we open our eyes to the one need, should we shut them to the other? Humanity's outer need does not justify the neglect of our own inner need, nor this the neglect of the other. No amount of humanitarianism can counterbalance the duty of devoting time and energy to spiritualizing our own self also, but this ought not become so self-centered as to become a total and exclusive devotion.

216

Philosophy offers a middle way between the self-centered obsession with spiritual development and the self-exhausting obsession with humanity's service.

217

The last marks of the ego's grip will linger on him in various subtle forms. Perhaps the willingness to be saved himself while leaving behind so many others entangled in illusion is the final mark to be erased. But it is a mark which only philosophical mystics, not ordinary mystics, are likely to be troubled with. Only a compassion of unparalleled depth and immense impartiality will put anyone on such a course as voluntarily to remain on liberation's threshold so as to help the unliberated.

218

When a man has been preoccupied with himself throughout his lifetime, when he is intent solely on his personal salvation, when he no longer thinks of other seekers' welfare because he is too engaged with his own, the danger is that his spiritual attainment, when and if it comes, will be kept for himself too. This is why Philosophy rejects the egocentric ideal of the lower mysticism and why it trains its votaries from the very start to work altruistically for humanity's enlightenment. No man is so low in the evolutionary scale that he cannot help some other men with a rightly placed word, cannot strike a flickering match in their darkness, cannot show the example of a better life.

219

The difference between the mystic and the philosopher is that although both are illumined by the same Overself, the former's limitations and narrowness limit and narrow the expression and communication of his state and his help. The philosopher, however, having all-around development—for instance, having well developed his intellect and activity—can explain to intellectual persons what they can understand, can work among active persons as one of them, thus showing that attainment is no bar to an intellectual disposition or a practical life. The mystic is often unable to do this, but talks as a simple fool or lives as a hermit or monk. Although this makes no difference to his enjoyment of the higher state, it makes a difference to other persons when they come into contact with him. But these differences merely belong to the surface, not to the inner core, where both mystic and philosopher enjoy the same realization. Hence it is a matter of choice, not necessity, which path is taken.

220

Philosophy may offer the mystic a better understanding and a fuller transmission of his own occasional mystical experience but it also faces him with a grimmer prospect when that becomes permanently stabilized. For it enjoins him to abstain from final entry into the last state, the utter mergence of all individuality in the great nothingness of the All. He is to become the Saviour of those he has outstepped, to wait and serve until they too are free from illusion and sin. Only an immense compassion could provide enough force to keep him from crossing the threshold.

221

It would be a great misconception to believe that this peace which he has found in his inner life is bought at the cost of a selfish indifference towards everyone and everything in his outer life. The contrary is the very truth. He attains the wisdom and obtains the power to do more real good for humanity than those who are still walking in darkness and weakness. If he is a philosopher, he will assuredly point out the way for others to light and strength, and may even sacrifice his rebirth on a higher planet to this purpose. He becomes a link between suffering humanity and serene divinity.

222

There is a fundamental difference between mystical escapism and mystical altruism. In the first case, the man is interested only in gaining his own self-realization and will be content to let his endeavours stop there. In the second case, he has the same aim but also the keen aspiration to make his achievement, when it materializes, available for the service of mankind. And because such a profound aspiration cannot be banished into cold-storage to await this materialization, he will even sacrifice part of his time, money, and energy to doing what little he can to enlighten others intellectually during the interval. Even if this meant doing nothing more than making philosophical knowledge more easily accessible to ordinary men than it has been in the past, this would be enough. But he can do much more than that. Both types recognize the indispensable need of deliberately withdrawing from society and isolating themselves from its activities to obtain the solitude necessary to achieve intensity of concentration, to practise meditative reflection upon life, and to study mystical and philosophical books. But whereas the first would make the withdrawal a permanent, lifelong one, the second would make it only a temporary and occasional one. And by "temporary" we mean any period from a single day to several years. The first is a resident of the ivory tower of escapism, the second merely its visitor. The first can find happiness only in his solitariness and must draw himself out of humanity's disturbing life to attain it. The second seeks a happiness that will hold firm in all places and makes retirement from that life only a means to this end. Each is entitled to travel his own path. But at such a time as the present, when the whole world is being convulsed and the human soul agitated as never before, we personally believe that it is better to follow the less selfish and more compassionate one.(P)

223

It is good for an ascetic or monk to sit idle and inactive whilst he contemplates the futility of a life devoted solely to earthly strivings, but it is bad for him to spend the whole of a valuable incarnation in such idleness and in such contemplation. For then he is fastening his attention on a single aspect of existence and losing sight of all others. It is good for a metaphysician to occupy himself with noting the logical contradictions involved in the world's existence and in the reason's own discoveries, but bad for him to waste a whole incarnation in fastening his attention on a single aspect. It is good for the worldling to accumulate money and enjoy the good things it can buy, marry a wife, and adorn his home with comforts, but it is bad for him to waste his valuable incarnation without a higher purpose and a loftier goal. Nor is this all. Mysticism, metaphysics, and worldliness are useless unless they succeed in affording a man a basis of altruistic ethics for everyday living. The average mystic does not see that his lapse into loss of interest in the world around him, his indifference to positive and practical service of mankind, in short his whole other-worldliness, is not a virtue, as he believes, but a defect. Hermits who withdraw from the troubled world to practise the simplicity, monks who retreat from the active world to muse over the evanescence of things, defeatists who flee from their failure in life, marriage, or business to the lethargy which they believe to be peace, thereby evidence that they have not understood the higher purpose of incarnation. It is to afford them the opportunity to realize in waking consciousness their innermost nature. This cannot be done by turning their face from the experiences of human existence, but by boldly confronting them and mastering them. Nor can it be done by retreating into the joys of meditation. The passionate ecstasies of lower mysticism, like the intellectual discoveries of lower metaphysics, yield only the illusion of penetrating into reality. For the world, as well as the "I," must be brought into the circles of meditation if the whole truth is to be gained. The one-sided, monkish doctrine which indicts the world's forms with transiency and illusiveness must be met and balanced by the philosophic doctrine which reveals the world's essence as eternal and real. There will then be no excuse for lethargy, defeatism, or escapism. A metaphysical outlook often lacks the spark of vitality; a mystical outlook often lacks the solidity of reasoned thought; and both often lack the urge to definite action. The practical failures of metaphysics are traceable to the fact that it does not involve the exercise of the will as much as it involves the exercise of the intellect. The intellectual failures of metaphysics are due to the fact that the men who taught it in the past knew nothing of science and those who teach it in the present know nothing of higher mystical meditation, whilst both have usually had little experience of the hard facts of life outside their sheltered circles. The failures of mysticism are due to the same causes, as well as others we have often pointed out. Finally, the failure of metaphysicians to produce practical fruit is partly due to the fact that they perceive *ideas* of truth and not truth itself, as the failure of mystics is partly due to the fact that they experience *feelings* of reality and not reality itself. The successes and services of the sage, on the contrary, are due to the fact that he perceives truth and experiences reality and not merely thoughts or feelings about them.(P)

224

From all these studies, meditations, and actions the student will little by little emerge an inwardly changed man. He comes to the habitual contemplation of his co-partnership with the universe as a whole, to the recognition that personal isolation is illusory, and thus takes the firm steps on the ultimate path towards becoming a true philosopher. The realization of the hidden unity of his own life with the life of the whole world manifests finally in infinite compassion for all living things. Thus he learns to subdue the personal will to the cosmic one, narrow selfish affection to the widespreading desire for the common welfare. Compassion comes to full blossom in his heart like a lotus flower in the sunshine. From this lofty standpoint, he no longer regards mankind as being those whom he unselfishly serves but rather as being those who give him the opportunity to serve. He will suddenly or slowly experience an emotional exaltation culminating in an utter change of heart. Its course will be marked by a profound reorientation of feeling toward his fellow creatures. The fundamental egoism which in open or masked forms has hitherto motivated him will be abandoned: the noble altruism which has hitherto seemed an impracticable and impossible ideal, will become practicable and possible. For a profound sympathy to all other beings will dwell in his heart. Never again will it be possible for him wilfully to injure another; but on the contrary the welfare of the All will become his concern. In Jesus' words he is "born again." He will find his highest happiness, after seeking reality and truth, in seeking the welfare of all other beings alongside of his own. The practical consequence of this is that he will be inevitably led to incessant effort for their service and enlightenment. He will not merely echo the divine will but will allow it actively to work within him. And with the thought comes the power to do so, the grace of the Overself to help him to achieve quickly what the Underself cannot achieve. In the service of others he can partially forget his loss of trance-joy and know that the liberated self which he had experienced in interior meditation must be equated by the expanded self in altruistic action.(P)

225

The peace to which he has become heir is not self-absorbed rest from old activities that he deserts, but a divine awareness that subsists beneath new ones that he accepts.(P)

226

When he first attains to this clear vision, he sees not only that which brings him great joy but also that which brings him great sorrow. He sees men bewildered by life, pained by life, blinded by life. He sees them wandering into wrong paths because there is no one to lead them into right ones. He sees them praying for light but surrounded by darkness. In that hour he makes a decision which will fundamentally affect the whole of his life. Henceforth he will intercede for these others, devote himself to their spiritual service.(P)

227

After the desire for the fullest overshadowing by the Overself, which must always be primal, his second desire is to spread out the peace, understanding, and compassion which now burn like a flame within him, to propagate an inward state rather than an intellectual dogma, to bless and enlighten those who seek their divine parent.(P)

228

Unfortunate is the traditional indifference towards the practical world and self-absorption in personal peace. Such an attitude is not the one taught by *The Voice of Silence*, which fitly represents the school of true sages and which inculcates compassionate service of mankind instead of self-centered isolation. The Tibetan doctrine is in this respect superior to the Indian doctrine.

229

The fourth part of this fourfold quest, which concerns moral and social tasks, ought not to be disregarded. It is only an unintelligent mysticism that promotes smug self-centered idleness whereas a philosophical mysticism inspires both useful and altruistic activity.

The condition of stolid indifference to humanity is not compatible with the condition of loving harmony with the divine soul of humanity. In Burke's eloquent phrase, it is "the offspring of cold hearts and muddy understandings." It indicates the attainment of an inferior stage of spirituality. How much nobler is the attainment of a true sage! He does not look haughtily down upon others from the cold pinnacle of his unworldly interests or disdainfully at their moral weaknesses. He does not stop with the self-engrossed type of mystic to wallow in smug peace. Jesus, for instance, did not disdain to descend from the Mount of Transfiguration to help the epileptic boy; that is, he did not disdain to interrupt contemplation for action. The philosophical type of mystic does not content himself with the non-cooperative ideal of personal salvation pursued by those interested in themselves alone and indifferent to mankind's darkness and misery. On the contrary, he takes on the supreme sacrifice of a continual reincarnation which shall be dedicated to human enlightenment. Only when he has done all he could for the service of suffering mankind, only when he has reached this stage, can he know true abiding peace. Then he truly can say, with Chuang Tzu: "Within my breast no sorrows can abide, I feel the Great World-Mind through me breathe." There is every reason why a man who accepts the gospel of inspired action should become a beneficent force in the world. Whatever role falls to him in the game of life, he will play it in a vital and significant way. More than ever before in its history, the world's need is for such active philosophers. It has little use for volitionally impotent visionaries. Their muddled ethos must share part of the responsibility for mysticism's failure to make more effective contributions towards helping mankind during their greatest crisis and most tragical times. When the world is in such a tremendous need of guidance hope comfort strength and truth during its hour of grave danger and terrible crisis, surely it is the course of a generous wisdom for the contemporary mystic not to seek his personal peace alone but to realize the importance of helping others to find theirs too? He should not seek to be detached monastically from the troubles of his country. On the contrary, he should seek to mitigate them, so far as it is within his power, by rendering wise helpful service.

What Winston Churchill once told the American nation, "The price of greatness is responsibility," is what may be said to the mystic. The Americans tried but could not escape getting embroiled again in European affairs, and the mystic may try but cannot escape his own duties to the rest of mankind. The esoteric explanation of this is the factuality of a deep interrelation and primal oneness of the human race.

230

The philosophic man's care for his own welfare does not make him insensitive to the welfare of others. His concern is not concentrated on, and does not end with, himself. Rather he puts both claims into sound balance and lets neither emotion nor self-interest run away with him.

231

Philosophy has never had a popular appeal and philosophers have always been small in number, but this is not to say that they have not affected the life of society and the trend of events. On the contrary, the intellectual capacity and moral character of philosophers have naturally made them members of the influential classes in their community, while the ideal of service, constantly thought about and acted upon, has by the law and power of recompense inevitably brought them into positions where there was opportunity to express it.

232

The mystic's own attainment certainly helps humanity but it helps only indirectly. The philosopher's, because it directly sets itself to benefit humanity, does so more widely and more markedly.

233

This ideal of a spiritualized worldly life on the part of an illuminate is held even where it might be thought the last place to be found—in Buddhism. For of the three Goals it sets before men, the last is that of the Bodhisattva. Linguistically, the term means one who is bent upon wisdom but technically the term means one who is destined to become a Buddha. Practically, it means one who stands on the very threshold, as it were, of Nirvana, but refuses to enter because he wishes to remain behind and relieve suffering humanity. This tremendous self-sacrifice indicates the tremendous spirit of compassion which actuates him. "I cannot have pleasure while another grieves and I have the power to help," said Gautama while yet a Bodhisattva. He has all the capacities and qualities, all the mental and ethical advancement to render him quite capable of swiftly attaining the Goal but prefers to use them only as far as its threshold and no farther. Hence, we find that Bodhisattvas are historically persons who practise pity, kindness, and charity to an incredible extent, but do not forget to use discrimination at the same time. He is soft-hearted but not a soft-hearted fool. Thus, he renounces the ego but he does not renounce the world. He may marry, as Gautama when a Bodhisattva sought to marry the princess Pabhavati (*Jataka* 531); he may live in luxury, ease, and comfort and say, as the same Gautama-Bodhisattva said: "Infatuated, bound and deeply stained am I with pleasures, fearful though they be, but I love life and cannot them deny. Good works I undertake continually." (*Jataka* 378) With all this, however, he does not drop his wisdom but holds perpetually to the meditation on the world's transience, suffering, and illusion but he does not hold to it to such an extent that he would fully realize Nirvana; here again, he pauses at its threshold. For he refuses to break his ties with common humanity. Thus, he is reborn in the most diverse bodies, environments, and ranks and undergoes the most varied vicissitudes, thus giving the benefit of his altruistic presence on the most universal and large-hearted scale.

Consequently, if we meet him in the flesh, we meet a citizen of the world, a man utterly free from all racial, colour, or class prejudice. He is ready to live in the world, therefore, even as a worldly person. He loves knowledge and will not disdain it when it deals with the things of earth alone; nothing that is human is unfit for him to learn. He will foster brains, practicality, self-reliance, strength, resolution, perseverance. He considers his word sacred and unfailingly keeps a promise and throughout the entire course of his worldly life he never cherishes ill will to anyone, not even to enemies who have insulted, injured, betrayed, or burnt him with their hate. For he remembers that he is a Bodhisattva—one who intends loving-kindness to *all*.

234

If it be asked how it is possible for the would-be philosopher to dictate in advance what attitude he is going to take after his final attainment, if it be objected that decisions made before this attainment may be discarded as unwise or unnecessary after it and that therefore the philosophic procedure of resolving to devote the fruits of attainment to the service of humanity is foolish, the answer is that these objections would be quite correct if the philosopher accepted attainment to its fullest extent—but he does not. He stops on the very threshold of it, and although bathed in its light and glory, does not accept it.

235

That which sustains each individual mind is a universal one. Therefore, that which is best for him in social and ethical action must also fulfil the requirement of being what is best for all. Otherwise it is incomplete.

236

If his earlier life has been self-centered, the attainment of this stage will provide him with the opportunity to escape from our miserable planet and to pass into a world of harmony, peace, and light, although this escape cannot in the nature of things mature until his physical body dies. But if his earlier life has been compassionate and altruistic in ideal—however unsuccessful in practice—the attainment will provide him with the power to implement this ideal, the strength to realize it in actuality. The thought will then present itself to him, "How best can I serve mankind?" This will lead him to seek for ways of helpfulness appropriate to his times, environment, and circumstances. Naturally the knowledge that helping others toward a similar enlightenment is the best service he can render them will predominate, but he will understand that their physical existence cannot be separated from their mental one and that it may sometimes be needful as a step toward that ultimate purpose to take up a duty which seems to belong solely to the external sphere of things.

237

Is it conceivable that just at the point in his history when a man has achieved the highest possible degree of power, of self-control, of wisdom, and of compassion—that is, when he has the greatest value for serving humanity—he is to be withdrawn from circulation and stopped from being helpful to those who most need him?

238

Those who engage in unselfish service are temporarily loosened somewhat from the ego. This of course is true only to the extent that the service is done with pure, and not with ulterior or mixed or quite selfish, motives.

239

Has it any moral realization of its responsibilities in the present world crisis? Can it say anything that is worthwhile and that will help humanity? What vital contribution does it offer to our generation? The answer to these questions is that philosophy is definitely alive to contemporary needs and extremely desirous of serving creatively. Although its votaries are primarily engaged upon spiritual studies, this does not mean that they must have a blank mind about other problems. They realize that their studies have an indirect bearing upon them too. However, the points of view being different, the conclusions are inevitably different too. For example, democracy says that public opinion should determine a government's course. Philosophy says that wisdom and virtue should determine it. At times, of course, the two coincide and then democracy is gloriously vindicated.

240

Those who have received its benefits will one day have to repay its obligations. This they can do only in the way suited to their individual circumstances. It is a duty laid upon them from within by no one but themselves, but it is not less imperative than if it had been laid from without, and by higher authorities.

241

He has no other course than paradoxically to separate himself from mankind if he is to serve mankind in the most effectual way—by living for it instead of being martyred by it.

242

The balanced view says that each individual has a duty towards society in return for what society has done for him. His right to draw something from society must be balanced by his duty to contribute something to it. Everyone should contribute something to the world's activity and not live parasitically on the labour of others. A genuine prestige should be attached to labour. It should be as dishonourable to be idle and mystical as it should be to be idle and rich. If anyone draws sustenance from society, he should help carry on society's work.

243

If those of higher ideals and unselfish character withdraw from society, leaving the world to be run by more materialistic and selfish persons, then society will certainly degenerate and thus bring karmic suffering upon itself. Wisdom, however, dictates the reverse policy.

244

There is a common goal for all of us. In the end nobody can attain redemption while his fellows remain still unredeemed.

245

The sage may invite co-operation in this work not for their personal aggrandizement but for the philanthropic enlightenment of the eager, questioning few.

246

The giving out of spiritual knowledge is best kept on such holy ground that it is done for its own sake entirely, and it should constitute its own reward.

247

If he gives his services to humanity, he does so without pricing them—without thought of or request for any external reward.

248

He is not a psychoanalyst who charges a hundred dollars an hour for consultations. He gives his services for nothing. Because he wants to conduct his life of service on the highest possible plane, he accepts no money for these consultations.

249

The mystic's error is to believe that his duty toward God cancels his duty towards man. Philosophy corrects the error and unites the two.

250

It is proper for the mystical novice to feel apathetic and lethargic about his duties toward and intercourse with society. He is trying to turn inwards and they would only disturb him. It is equally proper, however, for the mystical adept, if he has developed on philosophic lines, to feel led towards abundant activity and social service.

251

His ultimate aim is to enjoy the blessed presence of the Overself in his heart. But it is not, as with inferior mystics, to enjoy it alone. He ardently desires to share it with others.

252

The mystic feels he has accomplished his task when he has accomplished this blessed reunion with the Overself. The philosopher feels that it is not enough and that without ceasing to maintain this union, he must spiritually guide the few who seek truth and materially serve the many who do not.

253

When the better souls non-cooperatively stay out of worldly business because they dislike it, or regard it as soiled, or are too weak for it, they leave the field open to the worse ones.

254

If he serves a race, a nation, a class, or a group, his service will not be for them as such—his outlook is too wide for that—but as human beings.

255

The larger understanding and the greater compassion of philosophy bid him act differently. They bid him seek his own salvation, not outside of humanity's, but alongside of it.

256

He approaches men not as a beggar seeking help but as a benefactor offering it.

257

Philosophic altruism is not to be confused with its ordinary counterpart. Divinely inspired service is not the same as humanitarian service. The moral motivation and supporting consciousness are different. The sage practises the first, not the second.

258

If anyone can make a spiritual, aesthetic, reasonable, and ethical contribution to mankind, he serves God too, even if he belongs to no religion. For he is harmonizing himself with the World-Idea.

259

It must not be thought that a non-selfish actively altruistic attitude in his dealing with other men is the chief characteristic of the philosopher's practical life. If this were so then it would only be a good human life but not a divinely human life. Humanitarianism serves men whereas philosophy serves what is sacred in men.

260

Whoever wishes to attract people to philosophy must start by supporting its preachings with the attractiveness of his own personal example in day-to-day living. He must continue by practising love to all and depending on the power of truth. He must end by praying for others in secret and offering himself to the Divine as a pure instrument of service.

261

When the Higher Power leads a man to a position produced by his constant aspiration to serve coupled with his personal qualifications for it, the strength and wisdom he may need to fulfil it will also be granted.

262

To understand the mysterious language of the Silence, and to bring this understanding back into the world of forms through work that shall express the creative vitality of the Spirit, is one way in which you may serve mankind.(P)

263

The man who lives in the physical senses alone reaches and affects those other men only whom he can come into contact with physically. He is entirely limited by time and space. The man who lives in the developed intellect or feelings also reaches and affects those other men who can respond to his written or printed ideas or his artistic inspirations. He is limited only partially by time and space. But the man who lives in the godlike Overself within him is freed from time and space and uplifts all those who can respond intuitively, even though they may never know him physically. For in the spiritual world he cannot hide his light.(P)

264

It may be said that the world's supreme need is exactly what the illumined man has found, therefore his duty is to give it to the world. This is true, but it is equally true that the world is not ready for it any more than he himself was ready for it before he underwent a long course of purification, discipline, and training. Accepting these realities of the situation, he feels no urge to spread his ideas, no impulse to organize a following. However that does not mean that he does nothing at all; it only means that he will help in the ways he deems to be most effective even if they are the least publicized and the least apparent. He is not deaf to the call of duty but he gives it a wider interpretation than those who are ignorant of the state and powers which he enjoys.(P)

265

To wait until you have attained perfection means that then you will be able to serve humanity perfectly. But can the imperfect do nothing until then? No—they can help, only it will be imperfect help, limited help, and mixed with some seeking.

266

Imagination could not grasp, even if sympathy could sustain, all this planet's inescapable human misery and animal pain at once. No man living could ever measure the one or alleviate the other. During the 1940s, millions of men and women and beasts lived in torture or died in agony, starved in famine or were liquidated in explosion. He must perforce accept the quantitative limits which Nature, insulating his personality, sets for him here or else set up his own. However distressed a man may be when confronted by depressing national situations or by painful international tragedies, knowing that he can do nothing about them, that they are beyond his limited power as a single individual to influence, alter, or reshape, he will have to let the responsibility for them rest on the proper shoulders and accept the lesson in karma's working. He is not a second Atlas to bear the enormous burden of the whole world's accumulated agony on his little shoulders. Nevertheless, given a man who is at all sensitive enough to respond emotionally to all the piled-up misery that lies around him, imaginative enough to recall it even when he is isolated from it by good fortune, can such a one remain immured in his own individuality and become impassive enough to live undistressed by the woes of others, untouched by their cries? Hence although personally helpless in such present matters, he can at least work patiently to improve future ones by working to improve future humanity. He will seek to find a sensible balance between the good manners of attending to his own spiritual business and the compassionate duty of making his knowledge and experience available to others.

267

We must distinguish between those who have attained to the true self through purely mystical methods and those who have attained it through the broader philosophic ones. The first kind enjoy their inward peace and freedom but they are often content to stop there. The second kind likewise enjoy these things but are not content with a merely self-centered acquisition. They seek out ways of embodying in their social surroundings and stimulating in their human environment something of the perfect life which is its hidden heart. Hence they teach and preach to others the way of upward advancement which can lead them to share ultimately in this diviner life.

268

He will best meet those who come to him for help of whatever kind, but especially of the spiritual kind—whether they approach him in person or by letter—if he turns them over repeatedly to the Overself. He need not do so vocally or publicly. It is enough if he does it mentally and silently. For they come because they sense the current, however feeble, of Life flowing through him. He must get himself out of its way, otherwise he will be like a rock in its path. By instantly following this method of inwardly referring the supplicants to the higher power, he will safeguard himself and serve others more effectively.

269

It is not by overmuch fussy activity that we necessarily serve others best. We may, if we have opened ourselves to divine influences, become radiations of such influences. Merely by being faithful to them, we become the best missionaries for them.

270

The idea that he has a fancy for writing down his intuitions and inward experiences does not make him a whit greater than another who wraps the veil of silence around his ideas, his intuitions or experiences, which, though now unuttered, may yet dictate themselves through other channels to generations unborn.

271

His personal destiny or spiritual dedication will decide his future course—whether deliberately to remain obscure and avoid the notice which excites opposition, or publicly to accept a mission and bring inspiration to a particular kind of activity.

272

To come to a philosopher with expectations gleaned from religio-mystic circles, and to find that he refuses to play up to them, is to invite disappointment, perhaps even disillusionment. Yet, in being himself, in rigidly holding to the best he knows, the philosopher has really rendered the other a better service than if he had responded agreeably to anticipations. The ego's incapacity to recognize this does not destroy the seed that has been sown. Athens was handed truth by Socrates but handed him the cup of poison in return. But who knows what minds picked up thirty years later ideas he had left behind?

273

Spiritual work for the enlightenment of others is more important than physical-plane charity. The particular form it should take must naturally vary widely with different cases and different circumstances. It is understood that such service is limited by the extent of one's own development, the purity of one's motives, and the destiny of one's present incarnation. When external limitations permit nothing more, it might be done in the secrecy of one's own meditation chamber. It does not mean proselytizing others. It is not necessarily talking or writing about spiritual truths. It is a way of life and thought resulting from inward self-dedication and compassionate wisdom.

274

Philosophy *as a search for truth* must and does look at life as a whole, must and does take all human activities into its perspective, instead of leaving them outside. It is only because the philosophic teacher's human limitations prevent him from dealing with all things and compel him to specialize in one thing that he economizes time and strength by serving humanity as a spiritual educator rather than as a politician. Both services are needed by humanity, but one is infinitely more needed than the other. Save in the exceptional cases where he feels charged by fate and duty to render some public service in connection with them, he holds aloof from practical politics, theoretical economics, religious controversy, and social questions. He knows that the inner issue is really at stake behind all these others and this in turn depends on the metaphysical world-view. To formulate such a correct world-view and to guide men in the realization of their higher selves is then his chief and only task.

He reserves his best thought and energy for the fundamental task of, on the one hand, unveiling hidden laws of life and imparting a knowledge which improves mankind morally, mentally, and mystically and, on the other hand, to improving his own self so as to be better able to help change human character, reduce its selfishness, and dissipate its materialism. The social usefulness of teaching philosophy is ultimately on a deeper level than the social usefulness of stimulating worldly reform. For here man is dealing with causes, but there with effects. The philosophical mystic's work is limited in area to this single domain, but it is very much deeper and therefore very much more important just because of that limitation.

275

No other work could measure up, in eventual importance, to the work to which his life is dedicated, however insignificant his part may seem to him at any time. "God regardeth the duty of proclaiming His message as the most meritorious of all deeds," wrote the Persian prophet Baha'u'llah. Once fully engaged in this endeavour, he will feel more and more that he is part of a movement which is on the coming wave. Meanwhile, although he is to do whatever he can wherever circumstances allow it, in the way of such service, he is not to be over-anxious about results, on the one hand, nor utterly indifferent, on the other. A calm spirit, a patient mind, must never be deserted, yet a rejoicing heart over anyone that is guided to the Quest must never be repressed. His task is one of the oldest in human history—to convince men and women that it is worthwhile asking themselves: What are the ultimate values of human life?

276

The right way to help someone is to sympathize with the personal suffering, but to understand its inner necessity at the same time.

277

Whoever by speech or by silence, by art or by example, helps to improve mankind or increase knowledge of the higher truth, renders the best service. No other charity or philanthropy equals this upliftment of creatures struggling—unwittingly or deliberately—to a purified, disciplined, and refined consciousness.

278

The noblest calling in life and the most useful vocation is philosophical teaching.

279

The philosopher's work with others shines best in a literary function. There he gives light and healing, calm and hope to the many on their way who could never hope, owing to the lapse of time after his death or the distance in space before it, to encounter him in a consultative function.

280

He will not care to meddle in politics, for an arena of strife, struggle, the clash of selfish interests, lies, and libels will naturally be distasteful to him. But if destiny bids it, he will swallow his reluctance.

281

Philosophy tells us to work for the welfare of all men, but it does not tell us to work sentimentally, foolishly, unwisely, emotionally, and impulsively. It does not mean that a rich man should instantly give all his money to the poor; emotion may tell him to do so, but reason would not. He must use reason to check even universal pity.

282

It is not the duty of a philosopher to solve personal problems for others or to make decisions for them or to play the role of a healer. Leaders of religio-mystical sects often claim to do so but he has no such pretensions. Nor will he seek to attract disciples, making them more and more dependent on him, and form organizations, as those leaders often do seek. A clear distinction in thought and practice between these two departments is necessary.

283

No philosopher of wide-ranging vision and balanced mind dare claim to lead men into a permanent paradise. He knows that all beings and things are subject to change—except changeless Being itself. But he can claim to lead them into a supernal peace.

284

We need philosophers like Lord Haldane, whose services in the defense, education, and politics of his country were immense.

285

He is to expound truth and exemplify goodness.

286

If there is a call to an apostolate from a pure and deep source he will obey but if it originates in ego-serving shallower levels he will merely ignore it.

287

If the individual finds that he is best suited to help others through the medium of introducing them to meditation, then all other forms of service, such as writing for the public press, not being his true work, should be left to those who are specialists in that field.

288

So far as philosophy is to be saved from becoming obliterated, it must become embodied in a remnant of persons who understand, follow, and practise it, and it must also be recorded in writing for posterity.

289

If he cannot show a shortcut out of the jungle of contemporary spiritual bewilderment, he can contribute some valuable compass readings which may help to form a better notion where the way out lies.

290

Do not believe that every first meeting with a philosopher will necessarily enlighten you or even please you. The approach may be made with bated breath—such is the picture an aspirant, and especially a young one, often creates for himself—but the exit may be darkened with disappointment.

291

He does not claim to be a walking encyclopaedia nor ask for a halo of infallibility. There are many questions to which he does not know the true answers. He is neither pontifically infallible nor deifically omniscient. What the philosophical teacher seeks to establish are the basic principles in which all true seeking must end.

292

Whoever attains this, the topmost peak of the philosophic life, will naturally possess the capacity—rather the genius—to help the internal evolutionary advance of mankind. Indeed, it will be the principal and secret business of his life, whatever his external and conventional business may be. Those who stood closest to Jesus were asked to preach the gospel. Clearly therefore he conceived the spreading of truth to be their primary task. That other tasks, such as feeding and clothing the poor, had their own particular importance too, was acknowledged in his injunction to *other* persons. But that such tasks were secondary ones is clear inference from his instructions to the apostles. And in this critical passage of humanity from a used-out standpoint to a newer one which confronts it today, such a service is more than important. In his own humbler way and in a quiet unobtrusive manner, remembering always that people will find the best account of his beliefs in his deeds, even the neophyte who has still to climb the foothills of philosophy can and must communicate so much of this knowledge as he finds men may be ready for, but not an iota more. His task is not, like that of the apostles, to convert them but to help them. He may be only a firefly with little light to shed but he should desert the esotericism of former centuries and try to enlighten others because he must understand the unique character of this century and see the dangerous gaping abyss which surrounds its civilization. Moreover he may take refuge in the words of *Tripura*, an archaic Sanskrit text, which, if its archaic idiom be translated into modern accents, says: "An intense student may be endowed with the slenderest of good qualities, but if he can readily understand the truth—however theoretically—and expound it to others, this act of exposition will help him to become himself imbued with these ideas and his own mind will soak in their truth. This in the end will lead him to actualize the Divinity within himself."(P)

293

If the statements of philosophers are to possess meaning and value, they have to be related to the comprehension of men. This is why the philosopher assumes the function of religious prophet with the masses, dons the mantle of mystical leader or metaphysical teacher with the few, fills the role of a sage with the rare individual.

294

He has become, by virtue of his inner attainment, a responsible guardian of ancient truths. They are neither to be hoarded in a miserly way nor propagated indiscriminately.

295

Because he believes that a higher power is in very truth taking thought for men and taking care of the universe, he does not seek excitedly to convert them but simply to state the fact of its existence.

296

It is not enough to give people only what they are ready for, only to cater to unevolved mentalities. Some effort should also be made to develop them.

297

It is not by making a person—be he disciple or learner—subservient and dependent that we serve him best, but by helping him to help himself, to develop himself.

298

The truth-charged words of a philosopher are not for those who are neither seeking truth nor willing to accept it nor ready to understand it.

299

Appreciation of these truths is the beginning of the philosophic life. Application of them is the end.

300

Unless he puts his abstract principles into concrete deeds, unless his highest thoughts are reflected in his lowliest acts, the student is no philosopher. These teachings have not been easy to comprehend in theory; they will certainly be still less easy to follow in practice. Nevertheless these rarefied principles must be translated into terms of everyday living. The skeleton must now be fleshed out and the warm living blood of action must course around it. Hence the third path seeks to connect this knowledge with the practical obligations of mundane existence and to associate these practices with the social and personal responsibilities of men who lead active lives.

301

The reader has had most of this system now presented to him. His work in following these difficult abstruse thoughts has not been easy. Now he may face, if he wishes, an entirely fresh task, that of bringing ultimate truth down from theory to practice. It has to be made *real* to himself. It has to be fully and finally realized. Constant recollection and constant practice are the only way to do this. When he comes to this final frontier of all existence, he must bow his head in humble homage to the fact that here neither yoga nor religion can venture across alone. Here the man alone may pass who can *live* utterly and fully what he has thought in metaphysics, what he has felt in religion, and what he has experienced in the tense stillness of yoga.

302

The instruction which Moses received on Mount Sinai, "See that thou makest all things according to the pattern showed thee in the mount," is precisely the same as that which the initiate into *philosophic* mysticism receives from his Overself after his loftiest exaltation. That is, he is told to work out in the lower world, where good incessantly struggles with evil and where men are plunged in darkness and enslaved by animality, a pattern of applied truth, of divinity in action, of altruistic spiritual service.

303

The discovery that our existence as well as the world's existence is like that of a dream need not alarm us, need not cause us to become impractical, inefficient, uninterested in life and half-hearted in action. For as we should prefer a pleasant dream during sleep to a horrible nightmare, so should we try to live this waking world dream of ours as pleasantly, as profitably, and as successfully as possible. If these doctrines cannot be made subservient to the ends of living, then they are metaphysical and not philosophical. For the business of the metaphysician is to lose himself in abstractions, but the business of the philosopher is to find himself in common life.

304

That which he finds in deep eternity must be worked out in day-to-day life.

305

When what he receives from within at the intuitive level is transplanted without at the active level, it becomes complete.

306

He is still short of the ideal if he lacks the animating impulse which transfigures the thought into the deed.

307

There is a gratifying secret entwined with this injunction to serve mankind. Whoever gives himself in such service will inevitably receive a boomerang-like return one day when others will display a readiness to serve him. For karma is a divine law which brings back to him whatever he has given forth. The area and depth of his own service will mark the area and depth of that which mankind will extend toward him. Only the form of it will be different because this will depend both on prevailing circumstances and his own subconscious or conscious desire. It may take only a mental or emotional form. The moral of this is that the wise altruist loses nothing in the end by his altruism, although the foolish altruist may lose much as the karmic consequence of his foolishness.

308

A true power will inform the hands of those who will act at the behest of the god within, whose daily admonishment to him is: "Go out and live for the welfare of man the Light you find in the deep recesses of your own heart."

5

THE PHILOSOPHER

Although what Zen announces as "direct penetration to Reality" is what matters most, is the Goal of goals, no man's achievement will be any the worse, and each will certainly be all the better, at least as a human living in a society of other humans, if, along with it, scholarship and contemplation at depth, practical competence and metaphysical capacity, sharpness of reasoning and sensitivity to intuition, coexist completely.

2

The higher perception then unites with the intellectual function and the spiritual illumination does not cease despite the activity of thoughts.

3

In this unique state, which belongs only to the higher phases of mysticism, there is, at one and the same time, intense feeling but also intense thought, divine love in the heart and inspired understanding in the head, steel-hard strength in the will yet sublime surrender of it. The whole self is engaged in this holy communion and not merely a part of it.

4

If this attainment of radiant, inward glory is rare, it is not only because few consciously strive for it but also because few know the law governing the attainment itself. And that is a twofold law of balance and wholeness.

5

The goal of self-elimination which is held up before us refers only to the animal and lower human selves. It certainly does not refer to the annihilation of all self-consciousness. The higher individuality always remains. But it is so different from the lower one that it does not make much sense to discuss it in human language. Hence, those who have adequately understood it write or talk little about its higher mysteries. If the end of all existence were only a merger at best or annihilation at worst, it would be a senseless and sorry scheme of things. It would be unworthy of the divine intelligence and discreditable to the divine goodness. The consciousness stripped of thought, which looks less attractive to you than the hazards of life down here, is really a tremendous enlargement of what thought itself tries to do. Spiritual advance is really from a Less to a More. There is nothing to fear in it and nothing to lose by it—except by the standards and values of the ignorant.(P)

6

A fuller life will recognize not only the spirituality of man but also the individuality of man.

7

Resurrection—to die and live again—is a symbol. It means to leave the ego and enter the Overself *in full consciousness*.

8

He will unite with the Divine first by completely disappearing into it, then by discovering his higher individuality in it.

9

When the two selves become one, the inner conflict vanishes. Peace, rich and unutterable, is his.

10

He has extended his consciousness to the Overself, displaced the ego from its age-old tyranny, and become the full human he intended to be.

11

We who honour philosophy so highly cannot afford to be other than honest with ourselves. We have to acknowledge that the end of all our striving is surrender. No human being can do other than this—an utterly humble prostration, where we dissolve, lose the ego, lose ourselves—the rest is paradox and mystery.

12

Whether this other world of being is something into which he has advanced or into which he has retreated may be arguable. What is not arguable is that it is a world which the unequipped or the undeveloped cannot enter.

13

He may not rightly call himself a philosopher before he has gathered up and combined every single qualification needed for the title.

14

When he can speak out of a daily experience of the Overself, when it is something actual and present to him as a reality and not a mere theory, he may correctly call himself a philosopher.

15

Only when the Overself has illumined every side of his personal being can he be said to have a complete illumination. Only then has he attained the sagehood of philosophy.

16

It is out of such a splendid balance of utter humility and noble self-reliance that the philosopher gets his wisdom and strength. He is always kneeling metaphorically before the Divine in self-surrendering renunciation and often actually in self-abasing prayer. Yet side by side with this, he is always seeking to develop and apply his own intellect and intuition, his own will and experience in life. And because they are derived from such a balanced combination, this wisdom and strength are beyond any that religion alone, or metaphysics alone, could give.

17

Spirituality achieves its finest flowering in the individual who is emotionally adult, intellectually developed, and practically experienced. Such a well-rounded and admirably balanced growth is always best.

18

The philosopher will be a *karma yogi* to the extent that he will work incessantly for the service of humanity and work, too, in a disinterested spirit. He will be a *bhakti yogi* to the extent that he will seek lovingly to feel the constant presence of the Divine. He will be a *raja yogi* to the extent that he will hold his mind free from the world fetters but pinned to the holy task he has undertaken. He will be a *gnana yogi* to the extent that he will apply his reflective and reasoning power to a metaphysical understanding of the world.

19

From that moment when he understands human problems with the wisdom of the Overself, his thinking will become illumined from within, as it were. He will comprehend clearly the inner significance of each problem that presents itself.

20

When brain and heart are inspired and united, wisdom and love become perceptible.

21

In the philosopher, the sense of living in the Overself is continuous and unbroken.

22

In observation a scientist, at heart a religious devotee, in thought a metaphysician, in secret a mystic, and in public an efficient honourable useful citizen—this is the kind of man philosophy produces.(P)

23

His thoughts are guided by the Overself, his emotions inspired by it, and his actions expressive of it. Thus his whole personal life becomes a harmoniously and divinely integrated one.

24

He only is worthy of the name philosopher who not only possesses a knowledge of mentalism, and understands it well, but who reverently lets the higher power be ever present in, and work through, him. Otherwise he is only a student of philosophy.

25

A man acts philosophically when wisdom and service become the motive power behind his deeds. These are the two currents which must flow through his external life.

26

He will be active and creative if the infinite inspires him to that end, or he will repose in utter stillness if its direction is to that one. In this rhythm he will live and through it achieve the dynamic balance which philosophy prescribes. The movement from one end of the spiral to the other will then be no change of being for him but only a change of focus.

27

The philosopher has as little use for artificial professional sanctity as for morbid body-hating asceticism. Enlightenment must become "natural"—a living fact of the whole being—and its possessor inconspicuous. Neither the one nor the other is to be advertised publicly in any way.

28

The philosopher is a religious devotee inasmuch as he finds the Real sacred and holy. He is a respecter of science, one who tests theory against fact, belief against observation. He is a lover of aesthetic beauty, seeking its higher forms in nature, poetry, music, and other arts. He is a metaphysician, transcending materialism by responding to intuitive intelligence.

29

The true philosopher is conscious daily of the blessed inward life of the Overself, indescribable in its serenity, loveliness, strength, and sacredness. Keeping the mind in equilibrium, in a state of equipoise which remains undistracted and undisturbed by external forces and events, becomes perfectly natural in time, and is a state in which he continues until death. It is not a monotonous condition as some might believe, but one of such satisfaction that we can only faintly envisage it in comparison with our material joys deprived of their emotional excitements.

30

He is a philosopher who realizes to the full, and continually feels, the presence of divinity not only within himself but also within the world.

31

His wisdom must be equal to calamity or prosperity, the bad or the good—to all situations, in fact.

32

He has awakened from the dream of material reality, dissipated the illusion of the *I*'s personal consciousness.

33

He is a complete person who takes in the artist's contribution to beauty, the scientist's contribution to facts, the metaphysician's contribution to truth, the religionist's contribution to faith, and the humanist's contribution to goodness.

34

Because he has now enlarged his thought of self to include the Overself, it does not follow that he is therefore to disregard the personality and neglect its needs.

35

Emotion may point to one road, reason to another, and conscience to a third. Only in the matured philosopher does this trinity become a unity, does this inner conflict come to an end.

36

Wisdom blooms like a flower in the soul of one who follows this path.

37

The flower grows into a balanced and complete entity. This is the way he is to grow. It is perfect in itself, and nothing need be added to it. This is the ideal he is to realize.

38

In his practical life he will evidence a compassionate heart but a clear head, a strong will but a sensitive intuition.

39

He is a scientist to the extent that he respects fact, a metaphysician to the extent that he wants reality, a religionist to the extent that he recognizes a higher power.

40

Although he dwells in the Eternal, he lets the passing hour take from him what it needs. This is balance.

41

By starting to live from the core itself, we start to live harmoniously, undivided and whole.

42

The true philosopher does not fall into the errors of either ill-informed mystics or dogmatic materialists. The one glorifies either the ancients or the Orientals as being all-wise, thus idealizing what he has no experience of since it is so distant in time and space. The other ridicules this attitude and glorifies the moderns or the Westerners instead.

43

The philosophical attitude will appear in balanced judgements formed after clear and careful thought, in the harmonious way whereby idealism is tempered by realism.

44

Every act will then be in harmony with his own higher self. Wherever his attention may be focused and whatever the level on which it may be engaged, he will never become sundered from his deep lodgement in it. He will inwardly dwell in a hidden world of reality, truth, and love. None of his deeds in this earthen world of falsehood and animosity will ever violate his spiritual integrity.

45

Neither the life of action nor the life of reason is able to satisfy him, nor even their combination, however good it be. He comes, in time, to the last question and, with the finding of its answer, to the life of intuition. Henceforth he is to be taught from within, led from within, by something deeper than intellect, surer than intellect. Henceforth he is to do what needs doing under the influx of a higher will than his merely personal one.

46

The trained philosophic mind can quickly discern whether a statement of doctrine originates from the personal intellect, the personal emotions, or the spiritual Overself.

47

The philosopher's self-control is naturally achieved and durably settled. It hides no inner conflicts and leaves no harmful effect behind.

48

When he has silenced his desires and stilled his thoughts, when he has put his own will aside and his own ego down, he becomes a free channel through which the Divine Mind may flow into his own consciousness. No evil feelings can enter his heart, no evil thoughts can cross his mind, and not even the new consequence of old wrong-doing can affect his serenity.

49

In the true philosopher the distance between the thought of a right deed and the deed itself is nil. There is no inner conflict in such a man, no wavering between the lower nature and the higher ordinance. What he knows, he is. His wisdom has become welded into his moral outlook and practical activity. There are no schizophrenic dissociations or unconscious complexes. Righteousness is a profound instinct with him.

50

It is not that he sees beauty where others see ugliness—on the contrary, he recognizes the place of ugliness and its inevitability in this Yin-Yang existence—but that he sees all things, including ugly things, as manifestations of divine Mind.

51

There is a charm which emanates from goodness, a vigour which radiates from truth, and a peace which belongs to reality.

52

The philosopher does not hold any views. Views are held by those who depend on the intellect or the emotions alone for their judgements. His dependence is on the intuition, the voice of his higher self.

53

The philosopher lives in a great serene equilibrium upon whose boundaries rage and envy, greed and frenzy beat in vain.

54

He is above moods, neither exuberant nor restrained but always equable.

55

He combines the simple purity and direct honesty of a child with the discretion and prudence of an adult.

56

Sanctity is deep within him but his conduct and speech are never sanctimonious.

57

He will act according to the pressure of circumstances and the necessity of upholding principles. At times he may be so wrapped up in his own studies and meditations as to seem cut off from society altogether. But at other times he may keep so busy in the world as to seem one of its most eager members.

58

If such philosophy is lived by him, what he says cannot be valueless. Out of the deep stillness within there will emerge genuine truth, invisible substance, measured quality, or he will hold his peace and say little or nothing.

59

His conduct shows a calmness which seems invulnerable and a detachment which seems implacable.

60

In his mind he separates time and its trifles from the Himalayan massiveness of the Eternal. If he is forced by conditions to plan ahead for a few months or a few years, he never allows them to force him into deserting this inner loyalty to the timeless Now.

61

The philosophic mind is a civilized one. It is free from narrow prejudices, tolerant even when it disagrees, informed by wide studies, calm and controlled even in the encounter with provocative untruth, exaggeration, or fanaticism.

62

We would not expect an enlightened man to utter careless statements.

63

The discovery of a philosophic truth is, in time and as it is lived, a deeply felt thing even though its expression or communication may be quiet and composed. The stoical side of the philosophic character does not destroy the warmth of this feeling. It will be present in the communication itself as freshness and originality, as if heart were speaking to heart and, for those who need it, head to head.

64

A higher viewpoint will insert itself into thoughts and decisions; it will show up faulty ideas and defective decisions for the things that they are because it will show up the lower source whence they have arisen.

65

He feels released from the strain and tension of everyday life, for in its midst an enormous sense of well-being permeates him.

66

The divinely inspired mind may function in meditation or in action. If it has achieved the philosophic degree, there will be no difference between the two states.

67

He is a practical optimist. He turns rosy dreams to reality. He catches the bright but cloudy fancies of the optimist and ties them down to earth. He keeps his head among the stars but his feet are firmly planted on the ground.

68

He combines somehow the sophistication of the man of experience with the simplicity of the monkish ascetic.

69

The term *yogi* in the East has for centuries been almost synonymous with a man who has withdrawn from social life. Yoga aims at the suppression of thinking as a goal in itself, which means that it aims at conscious trance (for this is the only thought-free state apart from deep sleep) and hence at an inactive life. A philosopher is free to live like a yogi if he is led to do so or, on the contrary, to use both a developed thinking activity and a practical existence. Activity will then be quite spontaneous, not with the spontaneity of impulse or passion, but with that derived from the absence of merely animal motivation. It will indeed be inspired living.

70

He will possess the trained mentality and disciplined character which reacts swiftly to urgent situations, calmly to dangerous ones, and wisely to unexpected ones.

71

Having passed through the stage of lunacy which is communal and individual life today, he is at last enjoying the true normalcy of sanity, which yields its effects in comprehension and serenity.

72

He feels the truth deep within himself: his ideas are warmly held, not coldly intellectualized. Yet despite this love for them, the intellect is not absent, only it is put into a kind of balance with the heart so that light and power are combined.

73

He is idealistic without being fanatical, realistic without being materialistic, reformist without being obsessed.

74

When the full range of philosophic knowledge, experience, worship, and presence is gone through, the man ceases to seek: he is at peace.

75

He senses the power of the ever-accompanying Presence: it makes him sturdily independent.

76

The philosophic ideal is not to achieve a self-conscious spirituality but rather a natural one.

77

He will be more spiritual in an authentic sense than some others who, deliberately and consciously, try oft and long to be otherworldly.

78

A philosopher is not necessarily a man who lectures on philosophy, be it genuine wisdom or mere academic and scholarly word-spinning. He is a man who knows that life is not only for thought about it, and for insight into its deepest reality, but also for *living*. He is withal as sensitive as a mystic and feels nuances beyond the ordinary, but he cultivates calmness in the midst of normal activity and remains unflappable.

79

There is a singing joy in the Presence and a mental ease in the awakened consciousness.

80

The man whose thinking is unbiased by prejudice and whose feeling is untainted by selfishness is invested with a moral authority which others lack.

81

Attention is forever being caught by some thought or some thing, by some feeling or some experience. In the case of the ordinary man, consciousness is lost in the attention; but in the case of the philosophic man there is a background which evaluates the attention and controls it.(P)

82

The enlightened man may outwardly appear to live like others, a normal and ordinary life, but whether he does so or not, there will always be this vital difference between him and ordinary men: that he never forgets his true nature.

83

The results in consciousness will be to gain a new understanding of the world. The savage who sees and hears a cinema for the first time may believe that he is seeing flesh-and-blood people, but the civilized man who sees and hears the same film will know that he is seeing only their pictures. Again, whereas one man will believe the picture-people's environment to be of the same fixed size in space as the screen on which the perspective appears, another will know that—being made only of light and light in itself being quite formless—the perception of their spatial character is really a variable one. Great as is the difference in understanding between these two men, the difference between the world-understanding of the civilized man and that of the man possessed of this insight is even greater.

84

In the philosopher intellect is ruled by intuition whereas in the ordinary man intuition is dulled by intellect.

85

The Stoic, whose highest lights are his ethical principles, may attain cold neutral peace. The philosopher, who lives by trans-egoic awareness, finds a gracious tranquillity.

86

All men are subject to some effect from the people around them but only philosophers are able to be fully conscious of the influences impinging on them and to reject part or all of them if necessary.

87

Such a man can feel as joyfully enthusiastic about impersonal ideas as other men can feel only about personal fortunes.

88

Such a man is not plagued in society by self-consciousness.

89

He who has attained to this utter calm of the Overself, or come near enough to feel it every day, individualizes himself out of the crowd and finds his own soul. He no longer has to be with the majority to feel at ease.

90

The practical difference between a fool and a philosopher is that the first is always impatient with the second, whereas the second is always patient with the first.

91

Like men speaking in different languages, they are unable to establish any real intercourse with one another. Yet there is this difference, that whereas the philosopher has a clear enough perception of what is in their hearts they cannot comprehend what is in the philosopher's.

92

If they cannot make any inner contact with one another, the fault is not the philosopher's but the crowd's. He is ever ready to give every man he meets a mental handshake, ever ready to accept all people for what they are. Moreover, he is inwardly laid by his higher self under obligation to benefit mankind by what he knows and is.

93

His eyes look upon the same world as other men's but he sees much in it which they do not see.

94

It is the difference in world-view which explains why one man fills his heart with anger and hate at exactly the same mistreatment under which another man fills his heart with forbearance and forgiveness.

95

Philosophy takes into account the whole personality of man. The sage knows more about human nature than the psychoanalyst for, besides noting the structure of human behaviour, he takes into account both karmic factors of cause and effect and the higher reaches of the mind.

96

Sects who cling to their little fanaticisms with blind fervour show thereby their lack of balance. The philosopher also clings to truth with even more fervour because he *sees* what it is that he is clinging to, but he does so calmly, maintains a considerable self-effacing equilibrium, and keeps a large tolerance. He knows too that the truth is substantiated by observed fact, by the highest kind of feeling, by the oldest religion and the newest science.

97

Do not put a tag on the philosopher. To the observer staring at him and his life, he is a bundle of contradictions and inconsistencies. But whereas he reconciles them, they cannot.

98

Those who think that philosophy ends in a torpid indifference to life are in error. Rather does it end in a proper evaluation of life, which balances calm indifference against keen interest, so as not to be lost in either.

99

He lives in the world like other men and beholds all but, unlike other men, accepts all.

100

The philosophic attitude is to be in the world but not of it, to hold necessary useful or beautiful possessions but not to be held by them. It knows the transiency of things, the brevity of pleasures, the movement of every situation. This is the way of the universe, the ebb and flow of life, the power of time to alter the pattern of every existence. So the philosopher adjusts himself to this rhythm, learns how and when to let go and when to hold on, and so retains his inner equilibrium, his inner poise and peace. During stormy times he stands firm as a rock, he studies their meaning and accepts their lesson; during sunny times he avoids identifying himself with the little ego and remembers his true security is in the Overself.

101

He knows full well how illusory the *form* of the world is, yet he keeps this knowledge in perfect balance with his duties responsibilities and tasks in that world. He does what needs doing as effectually as any man of action, yet is inwardly as detached as any idle dreamer.

102

Is the philosopher affected by his surroundings like everyone else? He is, so far as they report their nature to his senses. But there the likeness ends. For his mind then steps in to work constructively on the report and to interpret it philosophically.

103

The aim is to develop an equable disposition which does not alternate misery with joy, friendliness with antipathy, or extreme with extreme. This is not the same as an inert apathetic disposition.

104

Some part of his mind and heart will always be elsewhere, out of all this activity, above and detached from it all.

105

It is not that he becomes a mere onlooker at life—although during the pre-philosophic period this temptation is present—but that the difference between absolute reality and relative existence becomes all too plain.

106

The ordinary man who loves comfort and desires possessions, property, or position is not acting wrongly. He is wrong when he lets himself get tied to them and suffers intensely at their loss. The philosopher may also have these things, but there is this difference: that he will be inwardly free of them.

107

The philosopher's duty leaves him free to live in the world or leave it. There are no compulsive rules for him. But if he decides to stay, or is compelled by his need to earn a livelihood, he will take care not to be of the world.

108

A perfect degree of impersonality is unlikely to be found because it is generally unsought and ordinarily unattainable. But a large measure of it may be arrived at.

109

The modern philosopher cannot fail to be a most paradoxical gentleman. He works as actively and apparently as ambitiously as other men, relaxes with entertainment or with the arts, but withal keeps his innermost self aloof and detached from the scenes and agitations around him.

110

In the philosophic experience, feeling is there and must be there, as it is with the unphilosophical. But it is more and more impersonalized—that is the vital difference. Yet it is a difference which repels, chills, or even terrifies some persons when the philosopher comes under their observation.

111

If the intellect of the philosopher is a developed one, it will be active in the creation of ideas if he is working with them, or of images if he is working in an artistic pursuit. But, in either case, he will still be detached from them, unbound by them, free to pursue them or to drop them.

112

The so-called dehumanized coolness of the philosopher is frightening to some, while to others its lack of negative passions and animal wraths is felt as a silent accusation, is catalytic in causing a feeling of guilt to arise—and so his company becomes uncomfortable.

113

He will grow into a great-hearted man with a clear insight into human motivation and a calm acceptance of men and women as he finds them. Something of Nature's patience in working out her evolutionary scheme will enter into his soul. When he thinks of those who have wronged him, he will spontaneously and effortlessly forgive them.

114

He will look at experience from a new centre. He will see all things and creatures not only as they are on earth but also as they are "in heaven."

115

He takes people just as he finds them and events just as they happen. He does not outwardly express any desire for them to be different from what they are. There are at least two reasons for this attitude. First, he knows that the divine thought of the universe contains the idea of evolution. So he believes that however bad people may be, one day they will be better; however untoward circumstances may be, divine wisdom has brought them about. Second, he knows that if he is to keep an unruffled peace inside him, he must allow nothing outside him to disturb it. Because he regards the outer life as being as ephemeral as a dream, he is reconciled to everything, rebellious against nothing.

116

Another characteristic of the philosopher is his capacity to see the point of view of all, of the sinner and the criminal, the weak and the ignorant, equally with that of the saint and the sage. This is born partly out of his developed intelligence, partly out of his profound impersonality, and partly out of his wide compassion. This leads to the consequence that when seeking practical remedies for social wrongs, or redress for private ones, he seeks beneath the surface for ultimate causes. A merely superficial view, which may deceive millions of people, is rejected by him. The punishment of a crime without accompanying ethical education, for instance, he regards as clumsy and inefficient brutality. Prison punishment, especially, should be set in a framework of ethical instruction which includes the doctrine of karma. Without such a setting its deterrent effect is not sufficient to make it more than a half-success and a half-failure.

117

The philosophic attitude, being a truth-seeking attitude, never criticizes merely for the sake of criticizing, and never seeks to uncover what is bad in a thing without seeking at the same time to uncover what is good. Its critical judgements are fair, never destructive but always constructive. Whatever it attacks because of the error and evil it contains, it also defends because of the truth and good it contains.

118

Even if he finds it necessary to give cautionary criticism, it will be philosophically balanced, truly constructive, and entirely free from condemnation.

119

His attitude is always fair and unbiased, because his sincerity is illumined by knowledge.

120

The philosopher will be patient with the moral and intellectual deficiencies of others. He will arrive at this patience not by a long training, but by immediate insight.

121

Feeling this sympathy with his fellow-beings, understanding why they act as they do, he can no longer bring himself to fear, hate, or condemn them.

122

A tender, world-embracing compassion overwhelms him.

123

He is able to determine precisely what ethical principle is their guiding and dominant force, and what mental status they have reached. Yet paradoxically enough, the greater clarity with which he can now view the souls of others does not diminish his tolerance but, on the contrary, increases it. For he understands that everything and everyone are the result of the previous experience which life has given them, that they cannot help being other than what they are, and that all occupy a certain place at some stage or other in the universal evolutionary scheme—even those who are actuated by devilish and evil characteristics. Instead of placing himself in inward opposition to the wicked and thus setting up conflict, he silently pities them in his own heart, for he knows that the karmic law will reflect back to its perpetrator suffering for every evil deed. On the other hand, he will not hesitate impersonally to perform a drastic punitive duty should it be his duty to do so according to his position in the outer world.

124

The philosophical attitude maintains fairness and courtesy even toward those who attack philosophy.

125

If the world is merely indifferent to these ideas he is not troubled. If it is actually hostile to them, he is understandingly tolerant, calm, and compassionate.

126

This is the paradox of the philosophic attitude, a paradox which few of its critics understand, that it directly faces or analyses its problems and yet turns away from them in utter unconcern. It is able to do this only because it functions on two levels, the immediate and the ultimate, because it refuses to leave either one of them out of its picture of life.

127

At last he will have reached a point where his thinking can be utterly free of past periods and present influences, where it can embody his own research and its independent results, where it is the voice of his own source.

128

He has discovered the strength which comes from self-control, the peace which comes from stilled thoughts, and the happiness which comes from the true self.

129

He enters into the mastery of philosophy when he not only sees its truth but also feels it fully and loves it deeply. He has attained peace of mind, yes, but he is still a human being, has known suffering and sometimes even tragedy, has blundered and groped his way through a necessary apprenticeship. He has acquired knowledge, yes, but with it a paradoxical sensitivity.

130

He will know R E A L I T Y, and know it too as his own ultimate being, indestructible and ever-existent. Amid the most prosaic surroundings, deep in the core of his own heart there will be perfect calm for himself and goodwill for all others.

131

He attains the beatitude of knowing his higher self.

132

His own fine balance not only saves him from falling into any one-sidedness but also allows him to recognize unhesitatingly and value justly whatever is worthwhile in all the sides of a subject or a situation. It keeps him inwardly free to admire without exaggeration or to criticize without prejudice.

133

The sanity with which he negotiates life's practical problems is impressive.

134

The philosopher, and the philosopher alone, can sincerely believe and accept two opposite points of view at the same time.

135

He will not gladly bear any label, for he considers truth a state of being rather than a set of dogmas, and he prefers the freedom to search and hold it to the shackles of sectarian connection. But if the world insists on his identifying himself, he will take the name of philosopher, as being broader, more universal, and less restrictive than any other. It is a name which links and limits him to no religious denomination, which detaches him from all intellectual schools, and which puts him under no organizational, party, or sectarian roof.

136

The philosopher has liberated himself from all the mental cages which are offered by time and tradition to seeking man. He is not the representative of any organized religion nor the advocate of any denominational sect nor the missionary of any proselytizing cult. He appreciates the past history of religion and extracts what he can find of value in it, but he refuses to let it burden him with what is not. He is determined to remain free from its debris and to find his way to the original source of truth.

137

When he reaches this understanding he will no longer look to any personage for inspiration, he will no longer take any guru at his self-asserted or disciple-asserted value; he will be attached only to principles, to Truth itself. Thus at long last he will achieve liberation from guru-hunting and find true self-sufficing peace.

138

Only the philosopher can move through the narrow world of conventional religions and remain strong in individuality and free in mentality. The same truth which gives him faith in religion also saves him from its limitations.

139

As the member of a social community he may prefer or find it necessary to wear a badge, to be joined to some religious organization, or he may not. But as a philosopher he cannot put such limits on his mind, faith, or practice, cannot commit his inner freedom into the hands of other men.

140

The philosopher is usually happier if his spiritual freedom is expressed in outer freedom from ecclesiastical cages or cultists' groups. That is why he is reluctant to identify himself with any single organized church or mystical society. But if particular circumstances or special service or inner direction call him to it, he will not refuse to surrender this outer freedom.

141

He is the true philosopher who neither falls into the trap of warring sectarianism nor allows others to push him into it, who looks for and accepts the flowering of what is best and truest in all the religions and movements, ideas and principles but himself remains unlabelled. He must refuse to restrict himself to or to conform with any single fixed and rigid faith. Whatever leads to a superior quality of consciousness is welcome, wherever it be found and whenever it originated.

142

The philosopher is usually too comprehensive in his outlook to confine his stand to one of two sides; he prefers to take a third position.

143

The philosopher more than other men is a cosmopolitan creature. He scorns the fierce nationalisms which run riot in the world and feels the truth of Jesus' message of goodwill towards all men.

144

If you have understood philosophy you will follow no spiritual leader, be he P.B. or anyone else.

145

The superior mind is marked by a universality of outlook which is the hallmark of development and spirituality.

146

The philosopher is non-partisan in the sense that he maintains his freedom to think independently and to make individual judgements throughout. He is free from bias and prejudice. If his conclusions happen to coincide with those of any group or denomination he will note the fact but does not necessarily support their other doctrines nor join their ranks.

147

All that is true and good and beautiful in every faith creed sect or school belongs to him yet he himself may belong to none.

148

When he has the confidence to speak from personal discovery and the authority to speak from a superior level, a few may then listen, but more will do so later.

149

Whatever the standpoint he will try to understand it even while seeing its falsity.

150

The man who finishes the Way must necessarily be solitary inwardly, for he has torn himself away from the common illusion.

151

The philosopher accepts his predestined isolation not only because that is the way his position has to be, but also because his physical presence arouses negative feelings in the hearts of ordinary people as it arouses positive ones in the hearts of certain seekers. The negatives may range all the way from puzzlement, bewilderment, and suspicion to fear, opposition, and downright enmity. The positives may range from instinctive attraction to a readiness to lay down life in his defense or service. All these feelings arise instantly, irrationally, and instinctively. And they are unconnected with whether or not he reveals his true personal identity. This is because they are the consequence of a psychical impingement of his aura upon theirs. The contact is unseen and unapparent in the physical world, but it is very real in the mental-emotional world. It is truly a psychical experience for both: clear and precise and correctly understood by him, vague and disturbing and utterly misunderstood by ordinary people as well as pseudo-questers. It is both a psychical and a mystical experience for those genuine questers with whom he has some inward affinity, a glad recognition of a long-lost, much revered Elder Brother. Unfortunately, despite the generous compassion and enormous goodwill which he bears in his heart for all alike, it is the unpleasant contacts which make up the larger number whenever the philosopher descends into the world. Let him not be blamed if he prefers solitude to society. For there is nothing he can do about it. People are what they are. Most times when he tries to make himself agreeable to them, as though they both belonged to the same spiritual level, he fails. He learns somewhat wearily to accept his isolation and their limitation as inevitable and, at the present stage of human evolution, unalterable. He learns, too, that it is futile to desire these things to be otherwise.(P)

152

Even the philosopher who goes out of his way to avoid provoking anyone in any way—who never shows hate, passion, wrath, or resentment, who keeps his ego out of his dealings with others, and who in short does all he can to diminish the chances of disturbing them—even such a man will nevertheless be criticized, attacked, interfered with, or abused, in spite of his good thoughts and good deeds. Such is the evil in men and so widespread is it. But this will happen only if he ventures into any dealings or any relations with them, if he appears publicly among them to teach or serve in some way. It will not happen if he prudently remains aloof, apart, secluded, obscure, a hermit—or, if that be not possible, if he goes out of his way in order not to attract attention. In that case, he will enjoy his peace undisturbed by the world's opposition. But it would then also be the world's loss.

153

The more he advances in power and consciousness, the more he grows in humility. Now, when he has something really worth being vain about, he takes especial care to be inconspicuous and not to seem extraordinary or holy above others. This is one of the causes of his secretiveness.

154

This silence which enwraps him does so only where his spiritual life is concerned. It is not quite the pride of feeling inner greatness nor a way of protecting that life against sneering laughter or inquisitive intruders. It is the sense of a holiness around it, the attitude of reverence for it.

155

It is not an exclusiveness born of spiritual pride but of spiritual humility. For the philosopher feels profoundly that he must respect other people's viewpoint because it is the result of their own individual experience of life.

156

The philosopher's inner life is an isolated one. It would be very foolish to blurt out all that he believes, thinks, or knows in any and every company. He recognizes the graded character of human mentality. This recognition compels him quite often to listen without dispute and with all tolerance to statements embodying extremely limited conceptions, half-developed ideas, or wholly biased views. A consequence of this attitude is that he usually understands more than anyone guesses.

157

If he has to live among those to whom his inner life would be uncomprehended, he guards his words, practises secrecy, and meets them on their own level.

158

He who seeks truth beyond the horizon of common humanity thereby sets up a difference which is no less actual and deep because it is invisible. But it is not merely because he is conscious that he is different from the herd that the philosopher wears a mask of secrecy over the face of his philosophy: it is also because he is conscious that there is little he can do about it, that the long discipline of life will do better whatever is necessary to bring the herd into the same perception.

159

What he carries within his heart and mind is, he feels, to be treasured. It is a spiritual treasure. He winces away from showing it to those who may despise it or even hate it.

160

The philosopher is not interested in drawing attention to himself but only to his ideas, his discoveries, and his revelations.

161

He will keep all mention of philosophy to himself and break his silence only when true need to do so manifests itself. He will do his exercises and practices in secret, unobserved, so that he may remain undisturbed. Where he must depart from the norm in public, as in following a fleshless diet, he will try to behave inconspicuously and thus draw no attention to his departure. From the standpoint of conventional society, he will not ordinarily be known as a follower of philosophy. In the Japanese phrase, "he will walk the Path as if not walking it."

162

He accepts his inner isolation and learns to live in it, realizing that he can do nothing about it. The compensation for such acceptance is that his serenity remains impregnable.

163

Philosophy touches life at all points. The philosopher willingly comes into contact with all kinds and conditions of men—to observe, to study, and to learn. But there are times when he may not do this, may not expose himself to psychic infections or disturbances.

164

Why should he confide this knowledge to those who are likely to treat it with either disdain or disbelief? Hence at the first sign of these reactions he draws back and says no more.

165

It is by the maintenance of such secrecy that they succeed in avoiding conflict with the prejudice and narrowness, the dogmatism and intolerance prevailing among those around them.

166

The earlier philosophic training in self-restraint enables him easily to conceal from the world what ought to be concealed.

167

Neither his speech nor his manner will divulge his secret.

168

He always makes it a point to behave civilly and sympathetically to everyone; nevertheless, if he deliberately lives a lonely existence, if he withdraws from the society of evolutionary inferiors, it is not only because he has no spiritual interests in common and familiarity could only lead in the end to boredom, but also because promiscuous intimacy would expose them to the perils of overstimulation which the forces present in him bring about automatically.

169

He does not want others to think of him nor like him. He believes in evolutionary grades of human mentality and is willing to accept with indifference the variety which is one result.

170

Whenever he happens to be forced into closer contact with worldlings, he will be polite to them but that is the end of the contact. His inmost thoughts will remain unshared.

171

His silence and reserve, his secrecy, become a kind of fortress for his protection.

172

With many persons he will feel only half of himself, with all his finest inner life closed up, and shut in with them he is physically present but spiritually far off.

173

Instead of proclaiming himself among the greatest of the Great, the philosopher confesses, "I am nothing." Instead of pretentiously gathering followers around his name as the High Prophet, he pushes them away, for this is related to his degree of inner development.

174

He has no banners to unfurl, so sure is he that the eternal truths can take care of themselves. Men and movements can try to destroy the belief in them, but given enough time it will reappear.

175

He who appears amongst humanity bearing the chalice of pure truth in his hands must expect insult and endure isolation.

176

The glory of his achievement is balanced by the memory of his past failure.

177

He will remain indifferent whether he be calumniated or revered, sneered at or glorified.

178

Whatever his task or profession in the world may be, he will so contrive that it will become a labour for the good of his fellow creatures not less than for personal profit.

179

To know the truth, to express it crisply with full calm authority—this is to be his mission henceforth.

180

The free soul has brought his thought and actions into perfect harmony with Nature's morality. He lives not merely for himself alone, but for himself as a part of the whole scheme. Consequently, he does not injure others but only benefits them. He does not neglect his own benefit, however, but makes the two work together. His activities are devoted to fulfilling the duties and responsibilities set for him by his best wisdom, by his higher self.

The world is necessarily affected by his presence and activities, and affected beneficially. First, the mere knowledge that such a man exists helps others to continue with their efforts at self-improvement, for they know then that the spiritual quest is not a vain dream but a practicable affair. Second, he influences those he meets to live better lives—whether they be few or many, influential or obscure. Third, he leaves behind a concentration of spiritual forces which works on for a long time, through other persons, after he leaves this world. Fourth, if he is a sage and balanced, he will always do something of a practical nature for the uplift of humanity instead of merely squatting in an ashram.(P)

181

He becomes in time, according to the measure of his development, a dynamic influence upon others. This is in part because people begin to see the benefits which he cannot hide, and in part because he wins their respect by the superior character which he manifests in times of crisis or difficulty. Among those who laughed derided or complained about his eccentric convictions, some live to tolerate or even accept them.

182

He will work from the Overself; he will move and serve the world from within his central being.

183

When he looks around at life from this fresh vantage point of the higher self, sensing the timeless while in the very midst of time, he becomes the bringer of an old-new hope for man.

184

He becomes an open channel through which flows the beneficent, educative, and redemptive power of the Overself.

185

In every situation where he is involved with other persons, he will consider neither his own welfare solely to the exclusion of others nor theirs to the detriment of his own. He will do what is just and wise in the situation, taking the welfare of all into consideration and being guided ultimately by the impersonal intuition of the Overself.

186

We may say of the true philosophers what one American author said of another American author. Herman Melville wrote in a letter to Nathaniel Hawthorne: "Knowing you persuades me more than the Bible of our immortality."

187

Whether he gives verbal form to the truth he has found is not, he discovers, important. Living it is his really important work and that he does spontaneously, naturally.

188

He becomes a centre of spiritual effluence.

The philosopher's view of Truth

189

Truth must be approached on its own terms. We are not to set up rules for finding it.

190

There are no statements of truth which can be called absolute on all levels of reference. Each is relative to the standpoint.

191

Although the pure truth has never been stated, nevertheless it has never been lost. Its existence does not depend upon human statement but upon human sensitivity. In this it is unlike all other knowledge.

192

There is but one God, one Truth, one Reality, although there are several different degrees in their perception by man.

193

The same doctrine which clarifies the game of life for one man, confuses it for another man. So long as truth is regarded from a personal standpoint this must inevitably be so. All schools of thought are tentatively correct *if* we assume the respective standpoints from which they look at a subject. The personal self possesses its own idiosyncrasies and peculiarities; its experience is circumscribed and it is guided by intellect, emotion, and passion alone. So long as we see things from this limited standpoint, so long shall we negate what others affirm, so long shall we now believe what we ourselves may later contradict. Yet the truth is more than a reconciliation of contradictory aspects, a bringing together of opposite tendencies. It is a final union which is higher than any of its separate elements. The process of attaining its height necessitates travelling a zig-zag path of alternating standpoints only at first. For when we leave the personal standpoint and win the higher self's insight, with its infinite perspective, we are able to harmonize all possible standpoints, we are able to give all other standpoints an intellectual sympathy without however regarding any one of them as possessing either universal or ultimate validity. But this need not lead to the silly conclusion that one standpoint is as good as another. For as one climbs up a hill the prospect varies, the outlook changes, and the field of view expands. He who has reached the crest is alone able to survey the whole landscape below, and to survey it accurately. Therefore the pilgrims of the Overmind refrain from letting themselves become covered by a crusted outlook, reserve their best exultations, remembering that ultimate Truth is of no party and yet of all, and hasten to that summit whereon they may stand serene, free at last from the noisy clamour of narrow minds. Then and then only the different world views which come into collision with each other in unphilosophical minds are spontaneously harmonized. Thus the simile of a search which we have used in the phrase "quest of the overself" is useful but does not cover the full implication of the undertaking which confronts aspiring man.

194

Is there a universal truth? Is there a doctrine which does not depend on individual opinion or the peculiarities of a particular age or the level of culture of a particular land? Is there a teaching which appeals to universal experience and not to private prejudice? We reply that there is, but it has been buried underneath much metaphysical lumber, much ancient lore, and much Oriental superstition. Our work has been to rescue this doctrine from the dead past for the benefit of the living present. In these pages we explode false counterfeits and expound the genuine doctrine.(P)

195

This truth is fixed, changeless, and eternal; it towers like the Great Pyramid over the flat desert sands of all other knowledge. It initiates us into a world of abstract being which paradoxically is not less real than that whose face is so familiar.

196

To arrive at great certitude is to arrive at great strength. Truth not only clears the head but also arms the will. It is not only a light to our feet but is itself a force in the blood.(P)

197

There is a buoyant cheerful quality in this truth; it acts as a tonic upon tired minds.

198

At the touch of truth falsehood goes, illusions fade, and deceptions—whether from within oneself or prompted by others—fall away.

199

Truth is the human knowledge of reality.

200

The coming of truth can be devastatingly cruel to some persons and immeasurably kind to others. Or it can be both to the same person at different periods of his life. It is not directly concerned with personal happiness.

201

Just as the sun can be seen only by its own light, so truth can be discerned only by its own self-revelation in the mind. That is, only by grace leading to insight. There is no other way.

202

The truth possesses its own force, but only for those who are ripe for its reception. The others can take nothing better than watery dilutions of it, nothing higher than elementary lessons in it, nothing subtler than symbolic revelations which obscure it.

203

Because this is the purest truth, it is also the most powerful truth. He who is possessed by it can do what others cannot. Therefore we cannot afford to water it down.

204

Truth is our only salvation, the final truth that in essence as Mind nobody is really disconnected from God, that the delusion of being alone and separate from the infinite life creates all our weaknesses, which in turn lead to most of our troubles, and that we are here to learn by experience what sort of stuff we are made really of.

205

Truth utters itself anew whenever a human mind comes fully to its self-discovery.

206

The depth of understanding at which men have arrived determines the grade of interpretation which life yields them.

207

Truth does not need man's support, for even if left unuttered it will survive and spread by the force which inheres in it. But man needs truth's support, for without it he remains insecure and peaceless.

208

Truth has always been present in the world but its acceptance has rarely been seen in the world.

209

All other questions resolve themselves in the end into a single one: "What is truth?" For this will not only have to include the world but also, and not less important: "What am I?"

210

Truth must be respected to the point of reverence before it will yield its deeper secrets. It must indeed be entangled with holiness.

211

This verity is trustworthy not because it is traditional ancient and venerable but because it is open to vindication by each man for himself.

212

All other truths need word or picture, demonstration or laboratory when they are to be conveyed to others, but the one truth which is an exception to this rule is also the deepest of all, the supreme wisdom. It comes to man, whether from another man or from God, only when the fullest silence reigns and when he himself is fully passive.

213

It has been said that man is too small mentally, too limited a creature, and too finite to be able to understand the supreme Absolute Being in all its greatness and grandeur. Therefore, however high his mystic experiences, he should be content with a kind of agnostic mysticism, a "thus far and no farther" in the realm of knowledge of this supreme entity. But there is some confusion on this subject. It has been the victim of speculation and miscomprehension. To get some clarity into it it is essential to free oneself from all religious and sectarian prepossessions—whether they be Indian or Western religions—and this is a service which philosophy alone can best render. Only after this is done can this subject be dealt with as it ought to be.

214

In the balanced mind which a philosopher trains himself to possess, and in the harmonious, felicitous working together of opposing qualities which he seeks to develop, the truth which he discovers—which must necessarily be the highest truth—will take the form of striking paradox.

215

Truth has too many sides to be held down fanatically in one alone. This may make it seem illogical, paradoxical, or contradictory. Do not ask any human mind to see what only a godlike mind can see—all sides all at once.

216

Paradox is an essential part of true religion, mysticism, and philosophy.

217

If the truth is that there is no truth, then those, like Jesus and Buddha, who claimed a transcendent insight were self-deceived fools.

218

Truth can frighten many by its high impersonality, but it can also warm their hearts by its putting order, and meaning, into life.

219

Truth is not only to be learned and known but also to be felt and worshipped.

220

"The teaching which slices through illusion," as the Oriental phrase puts it, is of course the Absolute Truth.

221

This truth can be confirmed by the great books of scriptural revelation, by the final conclusions of reason working at its highest impersonal level, and by the intimate facts of mystic experience.

222

The real Truth is so wonderful that it is what it is because "it is too good to be true" in the little mind's expectations.

223

It is a truth which can never be negated, save at the cost of letting in falsity. Nor can it be contaminated, save at the cost of letting in the ego.

224

Henceforth we must cease to associate truth with any particular race or people, country or man. Henceforth we must cease to look for it here or there. We must begin to comprehend its universality. It may manifest itself anywhere and amongst any people. Let us shed the delusion that Shangri-la has or ever had the monopoly of it.

225

What does it matter at this distance of time, either to us or to them, whether ancient Indians or modern Europeans have written down the truth? It does matter, however, whether we can recognize in both their literatures the truth as such and receive it into our minds.

226

Even if all written Truth vanished from the world, and all remembered Truth passed from men's minds or memories, a time would come again when someone, somewhere, somehow, and sometime would rediscover the knowledge.

227

Whoever claims to know Truth, God, Reality, must *feel* and love it too, or it is not Truth.

228

Most public attempts to interpret Truth to man have ended in misinterpreting it. This is sometimes because they have ended in compromises and sometimes because the interpreter's limitations got in the way.

229

Satisfaction invariably follows Truth, but Truth does not invariably follow satisfaction.

230

If he is seeking tranquillity alone he may get it, whereas if he is seeking truth the two together will be his reward.

231

It does not matter that philosophy is a lone voice now, for it is an enduring one. Other and more orthodox voices will make themselves better heard but they will also fade eventually into silence. The truth can never perish but its counterfeits and substitutes, must.

232

Truth can be neither antiquated nor modernized, but its formulation into words can.

233

Let us consider truth as an ever-receding horizon. Thus we achieve humility and keep the mind open for progress through these successive degrees.

234

These seven truths constitute the skeleton of a tradition which has been handed down from illuminate to pupil since prehistoric periods. The tradition itself is imperishable, being rooted in the divinity of human nature no less than in the sacred duty imposed upon the illuminati to preserve its existence among chosen inheritors prior to their own disappearance or death.

235

Truth does not display itself ostentatiously.

236

If any viewpoint has served its purpose but he refuses to advance beyond it, then it has become an obstacle in his spiritual path. The truth must be cautiously fitted to the receptivity of the learner. It is not everyone who can receive the same message. Hence we find it takes, in ascending degrees, the religious, the mystical, and the philosophical forms.

237

Philosophic truth has not merely a local or parochial significance, like some religions, but a universal one.

238

Even if only a single man in the whole world believes it, and all the others believe a falsity, truth still remains what it is.

239

The truth can take care of itself. Nothing can kill it although clouds of falsehood or illusion may obscure it. Therefore philosophers have ever been content to be denounced and reviled, while refusing to stoop to denunciation and revilement themselves.

240

Truth does not offer itself up to the call but awaits the right moment.

241

The persuasive character of truth exists only for those who are ready for it.

242

We may admire, respect, or even revere a man as a person, but still fail to admire—much less accept—his views. Truth forces us to separate personal emotion from clear reason, to deny sentimentality, to abandon intellect if intuition's light appears.

243

There are truths which are unalterable by the shifts of place, unmeltable by the discoveries of man.

244

These truths will continue to command the allegiance of remote posterity as they have commanded the allegiance of remote antiquity. Hence they may poetically be called eternal truths.

245

These truths must inevitably filter through from spirit into man's mind.

246

The great error of those who discover the relativity of truth, and are so overwhelmed by their discovery that they forget that it must be held together with other discoveries, is to overlook the progressive and evolutionary character of all conceptions of truth. It was so overlooked by the Sceptics' school of metaphysics in ancient Greece and by the Eel Wrigglers' school in ancient India. Life, experience, and reflection are at work in drawing us to higher and ever higher conceptions. Consequently these conceptions are emphatically not equal in value and we are emphatically not to evaluate all as alike. Philosophy does not fall into this error. While readily and fully acknowledging that all outlooks are relatively true at best, at the same time it sets up a distinctive outlook of its own. It shows that there is a definite ascent of progression through all these varying outlooks. They culminate in its own because its own is alone free and flexible, undogmatic and all-comprehensive.

247

He who wants the free Truth, unmixed with the suggestions and opinions of others, will not attach himself to any group: that is for complete beginners, who feel themselves too weak to search alone, who need the confirmations of others. Let them attach if they must but let them also regard it as a point of departure, not of arrival, not a stop.

248

If truth is unfathomable, those who claim its possession ought to remain silent. If its communication is however desirable for whatever reasons, including compassion, those who learn it ought to be warned in advance that they are receiving something else instead—symbolism or whatnot.

249

Truth is hard to come by, for not only must it be diligently sought after, but even when it is discovered the ego pushes its own beliefs and misinterpretations, dogmas and colourings, into the experience itself. Analysis and discrimination can only partly help to purify the result.

250

Finding the truth was the first great endeavour; holding on to it is as hard in its own way as the first.

251

The truth is not a form to be pictured—that merely shows how the physical body's senses dominate the mind—but a concept to be understood.

252

If we go far back in time and space, to Greece or India or China, we come close to the pure primordial truth. It is the same for Parmenides and for the *Upanishads'* seers.

253

Full knowledge of the Truth can be sudden or slow: the first way is through knowledge, the second through devotion and meditation.

254

Only the philosophically trained mind can respond, in complete truthfulness, to the Complete Truth that is the Overself's. All others can respond in part only, accepting some things, ignoring other things, even rejecting them.

255

It is a truth as fresh as this morning's shower yet, at the same time, as old as the Inca ruins at Cuzco.

256

Truth is a sword that hurts the sceptic, but a shield that protects the believer.

257

It is the conduct of children to accept truth only if it comforts them and to reject it when it disheartens them; to seek it when pleasant but to shun it when disagreeable. It is the conduct of adults to seek it for its own sake, whatever its effect upon their personal emotions may be.

258

If some aspects of the truth sadden us, other aspects cheer us.

259

Such truths can never become obsolete by time, although they may become hidden by it.

260

These truths belong to every mortal even though their discovery has remained in a select and enquiring group. They belong to no particular people, no special time. They are as ageless as they are universal.

261

They are paradoxes which discard outworn dogmas yet which attach themselves to ancient truths; which invite new modes of living yet offer practices which were known to the first Chinese emperors.

262

Truth existed before the churches began to spire their way upwards into the sky, and it will continue to exist after the last academy of philosophy has been battered down. Nothing can still the primal need of it in man. Priesthoods can be exterminated until not one vestige is left in the land;

mystic hermitages can be broken until they are but dust; philosophical books can be burnt out of existence by culture-hating tyrants, yet this subterranean sense in man which demands the understanding of its own existence will one day rise again with an urgent claim and create a new expression of itself.(P)

Part 3: MENTALISM

One thousand years ago the doctrine of mentalism was taught at Angkor, according to an inscription of that time which I saw there, the inscription of Srey Santhor. It likened the appearance of the doctrine in the world of faith and culture to the sun bringing back the light.

The philosopher today has a twofold path: to cultivate the gentle feeling of Overself in the heart within and to study the mentalness of the world without. A whole new generation is beginning to seek a better and higher life physically and emotionally, as well as more understanding of what it is all about. Here is where absorbing the knowledge of mentalism leads to dissolving the futility of materialism.

1

THE SENSED WORLD

The evolution from a world-view based upon the Eye to one based upon the Idea, is an evolution from materiality to spirituality. It is consummated when the vividness of sense experience is transcended by the truth of abstract conceptions.

2

The truth is that the hands touch and the eyes see but the surface of things. They do not touch nor see the completeness, the inner reality of things. In our ignorance we look upon forms as reality, we must needs have something to touch and handle if we are to believe in its real existence. The forms are alright where they are but they do not exhaust existence. That which tells us they are there, the consciousness which causes our senses to function and our ego to become aware of the results of this functioning, is itself closer to real being than the physical forms or mental images which are but tokens of its presence. We look always for mere forms and so miss their infinite source. We try to reduce life to arithmetic, to make one thing the effect of some other thing as cause, never dreaming that the sublime essence of both is unchanging and uncaused, formless and bodiless, the self-existent reality of Mind!

3

Our trouble is that our notion of what constitutes reality is incorrectly limited to the world of the five senses, with the sad consequence that we devise dozens of ways of finding happiness but never arrive at it.

4

We accept the first and chief suggestion of our senses without inquiry, the suggestion that we are dealing with a world totally outside us. It is an error which arises because we do not possess a deep enough understanding of ourselves. But this ignorance arises in its own turn because we do not penetrate deeply enough into our understanding of the world. Hence, the way out of it involves a twofold inquiry: into both self and not-self.

5

He sees that in the end the five senses are particular functions of the mind.

6

This thought that we are hermetically sealed in our five senses, that our sense-world is but a mere fragment of the total existence, and that such existence is itself a mere shadow of reality, is enough to awe us into a feeling of utter insignificance and helplessness.

7

Do the senses give you any real knowledge of a world outside your mind? Is it not rather that your sensations of such a world are only ideas inside that mind, and that you have no positive assurance of the existence of anything beyond those ideas themselves?

8

That which seems to be solid substance to the human touch is nothing else than a mental sensation. The testimony of the five senses is thus overthrown by profound reflection, and mind reveals its truth over the illusion of matter.

9

Thus our five-sensed experience of the physical world is really our remote experience of the divine world. The materialist's error is to take the first as a final experience.

10

He will come to see by experience, as science is coming to see by experiment, that this vast universe is real in its present form to his bodily senses only. As soon as his mind is freed from them, it takes on quite a different form, the old form having no further existence at all. He is then compelled to correct his false belief in the world's reality. If there were nothing more than the five senses, then this correction would make the universe an illusion. But the presence of mind in him makes it an idea.(P)

11

The distinction which is often made (especially by the school of Faculty-Psychology) between sensation and idea or between sense-data and thought was once believed to be an actuality, but it is now believed to be only a convenience for intellectual analysis. A compromise view now regards our experience of the world as being a compound of the two, but a compound which is never split up into separate elements. This view represents a big step towards the mentalist position but is still only a step. And this position is that there is only a single activity, a single experience—thought. The idea *is* the sensation, the sensation *is* the idea. The sense datum which our present-day psychologists find as an element of experience is really their *interpretation* of experience. Hence it is nothing else than a thought. And that which it unconsciously professes to interpret is likewise a thought!(P)

12

Men are not to be blamed for making the eye and the brain their measure of truth or reality: they are to be blamed for stubbornly refusing to heed the reports of those who have not so limited themselves.

13

It is a commonplace of scientific teaching to say that without the five senses man would know nothing of an external world. This is true, but only while science remains on a materialistic basis. For when it turns over—as it is now beginning to turn—to a mentalistic one, then it has to admit that both those senses and that of which they become aware are themselves mental products. Once this is grasped then it is possible to grasp why they do function during dreams and why we do know an external world in them.

14

Why is it that when an object gives rise to a sensation and is perceived as being *outside* the eye or ear which senses it, reflection shows that the process of sensing it could only have occurred within the eye or ear itself? Why is it that what is perceived as being outside the eye cannot possibly be reached by the eye? Mentalism alone can provide the answer.

15

What actually happens when you see something is that you become conscious of two pictures which are made upon the curved sensitive retinas of your two eyes. The reflected pictures—and not the solid thing itself—are all you directly know and hence all that you see. The whole world in which you really live and move is indeed only a picture-world!

16

All our ordinary experience of the world is derived from the activity of the sense-organs. But a conviction of mentalism's truth can only be derived from rational thinking or mystical experience. Consequently, he who limits himself to the evidence of the sense-organs and does not perceive its relativity will not be able to perceive the truth of mentalism.

17

Men who believe this world of five-sense experience to be the only real one can form only a mental concept—and that a wrong one—of the Overself.

18

Things seen or felt physically are technically called sensations or percepts in psychological jargon. And the ideas formed of those things are called concepts. But this is the materialistic view. Philosophy says they are one, not two.

19

That the outside world is reflected in our five senses as is our face in a mirror, is what those senses themselves tell us. That they participate in its making as a movie projection lamp in its screen pictures, is what deeper inquiry tells us. Nevertheless this only reveals the world's unreality, not its significance.

20

The fact that we do not perceive more than the world's appearances, never its realities, should alone be enough to dispose of old-fashioned crude and naïve materialism.

21

We have the illusion that here, in this sensory experience, we touch all of reality.

22

It is through his sense-organs that a man relates himself with the world and thus includes himself in it.

23

The real power to see, hear or feel, taste or smell does not dwell in the body. A deep unbiased analysis of the physiology of sensation will show that this power dwells in the mind.

24

In the process of sense-perception, registering impressions of the world are somehow transformed into mental states, that is, ideas. The world itself we never perceive, but only ideas.

25

All the muscle movements and nerve exertions and brain responses are themselves ideas to the mind.

26

It is not what most people regard as the world that the senses bring him into contact with, but rather the perception of it—an idea—or the projection of it—another idea.

27

All human experience is *known* experience. The world which comes to my attention *through* the five senses is known to me by the mind. Whatever the shifts of scientific knowledge may be at any time, this will remain as the central fact.

28

The power of sight in the eyes is to be distinguished from the eyes themselves, the perceiver of the world from the instrument of perception.

29

The totality of the immeasurably rich nature of the universe never reaches the human senses. This is not their fault. They cannot help but receive nothing more than a limited selection from it. There are numerous vibrations beyond their range and also beneath it. And yet we have the temerity to assert that the world of our experience, the only one we know, is the real world and that all others are illusory!(P)

30

In mentalism we separate the concept of the senses from the concept of the sense-organs. The two are not the same. The senses must be mentally active before they can be active at all. Although the physical sense-organs are the usual condition for this activity, they are not the indispensable condition. The phenomena of dreams, hypnotism, and somnambulism demonstrate this adequately. The physical sense-organs do not operate, and cannot operate, unless the consciousness takes them into its purview. Absent-mindedness is a common example of what happens when it does not do this. There are even commoner examples, however, of which we never think at all until our attention is drawn to them. A man sitting at his desk will not be aware for long periods of time of the sense of touch or pressure where his body makes contact with his chair; the nerve endings in his skin may report the contact but the mind does not take it in, and consequently is not aware of it. The sense impressions of touch are simply not there at all.

31

Men live tightly enclosed in the straitjacket of the human senses, so that they never know what is beyond these very limited and very restricted channels of perception. Yet their experience of the world is actually created out of this mysterious element which transcends their ordinary view. All that they get is their own idea of what is real, and never any contact with the real world itself. The lesson of atomic research is that such a world is completely different from the one that seems to surround them.

32

A curious example, but one helpful to the enquirer, exists in the case of bodily pain. It is utterly impossible for us to imagine pain in the abstract—existing without any mind to be conscious of it. The word becomes quite meaningless if we try to separate it from someone or something to perceive or feel it. Its very existence depends entirely on being thought of, on being related to a conscious percipient. The sensation of being felt, this alone gives reality to pain. This fact refers equally to past or present pain. It should be easy to apply this analogy to the case of mere ideas, for the latter, like pain, can never come into existence without something, some mind, to think of them. Consciousness, on the part of someone or something, alone makes them real and factual.(P)

33

There are sixty-four different points of the compass. Therefore, it is possible for sixty-four men to take up all these different positions and look at an object. Each will see a different appearance of it. Thus there will be sixty-four different appearances. Yet all the men will glibly talk, when questioned, of having seen the same object when they have done nothing of the kind. And if any one of them asserts that he has studied only the appearance of the real thing and the whole thing, he is obviously talking nonsense. Yet this is what most of us do when we say we have seen the world that surrounds us—this and nothing less. It is completely impossible through the instrumentality of the senses to see the whole of any object, let alone the whole of the world. They can only view aspects. But what cannot be done by the senses can be done by the mind, which can form an idea of the whole of anything. Therefore it is only through reflection—that is, through philosophy—that we can ever get at a grasp of the whole of life and the universe.(P)

34

It is natural for the materialist to ask how any sense can function without a sense organ. It is natural for the mentalist to point to the experience of dreams for the answer. All the senses are functioning during the dream but they do so without the apparatus of sense organs. This fact alone indicates in the clearest possible manner to anyone sufficiently perceptive to understand the indication that it is the mind and the mind alone which is the real agent in all the senses' experience. When, because of distracted attention, our mind is not aware of a thing which stands before our eyes, that particular thing temporarily ceases to exist for us. This means, if it means anything at all, that the thing receives its existence partly at the very least from us. It does not stand alone. Sense-experience actually takes place in consciousness itself: the five senses do not create but limit, canalize, and externalize this experience. We receive the various sensations of hardness, colour, shape, and so on, but they are not received from outside the mind. They are all received from within our consciousness. This is because they are received from the World-Mind's master image *within* us. The objects which cause those sensations truly exist, but they exist within this image—which itself exists within our field of consciousness. The things of experience are not different from the acts of knowing them. Hence the world exists in our thoughts of it.(P)

35

Everything happens in these organs, and all their highly complicated functions are carried out with the perfect precision of a finely made watch. Yet it happens without their owner knowing anything about it at all. Does not this show that there is something within the body that *does* know and does direct these organs?

36

The body's surface organs explain the nature and reveal the qualities of things in our environment. But without the mind such explanation and such revelation could never be possible. This is easily proven. When we withdraw the mind from the sense-organs, as in deep thinking or profound remembrance, we alienate the environment and hardly observe the things in it. In other words, we sense ultimately only what the mind senses.

37

The world-picture which the mind creates is, after all, a limited one for it is painted with only five colours. The senses we possess now do not exhaust the possible ranges of perception.

38

The two physical organs of sight, the eyes, causing two sets of sensation to be experienced, nevertheless produce only a single impression in my consciousness. The experience of an object and the thought of it are two different things. This means that the mind has its own separate existence apart from the body.

39

We wrongly fix our standard of reality by what we see, hear, touch, taste, and smell, by the senses which contact only a *part* of the great universe around us.

40

Mind is supersensual yet it is the ultimate activating agent in all sense experience. Hence the *Koran* says: "No sight reaches Him: He, the Subtle, the Knowing, reaches the sight."

41

The problems of illusory experience and truth and error really belong to epistemology.

42

The materialist who would confine all experience to sense-experience can no longer get away with such an antiquated argument. Without the instruments which convert these radiations into sights or sounds, his senses do not ordinarily tell him that infra-red and ultraviolet rays exist, for instance. This statement rests upon verifiable fact, not upon fanciful speculation.

43

The snake [seen in the place of a rope] may be an illusion, but all the same the perception of it was a factual experience. It is not to be ignored merely because it is an illusion, but to be explained.

44

When we say the world is not real, we mean that it lacks *intrinsic* reality for it is an idea only in a mind, an *appearance* only to something else.

45

We know the world through our thoughts and sensations about it, which are thus like a pair of spectacles. But we do not know what the world is like without these spectacles.

46

We are aware of the world only as it seems to our existing perceptions. Whole areas of it are therefore shut out merely because they lie beyond those perceptions.

47

The notion that one's own brain originates all one's own thoughts is shallow and erroneous. It may originate most of them in most cases, but only some of them in other cases. Four possible sources are one's physical surroundings, other people's thought directed to one, one's mental-emotional surroundings, and other people's mental-emotional atmosphere (aura) as it impinges on our own when brought close together.

48

In every physical illusion the bodily sense falsifies the mind's knowledge, yet this knowledge does not change the fact of deception, does not prevent the senses from continuing their operation even when their falsity has been exposed.

49

Even the physiologists tell us that the working of the mind is necessary to complete the act of seeing. Philosophy says, however, that the working of mind is necessary even to begin the act of seeing.

50

We see with our eyes forms and colours, we feel with our hands soft or hard things, wet liquids, large or small objects. All these observations are true ones; the body is not deceiving us but in certain circumstances appearances are doing so. That is, the use the mind is making of body is an interpretational one.

51

Those who say that *everything* in man's consciousness has come through the five gates of his senses, forget the consciousness itself.

52

Brain tissue is not mind. The five senses which are connected by nerves with it could not operate without mind, but mind can operate without the senses. Where are the senses when we work out a mathematical problem "in the head"?

53

Nature has placed the eyes in the highest part of the body, perhaps to signify that they are the most important of the five senses.

54

The materialist is also beguiled by his deeply cherished belief in the sole validity of sense testimony. What if Nature had given him ten senses?

55

Scientifically we never see the real light, but only its manifestations and reflections on various objects and surfaces. Light is invisible. We become aware of it only through its effects. Scientifically the eyes reveal only a part of the world in which we live; like all sense organs they are limited in function to a certain range and we cannot register beyond it. Science has had to invent and make many instruments to supplement this imperfect working of the senses. Detectors of X-rays and infra-red rays are cases in point. A German scientist once calculated that even the dense metal platinum would be reduced to a thousand-millionth part of its original volume if its molecules could be packed together so closely that they could not move. In other words, even the densest matter is mostly empty space! The eyes, however, see nothing of this truth and continue to testify to a platinum which exists more in appearance than in reality.

56

It is not the five senses which know the world outside, since they are only instruments which the mind uses. It is not even the intellect, since that merely reproduces the image formed out of the total sense reports. They are not capable of functioning by themselves. It is the principle of Consciousness which is behind both, and for which they are simply agents, that really makes awareness of the world at all possible. It is like the sun, which lights up the existence of all things.(P)

Body, brain, consciousness

57

He feels so firmly situated in the physical body that his whole being seems there alone. The first unthought, unanalysed impression supports materialism. But if he remains there he remains an intellectual child. It cannot be said that the brain knows the outside things *directly*; for it knows them through the intermediary service of the structure of nerves which connects it with the body's eyes, ears, skin, and so on. He hears, touches, or sees a thing or person through the body's senses. But although ear, finger, or eye is involved, analysis shows that in the end the experience is a concept:

it is there when he *thinks* it. Consciousness is involved in the act. For the mere fact that a man is aware of what he does and feels shows that *he* is a conscious creature in his own right, a *mind*-being apart from the fleshly form, however much he may be interlocked with it. This perception of the mentalist nature of all our experience of the world opens the way to deblocking the innate materialism forced upon us by the senses and the thoughts linked with them, a materialism which can be so subtle that even very pious persons are deceived by it.

58

We have the feeling of complete self-identification with the body. The five senses, the four limbs, the two eyes, and the entire torso report as parts of ourself. Yet mentalism shows that this feeling arises because they are really manifestations of our own consciousness, thoughts in our mind.

59

The mind issues orders to, and thus uses, the body. The transmission is staged through will, then energy, then nerve vibration, then muscle contraction, and finally, movement. Just as the mind does not act directly upon the body, so the body affects the mind by the same graduated process but in reverse.

60

The materialistic claim that all mental states, all spiritual experiences, and all ideas generally originate solely in the physical brain or in physical changes of the nervous system would be correct if the term "all" were replaced by the term "some." (This would still leave unsettled the mentalistic claim—which wreaks havoc with the whole underpinning of materialism—that the body, brain, and nerve system exist as a group of states of our *consciousness* and that we know of no other existence of theirs.)

61

From where does our consciousness come? The materialists say it is from the brain, and we cannot say that they are quite wrong. But what they need to learn is that although consciousness is expressed through the brain it does not start there. It has a prior existence.

62

Is it the body that tells you it is there, or the brain which informs you of its existence? No! Consciousness comes first and reveals their presence. If a dead man clutched a dissected brain for a whole year, neither of them would know of his own or the other's existence. Why? Because the mind which really knows has left.

63

No discoveries made in a physiological laboratory can ever annul the primary doctrine of mentalism. The mechanism of the brain provides the condition for the manifestation of intellectual processes but does not provide the first originating impulse of these processes. The distinction between mind and its mechanism, between the mentalness of experience and the materiality of the content of that experience, needs much pondering. (P)

64

The intelligence in the deeper human mind manufactures the bodily organs it requires for experience or development. In this way it has built the entire body itself.

65

Mind is an entirely different thing from body. How can it make contact and interact with it, and vice versa? Yet we know they do. The explanation is that there is no real difference in entity, only a seeming one.

66

Those who limit mind to the brain are unobservant. The entire body shows its presence, although not in the same highly specialized way that the brain does.

67

The materialist argument is essentially that mental function varies with bodily condition, that alcohol can convert the coward for a time into a brave man, that the increase in size and weight of the brain as man passes from infancy to maturity runs parallel with the increase of mental capacity, and that therefore mind is nothing else than a product of body. Mentalism says these facts are mostly but not always true but that even granting their truth, the materialistic conclusion does not necessarily follow. It is just as logical to say that mind uses brain as a writer uses a pen, that the body is merely instrumental and the limitations or changes in the instrument naturally modify or alter the mentality expressed. The thoughts and feelings, the ideas and memories, the fancies and reasonings which constitute most of our mental stock can be detected nowhere in the brain, can be seen by nothing physical, and can only be observed by the mind itself as acts of consciousness.

68

The scientist's statement that the workings of the consciousness are associated with physiology of the brain and the nervous system does not contradict in any way the mentalist's statement that our experience of the separate existence of that brain and nervous system is itself a working of consciousness—that is, an idea.

69

Philosophy follows a wiser path. Instead of setting up spirit and matter as eternally opposed enemies, it sets out to find the real and true relationship between them.

70

The man who refuses to acknowledge the fact of mind, as apart from brain, utters the ultimate rejection—of himself!

71

Mind is its own reality: it does not need "matter" from which to derive itself.

72

The most important of all metaphysical facts—the fact of their own consciousness—is entirely misinterpreted. The tremendous importance that ought to be attributed to it is instead attributed solely to the body.

73

The notion that consciousness is a sort of "gas" generated in the fleshy brain is the modern Western error, although an easy one into which to fall. There is, of course, a very close interrelation between body and mind, but it is one wherein the latter is expressed through the former, although narrowed and confined by the brain's limitations.

74

So much do human character, outlook, and mentality depend upon the physical body—its shape, condition, health, and fortunes—that the materialist identification of the self seems completely plausible. It is certainly part of the self, or an expression of the self; but if we analyse the notion of self as deeply and as abstractly as is possible, we find the materialist view to be a fiction. What then is left? Consciousness!

75

There is a difference—vast and deep—between the way Christian Science denies the body and the way mentalism affirms but changes the ordinary conception of the body.

76

That what takes place in the mind is only and solely a reflection of what takes place in the body—once a pillar of materialist doctrine—is hardly tenable in these days. It is quite other to say—correctly—that there is a close connection between the two.

77

The bread you ate last week became temporarily a part of your *body* but it never was *really* you at any time. That is, it was not your consciousness although it affected that consciousness.

78

Consciousness really does exist whereas the things which it makes known are present only when they are perceived, felt, heard, or otherwise sensed by one or more of the five reporting agents. This consciousness is in itself always the same, unvarying, the one thing in us in which thoughts and bodies make their appearance and from which they also vanish.

79

The world is both an experience in the mind and a picture in the mind. The brain is a machine for making thoughts; it is an expression of the mind and yet is itself in the mind.

80

The person is like an oyster shell, a mere house built around and existing for the living inhabitant within, yet a house that has somehow grown out of it and become inseparably a part of it.

81

The brain is in most cases the accompaniment and in some cases the condition of mental working but it is never the origin of such working.

82

It is a mistake to believe that the body, via the brain, makes its own thoughts. To correct it, reverse the assumption and perceive that thoughts are projections from Thought, that Consciousness comes first.

83

The world depends on the body's five senses for me to notice its existence. The body depends on the mind, without which I could not be aware of its existence. In the end, all is mental.

84

The consciousness which tells us that the physical senses are active is not to be mixed up with those sense perceptions, not to be mistaken for the sum of those perceptions. A deep, careful, and prolonged analysis will reveal that it is an entity in itself.

85

To grasp this mentalism, there must be continuous reflection on the differences between the body, the brain, and the mental consciousness which uses it as an instrument. Embodied consciousness uses instruments to get particular bits of knowledge: the body's five senses, the body's brain for thoughts. But the knowing element in all these experiences is his power of attention, which is derived from purely mental nonphysical being.

86

Mentalism affirms not only that consciousness is an immaterial thing but also that "no bodily activity has any connection with the activity of reason," as Aristotle taught.

87

The materialist who regards thought as solely an activity in the brain, and consequently as a physiological product in its entirety, has overlooked the thinker of the thought.

88

My life as a body is one thing, as a mind it is another.

89

If the blood, bone, and flesh of the human brain secrete thought then the wood and string of a violin secrete music.

90

So many use the word "mind" as if they knew perfectly well what they are talking about but the fact is that they confuse it with "body."

91

The materialist asserts that consciousness has no existence apart from the body, is indeed a product of the brain. A blow on the head may deprive a man of consciousness; an operation on the brain may change its mode of functioning. The mentalist says that these only provide the conditions which normally limit consciousness, thus making it seem as if the brain created it. But under abnormal states (like anaesthesia, hypnotism, drugs, or deep meditation) consciousness shows its own separate being.

92

The materialist who believes that not only are thoughts and ideas secretions of the fleshly brain but that mystical peace and divine revelation are as well, is wrong.

93

It is important to differentiate between man and his "garment," the physical body; that is, between mind and the thought of the body which it carries. It is important to make clear the distinction in thinking between the popular belief that man is the sum total of his physical attributes, and the philosophic revelation that mind is the source, projector, and substance of the man-thought.

94

If there were no such thing as consciousness in the body, we would be perfectly entitled to call it nothing more than a machine, albeit made of flesh and bone instead of steel and wood.

95

Mentalism tells us that the mind's activity is one thing and the brain's activity which accompanies it is another. Materialism asserts the contrary, that the mind's phenomena are produced by movements of the material atoms composing the brain.

96

Mentalism based on human experiences from the earliest Asian history right into our own time emphatically affirms that consciousness and brain are two different entities.

97

It takes keen deep thought to penetrate through the mass of often false and misleading suggestions received from so-called education which confuses two utterly separate things—brain and consciousness. The brain is what the dissection room of a medical school reveals; the consciousness is what enables the teachers and the students in that school to know what is being revealed.

The leap from sense to thought

98

There is a stubborn psychological problem, with profound metaphysical implications, which has remained unsolved throughout the whole history of science; but the range of data available today being greater, the prospects of its solution are brighter. Put briefly, this problem is as follows: is consciousness a property developed by the physical body in the course of its activity or is it a primary and intuitive part of the individual's nature? If the solution proved favourable to the theory of primacy of consciousness, then the effects upon our culture would be incalculable. The Christian teaching about the immortality of the soul would be vindicated, the value of religion in human life would be established, and the intellectual materialism of our time, which has given birth to such horrible evils as Nazism and Communism, would be eradicated.

99

The brain is physical—material, if you wish—but the mind, the private consciousness, is not. Most scientists, psychologists, and psychoanalysts would not agree with this statement, but the far-seeing ones would. The dispute can be solved only in two ways: having one's own personal experience of mind-in-itself, apart from brain, or awaiting the discovery of new, further extrasensory phenomena.

100

Psychologists have pursued the mind into that lump of greyish-yellow protein, that most complex of all organisms, the brain. They have triumphantly concluded that brain and mind are one and the same thing. Philosophy says that it is a mistake to identify the fact of general awareness—which no one can pursue simply because he *is* awareness itself—with a particular faculty of awareness as shown by some part of the brain. Brain is physical, consciousness is mental.

101

The study of man's brain and nervous system tells us a great deal about his brain and nerves; it tells us nothing about his mind, all the psychologists to the contrary.

102

Psychology, like all the sciences, has to turn itself into philosophy the moment it puts to itself such a radical question as "what is mind?"(P)

103

There is nothing a man knows more directly than the experience of his consciousness. He does not know a physical brain but a mental fact—that of being aware. Yet it is man alone who has produced that strange creature the materialist, who stubbornly denies the mentality of mind and insists on its materiality!

104

Because it studied the body first, it was inevitable that medical training should produce a group of materialists. But now that it is adding a study of the mind to its curriculum, it is only a matter of time before it will abandon its materialism.

105

No stimulus from any bodily sense, nervous system, or brain accounts for the existence of consciousness in many dreams and most imaginations. Its existence is independent.

106

Medical science still does not know how to answer with any certainty two questions which seriously affect its knowledge of how the body works. They are: (a) What is thought? and (b) Why do nerves—which are physical objects—feel pain and pleasure—which are not?

107

Those who believe that mental power and intellectual endowment are entirely products of the physical brain, glands, and nervous system will have to explain why Anatole France's brain weighed less than the ordinary man's. No, mind is an imponderable element.

108

Materialists who try to derive thought from a material brain and life from a material substance are fooled by the very accuracy of their observations. The connection in each case is close and definite, but it is not a causal one.

109

There is no adequate explanation why the nerves feel. The medical one only *describes* what happens; it does not explain. The mentalist one alone solves the mystery.

110

When we discuss these questions with medical men, they often raise the objection that the changes of thought and feeling as a result of liquor, drunkenness, drug narcosis, tropical fever, or brain lesion constitute a clear proof that mind is the product of body and that materialism is a true doctrine. We answer that they prove only that mind is closely connected with the body.

111

The old-fashioned medicine identified the mind's working with the brain's. The newer psychosomatic medicine begins to see how mind can of itself affect brain, that is, body. But its perception is unclear, its conclusions still shaky and uncertain.

112

Where the materialist scientists and psychologists have gone wrong is, first, the refusal to admit any other existence than the physical. Therefore they can offer no valid explanation for Consciousness in all its phases. If the body renews its cells every seven years, as was formerly claimed, or every one and one-half years, as others now claim, the very ordinary phenomenon of memory is inexplicable.

113

The researcher can most truthfully say that what he knows best of the world is its description as it appears to be. Under microscopic examination it is seen to be undergoing changes, however slight, all the time. But why does the feeling of its reality persist? Why does the feeling that the world is really present in our experience refuse to leave us? We have to say ruefully that there are really two levels of experience and therefore of truth—the common one and a higher one.

114

Scientists and psychologists who are trying to find the origin of mind by poking in the nervous system and the brain would do well not to make this one-sided research stand alone. They should inquire into the *nature* of mind—the very opposite of what they are doing.

115

The scientist's error begins when he assumes there is a gulf between the idea and the thing. For it is only his assumption. The experience of the thing and the idea of it are not two sunderable entities. If they were, we should register them as such. But actually we don't; we find that they form a unit of experience, a unit in consciousness.

116

Mind is the great mystery, so little known by the glib expounders of psychology who flounder within and never transcend the ego-bubbles thrown up to its surface.

117

In their haste to assert that mind is *only* a function of brain flesh they use the very mind whose existence, unnoticed and overlooked, makes their assertion possible.

118

Because there is an obvious connection and relation between consciousness and the brain, science cannot conceive how consciousness can exist separately. For the scientist, his life is in his body—nowhere else.

119

Nowhere in the physical brain can any anatomist find that which creates thought, although he may find conditions in it which prevent thought or distort it or weaken it. This is because the principle of consciousness exists before the physical body's brain exists, while it lives, and after its death.

120

The psychology which divides the brain of man into different centres of perception and reaction does not thereby explain the consciousness of man. And it is this principle of consciousness which alone makes possible all his perceptions and reactions.

121

Where is his consciousness when a man falls into coma? Or when an anaesthetic drug displaces everything from his mind?

122

Despite all its parade of learning and experiments, what science really knows about the real origin, the essential nature and inmost working of the human mind, is still amazingly little.

123

The process of becoming aware of the world makes a second thing of the world, objectifies it, and thus materializes it. Whoever proclaims himself a materialist cannot be blamed. But he is blameworthy for failing to go farther and recognize what has happened. What he experiences is the mentalness of the world. What he falsely understands by his experience is the materiality of the world.

124

Human experience of the world is the basis of the materialist theory of the world. But mentalism sufficiently explains that experience. This materialism cannot do, because it cannot account for the "leap" from sense to thought. The materialist theory collapses altogether when this simple analysis is made.

125

How can you convert solid lumps of matter into unseen intangible spirit? It is impossible without converting them into ideas first. For otherwise, you cannot get rid of their mass, volume, tangibility, and so on, nor reduce them to unity.

126

The attempt to regard Spirit and Matter as two separate self-existent substances must end in failure, for they cannot then be brought together, or interact together, either in man or in the universe. The same is true of Mind and Matter. But the opposing attempt, that of the materialists, to make Mind the highest product of the evolution of Matter, must end in equal failure.

127

If materialism were true, there would be no possibility of human memory and human imagination, from no physical origin could they be derived. Yet Descartes cut up the heads of animals, hoping thereby to find a physical explanation of memory and imagination!

128

If a man were made up of nothing more than brain and spine, blood and flesh, bone and skin, materialism could account for every phenomenon. But he is also made up of consciousness. And this is where materialism breaks down.

129

The powers of the mind increase with age in some men (as with Winston Churchill) even when the powers of the body decay. If thought were the product of flesh, it would *always* become enfeebled along with it. But this is not the case. Therefore the materialistic argument fails here.

130

The materialist tells us that the sciences of biology and anthropology prove man to be a thinking animal and nothing more. But we have already demolished the materialistic theory of the world. Therefore we cannot bow in complacence before such a solution of the enigma of human existence. How then shall we regard the materialistic view? Armed with philosophic preparation, we must now look within ourselves for an answer and subject the self to strict analysis. We must bring it up out of the darkness and look it full in the face. This alone when sufficiently prolonged and perfected can cause its meaning to appear.

131

When all mental facts are completely accounted for by corresponding physical conditions in the body, why look farther? Why not accept materialism as a perfect explanation? The answer is that this is not so, that certain supernormal, abnormal, mystical, and religious mental facts are not accounted for.

132

He who would make mind an incidental function of matter does not know what either mind or matter is.

133

How the electrical changes in the brain stuff which follow every activity of eye or ear, skin or nose, permit a man to acquire *conscious* knowledge of what lies outside eye or ear, skin or nose, is a complete mystery to science.

134

The critic may point out that all biology is opposed to mentalism, that when forms attain a particular level of organization they become thinking forms, that inanimate insentient Nature preceded living conscious form in the order of evolution, that the embryonic mind of animals appeared in the universe before the maturer mind of man itself, and that consequently it is quite absurd to suggest that the mind of man could have thought into existence what in fact was already in existence before it had itself appeared. He may finally observe scornfully that these are mere commonplaces of scientific knowledge, which now have long passed the need of being defended. We must give as a reply to our materialistic critic a fundamental counter-criticism. If the world's existence is completely and satisfactorily accounted for by its reactions to the physical senses of the human body, and if this body itself is a consequence of the evolutionary process of the larger world outside it, the materialist's explanation explains nothing, for it falls into a vicious circle. He forgets that if, according to his theory, the appearance of consciousness were the consequence of an evolution of material forms, then the cerebral-nervous structure of the sensory instruments—which are supposed by him to explain the possibility of consciousness—not having yet manifested themselves, *no sensations telling of a world's existence could have been possible*! *This dilemma cannot be got over except by mentalism*. The only world of which we can be certain is that constituted by sensations of colour, shape, breadth, bulk, taste, smell, solidity, weight, and so on. But sensations form the experience of individual minds and such experience, being always *observed* experience, is formed by thought. Hence if we talk of an uninhabited world—that is, of a world utterly devoid of a mind—we contradict ourselves. The error of materialism is to separate things from the thoughts of them. The consequence of this error is that it can speak of a world by itself as though the latter includes no such existence as thought. It forgets that each individual knows only its own world, because it knows only its own sensations, and that the identity between a Man's consciousness and the world of which it is conscious, is complete and indissoluble. We must place the mind inseparably alongside of the world. The world does not precede it in time. This is so and this must be so because, as the psychological analysis of perception shows, it is the constructive activity of the individual mind which contributes toward making a space-time world possible at all. An uninhabited world has never existed outside the scientific evolutionary theory. For sensations have never existed in separated form, as some celebrated metaphysicians of the eighteenth century supposed, but only in the combined form which they take in the individual's own perceptions.

135

It should be understood that by starting with the consideration of matter as something already existent and mind as something which has yet to come into existence, science has arrived at the impassable "gap" in its explanation of human world experience. This gap will remain forever impassable because unless consciousness existed previously, the sense-stimuli might strike on the brain incessantly but they would never get any response. However, by science retracing its steps, dropping materialism, and starting with the mentalist line first, the gap vanishes and science can proceed to wonderful discoveries which will bring it into fraternal relation with religion and metaphysics. It will then understand that all life becomes a play of consciousness.

136

A quarter century ago it was hoped that extended research into the colloidal material of nerve fibres would help solve the tantalizing problems that lie at the root of organisms having life and consciousness. Much progress has certainly been made since then. That the connection between the physical and the mental lies in the tiny nerve cell's colloidal structure will certainly prove indisputable eventually. But there is no *basic* solution of these problems without an adoption of the view that the physical itself is but an aspect of the mental. If this is done it is then possible to trace the building up of the individual's world picture through the ages by a combination of mnemonic images, associated ideas, thought tendencies, and habit energies; and his body picture through the evolution of functions like sight, digestion, and so on, which in their turn generated suitable sense apparatuses like eyes, stomach, and such. All these are memorized and conserved in a planetary mind which underlies all individual minds and without which indeed the activity of the latter could not be possible. Stromberg and Korzybski must eventually find themselves in a cul-de-sac unless they can comprehend that the wonderful synthesis which results in the actual perception of objects can be achieved by a consciousness which observes and interprets the reactions not only of the sense organs but also of the brain centres which, physiology supposes, give birth to or control the functions of thought, sensation, and memory. There is no use talking in terms of neurological structure or cerebral changes here, for with the detection of a principle of awareness one departs from everything physical and enters another world. If, therefore, he wishes to find just where a conscious connection with the nonmaterial energy can be made, he will have to detect this principle itself and not necessarily a particular point in his structure as an organism. And this can be achieved only by ultramystical methods.

137

By starting with the consideration of matter as something already existent, and mind as something which has yet to come into existence, nineteenth-century science arrived at this impassable gap in its explanation of human world-experience. It is still impassable and will remain so forever because the premise with which science started is wholly wrong. If a human being takes a wrong road and cannot arrive at his destination, the sensible course is for him to retrace his steps and take the right road. There is no other course open to science if it wants to arrive at a satisfactory explanation. It must go back from the materialistic line of thought and start with the mentalistic one, that is, with mind *first*. The essential point which must not be missed is that unless consciousness existed previously, the sense stimuli might strike on the brain forever but they would never get any response. There is no hope for success in solving this problem along the materialistically scientific road of explanation so long as it pursues a rigidly non-metaphysical course, no hope that the secret of consciousness dwells in a stimulated nerve or that the medium of interaction between thought and flesh is in colloidal structure. That secret dwells where it always has dwelt—in the mind alone—and both nerve and colloidal structure dwell there too. Once he grasps this fact, that the whole of his life-experience is only a play of attention, he will have grasped the essence of mentalism. This will liberate him intellectually from materialism.

138

The mentalist knot cannot be untied without arriving at the conclusion that the processes of sensation are mental ones throughout. In *The Hidden Teaching Beyond Yoga* the author deliberately led the argument to a gap and then said we must stop there, as science has to stop there, unless we drop the original premise that we are dealing with material objects which give rise eventually to a mental perception, and switch over to a new premise that we are dealing all the time with mental objects only. In other words, the gap does not exist except in the imagination of scientists.

139

The theory that we perceive the outer world through a sensing process which results in a picture arising in the brain, or on the brain's surface as it does on the eye's surface, still leaves unexplained how we are able to perceive this picture itself. The brain cannot see it for it cannot see colours—only the eye can do that. Nor can the brain feel it, for then it would have to touch it, which would be impossible in the case of large pictures of outer objects larger than itself. Nor can the picture look at, feel, or experience itself. The gap in this theory cannot be crossed. Only by reversing this theory and acknowledging that our awareness of the world really comes to us from within, that by a trick of the mind it only *seems* to come from without, can the correct and true explanation be found.

2

THE WORLD AS MENTAL

Mind, the projector

We can find no direct connection or immediate operation between a thought and a thing. We instinctively rebel at the notion that there could be one. And rightly so. For there are no things apart from the thoughts of them.

2

It was Plato who rightly pointed out that experience is really a medley of changing opinions and conflicting beliefs, thereby offering contrast with the orderliness and consistency of reasoned knowledge. This is why we have to begin intellectual analysis of the world by separating the realm of sense perception from the realm of reasoned perception, as though they were entirely different. But we must not end with such an artificial separation. For in the higher stages we climb to the viewpoint which reunites them again. The Thought is then the Thing. The Appearance is then also the Real!

3

The falsity of the view that the real world is outside consciousness and that the mental copy of it alone is inside consciousness, becomes known only after thoroughly deep penetrative thought. There is no world apart and separate to be copied, for the idea *is* the world.

4

We do not have a direct acquaintance with an external, material object; we have a direct acquaintance with our own perception only, the rest being a process of unconscious inference. We do not arrive at the notion of the man as a whole until we have experienced a compound of sensations such as his height, form, colour, and feel. A percept is the discrimination and combination of sensations, to which is added the assumption of extra-mental, separate, independent existence of the thing perceived. That a man is standing two feet away from our body in the domain of objectivity is an *inference* which we draw unconsciously, for the only experience which we have of him are these happenings in the eye and ear—that is, happenings which are ultimately within mind. It is only at the end of this whole process that we assume the object is in an independent, outside world. From these personal impressions our mind gets to work and makes a deduction that an outer man is there. What we really see is something mental, the existence of the material man being deduced from that of the mental experience. We do not immediately see any separate, independent, external, material man.

5

Things that can be seen and handled are not the less seen and handled mentally.

6

The first question which needs to be asked and correctly answered is: In what relation does our thought of a thing stand to the thing itself?

7

If a thing really stood aloof from consciousness, we could never obtain knowledge of it. Some relation must subsist between the two. To deny this, to assert that consciousness merely lights up the object's separate existence for us, is unconsciously to assume and take for granted as true a theory that still remains to be proved.

8

When we believe that we are experiencing the world outside, we are really experiencing the self inside.

9

The common belief is that the correct order is: first the world of things exists for us, and second we form an idea of the world afterwards.

10

We all firmly believe in the existence of this material world and we all appeal to common sense and common experience in support of our belief. Idealism retorts: That a world of which we are conscious exists is undeniable; but that this world is material in nature is disputable.

11

Only when an object is registered in consciousness is it really seen at all. Not even all the physical details of vision constitute the real experience of seeing it, for the *awareness* of it is not a physical experience at all.(P)

12

What we first become acquainted with are thoughts and sensations, feelings and percepts, memories and anticipations—that is, with mental things.

13

The mind deals directly with its objects and not through the intermediary working of ideas for the ideas are its only objects.(P)

14

Such is the make-up of our habitual outlook that we take it unquestioningly and immediately for granted that the presence of a sensation in our field of awareness indicates the presence of an external *material* thing.

15

All experience is thought-experience. What we know as the world is a series of thoughts, not a number of material things plus a number of mental thoughts. Consciousness runs through all of them as their common element: they originate from it, exist in it, leave it behind when they vanish.

16

The thought of a thing invariably *follows* attention to a thing, but the almost instantaneous rapidity with which it does so, together with the momentary character of both, produces the illusion of a single conscious act and we remain ignorant of the succession.

17

We have now been able to discover that our ordinary sense of self is a muddled one, confusing thought and thing, mind and body. It may be thought that the statement of mentalism contradicts our natural belief in the solidity of the material world. But as a matter of fact it does not really contradict either of the aforementioned beliefs; it merely corrects them. For it does not deny that the world is external to the body, and it does not deny that all tangible things are solid to the touch. What it does say is that the world is internal to the mind and that its solidity is likewise present in the mind alone.

18

The fountain pen, being a mental appearance, and one's awareness of it, being a mental activity, are therefore separated only within the world of mind and possess it as their common factor.

19

All we can rightly say is that the idea of the world is present in our consciousness. The moment we assert that the real world corresponding to it is outside, independent, and apart from us, we assert a supposition.

20

We form an idea of a table and unconsciously assume there is a separate object without us which corresponds to the image formed, but actually the existence of the external table is an assumption, for we know and have only known the mental table.

21

Does the world exist outside of and separately from the *mind* that knows it? This is quite a different question from that which deals with its relation to the *body*. Nobody could dispute its outsideness and separateness then. But the question we are really asking is not so simple. For the light-born image of the world which forms itself on the retina of the eye, the *awareness* of things touched, smelled, or tasted, is all that the mind actually knows. It cannot speak and has no right to speak of any world which possibly lies beyond its frontiers.

22

We are easily deluded by the solidity of things into a belief in "matter." The solidity is certainly there, it is real enough, but the "matter" is not.

23

The fact is we have never seen more than our idea of the external world, never known its physical nature, the latter being our own imagination or mental projection.

24

What is the use of maintaining that the universe has an existence of its own, entirely separate and apart from that which our minds give it, when we have never been able to know it and obviously can never know it except through our minds? Any such statement is a mere assumption for which we have no grounds at all.

25

The world is to be sought *within* consciousness, not outside it.

26

The objection is made that even if the world does not exist for us when we do not think it, it still exists for all the other human beings. The answer to this is: How does it exist for each of this multitude of persons? It is in his thought just as much as in ours.

27

The Chinese Chan-jan wrote, as far back as the twelfth century: "No objects exist apart from the mind."

28

The antique Indian division of manifestation into self and not-self and the labelling of the latter as *maya* because it wears a misleading garb is quite understandable on a mentalistic basis. For if the universe is really our thought of it, its seeming separateness and apparent externality do not make it, as a thought, any less a part of our own self.

29

Lao Tzu's definition of intelligence as the ability to see things in the germ is excellent, but the ability to see things as ideas is even better.

30

Philosophy is nondualistic in its view of mind and matter. They are not two separate things, it says, but one.

31

The notion that there is an inner representation within the consciousness of another world, a mental existence of this world corresponding to a physical one, is not admissible.

32

The statement that we can know only our own sensations and that we do not experience the world directly constitutes the very beginning of the doctrine of mentalism.(P)

33

The physical senses do *not* provide a picture of the object to the mind for the simple reason that all objects, including the senses themselves, are held in the mind. This is possible, this *could* only be possible, because the individual mind is not separate from the universal mind. As the Hindus say: Atman and Brahman are one. But that is carrying the discussion to a level that must be deferred for later study.

34

Our thoughts cannot be separated from our world. The two come into being together.

35

There is no difference whatever between the things of his experience and the thoughts whereby these things are known to him. In fact the things are the thoughts and vice versa.

36

There cannot be any contact with a world outside consciousness. This is a tenet fundamental to mentalism.

37

We are not asked to doubt the actuality of the ground beneath our feet or the music in our ears, but to understand that they have reached our consciousness because we have thought them.

38

What, beyond a continuously flowing stream of moments of sensation, do we really know as ourselves?

39

The view which critical reflection gives of an object does not coincide with the view which common sense gives of it. The first turns it into an idea whereas the latter retains it as something material.

40

No one can contest that the idea of the world surrounding us is in the mind. But that there is something else beyond the idea itself *is* contestable.

41

Consciousness presents its own products to itself, fabricating an entire world in the process. Mind makes and sees the picture.

42

The wall which I see is seen as something separate—as apart from my body. This is the external aspect of perception. The colour, the size, and the form of the wall are sensations which are experienced mentally and therefore within me. This is the internal aspect of perception. That a wall is without me I know only by something that happens within me. This may seem paradoxical but the truth is I do not know the externality of the wall but infer it. It is now necessary to attend closely to an examination of the mechanism of what follows. For having surmised the separate and external existence of a wall I have really projected part of my mental experience into the world outside. I have objectified an idea.

43

The mind has the power to externalize the very thing it perceives.

44

The world is apparently suspended in time and space but actually all three are suspended in the mind.

45

A distinguished musician once said to me that the effective power and reality of music lay not in the sensory impressions it causes, but rather in the mental ones, not in the sounds that enter the ear but in the thoughts provoked by those sounds. He added that its essential features of time and number are mathematical ones—that is, mental ones.

46

Mind constructs its own concepts and its own space wherein to set them up, and finally views them as different from itself and external to itself. Yet both differences and externality are illusions.

47

Herbert Spencer admitted the truth of mentalism in his *Principles of Psychology* (Vol. 2, Part 7). He admitted that the world we know is mentally constructed and mentally existent. Having got so far, he then fell into error, for he said that our experience of the resistance which objects in the world offer us proves that they also exist independently of and outside the mind. What was Spencer's mistake "of all of the objective idealists"? It was the failure to penetrate sufficiently far into the meaning of these two words: "independent" and "outside." How can the world have an independent existence when it has no significance for us before we actually experience it? It must touch our body or affect our senses before its existence comes to have any meaning at all for us. When this happens we have the feelings or thoughts which science calls sensations. Whether they are feelings of hardness, resistance, or weight, thoughts of redness, fragrance, or noise, they are still nothing else than our feelings and thoughts. Where is the independence here? The objects in the world are only objects of our consciousness. They may be independent in relation to our body but they are not independent in relation to our senses and hence to our mind. The sensations of resistance and hardness are no less mental ultimately than are any of the other sensations. Again, where is the outsideness here? Does the world really stand outside the mind that knows it? It is only at the cost of self-contradiction that we can answer that it does so stand. For whatever is in consciousness, whatever is mental, can be explained by the mind alone. It is the mind's own activity which makes resistance as it makes smells, sounds, and sights. Furthermore it is this same activity which creates the space-relationships between objects and hence the *thought* of their outsideness.

48

It is the starting point of all error to assume that at some point in time if not in space the mind suddenly made its appearance in the universe. This is the initial error of all materialism—whether it be scientific or theological or metaphysical. Mind is supposed by all these views to start functioning *after* matter has had a long inning on the cricket-field of the cosmos. Insoluble problems flow naturally out of this error.

49

All forms of the past have existed in time and place but many of them are now existing only in memory, that is, in thought. Mentalism says, "They were always in thought only."

50

All our experience is ordinarily confined to what the five senses present us—that is, to the sounds touches smells tastes and colours which are their objects. All these may conveniently be called our "sensations." These are what we really know, they are *ours* individually, and anything which we believe we know beyond them—such as separate and independently existent material objects—are mere suppositions and inferences. Therefore, there must be something in us which projects them so as to appear outside or interprets them as caused by something outside—which amounts to the same thing. Both projection and interpretation are governed by conditions of space and time. The obscurity in which all these operations are carried on does not cancel out the operations themselves. The world does not exist outside of our mind.

51

The existence of the world is not a testimony to the existence of a divine creator, but to the constructive capacity of the mind.

52

Stereoscopy offers an excellent illustration to help us realize that space is an illusion created before our very eyes. If two photographs of the same object are taken from different angles, placed in a simple stereoscopic apparatus, and looked at through its little window, the resulting picture is no longer a flat two-dimensional thing but a bulky three-dimensional one. There has been added to the height and width of an ordinary photograph the new element of depth, which makes the object stand out in relief. What seems to be a tangible space has been created behind and in front of the object. The consequence is that the image is transformed in a startling manner from a lifeless representation to something that seems vividly real. When such an apparatus so obviously creates space for us we ought not to regard it as fantastic when mentalism tells us that the human mind subconsciously creates its own forms and projects them into a fancied space.

53

All this vast and wonderful universe is in the end only the play of mind. We are imprisoned in our own involuntary creation.

54

The necessary action of human reason when at its best and sharpest, and when directed inwards upon itself, leads it to this irresistible conclusion—that the whole experience of this world is but the end-product of a process of the human mind.

55

It is not the clock or the sun which really measures time for us but the mind, by feelings and moods. Time, space, cause, and form are all of subjective origin.

56

Is it possible that the mere operation of thought suffices to produce this vast and wonderful universe in our field of awareness? We have only to study carefully, by way of illustration, the experiences of the dreamer, the novelist, and the hypnotic subject to understand that the answer may be in the affirmative.

57

"The mind, generated by thy ignorance, imagines the entire universe," says an old Sanskrit text, *Sankshepa Sarirake*, by Sarvajnatma Muni.

58

The molds of time and place, ego and its extensions, which shape human mentalism, the forms of thought, belong to this *maya*, this alchemically transforming power of mind.

59

How can you have movement without space? But if space is in the mind, so must movement be there too.

60

His difficulty may be self-created because he may think of the spiritual world as something still on a space-time level, only far finer than the physical world—something outside himself awaiting his entry. But like all the dream worlds, it is inseparable from his mind—only it is free from the space-time characteristics inherent in the present level of mental experience.

61

What I experience in my mind is projected out in space, but the ordinary person in his ignorance believes the very reverse is happening.

62

The world that you have is created by your mind. This applies to the after-death state and to the present state. Ideas manifest themselves in this world. Thus an architect's ideas manifest as a palace.

63

We experience the world as outside us not because we choose to do so but because we are obliged to do so.

64

The world seems to be "out there at a distance" but it is actually here within the consciousness.

65

The seeming reality of physical movement is not less yet not more than the seeming reality of mental awareness. Movement implies the existence of space in which it happens. Where is this space? It is in us, in our mind. All motion of the body is an item of the mind's awareness.

66

If the past is a memory and the future a dream, then both are thoughts. And if the past was once the present and the future will one day be the present, what else but a thought too can today's present be?

67

All questions about the universe's creation presuppose the previous existence of time and space since they unwittingly look for its beginning in a particular place at a particular moment which, in turn, suggests a previous one, and so on in an endless series. These questions defeat themselves: unaskable and unanswerable. Every experience of the world involves thoughts of it: this remains true when going backward into its past or forward into its future. Thoughts rise, or appear, in Consciousness. The universe is inseparable from this consciousness of it. This, isolated from every thing, should be the subject of our questions.

Mind, the image-maker

68

The difference between the chair thought and the table thought, the red thought and the green thought, the innumerable relationships among ideas, are all explicable by the fact that the mind's primary power is *image* making. This is a power which, in human beings, can be called into play deliberately and voluntarily, as we often do during wakefulness, or spontaneously and involuntarily, as we invariably do during dreams. The moment mind emerges from deep sleep and becomes active, it begins to *imagine* the wakeful world. What happens with men on a small scale happens also with the Universal Mind (God, if you like) on a cosmic scale. Its first activity is imagining.

69

The mind exists and develops on its own latent resources and needs nothing from outside. There is nothing outside. Nevertheless, its imaginative and creative power calls into play an environment which seems to be outside and which elicits those resources.

70

Two persons seeing the same fountain pen will experience two distinct sets of sensations and therefore what they actually see must inevitably differ. For each person perceives his own mental construction, despite the apparent reference being the same.

71

To have seen Himalaya's snows turn pink at sunset and the Taj Mahal's marble turn phosphorescent in moonlight, is to have seen beauty indeed. Yet after all it is not the place or the handiwork that really matters when we have gone, but the emotion evoked, the memory etched, and the taste refined. All these are *mental* things. We find at such high moments of appreciation, of aesthetic uplift, that the very essence of beauty is already present within ourselves, is an internal fact, made momentarily vivid by an external stimulus.

72

The mind *forms* its ideas and images. Hence "mental formation" would be a correct term to replace "mental construction."

73

I live in a world of Mind. The material forms which I see only *appear* as if they were non-mental.

74

If Matter has any existence at all, it is as the externalizing power of the mind.(P)

75

When we pierce through the illusion of matter we discover that his environment is as mental as the man himself.

76

The ego, the consciousness of the personal and physical "I," is that of which we are most vividly aware. And this essence is the mental, not bodily, part of us. But we are a part of the universe. Therefore the universe's own essence is also mental, not the physical part which we see and experience all around us.

77

Matter is merely something we imagine. Causation is merely succession and coexistence.

78

It is not possible to explain intellectually how sensations of the physical world are converted into ideas, how the leap-over from nervous vibrations into consciousness occurs, and how a neurosis becomes a psychosis. No one has ever explained this, nor will any scientist ever succeed in doing so. Truth alone can dispose of this poser by pointing out that sensations never really occur, but that the Self merely projects ideas of them; just as a man sees a mirage and mistakes it for real water merely by his mental projection, so people regard the world as real when they are merely transferring their own mental ideas to the world.(P)

79

His mind is much more a man's own than anything else could possibly be.

80

All other people throughout the world may apparently be sharing the same experience of its existence as our own but it is never really so. Each one's is wholly individual to himself and is lived only within himself, his consciousness.

81

We must firmly grasp this principle, that the only objects we know, the only world of our experience, have no existence apart from the mind. They do not and cannot subsist externally by themselves. That which projects them into space is mind, and as space itself is within the mind, their independent existence is sheer illusion, or *Maya* as Indians call it. We must look behind their illusory independence into the mind from which they spring.

82

Analyse your awareness of the physical world and, if your analysis is deep enough, you will be unable to avoid the conclusion that it is really a series of changes, or a group of states, of your consciousness. In other words, matter is something presented in my consciousness, whether it be now, at some time past, or in the future, even though it gives the impression of outsideness.

83

I see something, it may be a post or it may be a man. Then by the sense of agency one out of these possibilities is associated with *ahamkara* and I then know—I know I see a post.

84

"Thou art only thought," said the philosophic yogi whom Alexander the Great interviewed. He then proceeded to prove his statement by mesmerizing the king into believing himself to be a poor man struggling against destitution. I do not know if this anecdote exists amongst the Greek records of Alexander's adventures, but I found it amongst the Indian traditions about him.

85

If we do some act without attending to it but, on the contrary, with our thoughts engrossed on an entirely different subject which perhaps fills us with anxiety or joy, we are often later quite unable to remember whether we have done it or not. Here is an indication that if, as mentalism declares, it is not man's surface mind nor his everyday consciousness which presents the universe to him as an outside appearance then, in fact, he has a deeper unconscious mind which does it.

86

If the world is an idea, the ego which perceives it is itself an idea too.

87

The first step toward ceasing such wrong self-identification is to recognize the body to be but a state of consciousness, and the ego to be but an idea.

88

The life which is everywhere apparent, the forms in which it is constantly embodying itself are the effects of the mysterious movement which is the kinetic aspect of the Overself.

89

Mentalism tells us not only that matter is an unreal show but also that motion is just the same. The events and movements on a cinema film are not affecting or moving the white backsheet at all. Yet withdraw matter and motion and the whole universe will become nothing more substantial than a cosmic cinema picture.

90

The sensations of seeing, hearing, touching, smelling, and tasting things combine to make up our knowledge of the world around us in space and time. This knowledge depends therefore on egocentric personal experience. This is very easily proven by contrasting the statements made by a hypnotized subject about an object, and those made about it by a person in normal condition.

91

Every presented thing which is seen, smelled, heard, felt, or tasted, no less than every representative thought, idea, name, or image, is entirely mental. The streets of busy towns and the forests of lonely mountains are all, without exception, mere constructs of the imagining faculty.

92

He who doubts the power of mind to fashion its own world should consider such authentic instances of this power as those provided by the hypnotist's art. This has turned water into wine for its victim, chilling cold into heat, and volition into paralysis. The transformations are all imaginary ones yet are not bereft of their reality for him because of that.

93

The mind creates these images by its own power and their totality constitutes the universe of its experience.

94

His own past, once so intensely real, so vividly actual, has become only a faded and broken panorama of mental pictures. The "matter" of which it was made is now nothing more than "thought-stuff."

95

The chair which we see at an instantaneous and simple glance was really built up in the mind out of several separate elements.

96

The moods succeed each other—sometimes bright, sometimes dark—but who is the experiencer of them? It is the ego. The first stage of philosophy is to learn the secret of mentalism. Look upon every mood as a bunch of thoughts. The second stage is to look upon the experiencer as an object of those thoughts.

97

This is knowledge of the highest order, that everything around us and within us, every bit of Nature and creature, the experience of life with a physical body and of death without it—all are but forms of consciousness.

98

My experience of a thing is received from the body's senses. *Sight*: the eyes tell me its shape and colour. *Touch*: the skin tells me its hardness or softness, solidity or liquidity. Smell and taste may give more information. These perceptions make up the thing for me. But they would be non-existent if they failed to reach consciousness as thoughts. *It exists because my consciousness exists.* If this consciousness did not exist *by itself alone before the thought* my experience would be impossible. It is primary. It will continue to exist even between two thoughts, and, even more important, between two sensorial thoughts—sight and touch—connected with the physical body. But the brain is part of the body. So mind is not the same thing but exists as an independent entity, however close their working connection may be. This mind has no shape or colour, whereas the brain has. It being formless, no one can see or take hold of it, yet it is there. Now drop the term mind, the term consciousness, and let the term spirit take their place. Here psychological analysis of experience seems to cross the border into religion. For mind is a real thing, not a no-thing. It exists in its own right. *More, all experience is an uninterrupted spiritual experience, whatever man has done to degrade it.*

Every man knows that he is aware of himself, others, the world. But that awareness exists also in an unlimited uninterrupted way he does not know. Yet to the extent that he has this limited kind of consciousness he derives from It, shares the spirit, is part of it.

99

It would be absurd for him to deny the actuality, the living presence, of all that is happening to him in every moment of the day. They are there and they are real as experiences and he would be a fool indeed to deny them. Nor does mentalism ask him to do so. What it does say is that if he analyses the actuality of all these experiences, if he tries to trace out their beginning and end, their existence and continuity, he will discover that consciousness is their seat, that this consciousness can by profound thought be separated from its projections—the thoughts, the scenes, the objects and events, the people and the world—in short, that everything *including himself* is in the mind.

100

It is not merely a personal speculation but a commonplace fact of science, an item of the accepted physiology of the senses, a known result of anatomical research, that the *consciousness* of what we see and feel is what we really experience, not the things themselves. In the end all our facts are mental ones, all our surroundings are known only as our own thoughts.

101

The mentalness of all existence is not a theory nor a belief. It is an incontrovertible actuality.

102

If the world were not in the mind to start with, we would never know that there was world at all.

103

Just as the electric current must meet a second thing, resistance, before it can appear as light, sound, heat, or magnetism, so mind must meet with an idea before it can appear as consciousness, in the way we humans know the latter. Until then it must rest in the blankness of sleep, or the latency of subconsciousness.

104

It is not possible for sincere, scrupulous thinking to admit, and never possible to prove, the existence of a world outside of, and separate from, its consciousness. The faith by which we all conventionally grant such existence is mere superstition.(P)

105

The world is never really given to us by experience nor actually known by the mind. What is given is idea, what is known is idea, to be transcended only when profound analysis transforms the Idea into the Reality.(P)

106

We cannot help taking objects into our consciousness so long as we take the ego into it.

107

It is not because a thing is existent that you think it but because you think it, even if involuntarily, that it is existent. And this thought of it is a part of your own consciousness, not outside you.(P)

108

It is absurd even to suggest that there is an external world wholly outside of one's consciousness and wholly independent of it. One knows only certain changes of mental awareness, never of externals. The mind can only know its changes of individual consciousness. All its observations, each of its inferences, everything it knows—these lie enclosed within that consciousness and are never beyond it.

One's knowledge of anything whatsoever is simply one's *thought* of it. This is not to be confused with one's *right* thought of it. It is a conscious mental state, and even other persons are but appearances within this state, creatures in the cosmic dream. To follow this line of reflection to its inevitable end demands courage and candour of the highest kind, for it demands as ultimate conclusion the principle that knowledge being but ideas in the mind, the whole universe is nothing but an immense idea within one's own mind. For the very nature of knowledge is thus *internal*, and hence the individual mind cannot know any reality external to itself. It believes that it observes a world without when it only observes its own mental pictures of that world.(P)

109

It is a generative idea. Here is a whole philosophy congealed into a single phrase: the world is an idea.(P)

110

Unless we are in personal touch with the world, it is not present for us. The relation ends the moment our ego is withdrawn. Without it, without a viewing subject, the world as object simply does not exist. And nobody living in the ego-consciousness has any way of knowing what the world is in and by itself.

111

All experience is experience in the world of consciousness. There is no other.

112

So far as it appears in any creature's experience, the world is only a thought in that creature's mind. All creatures may banish the thought by sleep but only a human creature may banish it by yoga.

113

The only world we know, the only one we can ever know, is the one within our mind. The first proof of this is that when it leaves the mind in deep sleep, it has no existence for us at all; the second proof is that when it re-enters the mind on awakening, the sense-perceptions which tell us of its existence re-enter it also.

114

The hill or the star is a perception in your mind. You cannot now say exactly when your mind began to exist or when it will cease to do so, but only conjecture about it.

115

Such is the metaphysical importance of memory that it gives us the key to existence. For what is the once so real-seeming world of the now-shadowing past when recalled again into being by its magical power but a procession and collection of mental images of like texture to a dream? Did it not then exist like a common dream only in the consciousness of all its creatures? And do not the places and things and persons take on a curiously dream-like character when we bring it back into remembrance? Thus we have to step out of the past, which means to step out of the chains of time, before we can discover the essential mentalness of all our experience.

116

All that is real in human experience is the mind's experience; all that is received into the mind are ideas; all events of whatever kind are mental, that is, ideas.

117

Men talk of the solidity of their material existence yet a whole continent—Atlantis—vanished in a day.

118

What is experienced is nothing other than yourself, for it is nothing other than your thought and your perception.

119

When we give ourselves up to a desire or an attachment, why do we really do so? It is because we seek the state of happy consciousness which the thing obtained or the situation realized would, we believe, lead to. What we really desire is in the mind.

120

The doctrine of mentalism begins and ends with the bold pronouncement that all experience and even all being is in the mind.

121

How can a thought exist apart from its thinker? One can *imagine* this, but philosophy does not deal with imagination, only with known facts. The notion that thoughts are set out into space and that others tune into them is based on the illusion that mind is in the body or brain, whereas the reverse is true. Has anyone ever measured the mind and shown where it started and ended? The very notion of the world is *within* one's mind. This shows that he cannot say that thoughts are outside the mind merely because he believes they touch somebody who is hundreds of miles away. There is no more separation between thoughts and thinker than between dreams and the dreamer.

122

We have no other contact than with our own thoughts of the world, yet those thoughts are as truly and actually our experiences of it as anything else could ever be.

123

It is utterly impossible to explain the material world satisfactorily without reference to mind, and this reference must come first, not last, because it is the mind that tells that the world exists.

124

When the Naqshabandi Dervish Mullah (expounder and explainer of the teaching) says to a crowd around him, "You are here because of me!" his meaning can come alive only in a mentalistic sense.

125

We are able to think our surroundings only because ultimately they are as mental in substance as our commonly accepted thinking.

126

What fact is more certain, what part of human life more inescapable, than that of consciousness? What would become of our experience of the world without the awareness which is basic to it?

127

Mind is the foundation of all our existence. It is always there even when, as in deep sleep, we are not personally conscious that it is there. Any materialistic denial of its self-existence can be made only because mind is present to make it.

Mind, the knower

128

What is Mind? It is that in us which thinks, which is aware, and which knows.(P)

129

There is one natural capacity which is common to every human being and to every animal being—a capacity which is the very essence of its selfhood. It is consciousness. The most important of all states of consciousness is knowledge.

130

The only real existence is the mind's. But we ordinarily know only its projections and retractions, its phases and states, its consciousnesses and lapses.

131

Mind is that quality or capacity in man which enables him to be aware of both himself and his surroundings.

132

We are conscious of a world outside through the knowing faculty, the mind. The various ideas which we form of the world are simply states of the mind. These ideas are not separate from the mind itself and could not be. If they were, then we would have to become conscious of them, as we are of the world, through other ideas, through other states of the mind.

133

There is a region of mind which lies beyond the intellect's immediate reach. Because it holds so many lower but repressed desires, some psychologists have called it the subconscious. Because it holds so many laudable but vague aspirations, most religionists have called it the Soul. Because it is not ordinarily in the focus of awareness, other psychologists have called it the unconscious mind. All three groups are right, but each is limited in what it sees and what it understands, as if groping for knowledge in the dusk.

134

It is not that there are different minds in man, but different qualities of one and the same mind in each.

135

What we are is what we are conscious of. The mind makes its own reality. Consciousness is king.

136

Why is it that so many people are so unaware of their own higher existence? The answer is that their faculty of awareness itself is that spiritual existence. Whatever they know, people know through the consciousness within them. That in them which knows anything is their divine element. The power of knowing—whether it be a thought that is known, a complex of thoughts such as memories, a thing such as a landscape—is a divine power for it derives from the higher self which they possess.

137

The mind interprets its own experience in a particular way because, owing to its structure, it could not do so in another way. But these limitations are not eternal and absolute. When, as in dream, yoga, death, or hallucination, they are abruptly loosened, then experience is interpreted in a new and different way.(P)

138

To feel and to know are attributes of consciousness, not of brute matter.

139

We know only by inference or analogy that the *minds* of individuals exist, not by direct perception. Our social life is based upon this knowledge and, acting on it, we find it largely true.

140

Just as we first find water to be a liquid and later to be a gaseous combination, so we first find in vision that all the world is light, and later, in *knowledge*, that it is Mind.

141

Thinking is an act done mentally and, like all acts, points to the existence of someone who already exists or to something independent of it.

142

The writer George Moore was not particularly interested in metaphysics and usually left the subject alone. Yet half of a sentence he wrote upon writing itself contained the most important and significant metaphysical principle. It was: "My own mind alone is known to me."

143

There can be no thought without a thinker, and when we begin to search for that which thinks, we begin to follow a trail which leads to the Soul.

144

"I see" and "I know" are two very ordinary phrases. But what tremendous metaphysical meanings are hidden behind them!

145

When man turns to observe himself in the effort to know himself, what he first notices is not at all what he will have to notice later in the end: that is Consciousness.

146

By the light of mind, man is able to know, think, reflect, and feel.

147

If the human being finds that he has the capacity to think, to produce ideas, to discover the words or pictures in which he can clothe these ideas, he should remember that all this becomes possible only because of the primacy of the mind; that is, mind consciousness already existed, and hence they are able to exist. Without its prior existence they could not come to birth.

148

This deep unknown basis of mind determines its surface life and is the key to its conscious trends; therefore it should become our chief object of study.

149

That which enables us to know the world outside and to be aware of the self inside, is Mind.

150

Is man nothing more than nerve-stuff, flesh, and bone? Thought asks this question. Thought alone can answer it. No butcher shop, however crammed with nerve-stuff, flesh, and bone, will ever answer it. *Only the thinking principle in man, which is an emanation of his soul, can explain itself.*

151

It is mind which makes thoughts intelligible, things experienceable, and the thinker (the experiencer) self-conscious—Mind! the mysterious unknown background of our life.

152

We do not know the self directly but only through the thoughts it produces. It is impossible intellectually to examine it and equally impossible to exclude it from our examinations.

153

Things exist only in the character of known things. If they are absent from our senses they are present in our thoughts. If they are absent from our consciousness they must be present to the universal consciousness. Whatever is characterized as something known, cannot be the knowing principle itself.

154

Thinking is possible only where there exists an object about which to think, whether it be a material thing or a mere idea. We cannot think unless we have something in mind. This means in every act of thought there are two elements: the thinking itself and the object or idea thought about. These are so coupled together by the psychological constitution of man that the first cannot exist without the second.

This is equally true of the act of seeing. We cannot see anything unless there is some object, something to be seen. Hence sight depends upon both seeing itself and the object seen. Both are so interrelated that the former could not exist if there were not the other.

These statements may be more easily understood after due reflection, but it will be much more difficult to understand that the contrary ones likewise hold true. That is to say, no object or idea can exist without being thought of, and nothing perceptible can exist without something or someone to see it. In short, the factors which have been coupled together here are mutually dependent.

It is impossible for a thinkable object or idea to exist in a state where thought itself is impossible. It is impossible for a seeable thing to exist in a state where sight is impossible, as in deep sleep. And, since everything material is either thinkable or seeable or both, it follows that the entire material universe has its being in being thought of or perceived. It is only an appearance within the mind of the thinker or dependent upon the perceiver. No idea, no object, could have any conceivable existence if the perceiver himself never had any. Something living and conscious that can think and become aware of them must first exist through their relation to it. They cannot possibly exist in disconnection from a conscious mind.

If we imagine a universal state wherein there was no body present, no mind that could think of anything, perceive it, or be conscious of it, then we are quite unable to put any idea or object or sound or colour into this state.

This is true whether we apply it to mere ideas or to hard and heavy things which we see and feel, such as houses and trees. The point cannot be grasped by the understanding without previous reflection and meditation, for it appears to be contrary to common experience and common sense. In short, matter *is* a mental sensation and not the cause of a mental sensation.

155

Whatever thought, idea, image, or remembrance comes to us is not separate from our mind and consequently from us. And because every object, thing, or creature in the world around us is only a thought, idea, image, or remembrance to us, it is likewise not separate from us.

156

Anyone who is able to imagine or feel a real separation between thought and being, has done what I am quite unable to do. On the contrary, I find myself always constrained to imagine or feel that an essential and inevitable relation exists between them.

157

We never know things by and in themselves but only by and in the mind.

158

Mind can know only that which is of the same nature as itself, namely, thought.

159

If the object of my experience had nothing in common with my idea of it, it could not even stand in this alleged relation of cause and effect. If it does so stand, then what is the common thing between them? There is no answer to this question except the mentalist one.

160

Space is simply the way in which our minds see the world; that is, it is purely mental and not really outside us. The corollary to this is that as all things have their being in space, they must likewise have their being in the mind. But mind alone can only entertain *mental* visitors; it is too subtle to receive non-mental materials. Mind cannot receive that which is wholly dissimilar to it. Therefore all things must enter it as ideas only.

161

The mind can have dealings only with kindred objects formed from its own substance, that is, with thoughts, ideas. Therefore when it knows material objects they must really be ideas.

162

Mind and matter are incommensurables. Mind can enter into relations only with something allied to its own subtler nature, not with something wholly dissimilar, as matter is said to be. That which the mind knows must be relevant in relation to the Mind itself. There must be a community of kind between the two, a common identity of substance. The world as known cannot possibly be extra-mental in nature. Hence the characteristics of what the mind knows must be mental—that is, they constitute our ideas.

163

The human mind can enter into relation with—that is, become aware of—that which is of the same nature as itself, that which is correlated to it, that which is also mental. It is impossible for material things to enter directly into the immaterial consciousness of man.

164

Were our consciousness of the world and the world itself so essentially different after all, then no real contact between them could ever be possible. But contact does happen. And it does happen because the world is nothing less than the mind's idea.

165

If a man would be willing to think deeply enough, he would be obliged to agree with the assertion that he can know only the idea of a thing, and not the thing-in-itself.

166

Two things which are totally different from one another, quite unrelated, cannot work together or affect each other. This is mentalism's case.

167

The human mind is forever dealing with human conceptions of things under the belief that it is dealing with the things themselves.

168

Two lips utter a single word. The experiencer and the experienced object are a single stuff.

169

Mind is the knowing agent and mind is the object known. In the first case it assumes the internal form of self-consciousness, in the second case, the external form of experienced world.

170

When we analyse the experience of human experience itself, we find that it reduces down to the knower and the known, the mind and its thought. All attempts to separate the physical object from sense data and these from mental perceptions end in artificiality.

171

Mind cannot project itself outside itself to observe what it is. Only through what it knows or does or desires, only as its existence is expressed in any given situation, can it perceive itself.

172

The object seen, the eye which sees it, and the act of seeing are *all* part of a mentally created scene; all are idea.

173

The philosophical meaning of Einstein's discoveries—that the nature of the world depends on the nature of its relation to the one who sees it, that we cannot truly speak about any object independently of the observer, and that time is the hallmark of this relativity—is in perfect accordance with our own doctrine. Whatever is seen, is seen by the mind. Apart from the mind we know nothing of its existence and apart from the mind the thought of time could not arise for us. In short, every existent object is wholly relative to the subject—Mind.

174

Experience is a unity and cannot be broken into mind and matter. We cannot possibly separate the world from the mind that knows it. The two are always related. To object that such a relation need not exist outside the act of knowing the world, even though it must exist inside it, is to utter words which dissolve away as soon as their meaning is analysed. For the only world which human beings can ever discuss is one which they can think about and which is therefore an idea for their minds.

175

Because I am a conscious being I am aware of physical sensations and mental thoughts; but the consciousness which enables such awareness to exist itself existed before sensation and before thought, and this is as true of newborn babies as it is of dying men. This is what the materialistic anatomist dissecting the body fails to perceive. This is the forgotten self of the fabled ten persons crossing a river in Indian mythology, and this is the great secret which mentalism unveils for us.

176

The tenth man in the Hindu story, who failed to count himself when checking if all the party who waded across a river were safe; the Hebrew rabbi who said on his deathbed, "If there proves to be no future life, how I shall laugh!"; and the scientist who denied the existence of mind because brain-flesh produces consciousness—all three show how easy it is to forget the subject when looking at the object.

177

The object which the senses directly establish contact with is regarded as one thing; the mental impression they have when thinking of that object is regarded as another and totally different thing. This is a very simple and apparently very obvious view of the matter. To the ordinary mind, by which I mean the metaphysically unreflective mind, the statement is unarguable and its implied division of Nature into mental and material, uncontestable. But if you analyse the way you perceive objects you will find that both the perceiver and the perceived are inseparable in the act of perception. You cannot show a duality of idea and thing but only a unity of them.(P)

3

THE INDIVIDUAL AND WORLD-MIND

Philosophy does not treat the world as a shadow. So long as we do not treat our own selves as shadows, we cannot treat the world thus, since we as finite beings are parts of the world. Nor does Philosophy deprive man of his reality. It only shifts the centre of gravity without making him lose anything at all.

2

There is no other way in which we can think of things than as really existent. This will remain true whether we pause, reflect, and grasp their mentalness or whether, with the unthinking millions, we accept the appearance of matter for their sole reality and seek to penetrate no further.

3

He is quite right in questioning the usefulness of getting involved in an endless study of the intricate classifications of his surroundings, if they are illusory. From the standpoint of the Ultimate Path such a study is a waste of time and therefore is not indulged in. The aim of this path is to know the ultimate reality—knowing which, all its illusory reflections are naturally understood. However, he must be careful in the use of the word "illusory." The world is not illusory but the apprehension of it through the senses is. Each object regarded separately as an independent entity is illusory but regarded as what it is in its formless essence it is real. To put this in plainer language: everything seen is merely an idea in the mind. Ideas come and go and in this sense only are unreal; but the stuff out of which they are formed—that is, Mind—does not come and go and constitutes the ultimate basis of all ideas and therefore of their ultimate reality. He seeks to understand what this Mind is.

He may now begin to realize that all the theosophical teachings about the seven principles of man, the five *tattvas* (cosmic forces), and *prakriti* (root matter) are teachings given to beginners who are unable to grasp the great truth that all these are merely ideas and that Mind alone is what he should seek to know. H.P. Blavatsky gave these teachings because she knew that the nineteenth-century West was not metaphysically minded but rather scientifically inclined and science in those days was horribly materialistic. What else could she do but give out these lower grade teachings? She herself writes in one of her books that she has given only three or four turns of the key in the lock of universal mystery. The time has come in the mid-twentieth century to give the remaining turns which will make known the higher philosophical truth for which mankind is now better prepared.

4

To say that the world does not exist helps neither the cause of truth nor the seeker after truth. To admit that it does exist but to qualify the admission by adding "but not materially, only mentally" is to describe experience accurately. The dream exists in the dreaming mind as a series of thoughts, even though its world is not physical.

5

Whatever the five senses tell us about things and people, scenes and events, in our experience is certainly there and is not denied at all: such denial is emphatically outside the claim of mentalism.

6

The nature of world experience, such as moving, talking, or reading, must eventually be understood as mental or mind-made; but your *experience* of its activity or forms does not change, *only* your understanding of it: that is, that it is basically *mental* activity and these are *mental* forms. For whatever they do and however they behave or seem to behave, whatever you can know of them can be grasped only with the mind. They obviously have their own mental existence and activity even when you are not present to observe it. We must keep our common sense even when learning to reason philosophically.

7

But all this does not mean that philosophy asks us to mistrust the witness of our senses. That is correct enough for all ordinary, practical uses. But it does ask us to search more deeply into the significance of all sense-experience.(P)

8

As mental experience the world certainly exists but it is not the highest kind of existence. We can hope and look for another which transcends the present one. Nor is it necessary to wait for death to find it.

9

The laws of Nature remain still unchanged even when we find that Nature is mental, and not material.

10

To assert that the world is not there, that it does not exist, that the enlightened person does not see it, is to confuse beginners. Also it is semantically incomplete. Students would be more receptive, would understand more clearly, if they were told that it *does* exist but only in the way that a dream exists, as an idea in, and an experience of, consciousness.

11

Nothing of the existence of anything in the world is taken away by mentalism but everything of it still remains.

12

Any teaching which fails to concede the existence of this world not only fails to have any practical application to human life but also wastes our time in its study.

13

Mentalism is not so foolish as to deny the existence of our familiar world, the one we daily experience; it does deny that it is experienced independently of the mind or externally to the mind.

14

In the higher philosophy the existence of the world is not denied, as it is by Indian Vedantins and Christian Scientists. It is no less real than humanity. Only it must be understood that it is a *manifestation* of Mind, not an illusion. This being the One Reality, it follows that the world cannot be unreal. The form it takes is transient, however, but its absence is not.

Also, as far as world-manifestation is concerned, causality is not denied but accepted. However, it cannot be separated from succession in time. When, by ultramystic methods, the Mind-in-itself is known in its unmanifest state—that is to say, its timeless state—causality disappears.

The human mind as ordinarily known is certainly incapable of inventing so many marvellous processes in Nature. The world is the invention of Universal Mind. But the latter functions in and through the human mind. What it presents is common for all men. But it enters into humanity in consciousness only and is therefore an idea. Owing to individual uniqueness the idea is not quite the same for all; each gets an aspect, as it were. But even the disappearance of humanity from the earth would not entail the disappearance of all natural phenomena, for this cannot happen if other beings exist, such as animals.

15

Mentalism does not reduce our experience of the world to a shadow. It lets us keep the reality we feel but points to an ultimate reality from which that feeling derives.

16

How can a man neglect the presence of the world in which he lives, the body in which he thinks, and call himself a philosopher? How can he dare to assert that neither of them is present?

17

He who thinks in a balanced fashion can accept the world's presence as a fact of experience without accepting the crude materialistic theory which makes its physical presence the only one. He can find its reality in conscious-mind, not in matter, without running to the opposite extreme of rejecting that presence and denying that experience.

18

My fellow creatures are themselves but ideas, no less than the inanimate objects against whose background I see them. For they too are known to me only as reports of my mind. Nay, more, the very fleshy frames whereby they take individual shape before my eyes, and in which they are embodied, are but sense-images whose habitat is entirely subjective.

19

If they are only waves of energy, they are still recognizable as men and trees; if they are only ideas in consciousness, they are still taken for real men and palpable trees.

20

Unless a man is blind, deaf, dumb, and skinless, or anaesthetized by a chemical drug, his body will certainly register the impressions made upon it by the world outside. That is to say, he will become aware of the world's existence, be he philosopher or not. To a mentalist, the nature of this awareness is a different matter but the fact is still there.

21

It may be said that doctrines which try to persuade us that the world around us has no real existence are hardly likely to help us become efficient citizens.

The dream analogy

22

That life is a kind of dream is the hint given by religion, the experience felt in meditation, the knowledge correctly understood by philosophy.

23

Earth life is but a dream, lived out in a dream physical body amid dream environment. Dream experiences are only ideas; during sleep-dream man sees, hears, touches, tastes, and smells exactly as he does during waking-dream. Hence waking is but materialized ideas, but still *ideas*. God's cosmic dream: all universal activities are but different ideas of God, divine ideation made material and thrown upon the screen of human consciousness. The cosmic illusion is impinged upon man's sense and seen from within by Mind through consciousness, sensation, and bodily organ.

24

The world is neither an illusion nor a dream but is analogically *like* both. It is true that the mystics or yogis do experience it as such. This is a step forward toward liberation but must not be mistaken for liberation itself. When they pass upward to the higher or philosophic stage they will discover that all is Mind, whether the latter be creatively active or latently passive; that the world is, in its essential stuff, this Mind although its particular forms are transient and mortal; and that therefore there is no real difference between earthly experience and divine experience. Those who are wedded to forms, that is, appearances, set up such a difference and posit spirit and matter, *nirvana* and *samsara*, Brahman and Maya, and so forth, as antithetic opposites, but those who have developed insight perceive the essential stuff of everything even while they perceive its forms; hence they see all as *One*. It is as if a dreamer were to know that he was dreaming and thus understand that all the dream scenes and figures were nothing but one and the same stuff—his mind—while not losing his dream experience.

25

The common objections to mentalism may be summarized in three forms: (1) A thing does not cease to exist when we cease to think about it; thus, Australia is still to be found on the map even when we are not thinking about Australia. (2) The fact that we do not think of a thing does not prevent such a thing coming into existence. (3) Our awareness of things is largely quite involuntary; we do not choose to think them into existence—they just are there. The answer which mentalism makes to these objections, and to all others which may arise, is a simple one. It is this: consider your life as a dream! All possible objections will then have no ground on which to stand. They appear true while we are under the illusion of dreaming, but they are seen to be false as soon as we awake from the dream itself.

26

That man is already half-awake from the illusion of this World who knows that he is dreaming.

27

Life on the world scene was likened by Marcus Aurelius not only to a dream, but even to a delirium! Yet he was a man of much practical experience, a victorious soldier and a Roman emperor. And where the Greek poet Pindar and the Greek playwright Aristophanes used dream only as a metaphor to describe this physical life of ours, Plotinus used it as an actuality.

28

"Do not tell me that the bomb which destroys my home is only an idea!" To this there is the reply that once again we may call on the help of dreams to illustrate a difficult point: the tiger which mauls you in a dream is admittedly an idea. Both tiger and bomb are vividly present to your mind—but both are mental. How is it that sensations of pain in an amputated foot still occur although the external material foot is no longer there? In both cases we are clearly dealing with workings of the mind. That is undeniable.

29

Just as it is the dreamer himself who unknowingly makes the figures and creates the things which appear to him, so the waking man experiences only his own thoughts of the world. When those thoughts are not there, *he* is not there. And his world is not there: he and his experiences are contents of the mind. It is not, as commonly fancied, that he *has* a mind but that he—the ego-thought—is *in* the mind and never apart from it. The world comes before the waking dreamer just as it comes before the sleeping dreamer, only it comes more coherently and consistently and logically. The mystery of the universe is in the end the mystery of mind. The reasonable question to which scientists should address themselves, and will in the end have to, is "What is Mind?" To call it brain, flesh, is a misleading answer.

30

His physical senses tell him that this world is as real as anything can be. His intellectual reflection and intuitive experience tell him that it is dream-like.

31

Life is a dream, an infinite dream, without beginning and without end.

32

The young Swami Vivekananda could see the world only as a dream. While strolling in the public park in Calcutta, he struck his head against the railings several times, to see if they were real or mere illusion of the mind. Thus he got a glimpse of nondualism.

33

That pain is the mental end-result of a physical process is not denied by materialists, but that its mentalistic nature can exist independently of that process is denied. We must ask them to look at their dreams and especially at their nightmares.

34

To awaken from the world-dream and to tell one's fellow dreamers that its reality is a supposed one is to become a voice crying in the wilderness.

35

The grim illusions of a man's dreaming nightmare cause him trouble and suffering so long as he accepts them as real. If he arouses himself and awakes, they are seen for the hallucinations they are. The disciple's long-drawn endeavours at self-arousal throughout the quest meet with success when he knows and feels that waking life itself is like a dream, is after all only a thought that is taken up again and again.

36

Life is only a dream. Nothing we learn can change that hard fact. But we can be *conscious* dreamers.

37

They instinctively shrink from the notion that this entire life of theirs, the possessions, the family, the ambitions—all is like a dream, mere ideas. The ego winces at the blow thus struck at its own reality. The flesh rebels.

38

If life seems like a dream, as it does to him, even the dreamer—he himself—seems part of the dream, too.

39

It is true that only a person of much intelligence can understand the mentalist doctrine in all its fullness, but it is also true that the simple statement "Life is like a dream" can be understood by any ordinary intelligence.

40

Like a dreamer, we see a world around us and act in it but are mesmerized into accepting the reality of our experience so long as the dream itself persists. And, like a dreamer, we remain basically unaffected by all this illusory experience, for we are still the Overself, not the mesmerized ego.

41

A man's attempt to find significance in the universe's life (which must therefore include his own) need not prevent his holding it all—quest, self, the daily show—lightly. For the notion may be strongly implanted in him that life has the quality of a dream, that the world and its history is a flow of ideas through consciousness, and that all personality, including his own, is part of the entertainment.

42

In the end he will discover that man as Mind creates his own world of objects. To understand this let him just look at his dreams. He is not conscious of having created them, yet where else but from pure consciousness have they emerged? This shows how mind has the power to manufacture scenes, people, and such. The reference here is to what is called the Unconscious Mind.

43

Many have felt during meditation or even outside of it the dream*like* character of the world. As dreams are only thoughts, this means that they have felt the truth of mentalism. However, the world is only *like* but not actually a dream. When one meditates on the reason still more subtly he finds that it is really the substance of God reflected forth, the self-externalization of Cosmic Mind. It is there divine in essence. Its form is changing and an appearance but its ultimate stuff is, in reality, God. Life here on earth is divine in this sense. Once this is grasped, he finds a fresh basis for conduct, a deeper inspiration for activity. He cannot be a mere dreamer, cave dweller, or drifter. He must act. But actions will now be inspired by and performed for that deeper self within, and will therefore be impersonal and altruistic.

44

There is only one mind and all such names as cosmic mind, over-mind, and so forth are merely imperfect and partial concepts of that ultimate single mind which philosophy puts forth in order to help students advance to a higher stage. These concepts are not false, however. They represent aspects of the same ultimate mind as seen from different standpoints. As these standpoints are not the highest they do not yield the final truth. It will be well therefore for him to accustom himself to the highest standpoint and to remember always that there is but one mind, one reality, one principle, one substance, one being only. All things are forms or shapes which it appears to take temporarily. The key to the understanding of these admittedly difficult points is to think of the universe seen during dream and then to remember that that universe itself, its seas and continents, its peoples and animals, its happenings in time, its distances in space, do not exist apart from the mind of the dreaming person; that even if millions of people exist within that universe they are nothing else than ideas passing through the mind of the dreamer; and that their ultimate stuff or reality is mind although to the dreamer they appear real, as do also water, fire, gas, and even the ninety-odd chemical elements. Now he must try to regard the waking universe in the same way, with this difference: that because the ego is one of the dreamed-of figures in the waking dreams it must be eliminated if one is to break through the dream and ascertain that it is a dream in the universal mind.

45

When we realize how the mind weaves a whole host of creatures during sleep out of its own self, we comprehend a little of the meaning of the statement that the entire world is but a mental creation.

46

Only when we wake from a dream do we begin to grasp its significance, but before then we may be utterly deceived by it. Only when we wake from the dream of materialism do we begin to see how utterly it has deceived us.

47

If they discover the mentalist truth that this existence is like a dream, will not men's practical existence in the world become imperilled? Those who are already unbalanced will become more so. Those who are rigidly fixed in materialistic attitudes will become uncertain and unsettled. But those who come to it previously prepared by their intellectual and emotional history will be able to use their worldly life responsibly but without being mastered by it.

48

Mark Twain, the American novelist, wrote a book and promptly died when it was finished—even before it could be printed and published. This book was entitled *The Mysterious Stranger*, and in it he put forward the probability that all our life may be but a dream and that if this is so we can learn from it to support life's difficulties and endure till the end. Was it possible that Twain got some sort of intuition and guidance when the shadow of death was beginning to fall upon him?

49

To some who begin to suspect that all this may be like a dream—which is a hazy but imprecise glimpse of mentalism—it comes as a shock.

50

While he is under the spell of the World-Mind's magic he sees these pictures and experiences this dream as if they were the last word of reality.

51

Although to the mentalist the world appears *like* a dream it does not appear *as* a dream.

52

Sufi teaching is that the world is *Khayal* of *Khwab-i Khuda*—that is, the thought or dream of God.

53

Not only does one's past life turn all-too-quickly into the likeness of a dream but, what is worse, into a distant dream.

54

We are all like figures seen in a cinema show, where they and the episodes are illusory but the screen and projector real. Where do they go when the show ends?

55

The abstract idea that life is like a dream and that the world is but a thought-form is converted into a felt experience by the philosopher.

Individual mind and the world image

56

The thought of the external world comes from the Universal Mind (God) originally, while thoughts which pertain to personal characteristics come out of the subconscious tendencies developed in previous incarnations. In both cases the power which initiates thoughts is outside the conscious self but for that very reason is irresistible. The work of the Spiritual Quest is to enter into co-operative activity with God, on the one hand, and to conquer those subconscious tendencies, on the other.

57

How hard for the average mind to grasp this central fact, that the World-Idea *is* the world-creation. The one does *not* precede the other. The second is *not* a copy in matter of the first. Man has to work, with his senses and his intellect, when he wants to convert his ideas into objects. But the World-Mind does not need to make an effort in order to make a universe, does not in reality have anything to do at all, for Its thought *is* the thing. Some mystics and most occultists have failed to perceive this. Their realization of the Spirit did not bring with it the full revelation of the Spirit. This is because they have not thoroughly comprehended—usually through lack of competent instruction—its utter emptiness. Nothing can come out of the Universal Mind that is not mental, not even the material world which men believe they inhabit and experience. Science is on its way, through its delvings into atomic structure, to a suspicion of this tremendous fact; but so many scientists are so devoid of metaphysical faculty that they uphold materialism and deny mentalism!

58

For each man the world is what his thoughts of it give him, expressed as physical sensations and perceptions as they are in waking, or as dreams in sleeping. What holds them all together is a greater being—the World-Mind. Without such thoughts there is no universe *for him*.

59

The universe is mind-pictured, mind-made out of mind-stuff by the Great Mind. Even we, with little finite minds, must come into activity before we can get any experience of any world at all.

60

The world-image is duplicated in our individual mind but this duplicate image is entirely our own.

61

We receive as by hypnosis the World-Mind's master image because we are so intimately rooted in it. But we receive it only within the limits of our particular capacity and only upon the plane of our individual perceptions. That is, we think only a minute fragment of the whole thought as it exists in the World-Mind's consciousness.

62

All these little minds which people the universe and are active in Nature's kingdoms could not have come into being unless there were a universal originating Mind. They point to its existence, silently speak of their divine Source. The materialistic notion that individual centres of intelligent life could have been produced by non-intelligent "matter" is an utter absurdity.

63

It is the power of imaginative thought, both human and deific, which produces the world-appearance for us.

64

It is asked why, if the world is like a dream or a hallucination, we all have the same dream or suffer the same hallucination. Why do we project it in common instead of independently, since we all do have quite different dreams when asleep at night or quite different reveries when awake by day? The answer is that there is another and vaster Mind behind our personal minds which imposes the same world-image upon them all, so that all see it and live in it. Moreover, they are of necessity themselves projected by this Mind so that this image is not less real for them than their own selves. The mind makes for itself this world of illusion, this stage of space and time and form. But it does not make it independently of all prompting. For the image that it constructs is imposed upon it—or projected into it—by the Mind behind it.

65

The Theosophic doctrine that the physical world is an externalization of an astral plane or even the higher Platonic doctrine that it crystallizes a world of divine ideation is given to beginners as a help to give them a crude grasp, a first step towards the theory that the world is an idea, until they are mentally developed. When their mind is mature they are then told to discard the astral plane theory and told the pure truth that all existence is idea.

66

A popular misconception of mentalism must be cleared. When we say that the world does not exist *for man* apart from his own mind, this is not to say that man is the sole world-creator. If that were so he could easily play the magician and reshape a hampering environment in a day. No!—what mentalism really teaches is that man's mind perceives, by participating in it, the world-image which the World-Mind creates and holds. Man alone is not responsible for this image, which could not possibly exist if it did not exist also in the World-Mind's consciousness.(P)

67

The precise shape which the idea will take when it reaches consciousness will depend on the general tendencies of the person.(P)

68

Since the world is never found to be apart from our own minds, we are forced to relate it to them. And since it is equally obvious that the surface part of them does not deliberately bring it into existence we are further forced to deduce, first, that the deeper and unconscious part must do so and, second, that this second part must be cosmic in nature and hold all other individual minds rooted in its depths. This deduction, arrived at by reason, is confirmed by experience but not by ordinary experience. It is confirmed by sinking a shaft down through the mind in mystical meditation and arriving at our secondary cosmic self.(P)

69

The World-Mind is not a magnified man and the world-image is not "pushed" into our consciousness by its personal and persistent effort. The mere presence of this image in it is sufficient to produce a reflected image in all other minds although they will absorb only so much as their particular plane of space-time perception can absorb.(P)

70

The individual mind presents the world-image to itself through and in its own consciousness. If this were all the truth then it would be quite proper to call the experience a private one. But because the individual mind is rooted in and inseparable from the universal mind, it is only a part of the truth. Man's world-thought is held within and enclosed by God's thought.(P)

71

Are we, and the universe too, neither subjects nor objects but projects?

72

A metaphysical tenet which has previously been studied is that the stored-up karmic impressions of world-experience live powerfully and continuously within the personal consciousness as thought-forms of those external things and beings which form the basis of its own separateness. Indeed, without his knowing it they compel the individual to think this world into his personal experience. Therefore man cannot have the body-thought without having the world-thought at the same time. The reverse is equally true. His consciousness of the physical ego is interlocked with his consciousness of the physical world. This is why he loses the conjoint consciousness of both during sleep when the "I"-thought lets go of the body-thought and is itself withdrawn into the mind. If now we consider meditation again, we find that when attention becomes so concentrated on its object that it actually identifies itself with it, then the consciousness of the latter as a separate existence stops altogether. The process which begins with simple concentration gradually flows until it consummates itself in deep reverie. Mentally there is then only a single thought and physically a state of intense self-absorption is induced. The latter will indeed seem to an outside observer to be what he is likely to call a "trance" and it is generally so called by writers on the subject of yoga. Hence when an ordinary yogi is able to bring his thinking operations to a dead stop as the climax of his practices, all these karmic impressions are annulled. The five senses then cease operating because the mind's attention is absent from their organs, with the consequence that the entire external world disappears from his field of consciousness and he passes into a trance. Nature, however, reasserts herself and revives the impressions, with the consequence that he passes out of his trance and back into world awareness again. If now he ruminates over what has happened to him he feels, then, that the world is only a thought.

73

Just as religion is a foreshadowing of philosophy and just as an anthropomorphic God is a faint adumbration of the One for crude minds, so the divisions into matter and mind, objective reality and inner fancy, this world and an unseen world, are unconscious foreshadowings of the mind and its world-thought.

74

If each object of human experience is but an idea in the human mind, all the objects, including all the human beings themselves, constitute but a single idea in the divine Mind—the World-Idea.

75

Those who cannot accept the doctrine of mentalism have sometimes thought up very clever attempts to refute it. My friend, Professor Ernest Wood, once said to me that by leaving any object in a dark room and by turning a camera in its direction, fitted with a light and operated by a timing switch, so as to switch on the light in the absence of any human being in the room, a photograph of the object would thus be taken; and its existence apart from the thought of any human being would thus be proven. He said that an even simpler refutation of mentalism would be to walk over some rubbish in the dark which you did not know was there and to stumble over it. You could not possibly have thought of its existence, not knowing it was there, and yet it did exist! The answer to these clever criticisms is simple. Professor Wood, in the first case, had forgotten the person who had put the camera and the light in the dark room. That person had turned the camera towards the object and must surely have been thinking of the object. This, however, is only an answer to satisfy the requirements of logic; the real answer which philosophy gives is that the world-thought is given us by the Cosmic Mind—we do not create it. The presence or absence of any particular object within it does not therefore depend upon the individual thinking it, but his awareness of it *will* depend on this. The object in the dark room, the heap of rubbish in a dark street, exist for any individual's experience only so far as they come into his consciousness. Whether or not they exist for him at other times or for other men or for the Cosmic Mind does not and cannot alter this single fact—that his senses could never tell him about them unless his mind tells him about them, first and last.

76

Just as a man cannot lift himself up by means of his own shoelaces, so he cannot ordinarily get outside his own world-idea; the very faculty by which he sees and hears his surroundings selects some vibrations and shuts out others.

77

The language of the workshops is meaningless when applied to the world. The question of who "made" it simply does not arise for the man who has pushed philosophical enquiries to their farthest conclusion.

78

Consciousness, with all its wonderful attributes and capacities, is a faculty shared with the World-Mind, however shrunken it may be in man.

79

The experience gained through the physical senses is similar to, but not identical with, the experience gained through the imagination. That means they are both forms of mental experience but your imagination is entirely your own private affair, whereas the world-idea is a process wherein you participate with God, who holds this world-idea and you also with the Infinite Mind.

80

The individual person participates in this making of his world (although unconsciously and involuntarily) in this projection of the mind.

81

Supplementing the answer to your first group of questions, it should be said that *your* thought of things and people and surroundings makes their existence dependent on you for yourself alone. For other people, experience of the same objects depends on their thought and not on yours. The reason for this common experience is that there is one cosmic mind behind your mind and the other people's minds.

82

Are we to assume, as the unexamined and unanalysed experience tells us, that there is an external object outside us and an internal cognition of it inside us? No!—mentalism asserts that a cognition has only another cognition for its object, that the private and personal idea of the world "picks up" the cosmic and universal idea of it.

83

He who experiences the world, who touches, sees, and hears it through the five physical senses, actually gives it existence for himself. But this would not be possible if he were really, solipsistically, alone. He is not. For his little circle of mind is embedded in the larger circle of the World-Idea, itself the expression of the World-Mind. And it is from this fundament of all Being and, especially, Consciousness, that his personality gets its own consciousness. Man is literally in God but insists on holding to his littleness!

84

The interval between two thoughts is a very real thing yet not known for what it is because it is the merest fraction of a second. What is it? Consciousness. Deep sleep is the same but more continuous. It too is consciousness. Yet it too is not known for what it is. Why? The answer is that we have here a paradox. Consciousness not only gives us awareness of the world but also gives that world its very existence. We as individual entities share with the World-Mind in the making of that world from thought-stuff through the element of God in us but do not recognize this relationship, often denying it.

85

All the different kinds of phenomena which exist in the universe are all mental, manifested and received mentally by participation between the individual minds and the universal mind.

86

The faculty by which external contacts are perceived is not merely waking consciousness alone, nor even dream consciousness alone, but also the deeper mind behind both. Although the world exists for the individual because his ordinary consciousness perceives it, it does not exist for him only because of that. The deeper Mind is the universal element within him, above the personal and separate consciousness. The stimulus for his perceptions is indirectly derived from it too.

87

The existence of "archetypal ideas" or "divine thoughts" can be proven to exist nowhere else except in his own mind, therefore they have no more reality, no more value, and no more duration than other thoughts. The cosmic mind and his mind are ultimately one and the same. False habits of thinking cause false perception; hence he is not aware of this. The cosmic mind "created" all these ideas of objects in the universe, *including the self, the "I,"* in the same way that a dreamer creates his own dream universe. Mind is ALL we know, all we ever shall know. To discover what colour is, he must remember that the coloured object is itself but an idea; what can the colour be save an idea also?

88

When the mind is not active one is unaware of its existence—for instance, when attention is wandering or in deep sleep. A study of physiology shows that eye, nerve, and brain must combine to tell a person that he sees something and even then he does *not* see it until the mind pays attention to it. The truth is that the mind creates its own objects—but not the individual, finite mind; only the Mind which is back of it and which is infinite and common to all individuals. This is difficult to understand, so to make it easier one has to think of dream. In that state he can see cities, men, women, and children, mountains and flowers, hear voices, feel pain, and so forth. What is more, everything is so real then that at the time it is the waking state to him, not dream. Now who created all these scenes and things? Not his finite mind, for he is not conscious of having done so. Hence there is a larger mind within him which has this power of manufacturing scenes, objects, and events so vividly that he takes them to be real. This reality is a myth or, as the Indians call it, *Maya*.

Mrs. Eddy came extremely close to grasping this point and indeed of all the Western cults Christian Science stands closest to the ultimate teaching. Unfortunately it has mixed much error with truth and is ignorant of other vital teachings which are needed to complete the circle of knowledge. This impurity is due to the ego—the selfish, grasping personality which Mrs. Eddy possessed and which prevented her full initiation. The ego must be utterly yielded if one wants truth.

All this implies that matter is also a myth, unreal. Still more it implies that the ego is a myth, illusory. Here, then, is the first practice of the ultimate path: think constantly of that Mind which is producing the ego, all the other egos around, and all the world, in fact. Keep this up until it becomes habitual. The consequence is that one tends in time to regard his own ego with complete detachment, as though he were regarding somebody else. Furthermore, it forces him to take the standpoint of the *all*, and to see unity as fundamental being.

Those who have shown the worst features of hate, selfishness, brutality, and separateness are as much productions of this infinite Mind as others—only they have concentrated their full attention on the ego, and they have clouded reason by passion, while submitting to the stronger mental forces which propaganda has hypnotically let loose upon them.

89

Sensations belong to the subject himself; they are his own. But the same ones come to others, persist in all persons' world-experience. There is a consciousness, reflected in each one, which keeps the image intact. Hence part of the world-image does not originate with the person but with the World-Mind.

90

It may be asked: if mentalism is a true doctrine then why are we not able to alter physical things, such as our fleshly bodies, for instance, merely by exercising our thought upon them? We have to answer that it is the creative activity which gave rise to these things, and it is admittedly no less a mental activity than introspection, remembrance, and reverie, but whereas the latter occur in the individual conscious mind, the former occurs independently of us in the cosmic subconscious mind; and that the miracles which do unquestionably occur occasionally are primarily performed by the cosmic will and only secondarily because the necessary conditions of intense concentration or utter self-surrender have been successfully provided. In short, man's creative power is only a semi-independent one.

91

Everything in this world is a thought in the Cosmic Mind. Man himself is no exception to this statement. He knows himself and he knows the things of his experiences only so far as he thinks of them.

92

In the end all things finally come from World-Mind and for us come from mind, which itself comes from the same source.

93

So long as men fail to understand that they are able to know they are experiencing the world only because there is an infinite Consciousness which is behind and which makes possible their own little consciousnesses, so long will they spurn truth and sneer at truth-revealers.

94

According to the mentalistic cosmogony, the universe is a theatre wherein each actor plays many different parts.

95

We experience the world through the activity of a Power greater than ourselves, yet, in another sense, it is still our own activity.

96

The world-idea is *thought* by the individual mind and, in the process, inevitably shaped according to its limitations. But the first cause and ultimate source of that idea cannot be this mind. For the idea is "given" to it. It must be sought for in that wherefrom the individual mind derives its own existence. It must be sought, therefore, in the World-Mind.

97

It is not enough to say that the world is man's idea. We need to know *why* he has it at all. To be sufficiently explained, his world-idea must be brought into relation with the World-Mind's world-idea, because his individual mind is inseparably rooted in the World-Mind.

98

It is on account of this union existing between the individual minds and the World-Mind that we are forced to give our attention to the world-idea.

99

If the egocentricity of human beings were to have free and full play in the making of their world-environment, the consequence would be a disorderly, disharmonious chaos and not an orderly, harmonious cosmos. But the fact that they are unable to create or mold the world to their will shows plainly that they have only a very limited role in world-making. It just is not true that the human mind can build a new body for itself or transform an old one, or shape its surroundings entirely according to its desires.

100

I came across the following humorous piece in *The Triple Abyss*, by Warwick Fairfax. It refers to Oxford.

There was a young fellow named Todd
Who said, "It's exceedingly odd
To think that this tree
Should continue to be
When there's no one about in the Quad."

The reply:

There is nothing especially odd;
I am always about in the Quad.
And that's why this tree
Can continue to be
When observed by
Yours faithfully, God.

4

THE CHALLENGE OF MENTALISM

If materialism reduces man to mere physical substance, mentalism magnifies him to the grander stature of Mind.

2

The mere definition of mentalism startles the common mind, antagonizes the materialistic mind, but comforts the spiritually oriented mind.

3

Mentalism is the first and best way of breaking through the glamour which the world's materiality throws over most people. The Real is hidden from them. Consciousness is then supposed to be a property belonging to a lump of matter. This upside-down assumption is a false piece of knowledge. It must be dropped from possession, from held faith and reasoned conclusion—and each person must do this for himself: no other can take his place, not even a guru—or the illusion will return.

4

So long as a man does not see that his sense experiences are really mental experiences, so long will the truth of spiritual being remain effectually veiled from him.

5

In this doctrine of mentalism we come upon the central mystery of philosophy.

6

The mentalist character of all their experience is little or not at all understood by the great mass of people. Yet, curiously and paradoxically, this truth is the hidden basis of their religious beliefs, no matter what sect they belong to, for mentalism alone can make plainer the idea of Spirit, and make plausible the operations of Spirit.

7

If he does not wish to trouble his head, he can comfortably accept the appearances of things; but then he will be living only in the comfort of illusion. If however he wants to ferret out what is *real* in existence he must put himself to some trouble. He must persevere, read and re-read these pages until the meaning of it all dawns suddenly upon him, as it will if he does. It is perfectly natural for man to regard as the highest reality the experiences which impress themselves most forcibly upon him, which are those gained externally through his physical senses, and to regard as but half-real the experiences which impress themselves least forcibly upon him, which are those created internally by his own thoughts and fancies. But if he can be brought, as a true metaphysics can bring him, to arrive intellectually at the discernment that when he believes he is seeing and experiencing matter he is only seeing and experiencing thought, and that the entire cosmos is an image co-jointly held in the cosmic and individual minds, he will not unconsciously set up all those artificial resistances to the mystical intuitions and ultramystical illuminations which wait in the future for him.(P)

8

If negatively it rejects the teaching of materialism that all mental conditions have their origin in matter, it has good reasons for its rejection. If positively it finds that Mind is the reality which sustains our experience of the world, it has the high authority of a long list of illustrious names to support it—from ancient India, China, and Greece to modern England, America, and Germany.

9

We do not intend to deal here with some supernatural "spirit" which does not explain the world but only mystifies us, which is beyond all ordinary experience and whose existence cannot be irrefutably proved. We do not need to go beyond Mind—which explains the world as a form of consciousness, which is everyone's familiar experience at every moment of the day or night, and whose existence is unquestionably self-evident, for it makes us aware of every other kind of existence.(P)

10

It is because men are deceived by their senses into accepting materialism that they are deceived by their ego into committing sin. Mentalism is not only an intellectual doctrine but also an ethical one.(P)

11

Mentalism as the key to the understanding of the nature of the universe dissolves materialism. In this way it restores *real* religion to its rightful place and importance, but it does not restore the hollow semi-materialistic theatrical performance which passes for it. It restores a truer concept of God and brings back a solidly based faith in God.

12

If God is not the inner reality of this universe, then Matter is both its inner and outer reality. There will then be no room in the thinking mind for any belief other than materialism, no place for religion, no admittance to a spiritual metaphysics.

13

The notions of existence of fairies, *devas*, gods, goddesses, and especially of invisible worlds and planes and invisible beings and spirits are given through the form of popular myth and simple religion to primitive humanity partly to help them up from crude materialism and partly to foreshadow the doctrine that all worlds and all people are ideas. For ideas are as beyond the senses as are the invisible worlds and their beings. The early races of men would never have been able to understand idealism, and so an intermediate and understandable doctrine was given them; they could imagine heavens and hells and spirits as existing somewhere, even when they could not imagine that the solid earth was mere idea.

14

That man can hold the secret of this stupendous universe in his little head is something to be marvelled at.

15

The dematerializing of human belief has to pass through more than one stage before the process completes itself. All religious, metaphysical, and mystical systems which recognize the existence of Spirit but, side by side with it, the reality of Matter also, have passed through the earlier stages but not through the later ones. Only when they advance to mentalism will this final dematerialization be possible.

16

When a man begins to make Thought the subject of his thoughts, he opens a path to great discoveries.

17

Once rid of the basic error of materialism, once he has comprehended mentalism, the way is open for a real, and not illusory, progress.

18

How many riddles shall we solve, how many secrets unlock, when we solve the riddle of our own mind!

19

Man's search for an intelligible meaning in the universe can have no full success until he divests his thought of its materialistic assumptions and replaces them by mentalistic facts.

20

If the basic teaching of Mentalism seems too daring to risk acceptance, too impossible to be credible, he should look into the statements of celebrated persons who supported it—Plato, Plotinus, Chuang Tzu, Sir James Jeans, Bishop Berkeley.

21

Is mentalism suited to the world's present needs? On scientific, cultural, practical, and religious grounds, we reply Yes.

22

It was a favorite saying of my venerable old teacher, the late Subramanya Iyer, that you may measure the spiritual profundity of a people or nation by its appreciation and acceptance of the doctrine of mentalism.

23

Truth, in its higher reaches, is subversive of common sense, shattering to common mentality, and inconceivable to ego-cramped persons.

24

To be initiated into "The Mysteries" is to be introduced to the revelation of Mentalism, to what it means and to what startling consequences it leads; it is to discover that life, after all, no matter how thrilling, is like a dream passing in the night. But even the uninitiated are not allowed to stay in perpetual ignorance. For the tremendous event of leaving the body at death is attended by the enforced learning of this lesson, however much a man clings to his memories of this world.

25

With intellectual assurance, mystical experience, and the sages' confirmation, he can afford a wholehearted assurance about the truth of mentalism.

26

If it can make a man radiant and his aura vibrant, as mentalism properly understood can, it surely has sufficient inspiration behind it.

27

We may weep over, or laugh at, the human situation but whatever we do it is prudent to look at it through the glass of mentalism.

28

Unless there is a thorough understanding and appreciation of mentalism, several other important doctrines will remain incomprehensible to the human mind, or else will be incorrectly interpreted.

29

To understand this, to believe in the reality of mind and in the falsity of matter, is to escape from a delusion a hundred times subtler than the delusion that the earth is still, when in fact it is really moving quicker than the quickest train.

30

There are certain guiding ideas which are essential to a properly balanced life and one of them, however surprisingly, is that of mentalism.

31

To have his beliefs turned upside down and inside out may be painful for a man, but it could also be beneficial. This is certainly the case concerning the belief in mentalism.

32

Adherents of religion, practisers of meditation, and dabblers in spiritism, magic, or occultism can hypnotize themselves into believing anything, such as that there is no individual self, no physical world, and no physical disease. All these beliefs may be contradicted by their own experience or may be confirmed in temporary mental states. If the former, they ignore or explain away the contradiction. If the latter, the state passes away and they return to normal—a common phenomenon of hypnotism. Mind can play tricks upon itself, by itself, upon others. To understand what is true and what is false in such beliefs we must turn away from their parrot-like repetition to the study of mind in its various phases. This is supposedly done, and in great detail, in the academic world; but the central, the most important point is entirely missed. To learn what that is, study Mentalism.

33

When we ask what is the purpose of the individual's existence, we shall find that the physical world can give us neither a complete nor a satisfying answer.

34

This doctrine is the spinal column of the whole body of philosophic teaching.

35

Through mentalism he will learn to question the earth's seeming reality and his own personality's seeming identity.

36

From this single idea of mentalism, several others take their birth.

37

This thought, this idea, is as topical and living today as it was in the time of the Greek Proclus, the Chinese Chuang Tzu, and the Hindu Vasistha.

The effort required

38

The teachings of mentalism must be turned round and round, like a globe, until every aspect of it is seen and studied.

39

To appreciate the teaching that the world is an appearance is immeasurably easier than to establish its actuality in consciousness.

40

The road from mentalism as conception to mentalism as a conviction is a long one.

41

Few will welcome an astounding teaching like mentalism which turns their beliefs, ideas, even experiences, upside down.

42

When a man really understands this tenet of mentalism, he will admit its truth for he cannot help but do so. The defect in those who combat or reject it is a defect in investigation, study, and knowledge.

43

Faith in mentalism sometimes comes abruptly, on its very first presentation, when it comes with shattering force. More often it comes slowly, after having been fought by doubt and argument every step of the way.

44

If he becomes a real thinker he may also come in time to a self-conversion to the basic truth of mentalism.

45

Mentalism, the teaching that this is a mental universe, is too hard to believe for the ordinary man yet too hard to disbelieve for the illumined man. This is because to the first it is only a theory, but to the second it is a personal experience. The ordinary man's consciousness is kept captive by his senses, each of which reports a world of matter outside him. The illumined man's consciousness is free to be itself, to report its own reality and to reveal the senses and their world to be mere ideation.(P)

46

The spirit of true Science must be ours, too. We can accept nothing as true which is dubious as undemonstrable. The modern world, and especially the Western world, can sympathize with a teaching only if it will stand the double test of reason and experience.(P)

47

Only a highly educated mind can appreciate *intellectually* the truth which lies in mentalism, as only a highly intuitive one can *feel* its truth.(P)

48

If the Sphinx of mystic wisdom has kept her secrets well down all these centuries, she has not kept them from a few probing minds who have attained a sufficient measure of emancipation from the body to possess the proper equipment for such exploration.

49

It is seldom that the meaning of mentalism is immediately grasped; this is why it needs both explaining and approaching from various angles.

50

If we examine the world with the surface-faculties of the mind, we get a surface-result. If, however, we examine it with the deeper faculties, we shall get a deeper result.

51

It is not only a doctrinal belief to be accepted but also a metaphysical truth to be understood.

52

We dwell in a shadow world which seems to the unenquiring solid and substantial and therefore quite real. A man must do much to himself to make the journey from the illusion of the one to the illumination of the other.

53

How shall thinking man find his way out of the materialism into which his thought has led him? Consciousness is the clue. For if he will follow up this Ariadne-thread it will lead him into the liberating knowledge of mentalism.

54

In the beginning, Mentalism needs both study and thought, repeated again and again until the leap into understanding is finally made. When that happens there is a kind of intellectual catch-of-the-breath. From then onward it becomes a clear irrefutable doctrine. It is even more: it inspiringly opens the way to the major truths of real religion.

55

It is a truth which, because of its tremendous importance, its eternal unchanging character, clamours to be proclaimed to every age afresh but which, because of its very nature, is the least mentioned, the most unfamiliar of all. However late in his life a man discovers this truth for himself, its surprise is overwhelming. For most people are simply not ready to receive it.

56

Intellect, because of insufficient data or emotional distortions, may be misleading. Sense, whether touch or sight, because of physical and mental illusions, may be deceptive. Thus we are forewarned by the practical experiences of life not to reject mentalism hastily merely because it offends intellect or conflicts with sense. It is easy for the impatient to dismiss mentalism with an irritable stamp of the foot, as Dr. Samuel Johnson did the kindred teaching of Berkeley, but men who have given more time and thought to this subject are not so hasty in reaching a conclusion. After thirty years of teaching academic philosophy in London, Dr. C.E.M. Joad was forced to confess that the questions involved in mentalism are too difficult to be settled with any degree of certainty.

57

It is a doctrine which shocks common sense and clashes with simple experience. For it is ineffably subtle and immeasurably supersensuous. It can make its way into men's hearts only by struggling long and hard with them.

58

Every philosophy must *start* with things as they are, as we find them, and then it ascends up to higher and ultimate truths. We find matter to be real. So we do not assume its unreality, but proceed to *prove* that on the initial basis of its reality. But blind dogmatists reverse the process and start with unproved dogmas.

59

He should not rest satisfied with hazy notions of mentalism but should get its principles in sharp, clear focus. If necessary he should return and reconsider them until they are well understood. This may demand hard work but it is well worthwhile.

60

Only the unreflective man can be a materialist, for only he can accept the prosaic fact of the world's existence without enquiry into what lies beneath it. The man who can make his reflections deep enough and sustained enough mentally discovers that the world's appearance is illusionary and that the world's reality certainly does not lie in its materiality.

61

Mentalism has evoked disdain, ridicule, or attempts to refute it, but none has successfully done so.

62

The *idea* must sink ever deeper and deeper if it is to become strong and resurface later as understanding and conviction.

63

I have met very few people who really understand what is the simplest of all mystical, religious, and metaphysical tenets and yet, at the same time, the most important of them all—mentalism.

64

It is a measure of the depth, subtlety, and freedom of a man's mind how far he can follow the thread of mentalism to a point where he himself must refute materialism.

65

It is by repeatedly returning to an idea so utterly strange as this mentalism, learning to know it well and making oneself thoroughly familiar with it, that the materialistic resistance to it is gradually diminished.

66

Some are not so arrogant as to dismiss it with scorn. But it bewilders them all the same because it is too far from their experience and comprehension.

67

When the understanding of mentalism attains maturity the conviction of its truth attains finality. There will be no foothold for doubt. Thereafter the mentalist's attitude becomes unshakeable.

68

Everyone sees first only the absurdity of mentalism; some, proceeding to investigate, become bewildered by it; a few, persevering until they master it, see its truth.

69

They are victims of their experience: the world is solid, so it seems to be material; it is continuous and lasting, so it seems to be real. Only instruction, intuition, profound thinking, or profound mystical experience can dissuade them from their ignorant opinion and show them that it is the Consciousness behind their experience which is real.

70

We, the universe, everything, are pure Mind. This is unchangeable, hence unevolutable, or it could not be the Real. Once you awaken to IT you know it always was what it is; it can never evolve. All the rest was a kind of self-hypnotization, hence unreal. In that sense the Garden of Eden story is correct. We were then immortal, immaterial, innocent. We lost this by losing our awareness and accepting a limited idea of ourselves. We have been driven out of the Garden because we wanted knowledge. Knowledge presupposes "a second thing"—something to be known. Thus we lost unity, sought a world of objects, and got into oblivion of self. The happy Edenic state can be restored by right thinking and de-hypnotization of ourselves.

71

A rare few understand and *know* the truth of mentalism; they have validated it intellectually and verified it experientially: its mystical side is open to them daily and they pass into it nightly. But the great mass of people have never even heard of it.

72

Inevitably, as his reflections on mentalism continue and deepen and his intuitions assert themselves, a man comes to the time when it triumphs. Then, subtly, what he regards as reality changes and shifts from matter to mind.

73

Wide experience shows that it is not worth trying to convince those who deny this fundamental axiom. They lack the power to think abstractly and mere reiteration will not supply it. To expect them to be able to set aside their present standpoint and leap up to a higher one is vain; to explain what is incomprehensible to them is useless.

74

It would be better to keep silent than to make concessions out of weakness to the multitude's bias or incredulity. For mentalism is admittedly hard to apprehend until the last stages of meditation alters its level. The ego's heavy weight falls off his shoulders then: it imperceptibly lets go.

75

If the understanding of the truth of mentalism sinks deep enough, it will become lasting enough in the same way that the understanding of two plus two equals four remains an established knowledge.

76

The mentality which can carry its thought deep enough, and sustain the single line long enough, will in the end have to give intellectual assent to this grand concept.

77

Belief in materiality is natural because men need form and images, something touchable, whereas only developed minds can receive into consciousness abstract ideas like mentalism's truth and reality. Hence materiality—that is, *maya*, deception, illusion—is easily accepted.

78

The central truth of mentalism is both easy and hard to understand.

79

Mentalism is not to the taste of most people. It does violence to their common sense. It is too little known, hence has few followers. There are two kinds of truth: one is the truth of appearances, and the other is hidden deep down. The first is easy to understand; the other requires much work on one's own mind to get it sharp enough to recognize what is so elusive.

80

Put in the shortest way, mentalism is the teaching that all human experience is mental experience. But this truth does not come by itself to the uninstructed.

81

A special kind of patience is needed to gain a correct understanding of mentalism. The key idea that the world's existence (including our own, since we too are a part of it) is in the end a mental one can be set down in a single sentence. But the clear and full grasp of all its implications could absorb the larger fraction of a lifetime for many persons, or a few months only for others.

82

It is not easy to perceive the truth of mentalism: if it were, religion would not have been needed nor mysticism practised. Thought and feeling must struggle with themselves, and suffer, before illusion is shifted out of the way.

83

Many who tried to understand mentalism have complained that they could not do so. Such an intellectual failure is understandable. The old thought-habits need a total reconstruction. The new ones, bringing in new ideas, must be learned until acceptable and then practised patiently.

84

The fact is that there are few actual mystics but many more would-be ones. Consequently there are few who fully recognize, understand, and accept this truth of mentalism.

85

No man becomes a confirmed mentalist save after many doubts and some lapses, after strenuous reflections extending over years, and mystical intuitions manifesting in spite of himself. The strangeness and mystery of this doctrine are too baffling to be overcome either easily or quickly.

86

The acceptance of mentalist views is perhaps possible only after a great strain upon the intellect and the emotions has been passed through and left behind. This is comprehensible because the changeover from the familiar and conventional standpoint is so immense and so abrupt.

87

A modern man, educated in the scientific outlook, feels as a first reaction to such statements the impulse to reject them. A wiser reaction would be to take second thoughts and enquire into the reasons which prompted the seers to make them.

88

Unreflective minds are amazed, then scornful, when they first hear someone deny the existence of matter. Reflective minds are equally amazed but less scornful. If they take the trouble to investigate the assertion, they may be left with an uncomfortable suspicion that there might be something in it, even though they feel it too deep or too difficult for a final judgement.

89

A man needs to be extremely scrupulous about his own thinking, about what it contains of influences, suggestions, and preconceptions, before he can reflect philosophically about the Truth. That few persons arrive at mentalism is mostly because they fail to do so.

90

If in earlier eras a select tiny minority alone could take hold of the basic truths of mentalism, because they alone had the educational preparation, the intellectual development and emotional refinement, the personal leisure and the will to do so, in this era the ordinary man may, at least in part, do so. Teachings and revelations formerly regarded as inaccessible in his case can now have more interest and some meaning for him.

91

The physical world exists as a reality only with reference to the physical senses. For when insight is developed it is seen to be a mental state. How can the two views be harmonized? By analysis and study, by pondering over the very idea itself, and by deeper meditation. Spirit is thenceforth no enigma to the intellect.

92

The theory of mentalism is not understandable by the ordinary man when he is presented with it for the first time. It then seems puzzling as the hieroglyphics on an Egyptian papyrus. But if the same man will perseveringly study the explanations of it, eventually light will break in on his mind and he will see its truth.

93

The very idea that this world is not what it seems to be would yield an uncanny feeling did it not yield a derisive one much more to the vulgar mind.

94

In dealing with those who have not evolved enough to understand, much less accept, such a high doctrine as mentalism, it becomes necessary to modify, simplify, or even withhold it for a time.

95

Up to a certain point, the teachings are well within the mental grasp of any average mentality, but beyond that point they are not.

96

Whether we begin by accepting no knowledge not born out of common experience or whether we begin by accepting conclusions derived from transcendental dogmas, the end will be the same: mentalism!

97

It is the easiest of acts to reject mentalism but the hardest to refute it.

98

The sensation which a man experiences when he first begins to investigate mentalism is something like the one he experiences when standing on his head.

99

How few have reflected that all this multitude of different thoughts which stream through their consciousness presupposes the existence of a single Thought-stuff?

100

By applying either his belief in, or his knowledge of, mentalism and throwing everything into Mind, he practises nondualism and gets rid of the divided subject-object attitude. This work may take many years or it may not: it must be done calmly, patiently, without attempting to measure progress—itself an obstructive idea.

101

Those who have not had the inward revelation granted them, who have not awakened what the Hindu yogis call *antardrishti*, a kind of clairvoyant insight, often believe that mentalism is mere theory and that its talk of the world's unreality is mere verbalism. Even some among the seers have not seen this, although they have seen much else that fleshly eyes cannot. Sri Aurobindo in India, for instance, disputed mentalism, although his neighbour and contemporary, Ramana Maharshi, fully accepted it. Rudolf Steiner in Switzerland likewise disputed it although J.J. van der Leeuw, his Dutch contemporary, understood and explained it. This situation is strange, but among the sages with whom I found the deepest penetration into the nature of things and who were nearly all mentalists, some observed that the capacity to receive and understand the mentalist doctrine was the sharpest of all tests to which a truth-seeker could be subjected.

102

Many years ago Einstein was reported as criticizing Jeans and Eddington for their mentalistic views. He asked why anybody like the astronomer Jeans should trouble to look at the stars if he did not believe that they were really there. This is a tremendous misconception of the mentalist position.

103

If a study is made of the way in which we become aware of physical things, the process by which we perceive Nature around us, and if we put the collected facts into logical order and extract a logical conclusion from them, we shall understand a little better why the world's profoundest thinkers and most illumined mystics were mentalists.

104

No one yet has successfully refuted the *logical* truth of mentalism. Yet few people *feel* it to be true and therefore few can bring themselves to accept it. It is easy for a solitary mystic here and there who has been granted the revelation through his mystical experience, to adhere stubbornly to the statement that the world is a product of consciousness. But for others belief wavers and doubt undermines.

105

Tolstoy, when a mere youth, caught a glimpse of mentalist truth but fell into solipsistic fallacy. He thought he alone existed and that he merely had to withdraw his attention from the world-idea, and then it would completely vanish. Sometimes he even turned round abruptly, hoping to see this vast void!

106

It is strange how illuminated mystics have been unable to agree with each other on the question of mentalism and its truth. Among the moderns, Rudolf Steiner vehemently opposes it, whereas Ramana Maharshi strongly upholds it. Among the ancients, Patanjali deliberately attacked it, whereas Gaudapada specially advocated it. And if we leave the mystics for a moment and turn to the scientists, the same puzzling contradiction will be found: Thomas Henry Huxley and Sir Arthur Eddington bravely endorsed mentalism, whereas Einstein openly ridiculed it. How, when these great minds cannot settle the problem of mentalism once and for all, can the lesser ones of the mass of humanity hope to solve it?

107

There is one sentence in Professor Joad's book entitled *God and Evil* in which he mentions that after studying and teaching philosophy for thirty years he is unable to make up his mind either way about the truth of mentalism. This, if anything, should be a caution against its quick rejection, even though it is admittedly not an argument in its favour.

108

The mentalist position is the most acceptable of all to the philosopher not only because it has come down to him as a traditional teaching of the sages of antiquity, not only because it has proved itself to him in his own personal ultramystic experience, but because of the best of all reasons—it is irrefutable.

109

Solipsism is a belief into which a man more easily falls if he is a castaway alone on an unvisited island or lost in an uninhabited desert. Those who live in the world of action, who have obligations to and responsibilities in it, who are involved in social occupational and business relationships, are more protected against the solipsistic illusion.

110

We are moving in a subtle and delicate world when we are moving in the world of mind. It is necessary to comprehend our terms carefully and correctly if we are to understand the teaching of mentalism truthfully.

111

The Indians have built an entire metaphysical system—the Advaita—around the Upanishadic statement: "The Self alone exists." This might be called spiritual solipsism. To experience during meditation a state confirming this belief is their highest goal. The mind's power to create its own "inner experiences" is known, a power once alluded to by Ramana Maharshi as "expectancy" but which we in the West call "suggestion." The higher phases of Buddhist psychology refer to an almost identical experience as the Advaitic, but in their reference the Self does not enter the picture and its existence is never affirmed. In Mentalism it is understood that consciousness can shed its thoughts during the experience of Mental Quiet—also similar—including thoughts of the world and even of the individual ego, but it is not therefore claimed that these thoughts have no existence too and have never had any at any time. All this shows once again that mystic experience, even in its more advanced stage, is one thing and its interpretation—usually unconsciously made and religiously influenced—is another.

112

Mentalism leads neither to solipsism (one's own existence is the only existence) nor to Hindu Advaita's denial of the World's existence. The first is a misreading and consequent misunderstanding of it caused by a failing to see that the individual ego is itself a projection of Mind. The second fails to see that as an experience in the field of awareness of that ego, as a given and fundamental idea in that consciousness, it is a coexistent and not to be denied without impairing sanity.

113

We celebrate the tough logic of mentalism, its metaphysical truth and practical power.

114

The test of reality is non-contradiction.

115

There are cults which take the truth of mentalism but misapprehend and pervert it by fallacious reasoning. They do this in order to, as they believe, gain prosperity and regain health.

116

What even he cannot deny is the consciousness within himself. This, if he only knew, is part of the Universal Consciousness.

117

But if mentalism solves some of the major problems of existence, it raises some minor ones of its own. These perplex the beginner.

Accepting the Truth

118

All life is a paradox, being at once a combination of reality and appearance. An obstacle to the comprehension of mentalism is that one persistently, if unconsciously, views the world from the standpoint of the lower personality, which is extremely limited, and not from that of the higher individuality, which transcends both the intellect and the senses. Even life on earth in the body is really a kind of mystical experience from the standpoint of the mentalist but it is only a blurred, vague, and symbolic one. The thinking intellect finds it hard to grasp this situation because it is itself something which has been greatly filtered down out of the higher individuality. Mentalism can be understood up to a point through the use of reasoning but after this point it can only be understood through the use of intuition.

119

The first acquaintance with some of these ideas—especially the mentalist nature of the world and the future of the personal ego—alarms some people and makes them withdraw from any further interest in such frightening notions.

120

The simpleton is taken in by appearances. Whether he be a peasant in the field or a politician in the forum, he accepts what he touches, sees, or hears as being nothing more and nothing less than what it purports to be.

121

That mental processes are a function of the physical body, that they cannot be separated from one another, that thinking and sense-perception have neither existence nor meaning apart from physiology, that mind is identified with flesh and cannot be otherwise—this is the theory of materialism. And a plausible one, too!

122

Materialists of the scientific kind believe that there is a real material world of nature which is reflected, through sensation and thought, in the human mind. Materialists of the religious kind hold the same belief but add to it belief in a second real world—that of the Spirit. Mentalists reject this belief in a material world and declare the latter to be an appearance to sensation, an idea to thought; they know only a single reality—MIND—and a direct relationship only with its products—ideas.

123

We must understand that matter is not a thing but a thought within consciousness.

124

The truth of mentalism can be appreciated and accepted only by those who are either mentally competent to do so or intuitively ready for it. If any man cannot free his mind sufficiently from the erroneous suggestions with which either scientific materialism or religious dogma have straitjacketed it, he will reject the idea. And if he cannot ponder the questions involved with sufficient discernment and penetrate them with sufficient depth, he will reject it too.

125

Bertrand Russell in his book *Knowledge of the External World* came near to the metaphysical truth. In the end he couldn't make the leap over the gap. The reason why people can't make the leap is that they are so deeply identified with the body alone. This in turn depends partly on the way of life and partly on mental sensitivity.

126

The deceptions bred by an unreflective attitude towards the reports of sense and an unintuitive one towards the feeling of personality, enter so deeply into his mental principle because of their growing prevalence during a large number of births that they become almost an integral part of it. The melancholy consequences of this disposition are an inability to believe in mentalism and an incapacity to progress in mysticism.(P)

127

The illusions of materialism can in the end best be dispelled by the revelations of religious or mystical experience.

128

It is the incapacity of our thinking, the poverty of our perception, the vividness of our sense-experiences, and the encrustation of our habitual outlook which creates and maintains the illusion of the world's materiality and prevents us from noting that it is really a presence within consciousness. How can those who test reality like Dr. Johnson by using their feet or like any bricklayer by using their hands affirm any other doctrine than that of materialism? Contrarily, how can those who use their God-given intelligence to test reality arrive in the end at any other doctrine than that of mentalism? Those materialists who tell us today that the line of the soul is an unscientific one and that it is a legacy left to us by primitive simpletons are themselves unscientific and oversimple. For science, which began by repudiating mind and exalting matter, is being forced by facts to end by repudiating matter and exalting mind. This is why philosophy today must sharply emphasize and teach, alongside of ancient lore, the profounder mentalist import of vital facts of modern discovery which have not yet received their deserved reward of recognition from the world.

129

Some people complain that knowledge of mentalism or belief in it cuts off the enjoyment of life and blunts the keenness with which we meet it. I answer: Is their enjoyment of a play at the theatre cut off in any way by their knowledge that it too is only a series of ideas? Are their feelings blunted because the whole show is only the imagination of some author sitting in his study? Are they less able to appreciate its drama, its humour, or its pathos because they know that, like every other thought, it must pass and end?

130

Those who wish to evade these concrete facts commit a fraud upon themselves and impair their own intellectual integrity.

131

The doctrine of mentalism cannot be proved completely to satisfy the materialist, but then he cannot disprove it either. To end the dilemma, as a contemporary writer on mysticism ends it, by dismissing it altogether from consideration as an "idle fancy" is to oppose the personal affirmation of mentalism's truth by eminent ancient and modern mystics.

132

The materialist may turn all the knobs on his radio and adjust them as he will, but he remains unable to tune in to mentalism's wavelength. This is because he insists on missing the point, which is: What about the person who is doing all this?

133

Without the power to produce abstract thoughts, how can anyone understand that the self, or the mind, Consciousness, even knowledge or perception, is an entity by itself and not merely a by-product of the fleshly brain?

134

Those who have never thought *through* their physical experience find the tenet of mentalism incredible, its contradiction of sense-evidence imaginary.

135

They are willing to believe in mentalism but it is a belief subject to doubts provoked intermittently by apparent contradiction coming from sense-experience.

136

The mentalist meaning gets lost alas! before this constant confrontation with hard outside objects, reminders of a presumed material stuff out of which they are made.

137

It is doubtful if God created those strange creatures, the materialists. They arrive on the scene of life with eyes closed to their own existence as *mind* but wide open to the existence of something which is not there, which they call *matter*.

138

Mentalism startles us because our thinking habits are still coloured throughout with materialistic assumptions.

139

If he himself is a mere nothing who does not exist, who then is it who takes all this trouble to prove it?

140

He puts onto the body, its brain and sense organs, powers and attributes which belong to the mind. This is his error: this is materialism.

141

If a man persists in acknowledging his bodily self alone and in denying his spiritual self, he is not to be blamed for that. His experience of life has brought him to this point of utter materialism while his power of metaphysical reflection has not developed enough to carry him beyond it. He is to be pitied therefore, rather than blamed.

142

If matter were real, or as real as Mind, then the latter could no longer be the only reality. God would then no longer be unique, the One Being that alone is the infinite Mind, but there would be at least another alongside of it and identical in attributes with it. There would be gods, but no God, which is absurd.

143

They believe that matter has formed by itself its highest product—Man—who in turn has put forth his own highest product in Thought. The next step from this is to proclaim that man's happiness wholly depends upon his environment and not at all upon his inner life.

144

Most people, even most pious people, are materialists. To them tangible things in a tangible world are the realities.

145

To Albert Camus, reflecting the decision of the ordinary simple yet articulate man, it is enough merely to say that he can touch the world to conclude that it exists.

146

Those who uphold the sunless idea that matter is the only thing, as well as those who would insert a ghostlike thing called mind into it, deride the mentalist's position. Yet they would shake their complacency if only they could get unstuck from the limitation and incompleteness of their views.

147

It is important to note that "matter" has gone out of scientific thought but materialism has not gone out of popular life.

148

To follow closely an exposition of mentalist metaphysics is to put a great strain upon the attention. After a time, when it finds the solid earth seemingly deserted, it struggles to get away, unable to bear the thin rarefied air in which it finds itself.

149

That this World, so solid to our touch, so important to our lives, is "such stuff as dreams are made of," in Shakespeare's haunting phrase, is incredible to the ordinary shallow materialist, whether he be of a scientific or a pious mind. But then, we must allow that mentalism, even if true, is a bizarre, a staggering idea.

150

The world rarely finds reality for it judges mostly by appearances and externals; hence the wide prevalence of materialism, whether it takes an open self-confessed form or a covert religio-hypocritical one.

151

Half of our puzzling problems follow in the train of our naïve but erroneous belief that matter is itself an ultimate reality.

152

When we are directly confronted with the logical implications of this mentalistic discovery we are likely to withdraw to safer ground.

153

It is an extraordinary fact, and perhaps a paradoxical one, that he who states the simple scientific truth that the only objects man knows are mental ones, that is, ideas, is usually considered mad.

154

Life extends far beyond the narrow domain of this our flesh. Those who deride this truth will live to learn strange and surprising things.

155

The true picture of a man is to be seen in his mind and heart, not in his body. Yet the world generally believes in, and acts on, the very contrary of this truth.

156

We are conscious creatures only because our bodies possess brains: without them we would know nothing. Such is the notion implanted in us by those educators who had themselves received it in their turn. Mind did not exist by itself; Soul and spirit were imagined and inconceivable things.

157

The materialist's mistake is to exaggerate the physical facet of existence and then make a worshipped fetish of it.

158

Those who are spiritually blind, who have never felt the attraction of any higher forces than those which affect the body's senses, may consider such belief to be fantastic.

159

Those who have no better concept of consciousness than the usual one regard any other as a curiosity, as unnatural, and not as something which might be worth the trouble of investigating, much less of acquiring.

160

He is still a materialist, however formally and outwardly religious, who does not believe or perceive the truth of mentalism, does not know that consciousness is apart from brain.

161

It is difficult for the true adherent of the Quest to get over this hurdle of anti-mentalism, largely because of certain mystical world-views. Without these, a closer accord would be reached. But here, of course, one is up against the difficulties brought about by the contradictory nature of such experiences.

162

The materialist who says that we humans come from nothing and that if there is an infinite being, a God, he is infinitely indifferent to us, is thinking only of the physical body.

The position of modern science

163

That the majority of men have been unable in the past to perceive mentalism's truth is fully understandable, even pardonable, if we admit how stubbornly unshakeable is the human sense of material reality. The only successful attack on it hitherto has been that made by actual personal mystical experience—but mystics formed only a minority among men. This is why the mid-twentieth-century discoveries in nuclear physics are so important, for they must lead ultimately to the full vindication of mentalism, as they have already begun to do partially.

164

The time will come, and cannot be avoided, when both the new and the accumulated facts will force scientists to regard Mind as the real thing they have to deal with, and matter as a group of states of mind. But by that time they will be something more than mere scientists alone; they will be somewhat on the way to becoming philosophical scientists.

165

The belief that to touch a wooden stick is to touch matter is no longer good science. And it was physics, a science with its feet well on the solid ground, which brought about this striking change in outlook.

166

In this century the two streams of science and mysticism are converging into mentalism.

167

When a mystical seer proclaimed on the basis of his own insight that the reality of the universe was not matter but mind, educated people could afford to disregard his proclamations. But when leading scientists themselves proclaimed it on the basis of verifiable facts and rational reflections, they could not help giving their confidence to it. Consequently, those who have seriously absorbed the latest knowledge have been falling away from intellectual materialism. It is indeed only the uneducated, the half-educated, the pseudo-educated, and the word-educated who today believe in this miserable doctrine.(P)

168

His feet tell him that the ground he walks on is truly there. His four remaining senses tell him something about the other objects around him. All his physical experience confirms the factuality of the world. It is certainly an existent thing. How is it, then, that the Hindus and Chinese have celebrated thinkers who claim that this existence is illusory? Can Shakespeare's play *Much Ado About Nothing* thus be given a surprisingly different and tremendously larger reference? Were this so, these Oriental dreamers would be most alarming. Surely Western science would not deign to consider them even for a moment? Let us pause and see.

169

Shankara's Snake-Rope illusion is out of date. Science provides better illustration based on facts of *continuous experience* instead of exceptional or occasional ones. Indians ignore the fact that a thousand years have travelled on and away since Shankara's time. Human intelligence has probed and discovered much. Modern evidence for mentalism is more solid today. The tremendous advance of knowledge since his time has shown that the substance of which this universe is made turns out to be no substance at all.(P)

170

Is there some precise universal criterion of truth which will be applicable at all times and under all circumstances, in short, something unchanging and therefore supreme? For scientists know that the great principles which formed landmarks in the history of science were really successive stages on the route towards the precise truth. Science changes, its doctrines change, and its earlier approximations are replaced from time to time by more accurate points. We cannot hope to find an ultimate truth nowadays, when science itself is so rapidly on the march. There remains, however, one unfailing all-embracing fact which will forever remain true and which cannot possibly change. Indeed, every advance in experiment and theory made by enterprising scientists will only help to verify this grand discovery. What is it? It is that the whole world which every department of science is busily engaged in examining is nothing but an idea in the human mind. Physics, chemistry, geology, astronomy, biology, and all the other sciences without a single exception are concerned solely with what is ultimately a thought or series of thoughts passing through human consciousness. Here, therefore, we possess a universal law which embraces the entire field in which science is operating. This is an ultimate truth which will stand immortal, when every other hypothesis formulated by science has perished through advancing knowledge.(P)

171

Let us not be bewitched by Oriental futility and deny what is palpably factual. It does not benefit truth, reason, or experience to deny the world's existence. It does not help the spiritual life to do so. It is a waste of time and an unnecessary cause of bewilderment or confusion to Western students, setting vain problems for them which they need never have had. This does not mean that they should desert the idea of nonduality and fall back into dualism. It means only that they should not repeat, like parrots, what others teach them without having first got a satisfactory understanding of the teaching and tested its truth or falsity. To say that the world does not exist is either a clumsy semantic error or one of those incomplete truths which, unless fitted to its other half, misleads others and leads him into a labyrinthine maze from which he either never gets out or takes years in the process. By deep enough meditation he may get into a half trance which tricks consciousness, so that he wriggles out of his five senses and loses his awareness of what they normally tell him. The world is gone. But is it really lost? For after his meditation he must come back to his senses when the world reappears like a faithful dog. Instead of rejecting its claim to exist, the honest thing is to accept it and make a proper appraisal of it. For the world is a phenomenon: as an appearance it certainly does exist. But it appears in the mind, *not in matter*. In the decade after the First World War great scientific research was made. Einstein's formulations on relativity are justly praised. Heisenberg's work on the structure of the atom with its ions, electrons, and quantums brought him the Nobel Prize. The most advanced workers in nuclear physics know the mentalist position if they have the willingness to reflect deeply enough upon their observed facts and the mathematical capacity to support this reflection. Few possess both. Most refuse to go so far because they dare not abandon the last remnants of materialism which got so intertwined with science during the past two hundred years that getting rid of them now actually seems unscientific: Einstein deliberately refused even though he had the capacity. Heisenberg accepted but would not publish his acceptance of the truth until now. I believe he will do so before passing away. Professor Carl von Weizsäcker, who worked in both fields—atomic physics and academic philosophy—also perceives the truth about reality but must leave the immense labour of presenting publicly the mathematical formulas involved, to a younger man. The point of all this is that we do not have to swallow the incredible doctrine of the world's non-existence in order to deny its materiality. Science properly demands an explanation of the world. If it pushes this demand to the fullest possible extent, it comes to the same truth as philosophy, even though it be by a different way. The world is what it is, an appearance in the little mind; but behind both is Mind, the great unchangeable reality which transcends all human thought and touch and which alone is, was, and will be.

172

When Shankaracharya wrote his brilliant texts and commentaries more than one thousand years ago, he was compelled to quote the example (now so well known) of the rope mistaken for a snake. Today we have a better and more convincing example which nuclear physical science has produced by showing that almost invisible energies were being mistaken for solid material substances before the invention of highly subtle, high-magnifying apparatus and instruments which however were unable to omit the investigator's consciousness from the energies discovered.

173

The bomb, whose shadow darkly threatens the whole planet in our time, is itself the last and latest demonstration that matter is an illusion. The atomic physics which alone made the bomb possible has penetrated to a level where matter has disappeared into radiation. There is no matter there, only radiant energy.

174

In reducing matter to a mere formula of mathematics, Einstein destroyed materialism through the appeal to intellect. Thus he really brought a spiritual message, even though it was couched in the modern idiom of his time—as another Jew, Jesus, brought a message that destroyed materialism through the appeal to faith nearly two thousand years ago.

175

It was the keen thought of Gaudapada, with no equipment, which enabled him to set down the truth of non-causality which Planck and Heisenberg have reached in our own day through the use of the last word in laboratories.

176

Science has begun to establish the fact that the world is really mind; Truth established the fact that the mind is the Self. One of the *Upanishads* says: "This (universe) is myself, who am all, that is His highest state."

177

The tremendous implications of mentalism for science and metaphysics, its enormous significance for mysticism and religion will quietly come into prominence before this century closes.

178

Some scientists are approaching the position that the world is ultimately an idea in the mind of the beholder. What will follow? They must next proceed to the position that an idea has precisely the same value as any mental picture seen in dream and hence must be just as imaginary, which leads to the final position that the idea has no real permanent existence.

179

The simple notion that the world is just a machine, that God is the mechanic who puts its parts together and that matter is the stuff he began with and used to make these parts, belongs to the primitive levels of scientific thinking. It is for those who are just beginning to form the conception of an orderly universe in their enthusiasm for the early discoveries of science.

180

Matter is energy, pulsating as waves or formed into knots.

181

If so-called matter consists of the energy of the electron, whether as wave or particle, where is its existence as solid substance? Quantum physics has so far unveiled the truth about matter.

182

When there is no weight, no volume, no inertia to be found in the ultimate atom, where is "matter"? It is no longer existent. But was it ever existent? Obviously deep and sustained reflection upon this question could only turn a physicist into a metaphysicist—and that is not permissible! Science must remain science: having started with the dogma that it has nothing to do with metaphysics or religion it ends with it!

183

"What we know by our senses alone has reality," wrote D'Holbach, the French Encyclopaedist "All is matter and force." He meant that matter was the real thing, and force was what pushed it about to take a variety of forms. But how did he know that matter was there? Was it not his own mind that told him so?

184

The universe cannot be explained by a few scientific theories, notions, laws, or discoveries. It is unimaginably complex. Even with the help of the most amazing equipment, instruments, apparati, science discovers the merest fraction of the facts about anything in the universe. But even more important is the very limited nature of the physical senses. They seem to report the existence of matter, to give us substance and reality, when what is, is an entirely different level—that of Mind.

185

The ideas of the scientist combine into an intellectual outlook which increasingly influences the leaders, the teachers, the fighters, and, so far as it filters down—the masses. To the measure that science comes to understand that what it examines or investigates leaves out the unconscious contribution made by the examiner or investigator, to that measure its conclusion is incomplete. Further, that contribution is selective; it can deal with objects only as far as it can penetrate the material of which they are made. There is in consequence something missing from the scientist's knowledge of the universe. It is the philosopher's discovery that this missing element is vitally and fundamentally important.

186

When he comes to understand on what are really scientific grounds that belief in the materiality of the world is groundless, he may come to a better tolerance of the Quest.

187

Until lately, the education of medical students, their observation of mental consequences of physical conditions, and the general attitude of recent science led them into materialism and thence to agnosticism. But several factors have begun, or else will shortly begin, a reversal of this process.

188

A medical scientist declared himself opposed to any association of physiology with psychology. It would only harm both, he believed. He said that no one knows the link between consciousness and matter. This statement is quite reasonable for anyone, materialist or religionist. Only the mentalist can solve the problem.

189

Matter as an independent principle is non-existent, whether it be physical matter, ethereal matter, astral matter, or something else. All these are merely conceptions.

190

The book of Sir James Jeans entitled *Physics and Philosophy* reveals what is the actual case. He concludes, "As we pass from this phenomenal world of space and time to this substratum, we seem, in some way we do not understand, to be passing from materialism to mentalism and so possibly from matter to mind. . . . Modern physics has moved in the direction of mentalism."

191

Eddington went much farther in acceptance of mentalism than Jeans. He told science quite plainly that no satisfactory explanation of matter can be made without postulating mind.

192

The geologist, the biologist, and the physicist do not refute mentalism with their evolutionary stories. They only describe some of the ways in which Mind works to throw up its images.

193

To trace the working of the senses, to explore the problems of knowledge, and to understand the implications of nuclear physics—to do all these things to the fullest possible extent is to come under the compulsion of rejecting the claim of materialism that there is only a material world and that we human beings are only material bodies; that all mental experiences originate in material conditions only is the naïve conception which today only a child may form and hold; all things today point to the truth of mentalism.

194

It was a younger professor of biology in New Zealand who said in my hearing that recent discoveries by neurobiology in connection with the cell were undermining the materialistic view of it hitherto held and were pointing to something more like consciousness or mentality as its essence.

195

Matter, as an entity in itself, though so scientifically acceptable at the beginning of the nineteenth century, will be scientifically untenable at the end of the twenty-first century.

196

Science has long known that matter is able to change into wave-like energy or particle-streamed energy. Philosophy comments that what you see, this world of objects and creatures, is not really what you think it is. It seems still, solid, stable, but all the time it is vibrating with unbelievable speed *and we, the observers, with it*. Only when we penetrate the calm centre of being do we find the real stability, the true substance.

197

Those who are too intellectually dishonest and too morally unscrupulous to be willing to accept the deeper implications of the new scientific knowledge because it would so endanger their whole position, are like criminals who do not believe in accepting the law of the land because it is against their interests to do so.

198

There is nothing in these concepts that is essentially new, but parts of their restatement with the help of modern scientific knowledge inevitably are new.

199

Science has travelled far towards the mentalist position when, in the person of Niels Bohr, one of its most distinguished researchers, it admits that the human entity is both a spectator and an actor in the world drama.

200

No scientist knows what matter is in itself.

201

The last outcome of all scientific research and metaphysical thinking is, and can only be, mentalism.

Mentalism and related doctrines

202

The metaphysical doctrine called "subjective idealism" is a first step towards truth but not at all the last step. Taken by itself, leaving the universe within man's little finite mind alone as it does, it can even lead to serious misconception and error. Only by putting the world where it originates—in the World-Mind—and then alone bringing man's participating and limiting mind into the scene, can the doctrine be completed and corrected!

203

Berkeley said there was no object, only the thought of it and the thinking self. Hume said there was no object and no thinker, only the thought. Both men were approaching truth, guided by reason and intuition, but could not clasp it altogether. For only insight could have led them farther.

204

It is not enough, as the earlier Western Idealists did, to take the physical senses—parts of the body—into relation with the physical objects—the world outside them—and then remove the barrier between the two metaphysically, and thus remove matter itself. It is necessary to advance further, into a positive recognition of Pure Mind-in-Itself, and not merely consider the relations between the senses and their objects.

205

Berkeley said he could find no Matter. Hume agreed and went further by saying he could also find no Soul or Self. But neither Kant nor Hegel denied the existence of Matter, as Berkeley did, though they did reduce this entire existence to a form of thought.

206

Hume rightly pointed out that the mind is a mere series of sensations but he wrongly concluded that the series is destitute of any connecting thread. He saw nothing in the world but momentary perceptions, and in perceptions he saw nothing at all. They arose and faded into a void. Thus it might be said of the Scottish thinker that his doctrine was a Nihilistic Idealism and his universe a meaningless one. "Everyone keeps at a distance," he complained. "I have exposed myself to the enmity of all metaphysicians and even theologians; and can I wonder at the insults I must suffer?"

207

I have tried to study the nature of the mind and to understand its office in knowing. And the end of all my studies brought me to the sequel that I was compelled to testify to Hume's strange statements: "Nothing is ever really present with the mind but its perceptions. . . . We never really advance a step beyond ourselves. . . . Philosophy informs us that everything which appears to the mind is nothing but a perception, and is interrupted and dependent on the mind, whereas the vulgar confound perceptions and objects, and attribute a distinct, continued existence to the very things they feel or see. There is no question of importance whose decision is not comprised in the science of mind; and there is none which can be decided with any certainty before we become acquainted with that."

208

Whitehead has endorsed mentalism to the extent of admitting, in his work *Process and Reality*, that "apart from the experiences of subjects there is nothing, bare nothingness."

209

Now the realist assigns a greater degree of reality to that world than to its observer, because he says it will be there even when the latter has passed away. The idealist, however, assigns all reality to the observer because the world cannot be known apart from the latter.

210

"Thought and the object of thought are one and the same."—Parmenides, the earliest Greek mentalist

211

Kant's analysis of cognition was his supreme achievement. He traced back the true sources of our knowledge.

212

Plato, on Mentalism: "What a superior being would have as subjective thought, the inferior perceives as objective things."

213

Kant asked the metaphysicians of his time to cease their wrangling regarding the nature of the universe and the principles of Being until they understood better the nature of our knowing process.

214

The mentalistic schools of Chinese Buddhism existed only from 600 A.D. to 1100 A.D. They were named the Fa-hsiang and the Wei-shih. The mentalist school of Japanese Buddhism was the Hosso.

215

Kant as an idealist brought out two sides of idealism: that the world of experience is built up through certain processes, that is, it is a construction; and that the synthetic activity of the mind enables it to see the world as a finished thing. He was correct when he declared the known world to be mentally constructed, but not when he declared that there was an unknown world of things-in-themselves beyond it—unless we give that name to the karmic forces which became transferred into the known world.

216

Marcus Aurelius: "When thou hast roused thyself from sleep thou hast perceived that they were only dreams which troubled thee. Now in thy waking hours look at these things about thee as thou didst look at thy dreams."

217

P.B. Shelley, *Adonais*:

He hath awakened from the dream of life—
'Tis we who lost in stormy visions, keep
With phantoms as unprofitable strife,
And in mad trance, strike out with spirits knife
Invulnerable nothings—

218

Malebranche: "We do not perceive the objects which are outside us in themselves. . . . So by this word idea I understand nothing other than that which is the immediate object."

219

Mind is the one aspect or phase that one knows, in everything that exists. We can know nothing but mind.—Baruch (Benedict) Spinoza

220

Bradley has pointed out that the knowing self is itself only an idea and in that sense it is not distinct from the Predicate, the known object of thought.

221

"Are we actually alive in real surroundings or are we really only dreaming? Men, tired out with being fooled, have claimed that nothing is real outside our mind."—Voltaire

222

Ashtavakra Samhita: "The universe is but a state of the mind." *Panchadasi*: "The mind is virtually the external world." *Mahabharata*: "The mind is the essence of all things that are manifest." *Taittiriya Upanishad*: "From mind (*manas*) indeed are all entities born." *Brihadaranyaka Upanishad*: "This great, endless, infinite Reality is but purely mental (*Vijnanaghana*)." *Jivanmukti Viveka*: "The whole world is the result of mere mental construction in me."

223

"I was often unable," Wordsworth says, in the preface to his great "Ode," "to think of external things as having external existence, and I communed with all that I saw as something not apart from, but inherent in, my own immaterial nature. Many times while going to school have I grasped at a wall or tree to recall myself from this abyss of idealism to the reality."

224

"Only that day dawns to which you are awake."—Thoreau

225

"The Manifest is Mind; and so too is the Void."—Tilopa, *The Vow of Mahamudra*

226

Anaxagoras, the master of Socrates, taught that the real existence of the things perceived by the five senses could not be satisfactorily proved.

227

Oscar Wilde (in a conversation recorded by Lawrence Housman): "That surely is true philosophy. . . . You are what you are merely because they have made you a subject of thought; if they did not think of you, you would not exist. And who knows? They may be right. For we cannot get behind the appearance of things to the reality. And the terrible reason may be that there is no reality in things apart from their appearances."

228

Chuang Tzu wrote: "Confucius and you are both dreams; and I who say you are dreams—I am but a dream myself."

229

"Where are the pleasurable and unpleasurable moments after they are past? They seem to be like a sound, a shadow, a breeze, or a dream."—Su Tung Po

230

"I behold the world as if a picture," exclaims Sri Shankaracharya in the *Siddhantamuktavali*.

231

"Everything I see seems a dream, everything I perceive with the eyes of the body a derision."—Saint Teresa of Spain

232

William Blake, in his published *Letters*, reveals mentalist truth on the basis of personal firsthand experience. Blending the clairvoyant seer, the religious mystic, and the gifted artist, as he did, this is only to be expected. "I know," he writes, "that this world of imagination and vision is all one continued vision."

233

Berkeley used his mentalist discovery to restore the anthropomorphic God to its neglected shrine. His great errors were to introduce this personal deity as the author of man's ideas and to cling to the finite ego without suspecting that it was itself an idea.

234

We must expect that Roman Catholic metaphysics, following Saint Thomas Aquinas and, through him, Aristotle, accepting the material world's reality, will vigorously oppose mentalism.

235

"I came to the conclusion that consciousness is an undeniable datum, and therefore pure materialism is impossible. I fought every inch of the way against Idealism in Metaphysic—and that is why I was forced to understand it thoroughly before accepting it."—Bertrand Russell

236

Bishop Berkeley contributed valuably to these mentalistic teachings, and we of the West should be grateful to him. But there were a few weaknesses in them, which the best Asiatic thinkers immediately detect and consistently avoid. For instance, Berkeley accepted an experience as being true if the idea of it cohered and persisted strongly. Again and again Shankaracharya pointed out that these conditions were also present in powerful illusions.

237

The European thinkers who worked out the mentalistic basis of life with intellectual thoroughness—although not always with correctness—were German; Kant, Schopenhauer, Hartmann, Hegel, Schiller, and Fichte saw and taught that Mind was the primal reality and that the world was an idea in Mind.

238

Bishop Berkeley's metaphysical position is not easily classed. For, as the *Encyclopaedia Britannica* says, "There is some ground for the usual designation of his philosophy as subjective idealism. This interpretation however clashes with his often repeated avowal that he was trying to justify our natural belief that we have direct knowledge of a really corporeal world."

239

Despite the twisted condition of D.H. Lawrence's inner being he had moments of spiritual clairvoyance, of intellectual perspicuity. That is why he wrote somewhere: "All we know is shadows. Shadows of everything, of the whole world, shadows even of ourselves. We are all spectres. Spectre you are to me, spectre I am to you. Shadows you are even to yourself. And by shadow I mean, idea, concept, the abstracted reality, the ego."

240

It is an item of side interest that Berkeley's wife was a follower of Madame de Guyon, the French lady who, though not a nun, taught the practice of meditation and whose movement spread under the name of "Quietism." Mrs. Berkeley was a devout, earnest mystic who took herself very seriously and was very intent on self-improvement. In a few of the blank pages left by her famous husband, at the end of a rough draft of *Treatise Concerning the Principles of Human Knowledge*, she wrote, after she was widowed: "Who are you that you should fear man that is a worm of a day like yourself? Fear him only who will reward or punish you as you behave. . . . Let not imaginary goods as fame or riches charm you, the want of them, if you do, will distress you." Her use of the word imaginary is amusing, in view of her late husband's mentalistic doctrine.

241

Extract from the editor's (N. Rama Rao's) brief biographical introduction to the collected *Speeches of His Highness the late Yuvaraja of Mysore*: "Persons conversant with the evolution of his mind noted that he started with a materialist theory of the universe, but as his studies advanced and his thought matured, he came to hold a purely mentalistic conception that the universe is mind-stuff."

242

The Japanese Kukai, also known as Kobo Daishi (774–835 A.D.), in his work *Attaining Enlightenment in this Lifetime*, wrote: "Differences exist between matter and mind, but in their essential nature they remain the same. Matter is no other than mind."

243

Bergson said that philosophy must start with the problem of the existence of matter.

244

Dr. Samuel Johnson's erudition was admirably shown in the original dictionary he compiled, as was his talent for expressing common sense in pithy statements. But his metaphysical naïveté was equally shown when he stamped a foot on the ground in refutation of Berkeley's discovery. The foot's touch gave Johnson a physical sensation. He stopped there, not grasping that the sensation had given him an idea—solidity—and that without this idea his foot would not have felt the ground. He took it for granted that his experience testified to material reality. Science knows now that it was testimony to his sensations only, and the rest was theory and assumption: Berkeley took it as testimony to Idea-lism. But that is only a halfway house to adequate explanation, to Mentalism.

245

In a letter to H.W. Abbot, Santayana tersely defined what he called "the idealistic dogma" as being: "Knowledge of objects is but a modification of the subject." He then declares "the impossibility of being a thorough-going idealist, because consciousness of any kind implies the existence of something not itself outside of itself."

246

When, some years ago, I stayed in an ashram in Western India and idly looked through the volumes on its library shelves, I found a highly abridged version of a work called *Yoga Vasistha*; I realized that I had also found one of those Eastern writings which deserve Western readers too. That version had been made by an Indian scholar long before, had apparently never circulated beyond the Indian shores, and, try as I might, I could not secure another copy to take away with me. I think it had been privately published, but anyway it was out of print. The contents were so interesting that I never forgot the Sanskrit title. Now another and new abridgment is in my hands. Its reading has given me pleasurable hours, interesting hours, and thought-provoking hours. It is a book that should be also in the hands of every mentalist.

247

When Berkeley says "to be is to be perceived" (he means "by God"), it is equivalent, in philosophy, to "to be is to be known to the World-Mind in the form of World-Idea." But there are subtle yet important differences between the two outlooks. What did Berkeley define as God? Did he rise to the Ultimate Possible Concept, that of Nonduality? Did he understand that there is a distinction to be made between the Absolute Mind and the World-Mind?

248

Saint Thomas Aquinas' metaphysical outlook is coming more and more to be seen as Neoplatonism, with its mentalistic-mystical doctrine, rather than Aristotelianism, as so many have believed for so long.

249

That the last play written by Shakespeare was *The Tempest* is a historic fact which helps to explain why it holds the most mysterious truth—Mentalism.

250

"Consciousness gives unbeatable testimony to its own existence, but at first, unexamined, we limit that existence to *personality*. As an ever changing thing it is only Me: examined, inquired into, it becomes 'I-I-I,' that is, itself. The 'I' is not the 'Me'."—Coleridge

251

". . . as in your own Bosom you bear your Heaven And Earth and all you behold; Tho it appears without, it is within, In your Imagination, of which This World of Mortality is but a Shadow."—William Blake

252

Denis Diderot, although himself a staunch materialist, had to confess that Idealism "is the most difficult to oppose" [because] "we never get outside ourselves." There was an English lawyer who offered a large financial prize to anyone who could successfully refute the tenets of Idealism. But the prize was never won, because no one was able to provide a satisfactory refutation. Mentalism includes most of Idealism but goes farther and explains more.

253

Great Greek thinkers discussed whether brain and mind were two separate things or only one. But the greatest of them (such as Plato) ***knew*** the mentalist truth.

254

Objective idealism is based on error. The error is that objects have an existence separate from the idea of them. If this were true, and he formed his idea of the object from the object itself, then it should be asked, "What is it that tells him there is an object outside?" It is the mind which tells this. But the mind can give him only a thought. Therefore the idea which he forms and the object which reveals itself to the mind are *both* ideas.

255

Metaphysical idealism could certainly be argued about interminably, especially with the Neorealists. It is, however, just as worthy of consideration by the spiritually minded, and has, in fact, been held by a number of leaders in the mystical field—not merely through intellectual activity, but also through mystical experience.

256

It would be incorrect to state that the drift of science is away from Berkeley. It is true that Berkeley's view of mentalism was a limited and imperfect one, merely a beginning, in fact. But it was a beginning in the right direction.

257

Berkeley's clear thinking and clever statement of a noble truth were admirable. But he made one large mistake in formulating his views. This was to split the qualities of external objects into those which the mind contributes and those which belong to the objects in their own right. The fact is that everything, without exception, is derived from mind.

258

Even as a teenager the American poet Edgar Allan Poe felt something of the Truth and wrote in one of his verses: "Is all that we see or seem but a dream within a dream?"

259

Kant cleared the way admirably for other metaphysical thinkers by applying the notions of infinity and eternity to time and space, linking all to the human mind. Yet his own thinking was brought to a halt, baffled, and remained incomplete; he had to admit that "the existence of things outside of us must be accepted merely on faith."

260

"Are not the mountains, waves, and skies, a part of me and my soul as I of them—Is not the love of these deep in my heart?" wrote Byron as he gazed through windows of his hotel at Ouchy near Lausanne.

261

M.N. Roy: "Some leading scientists say, 'One has the idea of a tree, but one can never know whether the tree really exists or not because the content of the idea is the picture of the tree in the retina.' According to them, there is no way of ascertaining the connection between the picture in the retina and the tree supposed to be there at a distance; the latter may just as well be a projection of the idea. How do we know that the tree is the first and the picture on the retina is the second?"

262

Kant has written somewhere that our perception of the world is "of no more objective reality than a dream."

263

The materialistic position, that there is nothing in the world but matter, is as utterly devoid of justification as the most baseless theological dogma.—Thomas H. Huxley

264

In his play *The Tempest* Shakespeare has given clear expression to mentalism in the context of that famous line, "We are such stuff as dreams are made of."

265

Ariel: "Idealism has never been convincingly refuted. Bergson is the modern Idealist. All great philosophers have been idealists. Ideas are the only true things. That which is alone known is idea for it is that only which enters consciousness."

266

Berkeley dispelled the illusion that Matter exists outside of us by showing that the sense-elements, its primary qualities such as extension, form, and so on, and its secondary qualities such as hardness, colour, and so on, are mere modes of feeling, are subjective; that the existence of a hard, coloured, formed substance outside the perceiving mind was an illusion. Berkeley said God awakened these sensorial perceptions in us and the soul perceived them.

267

"We know that thought is the only reality in this world. . . . Nothing exists except that which is imagined."—Anatole France

268

Carlyle: "This so solid-seeming world, after all, is but an air-image over Me, the only reality; and nature with its thousandfold productions and destruction, but the reflex of our inward force, the phantasy of our dream."

269

Although Kant's primary work was to show that we live in a mental representation of the world, he also thought it likely that the world itself was mental too.

270

The twentieth-century metaphysical movement Neorealism, whose most brilliant exponents have been Bertrand Russell, A.N. Whitehead, and Samuel Alexander, took from materialism the postulate that the universe of our experience is independent of, and is unaffected by, our conscious experience of it. Nevertheless it also took from mentalism some of its epistemological and psychological features. It started out to demolish the mentalist position but in the end it came so perilously near demolishing its own that it has become almost bankrupt.

271

Yoga Vasistha: "There is a mind behind every particle of dust."

272

Hume, unlike the Advaitins, did not deny the world's existence, but he did deny that there was enough proof of its externality.

273

I did not work out the theory of mentalism intellectually until it had first been revealed to me mystically.

274

Many complained about my presentation of mentalism as being repetitious. Yet without such detailed reasoning and elaborate argument it would have been harder for the Western reader to understand, much more to accept, so unfamiliar a teaching.

275

A teaching like mentalism which does not agree with commonly accepted ideas must be carefully presented, for its very surprise may cause it to be deemed beyond, or not worth, discussion.

276

There are so many different points of view from which we can approach one and the same Truth, many different aspects to it. The mentalistic approach which I have emphasized was presented to the public quite deliberately.

277

The fundamental truth of the principle of mentalism is as clear to me as is the fundamental falsity of materialism.

278

The deep mystical background of mentalism is mostly a feeling whereas the form in which it has to be expressed is mostly an intellectual one.

279

The tenets expounded in my book *The Hidden Teaching Beyond Yoga* are of a kind which become more understandable as they become more familiar. It is really their intellectual strangeness which accounts largely for their apparent absurdity. And this strangeness itself arises because mentalism was originally discovered through mystical experience and has had to be translated into non-mystical intellectual terms.

280

To reach the masses with a doctrine as deep as mentalism is no little task, but this I have tried to do.

5

THE KEY TO THE SPIRITUAL WORLD

The living practice

Lack of a correct world view, and of the capacity to think logically and reason soundly from it, may easily be hidden when the aspirant has only to talk about his beliefs to his fellow aspirants, but it will become apparent when he has to apply himself to dealing with the necessary problems and everyday situations that arise in the course of human experience. In the face of such demands on his practical qualities, his theoretical shortcomings will then show themselves. If it is difficult to judge the truth of a system or a doctrine by intellectual means alone, it is much easier to do so by observance of its visible results in living.

2

Because Mind has always and universally existed so has its associated aspect, Energy, or Life-Force. And because Mind connotes meaning and creates purpose, my life has a meaning and a purpose linked with the Universe's: it is neither empty nor alone. Hope, prayer, truth, and Presence are my birthright. I am entitled to them. But I must claim the right, make it my own through faith at first, and possibly through knowledge later.

3

This invariable truth, that man does not exist in matter but in mind, blesses those who receive it. For it helps to console them in affliction, to guide them in meditation, and to illumine them in reflection.

4

Perceive these two things now: the dreamlike character of life in the world, and the illusory character of the personal ego. Hence the need of the "What am I?" enquiry, that the illusion of the ego may be dispelled. When you can see these things clearly, then you may be still and undisturbed, unentangled, and unillusioned amid the struggle of life. You will be wise, free, impervious to the petty persecution of men—their lies, malice, and injuries—for being no longer identified with the personality, you are no longer their target.

5

The doctrine will be his when feeling confirms what reason inculcates, when the figure and history of this world seem no more than a vivid thought in his mind.

6

Why does time take the sharp edge from our griefs? The answer usually includes at least three factors—the subsistence of emotional reaction to it, its placing in the long-range perspective, and the press of new experience upon our attention. But there is a fourth factor whose existence is generally unnoticed and whose importance is equally unknown. This is the fact that the grief tends more and more to become a past memory, more and more recognized for what it really always was, that is, a *thought*.

7

When we are free from the illusion that things are outside the mind, the way is prepared for an easier conquest over the desire for them—that is, for equanimity. "From desire of happiness men, enemies to themselves, blindly slay their own happiness," said Shanti Deva hundreds of years ago.

8

The practical value of grasping that the world is an idea is not only in the spirit of calm detachment which it gives but also in the liberation which it gives from various fears.

9

The value to the seeker after wisdom of comprehending the world's mentalistic nature is that it assists him to lose his fear of it as well as his attachments to it.

10

However much a Mentalist I may be by conviction and experience, I do not let it blot out the kind of world in which my body is living and active. The need for practicality, the keeping of both feet on the ground, is still there.

11

There is no reason why a mentalist should fail to regard the actual world as practically as any materialist. He is neither a fool nor a dreamer. He calls on both the scientific attitude and the mystical experience to support his view.

12

Through the disappearance of the world during mystical meditation he finds out its non-materiality. This is the Glimpse. But with his return to the world his glimpse changes into a memory only. How to establish it permanently, this harmony between inner vision and outer world, is discoverable only when living and active in the world yet thoroughly understanding the mentalistic nature of the world.

13

Such development comes only after many births. And since this truth has to be lived, it must be in practice and not only in theory. Before a man comes to this truth, this mentalism, much time is needed to enable his mind to develop and receive it.

14

The practical message of mentalism is not only to warn us of the creative value of our thought but also to bid us seek out the *source* of thought. For there lies our real home, and there we must learn to dwell habitually.(P)

15

The mental character of the world of our experience, once accepted, changes our religious, metaphysical, scientific, moral, and practical attitudes. Much in it does not need much thought for us to realize how grave is the importance of this fact, how momentous the results to which it leads!(P)

16

Inwardly and daily he returns to this idea that all is Idea, that the familiar world—its places and people, its city life seething with activity, its vaunted civilization and polished culture—has no other existence than in his consciousness and takes its reality from that. So to become conscious of Consciousness detached from its productions—thoughts—is his task, draws his strength and devotion.

17

Because mentalism is to become a vivid fact for him and not remain a mere theory, the advanced disciple will have to convert his joys and agonies into real-seeming dream-stuff. And he will have to achieve this conversion by the power of his own hard will and his own keen understanding. The higher self may help him do this, for he may find that some of the deepest sorrows which befall him are of a special kind. They may be extremely subtle or strikingly paradoxical or tremendous in vicissitudes. For instance, he may be estranged in the most poignant way from those dearest to him, from the master he reveres, the friends he needs, the woman he loves. He may be permitted to meet them *in the flesh* only briefly and only rarely, so that he will seek compensation by learning the art of meeting them often and long *in thought*. If these inner experiences can utterly absorb his imaginative attention, they will come to seem as actual as outer ones. If the capacity to introspect be united with the capacity to visualize in this intense way, the result will be astonishingly effectual. Thus he comes in time to see the Mental as Real. Thus he lifts himself from a lower point of view to a higher one. Thus he thoroughly overcomes the extroverted materialism of ordinary human perception.(P)

18

The way out is constantly to remember to think and to affirm that the world and all one sees and experiences in it has no other substance than Mind and gets its brief appearance of reality from Mind. When this is thoroughly understood and applied, its truth will one day stay permanently with him.(P)

19

Even though he knows it is like a dream, he must live, work and act, love, strive and suffer as if the dream were true.

20

The realization of the mentalistic character of our daily life need not curtail its interest, efficiency, or vividness. But there inevitably arises little by little an inward detachment from all things and all creatures, situations, and environments, which is the preliminary sacrifice required of the ego before the Overself's Grace can be shed down upon it.

21

The effect of a full and proper absorption of these ideas is to strengthen a man and invigorate his purpose, to make him feel that what is behind the universe is behind him too.

22

The illusion of materialism, of a world external to consciousness, could not be preserved if this practice of referring all objects to their source were faithfully and perseveringly followed. The truth of mentalism then becomes solidly implanted.

23

Confronted by the full meaning of mentalism, we are startled into discoveries of the highest importance. The world becomes a deception of the mind, its reality no longer a certainty. But the corollary is that the deception can be stopped, the truth revealed, the authentic reality recovered. This requires the corrective work first of the Quest and finally of the mentalistic techniques.

24

The illuminate sees objects as other persons do, only his sense of materiality is destroyed, for he sees them too as *ideas*, unreal. The illuminate's viewpoint is *not* the yogi's viewpoint. The illuminate finds all the world in himself, says the *Gita*. This means he feels sympathetically at one with all creatures, even mosquitoes or snakes.

25

Our pleasures and pains are not different when we realize them to be mentalistic, but our attitude toward them is different.

26

The constant practice of identifying himself with the mind rather than with the body-idea which inheres in it, leads in time to a certain freeing of himself from himself.

27

Just as a writer would convert imagined or lived experience into written work, so an instructed person would convert his vicissitudes into mentalist knowledge.

28

One need not seek out those unscalable heights for which the saints thirst, however much the purification of thought, feeling, and deed the philosophers welcome. Whoever understands Mentalism will also understand why.

29

The body is there but he is not present in it. Activity goes on but he does not seem to be the actor. It is as if he were not present at all, except as an observer. Somehow he is in society, for they see and hear him, but he does not belong to society. Now at last he understands perfectly dying Socrates' celebrated phrase: "Yes, if you can catch me." For he understands the "I," comprehends mentalism. Now at last Reason governs him and truth is revealed plainly to him.

30

The Oriental notion that escape from life is escape from bondage is an opinion which admittedly has its point, but is not cared for in the mentalist outlook. Instead, a divine order, a meaning-purpose, replaces it.

31

There are great possibilities open to the man who believes in and applies mentalism. This is indirectly evident by the history and state of the Christian Science movement, for it will be found that many Christian Scientists, if they have really understood and constantly applied their doctrine, have risen to high executive positions. Why is this? It is partly because they have obeyed the higher moral law and partly because they have used the creative power of meditation. They have tried to run their businesses on the Golden Rule, and they have positively affirmed ideals in their business and work. Thus they have made good karma for themselves not only by acting morally but also by acting creatively through using their thoughts in a constructive, healthy manner. They do not believe that business is a struggle of wolves but an opportunity to serve and to profit by such service. They do not believe that it is an opportunity to get the best of others unscrupulously but that it is an opportunity to practise ideals and to express ethics. They do not believe in depending solely on their own little selves for results but they also look up to a higher power, God, in prayer and thought. They increase their openness and receptivity to this higher power by trying to purify their characters and to ennoble their personalities.

32

To the degree that we are able to transcend the world-thought within our consciousness, to that degree we are able to transcend the gravitational force of worldly desire itself. But this presupposes a knowledge of the mentalistic doctrine. Therefore, even in the sphere of ethics can be seen the usefulness of such knowledge.

33

Mentalism does not teach us to ignore the world and to dismiss the body. It does not tell us to cease from activity and to deny life's utility. It simply gives us a new and truer way of looking at these things.

34

Those who can lay proper hold of its knowledge will find that it carries power instead of depriving them of it as superficial critics believe.

35

We begin to be about our Father's business when we begin to seek life in Mind, not in matter.

36

What is the hidden meaning of Saint Paul's words which are so often quoted but so little understood: "For to be carnally minded is death, but to be spiritually minded is life and peace"? Do they refer only to sexual morality? Do they refer to pious feelings? For those who are children in the quest of truth, the answer is obviously in the affirmative. But for the mentally mature and philosophically enlightened, there is a totally different meaning in this statement. To be carnally minded means to apprehend the flesh, that is, matter, as reality. To be spiritually minded means to take nothing else than the egoless Mind as reality. Whoever does this and seeks beyond both matter and ego, obtains the result which Paul indicates—that is, true life and unbroken peace.

37

At this level he becomes a spectator who sees the actions and notes the thoughts of body and intellect. He registers the emotions too but does not join with them.

38

He begins to perceive for the first time the inner nature of people and the inner purpose of events.

39

When we begin to realize the mentalist nature of our whole life-experience we begin to take its varied impressions like water on a duck's back.

40

We are in part fleeting pictures in each others' minds. Every night the canvas is rolled up, the show comes to an end, the cinema screen is left blank, and we vanish as though we never were. Is it worthwhile being too solemn about this brief business of living?

41

He now sees what he did not see earlier, that the outer happenings of his life are often connected with the inner trends of his thought and that a change in the latter will often produce a change in the former.

42

The mentalist view of man is neither a romantic approach to life nor a neurotic escape from it.

43

The impact of this discovery that the mind is merely dreaming the world around him and that the senses are merely contributing to this dream, may be quite unsettling for a long while afterwards. Our life may be deprived of purpose, our existence of reality, our will of its power, and our desires of their vitality. For those who have been too attached to earthly things, such a mental state may be useful medicine to cure them of their excessive attachments. But man does not live by medicine alone; he needs bread. Therefore, we must put this discovery eventually in its proper place along with all the rest of philosophic truth. If we succeed in doing this we shall recover our balance, we shall live in the world but not be of it, we shall be adequate to our responsibilities but not be enslaved by them, we shall be active but not let activity destroy our inward peace.

The powerful knowledge

44

Power, whether it be worldly or spiritual, always brings responsibility with it.

45

Our existence as human beings is conditioned, and at times even dominated, by circumstances. Often we should like to remold these, but to do so requires control, and control indicates the need for power, and power depends upon knowledge. This is the justification of philosophy. When we understand its doctrines aright, that mind constructs its experience, its environment, its world, we understand the implication that an amendment in our environment can come only through amendment in our thinking. Thought is creative, and we are continually building both ourselves and our environment by the characteristics and qualities of our thoughts.

46

What to do with the spiritual force current when you feel it—it should be mentally directed into any channel you think advisable or towards any person you wish to help. It will not, however, be wasted if you fail to do so because it will be drawn upon without your conscious knowledge by those who look to you and think of you when they need the inner help. If, however, you deliberately direct it, it will naturally have much more possibility of reaching this objective successfully and effectively.

47

When the mind is fully withdrawn from the physical body and turned in on itself, the thoughts which are then entertained become creative and dynamic on their own plane. What is desired or expected immediately manifests itself. It is a wonderful dream-world where imagination rules supreme and assumes the fullest reality, externalizing itself instantaneously and bringing the man face to face with his own thought as though it were some thing outside himself.

48

While the senses are in abeyance, the deeper level of mind where lie its creative roots can become more easily active.

49

Thus thinking is used as a means of going beyond it, and imagination as a means of suspending it. These two faculties, which hinder the ordinary man from attaining spiritual awareness, actually help the philosophically instructed aspirant to attain it.

50

It was not Jesus' thorn-crowned corpse that was resurrected but the man himself, not his transient body but his immortal consciousness. For mentalism teaches us that a mental form can be seen by others so vividly, so objectively, that it can easily be taken—or mistaken—for a physical one.

51

You triumph over conditions in the moment that you triumph over the thought of them.

52

Remember that Emerson said of Napoleon: "He never blundered into a victory. He gained his battles in his head before he won them in the field."

53

Whoever can understand that substance is inseparable from life and that life is inseparable from mind, whoever can intellectually perceive that the whole universe itself is nothing less than Mind in its different phases, has found the theoretical basis for an appreciation of the wonderful possibilites which dwell behind human experience. The mind's powers can indeed be extended far beyond their present puny evolutionary range. He who reflects constantly upon the true and immaterial nature of Mind and upon its magically creative powers tends to develop these powers. When he becomes capable of successful and ego-free concentration, these powers of mind and will come to him spontaneously. It is natural that when his will becomes self-abnegated, his emotion purified, his thought concentrated, and his knowledge perfected higher mental or so-called occult powers arise of their own accord. It is equally natural that he should remain silent about them, even if only because they do not really belong to the named personality which others see. They belong to the Overself.(P)

54

Telepathy is possible not because thought can travel in space but because space is actually in thought.(P)

55

The human body is a part of consciousness, indeed a major part, but consciousness itself is only a part of a larger and deeper consciousness of which we are normally unaware. Yet it is in this mysterious region that the creative origin of the body-idea lies. If the ordinary "I" cannot make the body keep well by merely holding the thought, this is because the creative power lies in an "I" which transcends it. The ego which identifies itself with the body thereby stultifies its latent powers. But as soon as it begins to identify itself with pure Mind, certain powers may begin to unfold. Many cases of mystic phenomena, such as the stigmata of Catholic saints, confirm this.(P)

56

Whoever develops these powers of the Overself must develop a strong sense of responsibility with them, an awareness that they have been entrusted to him as to a custodian. The grace which allows them can also disallow them.

57

A thought will annihilate distance and reach here or elsewhere provided it is sufficiently concentrated and provided there is attention to its reception. This naturally results from the universality of Mind. But it is much easier for telepathy to operate *after* there has been a single meeting on this material plane. Even a letter which has been read and signed by one person acts to some extent, vicariously, in place of such a meeting.

58

It is not easy to authenticate the belief that the violent emotion—that is, the strong ideas—of a pregnant mother may influence the form of her unborn child. It is much easier to authenticate, however, the appearance of stigmata on the physical body in the historic cases of nuns immersed in empathic contemplation of the crucifixion of Jesus. Once we understand something of the secret of the concentrated mind we understand something of the secret of the magic.

59

If a man does not use his mystical gifts in a disinterested way, if he exploits them for selfish or immoral purposes, then the inescapable divine law is that he shall slowly or suddenly lose them.

60

If abnormal powers appear in a person who is still without philosophical readiness for them, they will prove themselves unreliable, either for accuracy or permanency.

61

It is better to be over-cautious than over-dogmatic when considering the miraculous and the supernatural. It is useless for people to set up limits for what is or is not possible in Nature. To do so would mean that they have got a full knowledge of Nature's laws—a claim nobody dare make in these days and expect any sensible person to accept it. We have lived to see several nineteenth-century so-called laws of Nature abrogated by man himself, not to speak of earlier ones like the "laws of gravity."

62

He knows now that his life-experience can be as boundless or as confined as his own thought.

63

It lies *in your mind* whether or not you shall make something worthwhile of your life. What you have learned from the past, what you think of the present, and what you seek from the future—all these *ideas* combine and influence the achieved result.

64

We sin in thought first and then only in the body.

65

That which we experience inwardly as thought must, if it be strong and sustained enough, manifest itself outwardly in events or environment or both.

66

We are nearly (but not quite) as much in the dark about these higher worlds of being as an infant in the womb is about our own natal world.

67

There are extraordinary capacities in the human mind which are occult only in the sense that they are untapped and uncultivated. If we take the trouble to discover their existence by means of mystical concentration and to utilize them by constant experiment, we may obtain surprising results.

68

Just as the galvanometer will detect surrounding forces which escape man's own senses and which are both invisible and intangible to him, so one who is trained in the art of mental quiet becomes able in time to detect, through the activity of the mind's powers, things which are beyond the range of those to whom the art is unfamiliar and who lack the sensitivity it affords. He finds himself in a mental world of extraordinary manifestations. Mental images which appear to the mental touch, sight, or hearing will manifest themselves first because, being based on the senses, they reach the ordinary consciousness more easily.

69

It is said that power corrupts men—but this may be also true on the spiritual plane. Few men can develop occult power and not be corrupted by it.

70

When these telepathic incidents keep on happening with regularity, the connection between them and the higher power now at work is impossible to miss.

71

The creative artist achieves inspiration when he forgets himself and lives in his created forms—that is, when he accepts his thoughts as realities.

72

He who can arrive at the standpoint of *realizing* his own body as a thought structure can work wonders with it. He who can realize that things in space are ideas can annihilate space at will. And he who can regard present time as he regards past time can work marvels now.

73

He will discover how much his environment, even his work, is a projection of his personality and of the thoughts that go to make it.

74

The true meeting of individuals does not occur in the daily world, but in the world within thought—nay, deeper than thoughts. This world has become real for many and will become increasingly so for others.

75

The creative power of mind was evidenced at the beginning of the nineteenth century by the case of Joanna Southcott. She was a prophetess and also the founder of a Christian sect in England. In one of her visions Jesus appeared and promised she would bear a child, in which he himself would reincarnate. For some months her body showed all the outward signs of pregnancy, both to examining matrons and to inspecting medical men. She herself felt something moving and growing within her. Then she died, exactly nine months after her supposed conception. Surgeons conducted a post-mortem examination but could find no cause whatever for the previous appearance of pregnancy. Her fervent wish, ardent faith, and continuous concentration on the idea had released subconscious forces which materialized it.

76

A man's face becomes white when a strong thought of fear enters his mind; another time it becomes red when a strong thought of shame enters it. Thus mind changes the expression on his face and reveals its influence on the body.

77

Once we perceive the truth and implications of mentalism, the tremendous practical and persuasive value of good suggestions and creative imaginations will also be perceived.

78

No man knows how deep is the reservoir of forces—mental, volitional, or psychical—within him untapped and unused.

79

The idea which a man has of himself is important to his inner life and growth.

80

In Jerome K. Jerome's play *The Passing of the Third Floor Back*, when the part of "The Stranger" was played in London by Forbes-Robertson, the latter was so overcome by the lofty spirituality of the principal role that he had to cancel a long-standing arrangement with fellow-actors to go out after work in the theatre for a glass of wine at a tavern and thence to a restaurant for dinner. During the run of the play, F-R could not bring himself to do anything so material while his mind was still so exalted with the afterglow of "The Stranger's" character. A lady with long experience as an actress, both on the theatrical stage and in radio broadcasting, once told me that she had found the work of acting could become a path to spiritual self-realization. She said that she found it necessary to act so intensely on the stage in order to be thoroughly convincing that she lost herself in the part she played. It was a complete concentration. She became so absorbed in it that she really did identify herself with it, become one with it. In other words, she lost her own personal identity for the time. She projected herself so fully into her characters that there was no room for her own familiar ego. She concluded that acting was a yoga-path because the same capacities for self-absorbed thought, if sufficiently directed in spiritual aspiration towards the higher self and not towards some weak human character, could one day turn an actor into an adept. Henry Daniell denied all these assertions and told me his own experience refuted them. A point of view which partially reconciles these two conflicting ones is that his theory is correct for the great mass of actors, whereas the lady's theory is correct only for the geniuses among them. The first are always conscious of being witnesses of their own performances, being too egotistic to do otherwise; but the others are not, being able, like all true geniuses, to rise during creative moments above themselves. In confirmation of this point of view is the fact, noted by Charles Lamb and confirmed by the actress herself, that Mrs. Siddons, one of Britain's supreme theatrical geniuses, used to shed real tears (not fakes) when she played the part of "Constance" at Drury Lane. Henry Daniell's belief that the actor always remains apart in his inner consciousness is thus refuted. He may do so but the perfect actor, the genius, does not and cannot. He must live his assumed character perfectly if he is to succeed in completely putting it over to the audience.

This lady said further that it is well known in the theatrical world that certain actors become what is technically called "typed." That is, in their personal character they tend to become more and more like the kind of part they have mostly played during their career. If a man has been cast as a villain year after year throughout his life, he actually begins to develop villainous traits in his moral character as a result. This, she said, was the effect of his intense concentration while upon the stage reacting later on his off-stage mentality. Another extremely interesting thing which, she said, helped to convince her of the truth of mentalism, was that when she had given herself with the utmost intensity to certain situations in which she played on the stage, and played repeatedly over a long period of time, situations somewhat similar would enact themselves in her own personal life later on. The discovery startled her for it revealed the creative power of concentrated thought.

Finally, she told me it was common knowledge in her profession that the most effective way to learn the words for a part is to learn them at night in bed just before sleep. No matter how tired she was at that time the lines would sink into the subconscious with a couple of readings and emerge next morning into the conscious with little effort.*Critical comment on the above*: E.Y. says that it is true that most actors do lose themselves utterly in their roles. Nevertheless, this happens only if they are mediocre artists or unevolved spiritually. The supreme artists, as well as those who are highly developed spiritually, do feel perfectly able to play the observer to their acting part, to stand aside from the role even in the very midst of playing it.

81

Where these mental powers are used for evil purposes, such as to suborn the free will of another person to make him act against that person's own interests, the results will act like a boomerang one day to punish the evildoer.

82

There *is* such a thing as telepathy. A fine concentrated thought, a strong emotion, once born, will float through the air and pass into some kindred mind which will discover and use it, just as the etheric waves which carry wireless speeches are flung around the world and picked up by receiving sets which are able to tune in, under appropriate conditions and within certain limitations.

83

Why do stigmata not appear among Hindu Yogis, Chinese Taoists, and Persian Sufis? Why do they not even appear among Protestant Christians and the Greek-Russian-Syrian Eastern Church? Why do they appear only in the Catholic Church *which alone puts strong emphasis on meditation upon Christ's wounds*? How perfectly this illustrates and vindicates the truth of the Lord's declaration, in the *Bhagavad Gita*, that "By whatever path a man approaches Me, by that path I receive him."

84

We are influencing the coming years by our thoughts. The importance of thought in forming external environment, the value of imagination in ultimately creating circumstances, and the use of visualizing the sort of life we aspire to have, are to be impressed and re-impressed on a generation which has to escape from the materialistic outlook. By this twofold process of rising to our divine source and controlling our intellectual ideas, we can begin to control our outward life in an extraordinary manner.

The mystic experience

85

If students can understand the way the mind and the senses really work, what the results of this working are, and what direction they point to . . . if they can break through that barrier between flesh and thought which favours materialism and agnosticism and even atheism, then the perception actually becomes a spiritual experience. It is the key opening the way to mentalism's discovery and acceptance.

86

Those who have had the profounder kind of spiritual experience *and* have *understood it*, not only can *not* interpret life in terms of dead matter or mechanical dynamics, but must interpret it in terms of *mind*.

87

Kept down to his little cares and petty interests, confined within his own ego held under delusion that this is all there is of him, of his being and consciousness, and finally stupefied by the power of sexuality, what wonder that he is ignorant of his higher nature, his connection with the divine? He can come into this knowledge by correct deep thought or by purified cleansed faith or by the influence of someone else who has discovered it. Whatever the way, he has the practical possibility of lifting himself up to a new awareness.

88

The enigma of what we are can get its first convincing answer by mentalistic study and practice: it brings a man into awareness of his soul.

89

Until he acquires firm possession of the truth of mentalism, the mysteries which lie beyond it can be only hazily grasped.

90

If they would only stop to think over the meaning and the importance of self-consciousness, they might get at the Great Secret.

91

The doctrine of mentalism is understood personally or confirmed practically by an advanced mystical experience, provided the experience itself is not misunderstood through overstrong preconceived notions which are brought to it.

92

We do *not* dream the waking world as we dream during sleep. For the latter is spun out of the individual mind alone, whereas the former is spun out of the cosmic mind and presented to the individual mind. However, ultimately, and on realization, both minds are found to be one and the same, just as a sun ray is found to be the same as the sun ultimately. The difference which exists is fleeting and really illusory but so long as there is bodily experience it is observable. It is correct to note that the present birth-dream is caused by past tendencies; we are hypnotized by the past and our work is to dehypnotize ourselves, that is, to create new thought-habits until the flash comes of itself. But the flash itself comes during a kind of trance state, which may last for a moment or longer. It comes during the higher meditation of supramysticism.(P)

93

In one of those apocryphal books which was rejected by those men who formed the canonical collection called the New Testament—a rejection in which they were sometimes wrong, and certainly in this instance—there occurred a saying of Jesus which runs, "When the outside becomes the inside, then the kingdom of heaven is come." Can we expand this mystical phrase into non-mystical language? Yes, here it is: "When the outside world is known and felt to be what it really is—an idea—it becomes a part of the inside world of thought and feeling. When its joys and griefs are known to be nothing more than states of mind, and when all thoughts and feelings and desires are brought from the false ego into the true Self at their centre, they automatically dissolve—and the kingdom of heaven is come."(P)

94

When you stop putting borders around your consciousness by holding it to bodily and mental experiences, you give it a chance to show itself for what it is—infinite—and you give the world which plays the role of object to consciousness's subject a chance to show its own mentalist character as idea.

95

Think of yourself as the individual and you are sure to die; think of yourself as the universal and you enter deathlessness, for the universal is always and eternally there. We know no beginning and no ending to the cosmic process. Its being IS: we can say no more. Be that rather than this—that which is as infinite and homeless as space, that which is timeless and unbroken. Take the whole of life as your own being. Do not divorce, do not separate yourself from it. It is the hardest of tasks for it demands that we see our own relative insignificance amid this infinite and vast process. The change that is needed is entirely a mental one. Change your outlook and with it "heaven will be added unto you."(P)

96

To arrive at the understanding that the universe is non-material and is *mental*, is to be liberated from materialism. It produces a sensation like that felt by a prisoner who has spent half a lifetime cooped up in a dark and dingy fetid dungeon and who is suddenly liberated, set free, put out of doors in the bright sunshine and fresh clean air. For to be a materialist means to be one imprisoned in the false belief that the matter-world is the real world; to become spiritual is to perceive that all objects are mental ones; the revelation of the mental nature of the universe is so stupendous that it actually sets mind and feeling free from their materialistic prison and brings the whole inner being into the dazzling sunshine of truth, the fresh atmosphere of Reality. All those who believe in the materiality of the material world and not in its mental nature, are really materialists—even if they call themselves religious, Christians, spiritualists, occultists, or Anthroposophists. The only way to escape materialism is not to become a follower of any psychic cult or religious faith, but to enquire with the mind into the truth of matter and to be rewarded at length by the abiding perception of its mental Nature. All other methods are futile, or at best are but preparatory and preliminary steps.(P)

97

Reality is inaccessible to thought so long as we regard the latter as separate from it. The moment this illusion is dropped, the truth is revealed.(P)

98

Whoever understands that every object and every person he sees around him is separate only in appearance, and appears so only through the unexamined working of his mind, is becoming ripe for realization. But very few are those who have come to such advanced understanding.(P)

99

There are strange uncommon moments when we seem to be lifted out of ourselves, when the whole of the past and present existences seems but a picture in a fitful dream and when the entire stuff of the universe seems nothing other than momentary thought. At such moments we may understand by an act of intuition rather than of reflection that the world is a product of Mind, not of Matter.

100

If a materialist would stop to think about this mystery of the ultimate observer and if his thinking faculties were sufficiently sharpened, purified, and made capable of dealing with such an abstract subject, he would lose his materialism and become a mentalist. Let him ask himself who it is that speaks when he speaks about himself, what is this "I," this thing that bears his name. Since that which speaks and that which is spoken of cannot be the same but must be separate, then he would have to admit a further "I" behind the one that speaks about himself. He could go on analysing backwards in a never-ending series in this way. Each time the "I" would seem to have some other "I" to which it was an object and to which it could refer as the subject. The existence of his ego would be established in relativity, for it would seem he could move infinitely and indefinitely through this mystery of what is meant by "I." This is because the instrument which he is using for such analysis is the logical intellect, which would thus reveal to him its strict limitations.

Observing these limitations he would then have to ask himself whether or not it were possible to use a subtler instrument, and then mystical metaphysics would tell him: Yes, such a subtler instrument is available—it is your intuition. Cultivate this rightly, shun its counterfeit, subject your feelings to the philosophic discipline, and then practise meditation. You will find that your intuition will lead you back and back to the one element which is the final "I" and which directs every operation of the subconscious functions of the body, and which gives your personality its consciousness of existence. This "I" is non-physical; it is the inmost part of your mind. Understand this and you will necessarily have to give up materialism. You will become a votary of mentalism. Even more, the realization of this truth in actual experience makes you aware that the universe is friendly to you because you are intimately related to it. Your own mind grows out of the World-Mind. It is this relation which enables your mental nature to think and to know, your emotional nature to feel, and your physical body to act. Without it you would be dead in the fullest sense of the term. Everything inside of you, like everything outside you, changes; but this real Self never changes for it dwells in the kingdom of the World-Mind, the kingdom of heaven which is an everlasting one.

It is a phenomenal feat to understand Einstein's law of relativity as it applies to the physical world; but, after all, this understanding does not bring peace of mind or strength of life. It is quite another thing to understand the law of relativity as it applies to the inner Self and such understanding does bring these things. Our knowledge of physical relativity has led us to control of the atom, whose reward seems to be the likelihood that we shall destroy ourselves, but our knowledge of spiritual relativity leads us to control of the mind, whose reward is to save ourselves.

101

If mentalism turns our universe upside down for us, further comprehension of it brings the universe back again into position, but transformed, divinized, and divinely supported.

102

We have the authority of Indian texts for our assertions. Thus: "Through the *mind* alone It is to be realized," says *Brihadaranyaka Upanishad* (IV.4.19). And in Shankara's *Commentary on the Gita* (II.21) we read, "The mind refined by subjugation of body and senses, and equipped with the teachings of scripture and the teacher, constitutes the sense by which the Self may be seen." Finally, *Mundaka Upanishad* (III.1.8) says, "When a man's mind has become purified by the serene Light of knowledge, then he sees Him."

103

The word *gnana* means "knowledge" and is generally translated as such. But it has a secondary and allied meaning: "that which reveals." When the truth of mentalism finally dawns on a man, not only as an idea thought out, an emotion strongly felt, and an experience shattering the last remnants of materialism for him, what happens is the greatest revelation of his life—as sacred as any gospel.

104

How mentalism lights up those deeper and darker sayings of Jesus! "The kingdom of heaven is within you" is then seen to be both a joyful proclamation of spiritual hope and a statement revealing a little-known fact. It proclaims a heavenly existence as being within reach of the mind that is the real man and it tells of such existence being hidden within the mind itself. Heaven is then no far-off place or no post-mortem condition but a state attainable in this life.

105

With this progressive deepening of consciousness, the body will come to seem only a part of himself and the physical life only a part of his true life. If he perforce feels that he is the flesh, he also feels that he is much more the spirit. If in the one he is aware of the evanescence of existence here, in the other he is aware of its eternity there.

106

When this truth of mentalism strikes our mind with vivid lightning-flash, we have gone a long way on the quest.

107

He discovers the nothingness (no-thing-ness) of matter.

108

From these mysterious layers of the mind, he may draw up supernal knowledge and divine love.

109

Our knowledge of the meaning of life ascends progressively with our knowledge of the nature of our own minds.

110

Hitherto he has accepted the interpretation of his world experience which the lower self has thrust upon him with overwhelming force and great immediacy. Now he must reinterpret it mentalistically under the gentler and slower influence of the higher self.

111

We not only know that there is a world, with objects and creatures, but also that we ourselves exist. But unless we analyse psychologically and physiologically the "me"-thought and the objects, the consciousness which tells us all this is confined with them and its prior existence is never discovered. The "me"-thought appears simultaneously with the world. We identify with the "me" and with its physical senses, never pausing between one thought and the next to learn what consciousness in itself unmixed with one or the other really is. For here is the basic "I," the holy Spirit, the God-particle within us. Here too thinking as a process slips into contemplation as a stillness.

112

The mind which is aware is a distinct and separate thing from the things which appear in the field of awareness. That mind is the true self, but those things—which we know only as thoughts—are not. The emotions and thoughts that we commonly experience are outside the ring of the real "I," yet are always taken—or rather mistaken—for it.

113

Outside of the mystical experience wherein the whole universe rolls up and vanishes away, leaving the man "conscious only of consciousness," the next overwhelming realization of mentalism comes to dying persons.

114

Why is it that during our most exalted and purest emotional happiness, such as that which comes from listening to fine music or looking at a landscape of wild grandeur or giving ourselves up to mystical rapture, time seems to be blotted out and we remember its existence only when we are recalled to our ordinary prosaic state? Consider that this strange feeling never arises during our more worldly or more painful episodes. The explanation lies in mentalism. All human experience, including the physical, takes place in the mind. Each episode must be thought into consciousness before it can ever exist for us. If the episode is a happy one, we love to dwell on it, to linger in it, and to become absorbed by it. Such intense concentration greatly slows down the tempo of our thoughts and brings us nearer the utter thought-free stillness wherein our spiritual self forever dwells outside time and space.

This kind of experience demonstrates vividly to those who have not yet been able to practise the meditation required for, and leading up to mystical rapture, what mystics find during such rapture—that man in his true being, in his Overself, is not only timeless but also sorrowless.

115

The truth of mentalism may become intellectually convincing, but it will be subject to doubts so long as it is not carried into the heart and deeply felt like a living thing. It should attain the force of personal experience.

116

For those of an intellectual inclination, Mentalism, well-absorbed, can become the forerunner of spiritual awakening.

117

Mentalism makes it possible for each man to understand why there must be a god. And what is more, it also makes it possible for each man to transcend his intellectual discovery by the mystical experience of the presence of God within himself.

118

The mystic penetrates the level of ordinary consciousness and thus becomes aware that it has a sacred source.

119

The faculty of memory is valuable only to the extent that it enables us to remember the Higher Power.

120

The fact is that the mere awakening to the truth of mentalism is itself a joyous event, while the final realization of it establishes him in a great calm and a decisive insight. It will set him free from leaning on outside supports, on books, however sacred, or men, however respected—if life and development have not already done so.

121

Whoever continues to regard the world as a material thing continues to obstruct his own efforts to attain the higher mystical experience. This obstruction is only reduced but not removed if he believes the Universal Mind to be behind the material world. Only when he resolutely discards all materialistic and semi-materialistic standpoints, only when the world ceases to be something outside the mind and becomes directly present to it as a thought, can he end this groping in the dark and begin to move successfully forward.

122

Another truth which follows from the truth of mentalism is likely to be an unexpected one. To materialist atheists and their kind, it will also be an unpalatable one. Because all our human existence, including even our outward experience, is ultimately mental, there is no other way to a genuine and durable human happiness than that which is for all human beings the ultimate one, that irradiation of the thought-bereft mind, that inner peace which passeth (intellectual) understanding which Saint Paul called entry into the kingdom of heaven.

123

The impact of this truth, coming at the right time to the proper person, has the force of a revelation.

124

He may go as far as thought can carry him, limited only by the limits of imagination and logic, conjecture and clairvoyance, but in the end his mind must return to the exclusive consideration of itself.

125

When we understand this truth, we shall understand that the Overself is forever present with us and that this presence is more immediate and intimate than anything else in life.

126

Thought acquires a right knowledge of itself when it turns back all its attention from the thought-series and seeks its own being.

127

Mind as man is largely self-ignorant, but Mind as Mind is wholly self-illumined. For man is shut up by the body, imprisoned by the very senses to which he is so grateful for sight, hearing, and feeling. But when he comes into self-awareness he is liberated.

128

If you believe that the world of material things is outside you, that matter is a separate and solid entity, experience will confirm your belief. You will be a materialist, no matter how pious your life. If, however, by profound thought, deep meditation, and other preliminaries, you have removed some of the obstacles which surround and entrap most people, then you may be more likely to let light dawn within you. You *may* get the shattering experience of the mentalist revelation: many many discoveries will then be made. You will discover that the world is a form taken by consciousness. You will learn the meaning of the void.

Consciousness as world

129

If we could reflect profoundly enough about the nature of the *I*, or the activity of the body, or the composition of the ground upon which we stand, we could arrive at a preliminary but immensely significant solution of the mystery of existence. Gotama did this during a single sitting under a tree and became a Buddha, an enlightened one.

130

The mystery of Mind is undoubtedly the biggest mystery of all, for when he understands that he will have the key which unlocks the door to all the other problems. However, it is necessary to grasp the following: there are two phases of Mind. The first is *Consciousness* in its everyday form, that is, the consciousness of this time-space-matter world. He has the illusion that this consciousness is a continuous and unified whole, but actually it is like a stream of machine-gun bullets, being made up of an incessant series of disconnected thoughts. Because these thoughts arise and disappear with extraordinary rapidity, the illusion of continuous consciousness, the illusion of an unchangeable, solid world, and the illusion of a separate ego are born. The word "illusion" used here must not be misunderstood. The existence of this amazing trio is not denied for a single moment, because they are there staring him in the face. But this existence is purely relative. It is not absolutely permanent and therefore not real in the Oriental definition of that much-abused word. He must not confine the notion of Mind to that fragment of it which is used in everyday consciousness. What is called Consciousness is merely a portion of what is called Mind, or, functionally regarded, merely one of its faculties. It is the transient and relatively less important portion too. Whether consciousness lives or dies, Mind will always go on because it is the hidden source. Now this Mind in its own pure stage (i.e., unexpressed through everyday human consciousness) is utterly beyond the range of human thinking because it is Absolute, timeless, spaceless, idea-less, and matterless. It has no shape to be seen, no sound to be heard. Consequently from the average human standpoint it is a great Nothing and as a matter of fact some of the Tibetan sages did call it a Great Void. As he cannot pull it down to the grasp of his little human mind and therefore is not ordinarily aware of it, it has sometimes been referred to as the Unconscious Mind, for want of a better term. But such a description is not a good one, as it may lead to dangerous misunderstandings. A better descriptive term must be found. To quote a phrase from one of Disraeli's novels: "The conscious cannot be derived from the unconscious. Man is divine."

It is this Infinite Mind which has been called God, Spirit, Brahman, and so forth. He has to get the *knowledge* that his own little individual stream of consciousness has flowed out of this great source and will eventually return to it and disappear into it. This is Truth. This universal, impersonal Being is what all are after. The ones who seek it consciously are the people who have taken up the Quest. Those who are after it unconsciously take to drink and other sensual enjoyments and pursue the allurements of this most alluring world.

131

Thoughts could never come into existence if Mind were not also here primarily. Nor could we humans become aware of the universe without Mind's priority.

132

Mind is governed by its own laws and conjures up its own creations. The universe, at any particular moment of its history, is formed by the action and reaction of these creations.(P)

133

Mental activity need not be conscious.(P)

134

The ideas pass, the Mind remains. But while they exist they are included in and share the Mind's reality. The world's appearance is therefore and in this sense real enough to the conscious beings within it while it lasts. Thus the distinction between inner reality and outer appearance, while not effaced, is nevertheless reduced to secondary status.

135

Chandrakirti, a Mahayana Buddhist guru, said, "We teach the illusion of existence only as an antidote to the obstinate belief of common mankind in the existence of this world." What he means by this is that the world is only relatively existent in relation to the physical senses and the physical brain. The senses report its existence quite correctly and Mentalism agrees with mankind in the factuality of this experience. But it says this is only a relative truth, that the basic or real truth is that both world and self exist in consciousness, that they are nothing else than Consciousness itself.

136

It is a large error to take, as so many do take, consciousness as being the total sum of personal states known in experience, and nothing more, to regard it as so many separate pieces of awareness put together.

137

You *live* in consciousness; your body merely moves about; but few persons will pause long enough to perceive who they really are and what they are really doing.

138

Not only is the world an appearance-in-Consciousness, but so is the ego. It is in the end a thought, perhaps the strongest of all; and only the Consciousness-in-Itself is the Reality from which it draws sustenance, existence, life.

139

So long as there is something, whether it be a physical object or a mental idea, which forms an *object* of our thinking and is, therefore, still not the power that thinks, so long do we prevent ourselves from knowing mind as it is in its own naked purity.

140

The mysterious question "Who Am I?" is certainly deeply important, which is why it was put forward from the very beginning of his career by Ramana Maharshi. There is also another question which one may venture to state: "Where Am I?" Am I here in the fleshly body or in the invisible mind?

141

The ego's world of experience is ultimately due to the Overself, present at its base, limiting and determining a fragment of its own consciousness by its all-imagining power. Both the ego and its world are mentally created.

142

The world looks just as it did before; being understood for what it is—a thought-series—does not alter its appearance. The sage's perception of it is like other men's; his senses function like theirs; but he knows that his experience of it depends on the ever-presence of Consciousness; *he is never without this awareness*. This is the large first difference.

143

Every human being is first conscious of his own consciousness. If he traces out its implication, he may see that this is the best proof of the mind's reality as a separate existence.

144

We may note the fact of being conscious, but we can never ordinarily note the fact that we are conscious of being conscious in the same way that we are conscious of everything else.

145

The ordinary man thinks he is the ego because he identifies with his thoughts and his body. The awakened man knows that he is the Consciousness behind both.

146

Philosophy does not limit mind to mean the outer behaviour or inner consciousness, although it must necessarily include them. No, mind is that primal element which manifests to us through behaviour-patterns and conscious states.

147

When I say that I am my own mental existence then I imply I am also the whole universe. Nature exists within me, for Nature is but my idea. The world is my creation. This is no empty vagary but the veritable truth, the grandest which ever entered the half-taught mind of men.

148

Consciousness produces the experienced world and gives or deprives it of reality.

149

What else does anyone really own except his consciousness, of which his ordinary self is only a changing product? What else can he take with him unfailingly to any part of the world, and perhaps—if the seers know what they assert—even to that other world beyond?

150

If the ego-mind is that which knows the objective world, it is itself that which is known by a transcendental Mind.

151

Scientifically, it would seem that each human being is just a collection of various physical sense-perceptions which quickly change and flow, and that he is nothing more. The religious person would protest and add his spiritual self, or soul, to this collection. Here the philosopher would come along and ask both persons, "What about a consciousness which tells you all this?"

152

So long as he does not comprehend that he himself is the real seer and that all these objects are seen *within* the consciousness, so long will he commit the error of taking the ego for the "I."

153

"In the beginning was the Word" is the New Testament's way of expressing that the universe is a mental one. The whole cosmos was, from the very beginning, a thought, a word in God's mind.

154

It is true that the knower of the outside world is within man's mind, and that this element is also the Knower of himself, and that the knowledge of the self is the key to the knowledge of the world—as even an occultist like Rudolf Steiner concedes. But this does not exempt man from using that key. It does not mean that it is enough to know the self, that we may stop with that. The key must still be used because the self does not exist in a vacuum; the body is there, and the world is there. (*Memo to PB*: Add here the notes about the two paths and the necessity of combining them. The *Who Am I?* path and the *What is the World?* path.)

155

The two analyses must come together now, simultaneously: the "What Am I?" and the "What is the World?" Then only can they be unified by mentalism, reappearing in, and as, the One Consciousness; the duality of self and non-self vanishes.

156

Consciousness came first: all thoughts came into being later. It made their existence possible. It is the permanent principle in man whereas they appear and vanish.

157

Consciousness is more important than doctrine.

158

The body observes the world outside it and the ego-mind observes the body. That which stands apart from both, as the third observer, is the Overself.

159

When we look for the last explanation of the universal phenomenon, we find one persistent and ultimate reality . . . Consciousness.

160

Mind as we humans now know it is but the frothy tossing wave on the surface of a mile-deep ocean.

161

The conventional definition of consciousness, which makes it the total of all the mental states of a person, is satisfactory only as far as it goes, but it is unsatisfactory because it misses the most important element—awareness—which is not a state at all, and not even an item in it.

162

The awareness of the thought series itself bespeaks a prior existence of consciousness.

163

That which is most important to us, in us, and for us, is consciousness. Yet it is the one thing about ourselves of which we know least and ignore most.

164

The human entity is not only the thoughts and images found in his consciousness; he is also and much more that consciousness itself.

165

In the last analysis, the only thing that he really knows is consciousness. It is that which he regards as self, though it may assume different patterns at different times.

Consciousness and pure Mind

166

Our own mind is a human analogue of the Universal Mind. Thus in its character and working, Nature provides an easy lesson in divine metaphysics. If we wish to obtain some slight hint as to the nature of the highest kind of mental existence, that is, of God, we must examine the nature of our own individual mind, limited and imperfect though it be. Now philosophy is not afraid to admit pantheism but does not limit itself to pantheism. It also affirms transcendentalism but does not stop with it. It declares that the Unique Reality could never become transformed into the cosmos in the sense of losing its own uniqueness. But at the same time it declares that the cosmos is nevertheless one with and not apart from the Reality. The easiest way to grasp this is to symbolize the cosmos as human thoughts and the Reality as human mind. Our thoughts are nothing other than a form of mind, yet our mind loses nothing of itself when thoughts arise. The World-Mind is immanent in but not confined by the universe in the same way that a man's mind may be said to be immanent in but not confined by his thoughts. Furthermore, not only may we find it helpful in the effort to understand the relation which the cosmos bears to the World-Mind, to compare it with the relation which a thought bears to its thinker or his speech to a speaker, but when we consider how our own mind is able to generate thoughts of the most multivaried kind, we need not be surprised that the Universal Mind is able to generate the inexhaustibly varied host of thought-forms which constitute the cosmos.(P)

167

The word "Consciousness" is ordinarily taken to mean the totality of thoughts and feelings and knowledge held by anyone at any time: all his perceptions, ideas, remembrances, imaginations—in brief, his total awarenesses. But in this philosophy, by capitalizing the initial "C," the term is given a fresh and deeper, still more abstract and subtler meaning. It then becomes the self-contained being or entity which is aware. This is the profound sense in which the word was used by Brahmin thinkers and mystics thousands of years ago, speaking and writing in the Sanskrit language. The man who introduced it into the English language in 1690 was John Locke when he wrote: "Consciousness is the perception of what passes in a man's own mind." This definition shows how long is the distance between those profounder Indians and the less metaphysically minded Europeans.

168

That we know this awareness exists means only that we have an *idea* of awareness. We do not *see* that awareness as itself an object, nor can we ever do so. If we are to know the awareness by itself, first we would have to drop knowing its objects, its reflections in thought, including the ego-thought, and then *be* it, not see it.

169

Mind must be distinguished from the states of mind, as the object must be separated from knowing it, the act of knowledge. Spinoza opposed the phenomenal world to the substantial, phenomena to substance; what others call relative to absolute; what the Hindus call illusion to reality; and what the religionists call matter to spirit. But all these statements can only be made because the mind originally makes them, for the mind is the witness of both. We must give the primacy to mind, for it Is. Whether illusion exists or not, whether the absolute exists or not, Mind IS. If the world is constantly present to me, it is a *mind* which is making it present, for awareness is a power of mind. It is *mind* which makes the thought of material objects possible for us; and to make mind a by-product of an alleged matter is a contradiction in itself.

170

The mind can know as a second thing, as an object, that which is outside itself. This applies to thoughts also. If it is to know anything as it really is in itself, it must unite with that object and become it, in which case the distinction of duality disappears. For instance, to know a person, one must temporarily *become* that person by uniting with him. Otherwise, all one knows of that person is the mental picture, which may not be similar to the real person. Similarly, the Ultimate Consciousness is not something to be known as a second being apart from oneself. If he knows it in that way he really knows only his mental picture of it. To know it in truth he has to enter into union with it and then the little ego disappears as a separate being but remains as part of the larger self. The wave then knows itself not only as a little wave dancing on the surface of the ocean, but also as the ocean itself. But as all the water of the ocean is ONE, it can no longer regard the millions of other waves as being, from the standpoint of ultimate truth, different from itself. To render this clearer still, during a dream he sees living men, houses, animals, and streets. Each is seen as a separate entity. But after he awakens, he understands that all these individual entities issued forth from a single source—his own mind. Therefore they were all made of the same stuff as his mind, they were non-different from it, they were not other than the mind itself. Similarly when he completes the Ultimate Path he will awaken from the illusion of world-existence and *know* that the entire experience was and is a fragmentation of his own essential being, which he now will no longer limit to the personal self, but will expand to its true nature as the universal mind. The dream will go on all the same because he is still in the flesh, but he will dream *consciously* and know exactly what is happening and what underlies it all. When this happens he cannot go on living just for purely personal aims but will have to enlarge them to include the welfare of all beings. This does not mean he will neglect his own individual welfare, but only that he will keep it in its place side by side with the welfare of others.

171

Human existence cannot have its goal in meditation alone, however rich the experiences may be which such meditation brings. For the deepest possible experience of meditation is to empty consciousness of the world-experience and thus to point out its unreality. But That which does the pointing, and that which is having the experience, and the experience itself—all, in the end, originate from the Real. The discovery of the unreality of the world is useful, for it offers the needed complete detachment from our bonds. But this cannot be the unique, the sole highest purpose of our existence, for then there would be no need to continue existence in the body after the discovery. A mystic must move on and seek the still farther realization which shows the world under a new light and offers an entirely new standpoint for understanding it. And this is that the uniquely real is not less present in the world than in his meditation, only it is present in a different way. It is like the dreamer who wakens to the fact that he is dreaming and who continues to dream but knows all the time that it is a dream experience. In just the same way the highest realization is that the Real is Consciousness—the pure, the ultimate Consciousness—but this consciousness can take different forms and yet still remain what it really is.

172

"The universe is my mind; my mind is the universe," said Lu Hsiang-shan. There is no end to the number of things to be learned about the universe, he argued. Learn therefore to know the one great principle—the mind—behind it.

173

It is a pity that one word is used for opposite methods. We separate *drsyam* from *drik* only in preliminary stages, only temporarily in order to be able to point out later that this *drsyam* is Brahman (as every dream object can be pointed out to be only mind) and thus the ALL is explained as Brahman. The final stage of Yoga (*asparsa*) is emphatically not to get rid of *drsyam* (thought objects) but to recognize all of them as Brahman. The lower yogi suppresses them, but our aim is entirely different. We do not kill the thought but examine it. To carry out this examination we must have concentrated sustained thinking, and this is the use of lower yoga; then we have first to separate it—this is preliminary. Afterwards we discover all thoughts to be as waves of one ocean, to have Brahman as their real essence or nature.

174

There is no other conclusion for the profound thinker than that mind must come out of Mind.

175

What is the reality behind all our experiences? Since they are thoughts, and since thoughts are made possible by Consciousness, it must be the Consciousness. This remains true even when the "I" is unaware and unconscious, because limited and little, being only a thought itself, an object known like other objects; the Real is still there but hidden.

176

The Vedantin tells you, "Your experience of the world is illusory; you take it to be existent; you see a snake when there is only a rope." But the philosopher comments: "It is misleading only if while you are in the body you take it to be utterly and ultimately real. The world is actually there, but what is it that makes it there for you? Consciousness! *That* is the reality. But what you call consciousness is only a fragment, a very small confined thing, compared with its source."

177

Materialism is strongly repudiated by those who understand that Consciousness at its highest is itself the Supreme Reality, and not merely a by-product of the material body.

178

When we come at last to perceive that all this vast universe is a thought-form and when we can feel our own source to be the single and supreme principle in and through which it arises, then our knowledge has become final and perfect.(P)

179

To man's physical senses the Real offers no evidence of its existence. Therefore, to him it is as Nothing.

180

We never know Consciousness. We can claim to know objects and thoughts, impressions and feelings, because each being separate from the other they can only be known by a person, an individual, a separate and distinct knower. But Consciousness, being the light behind all thoughts, cannot be reduced to an ego-thought, confined with a little "I."

181

The mind which forms such a multitude of images of the things outside the body, can nevertheless form no image of itself.

182

In the ordinary man's cosmic picture any one object is separate from any other object. In the scientist's cosmic picture they are also separate, but intellectually he may have arrived at the point of holding them together in the idea that they are all different forms of one and the same ultimate Energy. But this remains only an idea. In the philosopher's picture, the ordinary man's and the scientist's are both included, but there is an addition, namely, he knows by his transcendental experience that these two are projections of Consciousness and that this Consciousness *is* the reality.

183

Thinking man needs the concept of pure Mind, infinite formless consciousness, timeless being, as absolutely necessary to complete and perfect his thinking. Everything in the end points to it, from his own existence to the universal existence. The religionist and the mystic may call it God, satisfied with faith; and even if he himself cannot enter into it, he knows it must be there and has always been there.

184

Those who make consciousness a physical product or effect, to vanish forever long before its physical originator vanishes, need to try the Art of Mental Quiet with the specific object of going in quest of Consciousness itself, separated from all mythology, whether religious, scientific, or esoteric. They then discover that the *forms* taken by consciousness may change or pass into dissolution but THAT out of which they originate cannot.

185

Whatever becomes an object to consciousness cannot be the conscious self which notes it as an object. Every thought, therefore, even the thought of the person, is such an object. The real self must consequently inhere in a consciousness which transcends the person and which can be nothing other than pure consciousness itself. The keen insight of the Chinese sages perceived this and hence they used the term *Ko*, which means "to be aware," as representing the transcendental knowledge of real being, and the same term, which also means "he who is aware," as representing a man like the Buddha who is possessed of such knowledge.

186

The personal consciousness has no more reality than that of a reflection in a glass mirror, for it is Mind which illuminates it. The personal life may be as transient as foam.

187

Where does this Consciousness come from? This will never be discovered, because it is itself both the asker and the answer; it was there before the question arose, it made the question possible, it will be there when all else has passed away. This thin ray of conscious being which is the questioner's known self contains in itself the ultimate solution of all his self-made riddles.

188

The element of consciousness, *Vijnana*, is not subject to death: this is asserted in an old Buddhist text, *The Saddha-tu-Sutta*.

189

That which is always in the background of *all* thoughts is Consciousness. Without it they could never appear nor exist, whereas Consciousness exists in its own self-sufficiency.

190

The form of consciousness may change, the fact of consciousness may be temporarily obscured, but the reality behind consciousness can never be annihilated.

191

The true being, World-Mind, was there before men's thoughts began.

192

In ordinary experience consciousness is not found by itself, independent of what it holds, separate from what it perceives and experiences, distinct from the things given to it by the world outside. That is to say, it is not isolated from its contents but always inclusive of them. And not only is it connected together with physical objects but also with different ideas that are merely thought about, with reasonings and imaginings. There is further evidence of this relationship to be found when we turn from the waking state to the sleeping one. When this is really deep, without dreams, there is no world and there are no imaginings. At such a time consciousness does not exist. When thoughts come into being within a man, the world comes into being for him. When they die down, he loses his consciousness and his world too. But the opening of this paragraph was qualified by the three words "In ordinary experience." For a few men, consciousness without thoughts has become a practical realization: for the whole race of men, it remains in the future as an evolutionary possibility. These adepts find Consciousness-in-itself *is* the reality out of which thoughts rise, including the world-thought. It is not easy to adduce evidence for this since these are events in private personal biography, not scientifically verifiable.

193

There are two ways of knowing, and two kinds of things to be known: the first is on the ordinary level, and deals with physical and intellectual things: this I have called immediate knowledge; the second is on the deepest possible level, and deals solely with the essence of *all* things whence they unfold, the divine Mystery, where knower dissolves into the known. This is metaphysically known as the ultimate level.

194

What is energy? Its transformations are known as sound, light, heat, and so on. But these are only appearances of something else. One never catches an isolated pure energy-in-itself. It is about as detectable as pure matter. There is therefore something behind energy and behind intellect, or shall it be said, behind life and behind thought. Energy cannot be reconciled with an eternal state. But if energy itself springs up as an emanation from the deeper level of mind it may be possible to effect such a reconciliation. Neither intellect nor energy can be the eternal soul but both could be ever-changing emanations of something which might itself be relatively changeless. Light is the highest of the energies; the Sun is the father of all things. Matter is scientifically reducible to light. In the depths of some mystical experiences one may find oneself surrounded by an ocean of light. Light is then the manifestation of this deeper mind but it is still only a manifestation. Consciousness must be interiorized so deeply that even a thought or an idea, a psychic image or a clairvoyant vision must be recognized as something outside the true being, something objective, separate, and away from the true self. Many mystics do not feel such a need, but all philosophic mystics ought to do so if they are to attain a pure spiritual experience in its perfect integrity.

195

It is absolutely certain and quite unquestionable that consciousness is primary, the beginning of all things, the only God there could be and the only one there has ever been. If anyone doubts it, it is because he is blinded, so does not see; he is befogged, so does not understand. From what or from whom else did he derive his own consciousness, his knowing power, and his thinking capacity?

196

The teaching divides consciousness-in-itself from consciousness of the self. Such a division would, of course, be totally rejected by the materialists.

197

Anterior to all things is Mind. Electronic energy and material being are but its aspects.

198

It is not possible for consciousness to know anything greater than consciousness.

199

Mind offers its own certitude. It is completely self-posited.

200

Consciousness runs deeper than its contents, subtler than its thinking activities, and serener than its surface agitations.

201

Who is it who becomes aware of all these things which make up his world? *What* is it that perceives objects? *What* gives its attention to thoughts and things? *Wherefrom* does consciousness arise, or is it there *first*, thus making the known world knowable?

202

Because it is known directly—and not through the medium of thoughts or words—it is called immediate knowledge.

203

The world-thought holds in a kind of spell; every possible state of consciousness short of the Overself is still an *idea* in the human mind.

204

To the extent that any man discovers this for himself, to that extent he is said to be enlightened. Outside of this enlightenment, what he gets or produces is his own mental creation: it may be entirely false or quite correct, but it still remains no more than a mental creation.

205

Every kind of experience, whether it be wakeful, dream, hypnotic, or hallucinatory, is utterly and vividly real to the ego at the time its perceptions are operating on that particular level. Why, then, amidst such bewildering relativity, do we talk of divine experience as being the ultimate reality? We speak this way because it is concerned with what bestows the sense of reality to all the other forms of experience. And that is nothing else than the central core of pure Mind within us, the unique mysterious source of *all* possible kinds of our consciousness. This, if we can find it, is what philosophy calls the truly real world.(P)

206

The mental images which make up the universe of our experience repeat themselves innumerable times in a single minute. They give an impression of continuity and permanency and stability only because of this, in the same way that a cinema picture does. If we could efface them and yet keep our consciousness undiminished, we would know for the first time their source, the reality behind their appearances. That is, we would know Mind-in-itself. Such effacement is effected by yoga. Here then is the importance of the connection between mentalism and mysticism.(P)

Index for Part 1

Entries are listed by chapter number followed by "para" number. For example, 5.8 means chapter 5, para 8, and 3.43, 79 means chapter 3, paras 43 and 79. Chapter listings are separated by a semicolon. Please note also that, for the reader's convenience, the first number in the right-hand running heads throughout the text indicates chapter number.

R

S

T

U

V

Index for Part 2

Entries are listed by chapter number followed by "para" number. For example, 4.33 means chapter 4, para 33, and 1.357, 442 means chapter 1, paras 357 and 442. Chapter listings are separated by a semicolon. Please note also that, for the reader's convenience, the first number in the right-hand running heads throughout the text indicates chapter number.

E

F

G

H

I

N

O

P

T

U

V

Index for Part 3

Entries are listed by chapter number followed by "para" number. For example, 4.245 means chapter 4, para 245, and 4.234, 248 means chapter 4, paras 234 and 248. Chapter listings are separated by a semicolon. Please note also that, for the reader's convenience, the first number in the right-hand running heads throughout the text indicates chapter number.

T